PRIVATE SECURITY
in the 21st Century
CONCEPTS AND APPLICATIONS

Edward J. Maggio, Esq.
Assistant Professor of Criminal Justice
New York Institute of Technology
Director
NYIT Center for Security Disaster and Response

JONES AND BARTLETT PUBLISHERS
Sudbury, Massachusetts
BOSTON   TORONTO   LONDON   SINGAPORE

World Headquarters

Jones and Bartlett Publishers
40 Tall Pine Drive
Sudbury, MA 01776
978-443-5000
info@jbpub.com
www.jbpub.com

Jones and Bartlett Publishers
Canada
6339 Ormindale Way
Mississauga, Ontario L5V 1J2
Canada

Jones and Bartlett Publishers
International
Barb House, Barb Mews
London W6 7PA
United Kingdom

Jones and Bartlett's books and products are available through most bookstores and online booksellers. To contact Jones and Bartlett Publishers directly, call 800-832-0034, fax 978-443-8000, or visit our website www.jbpub.com.

Substantial discounts on bulk quantities of Jones and Bartlett's publications are available to corporations, professional associations, and other qualified organizations. For details and specific discount information, contact the special sales department at Jones and Bartlett via the above contact information or send an email to specialsales@jbpub.com.

This publication is designed to provide accurate and authoritative information in regard to the Subject Matter covered. It is sold with the understanding that the publisher is not engaged in rendering legal, accounting, or other professional service. If legal advice or other expert assistance is required, the service of a competent professional person should be sought.

Production Credits

Acquisitions Editor: Jeremy Spiegel
Editorial Assistant: Kyle Hoover
Production Director: Amy Rose
Production Assistant: Julia Waugaman
Assistant Photo Researcher: Meghan Hayes
Marketing Manager: Jessica Faucher
Manufacturing and Inventory Control Supervisor: Amy Bacus
Cover Design: Kristin E. Parker
Cover Image: © Digital Vision/age fotostock
Chapter Opener Image: © Stephen Sweet/ShutterStock, Inc.
Composition: Lynn L'Heureux
Printing and Binding: Malloy Incorporated
Cover Printing: Malloy Incorporated

Library of Congress Cataloging-in-Publication Data

Maggio, Edward J.
  Private security in the 21st century : concepts and applications / by Edward J. Maggio.
    p. cm.
  Includes bibliographical references and index.
  ISBN-13: 978-0-7637-5190-6
  ISBN-10: 0-7637-5190-1
  1. Private security services. 2. Security systems. I. Title.
  HV8290.M34 2009
  363.28'9--dc22

                              2008035266

6048
Printed in the United States of America
12 11 10 09 08   10 9 8 7 6 5 4 3 2 1

For my father, Edward I. Maggio, for his service to the City of New York and to the American business community.

For my mother and sister for their continued love and support.

For Anthony.

Contents

9   Riots, Domestic Terrorism, and Maritime Security Issues 241

Preface

If you asked an American to define *security* prior to the events of 9/11 and the Iraq war, the explanation would focus on retirement packages or financial status. To note that the 9/11 tragedy changed the American understanding of the nature of security would be an understatement. From the people at ground zero to the testimony before the 9/11 Commission, a harsh message and lesson were sent throughout the country. No longer can the business community and citizens of this country expect that government will be the sole provider of safety and security. As man-made and natural threats from within and abroad create both financial and mortal threats to our society, the need for more protection beyond what government agencies provide is paramount.

A US business, whether a small enterprise or a major conglomerate with huge corporate headquarters, must take steps to train and prepare for threats to the company's existence. Hospitals have increased security for their facilities owing to the increased number of people needing health care. Grade schools and universities have also had to increase the level of security at their facilities in light of tragic events such as those that occurred at Columbine High School and Virginia Tech. The legal system has also pushed for the use of more private investigations in lawsuits and investigators as gatherers of information for civil matters. Crime, particularly theft in the business environment, is evolving in the business community and is taking on new forms that require new methods of detection and training for security personnel. Although disputed by numerous experts, the possible damage to our environment has now placed businesses at risk for damage caused by natural events of a possible catastrophic nature. The rise of Islamic fundamentalism and homegrown domestic terror groups has also changed the landscape of security issues in the United States. Not since World War II have private security personnel been needed in such large numbers in this country. It has become clear to everyone that we live in a dangerous world. The growth experienced in the private security industry is also warranted because of the demand by the public for more security professionals.

Today the security and investigations industry is a $100 billion business worldwide. It has been in existence for nearly 130 years in America, growing in the late 1800s to its current state. In the United States, there are approximately 15,000 businesses that make up the $29 billion contract security industry. The demand for US private security services is expected to exceed $45 billion in 2010. Private security will continue to expand and grow for a number of major reasons:[1]

- Insider threats—This threat has been recently pushed to the forefront. In one study by Intelomics, up to 80% of all security breaches are done by insiders with access to business systems (e.g., employees, consultants, and temps). In the same report, nearly 78% of those breaches go unreported owing to fear of negative public reaction. More and more individuals, businesses, and organizations are looking to private security forces for protection.
- Corporate espionage—It seems as if you cannot pick up a paper without seeing a story about corporate crime and espionage. Corporate espionage, the theft of corporate information that is valuable, is estimated to be nearly a $1.5 trillion per year problem globally. Private security forces and investigators are often the first line of defense against corporate espionage.
- High-tech crime—Businesses and organizations are both struggling to cope with high-tech crimes. Computer crime, cybercrime, identity theft, electronic money laundering, counterfeiting, smuggling, and other offenses are all on the rise. It is estimated that an identity theft occurs in the United States every 30 seconds, and it is reported that more than 12,000 serious computer attacks occur each minute. Private security investigators must become more engaged than ever to combat this threat.
- Terrorism—The federal government has warned of future possible acts of domestic terrorism against the American business and industrial community. If you look at the list of the top 100 terrorist targets, it is laden with private-sector assets. No longer can business and industry afford to be lax with security preparedness. Approximately 85% of critical infrastructure—water systems, power grids, bridges, and tunnels—in the United States is privately owned, and private security forces are becoming the primary protectors of America's vital infrastructure.

While the need for private security is high, the information and training is still in a stage of development for private security personnel pursuing careers in this field. While public-serving police organizations have formal academies, private security is developing and growing in new areas where training is still not widely available to all entry-level private security personnel. Private security training in the United States is still rudimentary compared to our European and Middle Eastern counterparts. Generally, American businesses are reactive in investigating and becoming aware of threats, creating new procedures, hiring personnel, and more importantly, investing in advanced training for security personnel. Many American businesses do not realize global events or the ever-changing security environment should influence their awareness and possibly create a

---

1. Spy-Ops. 2006. Quarterly intelligence update. http://www.Spy-Ops.com.

change in company policies. An estimated 44% of private security personnel have not been trained to handle terrorism-related emergencies. That equates to nearly 500,000 security personnel not prepared for worst-case scenarios when our country needs them most. The work of private security personnel in handling terrorist scenarios is coupled with the added responsibilities of addressing high-tech crime, corporate espionage, and insider threats. The current training of personnel to handle these problems falls woefully short of that which is necessary. Additionally, the threat, techniques, and crimes are constantly changing in our nation, increasing the need for continuing security education.

There are also significant issues facing the nature of the private security industry. In a 2005 report by the public advocate for the City of New York, several critical issues the industry needs to immediately address were identified:[2]

- Security personnel wages are low, and healthcare benefits are unaffordable or not offered.
- Turnover is rampant: nearly one quarter of security personnel stay at their job one year or less.
- Most security personnel report having less training than required.
- Training fails to emphasize terrorism, working with police, or firefighters.

Security personnel wages range from minimum wage to over $17 an hour. The difference depends on location and training and the field specialty of the private security person. The wage issue drives the second issue that has been around for a long time: turnover, people entering and leaving the profession at a rapid pace. One recent report on the industry in the United States estimates that employee turnover is as high as 400% annually based on private security employees being terminated, retiring, or resigning from their position.[3] Second to turnover is the ability of individuals who want to become security guards to pass the background screening. While no conclusive studies have been done, a random survey of those in the field found turnover as high as 31% of candidates washing out because of their credit or criminal history. Attracting, educating, and retaining private security staff must become the number one priority of every organization in the private security industry. Private security personnel will continue to be needed as protectors of American businesses.

Businesses in our country are the front line to the stability and security of our nation. The private sector of American business controls 85% of the nation's infrastructure. Security and national preparedness for crime, terrorism, and natural disasters therefore often begin with the private sector as the front line to handling difficult situations. The ability to be prepared and to actively prevent financial and physical threats therefore not only protects their organization, but also secures society. American businesses and other organizations can prevail and save the lives of others with a well-trained security team

---

2. Lovato, R. 2006. Security guards demand better pay to protect US against terrorism. *New American Media*. February 28.
3. Orlov, R. 2006. Upgrades urged for security guards. *LA Daily News*. April 7.

and well-developed security planning. The events of the Katrina tragedy also demonstrated how the corporate world was more prepared to respond to a natural disaster than US government agencies. Additionally, American businesses and corporations are now working together more than ever before to share the best practices and information for protecting their respective industries. The American business community is also working together with government agencies to learn how their security and contingency plans fit in with a larger government response to a major crisis or a smaller criminal act.

In the past, many scholars and policy makers have thought of domestic and international security and emergency and public health issues only by separate respective fields of criminal justice, business, government, and the medical community. Unfortunately, many still do. In addition, respective disciplines in recent years have expanded beyond the scope that many realize at this time. For example, private security under the criminal justice academic field since 9/11 now involves the following:

- Private investigations
- Advanced business security
- Emergency management/public health crisis control
- Corporate espionage
- Counterterrorism
- Counterinsurgency
- Computer crimes
- Business continuity and risk assessment
- Money laundering
- Corporate and industrial terrorism
- Information warfare
- Computer hacking

The engineering and technology fields are now adapting at an increasing rate to handle security problems emerging in the world community. Leadership development is crucial to prepare individuals to enter new security fields and to lead government and corporate businesses in these crucial areas. By and large, the academic community has done a poor job of providing the necessary information to policy makers on domestic and international security, information and data protection, emergency management, and world health issues. With the exception of a few dedicated and noted experts, many scholars and business professionals are uninterested in developing policy recommendations and strategic networks to deal with long-term real world problems as well as short-term challenges. At the same time, many policy makers and corporate professionals focus almost exclusively on short-term issues. Long-term threat planning and the researching of new ways to apply technology to crises and threat situations are largely nonexistent until actual problems become uncontrollable or receive negative societal and media attention. As a result, there is a large and growing gap between academia, policy makers, and corporate professionals with respect to security and health emergencies. This gap has only recently been bridged by other educational institutions that are focusing on marketing their university name while developing the networks with businesses and government agencies for prestige, funding, and the benefit of their students.

An effective member of any private security team can no longer just be someone who knows basic facility security and guarding practices. They must be multidisciplined and prepared to handle a number of tasks as a member of a security team. Technology and efficient educational methods now allow security personnel to be trained in ways that are cost-effective and in a manner that does not take them out of the workforce during the education process. To train security personnel in just a small set of skills is not only foolish; it is possibly legally negligent, thus imposing liability on a business entity when a breach in security in some form occurs. An entry-level security person may wish to work in other arenas that require specialized knowledge and skills. Ultimately, comprehensive training and better compensation will decrease turnover and make security personnel more familiar with their buildings, coworkers, and emergency procedures, and thus increasing security.

This textbook provides new information for educating and training private security personnel in the beginning stages of their career, whether they are a full-time students or entry-level security workers on the job. This text will not only provide background information that a prospective security person should know, but also basic operational procedures that should be understood by a student. The first chapter serves to inform the reader about the historical development of private security as well. The extensive number of topics also allows a security person to adapt to a business environment as the organization grows. The style of this book is to slowly provide information that, step by step, increases the knowledge and skill set of a private security person in training or student interested in security.

Historical Development— Private Security: Past to Present

CHAPTER

1

▶ ▶ OBJECTIVES

▶ ▶ OBJECTIVES

When you finish reading this chapter, you will be better prepared to:

- Understand the development of private security from ancient times to modern times.
- Examine the development of public-serving law enforcement agencies along with private security fields in Europe and America in the 1800s.
- Understand the increased need for private security personnel as a result of WWII and the 9/11 attacks.

■ Introduction

If you speak to most people and ask them when they first noticed private security personnel appearing at local businesses and various other locations, you are likely to receive a great variety of different answers. Older people in the United States would say private security personnel emerged on the scene following WWII, while others would say they noticed private security personnel following the 9/11 attacks. In reality, private security personnel have a rich world history and a calling full of traditional origins. Just as humankind developed all over the world, so did the private security field in a local area in some shape or form. Historically, wealthy members of a society relied on their private security personnel to ensure safety and economic order in a given region. In the modern world we take banks for granted in terms of the security services they provide for people. People historically had no place to secure their wealth and valuables other than in their own homes. Therefore, wealthier families and their homes were constant targets of roving thieves, invaders, or their neighbors who coveted their wealth and land. In ancient and medieval times, every journey far from home could be a venture into unknown danger. People would often seek protection in the form of hired personnel when traveling. There were no public law enforcement agencies that could be contacted by telephone when people needed help and assistance. It is only in the last 300 years that law enforcement agencies, charged with guarding the welfare

1

of the entire public in a community, have become the norm. To give you a better understanding of the development of private security, it is important to examine some of the earliest beginnings of private security.

▶ ▶ CASE STUDY

Imagine taking a walk through your local neighborhood. You see a private security person working at one of the local businesses in your town. The private security person is in uniform and observing people. People notice the guard as they enter or leave the business. The private security person noticeably observes people entering and leaving the business and receives messages over a radio receiver on their person. Imagine further that while walking around your neighborhood you observe a local police officer sitting in a police vehicle looking straight ahead and appearing very attentive to people walking by the vehicle. Both the private security person and the local police officer have similar uniforms and have been engaged in similar behavior while on duty.

1. In what type of business would you find private security personnel at this very moment in your town?
2. What type of activities do local police perform in your community?
3. What do you think is the difference between local police and private security personnel?
4. Think about world history, imagine hundreds of years ago; what did communities do without local police? Who protected people from harm?

■ Ancient Egypt

One of the first uses of hired guards and private security personnel can be dated back to Ancient Egypt. During the 13th century BC, Pharaoh Ramses II oversaw the growth of Egyptian civilization, notably the building and expansion of the Egyptian military on an unprecedented scale. Egypt's military campaigns and security needs under this pharaoh provided true security innovation in the ancient world. During his foreign campaigns, Ramses II relied heavily on a foreign corps of Nubians known as the **Medjai,** a generic term for *scout* or *guard*.[1] Unlike local Egyptian people that could be conscripted or inspired to fight for the Pharaoh on the basis of patriotism and loyalty, these guards were hired specifically to supplement the Egyptian military and security forces.[2] They were instrumental in the protection of Thebes and the royal complex at Deir al-Madinah.[3] The Medjai have recently entered popular American culture as a result of recent movies. The Medjai have a fictionalized portrayal in the popular Stephen Sommer's *Mummy* movie franchise in which Medjai demonstrate themselves as a loyal and superior security force for the protection of the Egyptian people. Besides the Medjai, Ramses II hired Libyan, Syrian, Canaanites, and Sherdens from Sardinia as private soldiers and bodyguards for the pharaoh and his family. Such images of privately paid bodyguards can be found on wall paintings and ancient buildings in Egypt even today.[4] It is not surprising that by maintaining security at home for vast building projects for the Egyptian people, after his death Ramses II earned the title Ramses the Great.

■ Ancient Rome

The Roman Empire also was innovative in terms of law, architecture, medicine, and the use of private security personnel in the ancient world. The practices Rome helped foster exist today. The more privileged members of Roman society began to hire personnel to protect their increasingly growing property, estates, and members of their family. It was not uncommon for wealthy people to hire gladiators to defend their property or to have organized criminal bands at their disposal for protection services.[5] During the spring and summer months, well-trained and well-known soldiers could also find employment as private security personnel when not on a military campaign. In many cases, the reputation of such personnel alone would be enough to deter criminals from targeting their employer. Slaves were often used by their masters to protect buildings. The slaves were a cheaper alternative to a well-trained and seasoned fighter. Slaves had the advantage of being familiar with the normal people who entered and exited their master's home.[6] A slave guard posted at the entrance to a Roman building would be called a **janitor** in honor of the two-faced Roman god Janus who protected Roman entrances. Often a janitor would be a castrated eunuch slave. Low-level slaves working as janitors in a private home would occasionally be chained to the building's doorway and supervised by a higher-ranking slave. A higher-ranked slave could also monitor and direct the security of the slaves that manned the doors of a building, especially during times of turmoil or even a very large gathering at a Roman party. With the aid of other slaves or a vicious guard dog, a wealthy Roman would have private security in place.

The Roman emperors also had an elite bodyguard corps of soldiers known as the Praetorian Guard that formed an additional check against crime and turmoil in Rome. As bodyguards, they took an oath of loyalty to the emperor. When off duty, they often roamed through the streets of the city in civilian clothes because of the resistance of people to military control. As soldiers, they could obtain information in the respective neighborhoods as to prospective crime problems, possible invasions, or direct threats to the life of the emperor himself.

Over time, the Praetorian Guard became more established as leaders in the regular Roman army legions that were expanding through Europe, Africa, and Asia. They soon formed part of the often uncontrolled military force that enthroned or assassinated emperors at their political will. A quick examination of Roman history reveals the frequency with which the Praetorian Guard could end the reign of a Roman emperor at the point of a sword.

In Rome, the task of urban control of the populace itself fell to the **urban cohorts**.[7] The urban cohorts served as a form of **gendarmerie**, a type of armed police unit. Primarily, the urban cohorts were focused on maintaining order and control among slaves that could escape, representing a property loss to the Romans who owned them. Also, the common unruly citizens of Rome who caused mayhem in the streets could also be controlled through the cohorts. Just as people becoming inebriated and causing trouble is a concern for communities today, the urban cohorts could restore order and peace when drunken Romans began to cause mischief at the end of a night of festivities.

In ancient Rome, soldiers were often assigned to guard the Roman capital's **infrastructure**. The infrastructure is the facilities, services, buildings, and structures needed for the community's survival. The Roman soldiers assigned to protect vital areas such as roads, buildings, and water facilities controlled the life of a Roman city. Any severe damage to such areas would have resulted in doom for the Roman population. In Rome itself, the task of such important work soon fell to a group of men known as the vigiles. They are often credited as the origin of both private security personnel and public law enforcement in Roman history. In reality, they were more of a semiorganized fire brigade in the Roman capital. They were established by the first emperor of Rome, Augustus Caesar, who consolidated his power as an absolute ruler following a brutal Roman civil war. As the Roman Empire expanded, so did the amount of buildings and the population of the capital Rome. The vigiles were ultimately assigned the overwhelming task of fighting the devastating fires occurring in Rome as part of the general disorder and overcrowding in parts of the city. From the vigiles, the word *vigil* entered the English language as those who watch for dangers or perils in the local community.[8] Soon the vigiles were mandated to handle not just fires, but to carry out low-level policing duties in Rome. Archeologists recently discovered a vigiles headquarters. The building served as one of the earliest fire and law enforcement stations in history.

It must be understood that with no single unified police or fire rescue department in Rome, a mixture of groups provided safety to Roman citizens on a regular basis. Security therefore was a combination of slaves, free Roman citizens, soldiers and gladiators-at-large, Praetorian Guards, and vigiles. Security, although mostly private in nature, was reactive to crime and security problems as they happened. In many situations it would have been up to someone acting on their own to make an arrest or report when they observed lawless behavior.

■ Byzantines

By AD 400, the Roman Empire slowly began to fall into chaos and lawlessness, while the Byzantine Empire in the East thrived and continued to grow. The Byzantine Empire emerged as eastern provinces of the old Roman Empire consolidated into one empire under the control of its own emperor. As the Byzantine Empire continued to grow, its emperors followed the practice of hiring contracted foreigners for their personal security forces. The Byzantines called these privately paid security forces the **Varangian Guard**.[9] Members of this unit were generally chosen from war-prone civilizations, with a general preference for men from the northern Viking region or the Eastern steppes of Europe and Asia where men were known for their wild appearances and love of battle. The general mandate of this group was to protect the emperor and Byzantine Empire from threats. Since these foreign guards did not have family connections to the Byzantine people, they would be able to suppress rebellions of the masses without hesitation in the Byzantine capitol of Constantinople or throughout the Byzantine Empire in the east.

■ Middle Ages: Western Europe and Asia (476–1500)

After the fall of the Roman Empire in AD 476, communities in Western Europe lost all previous security forces and the resources available for security. Over time, local families banded together to wall up or fence in their local areas for their own protection. As groups such as the Huns or Vikings continued to raid Western European communities, wealthy members of the community looked for ways to protect themselves while also fighting with others for land and power. In Asia, the growing Mongol hordes led the Chinese and Japanese civilizations to expand their military forces and its citizens began to use private security personnel. Eventually, the instability in both Western Europe and Asia led to the development of walled cities during this chaotic time in world history.

Italy and China relied heavily on private security personnel during this time both to guard and to act as fighters for military warlords. Military personnel in these areas eventually organized into private organizations with a leadership caste and organized structure. Over a period of years, these warlords consolidated their power in their respective regions in Europe and Asia and established themselves as rulers. Such leaders would offer tracts of land to the noblemen along with the poor peasants who lived on the land. A nobleman or leader would then provide security to the peasants who worked the land so that it could be harvested, and livestock holdings increased without any risk of being attacked by outside forces. This system became known as **feudalism**.[10]

With security in place, the majority of food and profit produced in a community would go back to the ruler and his noblemen to fill their pockets before trickling back down to the peasants for their own survival. The ruler of an area would use his significant share of food and profit and put it towards procuring more arms (military and police support), to engage in warfare, or provide additional security to the region.

Because everything focused on the notion of war and survival, castles and building security technology developed in different parts of the world as extra sources of security for lords and rulers. The lives of individuals in a society under a feudalist

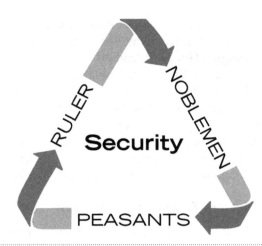

Figure 1-1   Feudalism Chart

system were fairly similar, whether they were in feudalistic Europe or an area in Asia that also operated under feudalism.[11] The feudalism system provided the necessary security after the fall of the Roman Empire for Europeans (see Figure 1-1).

England

To understand the developments of private security in America, we must further understand those of England following the end of the Roman Empire. In the case of England, the Anglo-Saxon German tribes that invaded the British Isles fostered new security developments. The Anglo-Saxons brought to the English landscape a more sophisticated local system for providing civil and military protection. Organized systems of 10 English families known as **tithings** banded together for security and to provide community responsibility for law and order. The 10 families would therefore ensure on their own that security functions would be carried out by their respective members in an organized and more accountable manner.[12] This system proved invaluable to the safety of the native British. This system however, would soon change due to a new invader from across the English Channel.

A Norman ruler nicknamed "William the Bastard" invaded England in AD 1066 from Normandy, what is today known as Northern France. William engaged in warfare for complete control of the British Isles. After winning the battle of Hastings in AD 1066, the newly crowned William the Conqueror consolidated his control over Britain as fast as possible with security as a major priority. As Norman outsiders with their own language and customs, William and his fellow Normans expanded the tithing system in England into the **Frankpledge** system. The system was one of oaths and pledges. William, as the king of England, along with his future successors to the throne were to ensure safety and security in the kingdom by demanding loyalty from the people. In particular, the lords of the land were expected to make an oath as proof of obedience and acceptance of the king's autonomous power in Britain.

Over time, the English lords and wealthy members of English society grew tired of the power and actions of future English rulers. English monarchs would pass random edicts and laws often based on their own self-interests and not for the benefit of England itself. The upper class silently grew more distrusting of the English kings after William and the seemingly limitless power they possessed. Eventually, the lords and upper class banded together in continual opposition against their English rulers and their mismanagement of the lands.

By the reign of King John in 1215, the English lords revolted and in the ensuring chaos that shortly followed, they forced the king to sign a pledge known as the **Magna Carta**. This governing document established for the first time in the English feudal system of governance the supremacy of established law and order over random and arbitrary orders of a king.[13] In particular, the document laid out the responsibilities of the state to its subjects, notably in the area of individual rights, privileges, and security. Although the Magna Carta focused more on the rights of English lords and wealthy members of society rather than the masses of poor English peasants, it was a major hallmark towards the notion of protection of safety and property by a government. It was the first modern document to provide "due process" or opportunity to claim injustices before a person is deprived of life, liberty, and property.

By 1285, King Edward I took steps to formalize security on a more local level in terms of English villages and towns. King Edward I declared the **Statute of Westminster**, which established the precedent that any person had a right to stop in their current activities and act affirmatively towards the apprehension and pursuit of felons when a crime was committed in front of an English citizen. It is important to note that not just a knight or a royal official, but any free Englishman now had royal authority to prevent crime and to act to restore security when order and peace was disturbed by others.

In examining the Statute of Westminster further, it is clear that it established three major practical security measures for the average English person:

- watch and ward,
- hue and cry, and
- assize of arms.

First, a **watch and ward** measure provided that local town residents were to act as **watchmen**. These watchmen were to be chosen or assigned to patrol walled cities in the evening for criminal or unruly behavior.[14] Watchmen had specific orders to be followed. They were positioned at every gate of a walled town or city between sunset and sunrise. They had civilian authority powers to detain strangers to a community during darkness and to hand them over to the royal authorities in the morning with an oral report of why they detained the individual.[15] They could also serve as witnesses in formalized English criminal justice hearings against an accused person. This system of security was a form of required civil service that was essential to the security of a large village or English city. Any person who refused to serve as a member of the watchmen on their scheduled assigned time and date would be punished publicly or fined. Therefore, the watch and ward measure established an early private civilian auxiliary force for community protection as royal authorities could not always be present in locations throughout England at all times. With threats of constant invasion from foreign armies or uprisings from the people themselves, the more security that the English Crown could have available for a crisis situation, the better.

The Statute of Westminster also brought a return of an ancient Anglo-Saxon custom known as the **hue-and-cry system.** In this system, a watchman facing resistance from people to restore order, especially in the case of drunken or unruly citizens, could yell for assistance from the local citizens to come out of their homes and act affirmatively to assist the watchman.[16] The old custom applied towards any individual who refused the orders of a watchman or resisted arrest. This was useful in both disrupting a group of bandits attempting to enter an English town or to put down a group of disruptive citizens making too much noise and trouble. This system was also paramount in the case of a fugitive on the run or a watchman who was outnumbered by a gang of criminals. Such a situation would require more people to adequately handle this matter in which the life of the watchman was in danger. Lastly, to adequately enforce the hue-and-cry system under the Statute of Westminster, the statute further established the **assize of arms,** which by royal English decree required that every male citizen between the ages of 15 and 60 keep a weapon in his home. By having weapons available, residents could arm themselves and quickly respond to a crisis or create a show of force as a way to restore peace.

The reality is that the systems of security provided by the English Crown, and similar feudal systems around the globe, were not adequate for the needs of merchants and aristocrats of the society at the time. The rise in populations in different areas created an increased demand for people to serve others as security personnel. However, the lower economic classes (peasants, serfs, slaves) soon began to resent compulsory watch service or any type of security work and rebelled when they could. To a peasant, serving as a security guard or in any type of security role meant one less person was able to tend to the crops, raise livestock, or tend to activities that produced food and ensured survival for their family. In some cases, the locals who wanted to avoid any type of community security work were willing to pay others to take their place guarding locations, gates, or patrolling along a city wall. For those members of feudal society who desired to get out of agricultural work and work in some form of security position, the possibility for pay and opportunities was now available. As the wealth of aristocrats and rulers increased, so did the chances for others to be hired as private security personnel. However, as the world progressed through additional conflicts, private security personnel would present problems of their own for society.

The Rise of the Mercenaries

If you were to examine the medieval period in Europe and Asia, economic changes and the conflict between growing city-states continually left communities in a cycle of prosperity or desperation. With entire populations often falling prey to disease and war, the need for security among people pushed the eventual organization of armed bands of men seeking employment as security personnel. A new term, **mercenary**, emerged in Europe from the Latin word *mercenarius,* one that serves merely for wages. A mercenary is a person who is motivated by the desire for private gain to take part in armed conflict or in providing security.[17] A mercenary is not a party in a conflict and is generally not interested in who the ultimate winner of a conflict is. For gold, jewels, food, or land, veterans of military conflicts could be hired for private security duty.

During the later Middle Ages, the development of mercenary free companies or "free lances" emerged consisting of organized groups of mercenaries with a formalized structure established and an agreement among its members on how to operate. Such companies of mercenaries generally only formed when a long war came to an end and individuals from active duty military groups were no longer needed by their ruler.[18] From Europe to Asia, the hiring of veterans for security services during the Middle Ages became more common as villages and towns became more prosperous or feared constant threats from bandits and their neighbors. When a new war broke out between two towns, city-states, regions, or groups of people, mercenaries were necessary. If one side lacked the money necessary to maintain an actively trained and ready military force, a free company could be contacted and hired after a negotiation. This cycle repeated itself for hundreds of years. We must understand that until the rise of Napoleon and his Grand Army following the French Revolution, the use of standard full-time armies on active duty was not typical. Privately hired personnel serving as both security and fighting units was the norm for most of human history.

Often free companies or mercenary groups offered specialized forms of combat and protection services to clients as part of their offerings. Therefore, a newly joined mercenary could receive training and learn skills not available to regular soldiers under an official banner.[19] Despite the advantages of advanced training and skills, mercenaries occasionally created new problems for those seeking a quick fix to their security difficulties in a town. During the times of major turmoil, it was not uncommon for mercenaries to change their loyalty and serve the opposing side of a conflict if a higher fee was offered by another party. Even today, the term *mercenary* still calls to mind negative images of people who put profit before loyalty to their mission and client.

While the use of hired security forces is still a topic that causes debate, it is important to remember that scholars have been debating the issue since the moment organized mercenary groups first emerged. Scholars such as Thomas More noted the positive advantages to using hired security and military forces in a society. In his masterpiece, *Utopia*, More advocated the use of mercenaries instead of citizens to provide military and security functions. He preferred that a group of unknown barbarian mercenaries be employed to protect the masses while the rest of the people living in his proposed Utopia were free to seek other pursuits such as art and music.[20] Since unknown barbarians would not know the established citizens, all people would be treated equal in terms of security and protection. It is believed the popularity of using Swiss mercenaries during the Middle Ages inspired this notion.[21]

Around the same time period, negative criticisms of mercenaries were rampant and widely held among people who experienced their services firsthand. Noted political and military strategist Niccolò Machiavelli argued against the use of mercenary forces in his political work *The Prince* based upon very sound reasoning. Machiavelli focused his concern on the profit motivation of armed men providing military and security services in a warring Italian city-state. He rationalized that a man whose sole motivation is money will not be inclined to take the risks necessary to turn the tide of battle or protect others under his protection at all costs. Citizens, however, would die to protect their home and way of life in an Italian city-state. Therefore, a dedicated citizen would sacrifice their life for the greater good of the city-state while a mercenary would abandon his post in the face of greater opposition.

It is important also to realize that mercenaries, after protecting a town or city-state in Italy, often would decide to rob or simply terrorize the town for additional funds and resources. This is a major reason for Machiavelli's concern of force dynamics in terms of hiring personnel to fight or provide security services. As an observer of political intrigue and power in Italy, he noted that a mercenary who failed was obviously no good, but one who succeeded may be even more of a threat than even imagined by the employer of such mercenary forces.[22] If a group of hired security forces could successfully protect a ruler and had more military power than the ruler, then a mercenary group would be inclined to take control from a ruler and put themselves in power. It is important to note that Machiavelli was writing at a time when frequent betrayals by mercenary units were commonplace in Italy. Therefore, citizens of a city-state would be preferred.[23] However, the problem of turning a person that is a farmer, artisan, or student into a trained security professional would be a dilemma not solved until the 1900s.

Controversies in Private Security   In this century, there is now a repeat of a previous historical cycle. Following the end of the Cold War and the demise of the Soviet Union, more Western nations have been decreasing the size of their military forces. The conflicts in Iraq and Afghanistan along with the new war on terrorism has now led former military officers and soldiers to join corporate security groups such as Blackwater and Dyncorp to provide security services to clients alongside conventional military forces. Many of the security duties currently being carried out in Iraq and Afghanistan are now being provided by corporate security groups; the newest incarnation of the mercenary units of the past. In addition, the concept of compensation for private security work has also reemerged. Despite the contentions by Machiavelli, it is now firmly established in the corporate world today that a member of a security team that works within a company and wants the company to be successful is generally going to be paid less than an outside security consultant brought in to increase security at the same location.

The change just in the last few decades has shown an additional return to more medieval traditions besides mercenary units previously mentioned. In the 1900s, private security personnel were often guarding or protecting the specific needs of wealthy citizens and companies around the world who required extra protection of assets and human lives. However, currently the return of specialized private security personnel and military style protection is once again present in security firms and companies. Such organizations can tailor the advanced training of their personnel to meet the specific needs of a paying client, whether on a temporary basis, or on a contracted permanent basis. While the negative disloyal mercenary image continues in modern times, the growth in the use of private security personnel in the last two centuries has helped to change the image and the role such personnel play in terms of security. To understand the massive growth of the private security field in the last few years, we must also examine the rise of contemporary public-serving police organizations.

■ The 1700s and 1900s: The Rise of Private Security and Public-Serving Police Organizations

Public-serving law enforcement agencies and organizations are a recent human innovation. With growing populations around the world and increased demand by people of their leaders for safer environments, the development of public-serving law enforcement personnel answerable not just to leaders of an area, but to the general public as a whole was inevitable. While scholars argue as to the first modern police organization, one can look back and see the developments emerging in Europe.

France

The first police force in the modern sense was created by the French government of King Louis XIV in 1667. It was created to enforce the king's rule and provide control of the masses in the city of Paris. Paris at that time was one of the largest cities in Europe and one of the most dangerous places to live because of the turbulent socioeconomic structure at that time, namely the difference between the rich and the suffering French poor. The royal edict by King Louis XIV, registered by the Parliament of Paris on March 15, 1667, created the office of *lieutenant général de police* (lieutenant general of police). This chosen individual would now lead an organized Paris police force. It is important to note that the ordered mandate of this new group of officers was "ensuring the peace and quiet of the public and of private individuals, purging the city of what may cause disturbances, procuring abundance, and having each and everyone live according to their station and their duties."[24] This organization's focus was to prevent people from engaging in any activity that disrupted the ability of the rich to control the poor. Gabriel Nicolas de la Reynie became the chosen lieutenant general with absolute control of the police force. In addition, he was provided funding for 44 *commissaires de police* (police commissioners) under his authority. The city of Paris was divided into 16 districts policed by these 44 *commissaires de police*, each assigned to a particular district and assisted in their districts by clerks and a growing bureaucracy. The scheme of the Paris police force was extended to the rest of France by a royal edict in October 1699. Soon the French government created police organizations in all large French cities or towns based on this Parisian police organization. In 1709, the commissioners were assisted by newly appointed *inspecteurs de police* (police inspectors).[25]

While innovative, this deployed police force in Paris was charged with additional duties as time passed that extended beyond the maintenance of a quiet street or arresting thieves. Its functions took on a more social and economic focus. The work of this organization expanded from law enforcement duties to include urban planning, cemetery maintenance for the prevention of plague epidemics, monitoring the prices of goods, and other quality-of-life issues. In reality, the concern was to serve the aristocracy and guarantee the lower classes continued to function under a banner of law and order for the benefit of the king and his court; there was a lack of trust of the general public. What began in France and what would later spread through Europe was the development of organized police groups that, with the mandate of the ruling power, could exert power over the people in the interest of maintaining law and public order.

England

The next development of the concept of the modern police force can be seen in England. By the 1800s, inadequate law enforcement over much of England prompted a need for increased security. As England entered the industrial age, the factory emerged. The need for workers in factories resulted in a mass movement of people from the open spaces of the country into densely populated areas near the factories. Factory conditions at large industrial firms of that time were often filthy and dark. Workers in a community were often working long hours for little pay despite the drab and sometimes dangerous work conditions. This led to groups of workers in different industries becoming dissatisfied and unruly with a propensity for halting work when pushed too far by their superiors. Out of fear of their workers, industrial firms began creating their own security units to counter possible activities such as strikes or violence. With visible or known security personnel in place, incidents of violence or striking could be prevented out of fear of a security person's response.[26]

With the expansion of the railroad throughout England, large numbers of people traveled quickly to other parts of the nation for the first time. The crowds at railway stations created security problems, as did the arrival of criminal gangs, possible stampedes due to people struggling to get to their train, or the occasional incident that could disrupt trains from departing or entering a station. Soon the newly developing railway companies began to hire private employees to maintain order and control for the sake of the public and the railway companies themselves. As English people saw the effectiveness of hired security personnel, they turned to their government to criticize the public law enforcement agencies in place at that time. It must be remembered that at this time, private security personnel were often better trained and more effective than their public law enforcement counterparts. In London, in particular, the demand for public-serving police soon became strong as densely populated city areas became havens for criminal activity and vice.

With no formal police force, London residents had to protect themselves. Neighborhoods appointed householders as **constables** who had the authority to arrest criminals or summon assistance. Citizens were still required by law to heed the "hue and cry" of a person and help defend against criminal activity. With such rudimentary policing of public areas in place, the government focused on deterrence of criminal activity under the so called **Bloody Code**, a succession of laws enacted through the mid-1700s in which more than 200 offenses carried the death penalty.[27] These included not only violent crimes, but also criminal activities ranging from forgery to shoplifting and pick-pocketing.[28] Even with the Bloody Code, there was no formal system of investigation or prosecution of criminal suspects. The English government soon began offering large bounties for conviction of those guilty of serious criminal offenses. As the industrial age progressed and the railroad brought more people to London, crime became more violent. It became evident to the people of London and to the government that new methods of law enforcement and security were needed. One of the innovators in providing a solution to the London crime problem was Henry Fielding, who with his half brother John, served as a mid-century magistrate at Bow Street, near Covent Garden in the city of London. In 1753, the Fielding brothers induced the English government to fund the **Bow Street Runners,** a corps of ex-constables, to track down criminals and bring them to justice in the English criminal justice system.[29] Originally numbering just eight persons, they were the first detective agency in the city of London created under the banner of government authority. The Bow Street Runners represented a formalization and regularization of existing policing methods in a time when chaos and uncertainty were prevailing. What made this organization different was their formal attachment to the Bow Street magistrates' office and the fees paid by the magistrate with funds from the central government.[30] The detectives in this agency soon began receiving extreme amounts of criticism from the general public for their harsh and unruly tactics. Although considered authorized government agents, they were known to spend their leisure time at places frequented by London's most notorious criminals.[31] With private police providing more effective security to customers and employees than the public police, the public put pressure on the English government for dynamic changes to this form of public policing.[32] Heeding the demands of the public, in 1829 England's home secretary Sir Robert Peel introduced to the English parliament the "Bill for Improving the Police in and near the Metropolis." The bill proposed a return to the Anglo-Saxon principle of individual community responsibility for the preservation of law and order in a given community through prevention.[33] The bill also proposed that London in particular should have a body of civilians appointed and paid by the local community to serve as full-time police officers. These police officers would receive more organized training and a clearer understanding of their police duties as ordered by their chain of command. The English parliament agreed and in 1829 passed the proposed bill and created the London Metropolitan Police. This more formally trained police force promoted the notion of prevention of crime. These police officers served as deterrents to urban crime and disorder by their mere presence on London streets.[34] This concept in policing is still used by public-serving law enforcement organizations today—the idea that people will not commit criminal activity when a police officer or security professional is nearby. The development of private security and a new public-serving police organization in London would soon spread its popular influence across the sea to the United States of America.

American West: 1800s

In America during the 1800s, the rapid expansion westward by pioneers, businessmen, and tourists alike was made easier by the expansion of railways. As the railroad expanded into new areas, it often moved into unexplored and dangerous territory. Towns went up along the railways even before law enforcement personnel could be recruited and set up to protect individuals. Departing at a certain railway stop meant possibly walking into the unknown and taking your chances with whatever threats were present. Therefore, as the American railways expanded, it often meant that people moved or lived in areas with little or no public law enforcement personnel at all to protect their lives and property.[35] As people went westward as a result of the California gold rush, so did criminals following trains full of potential victims.

This was the age in American history when trains were attacked by outlaws and thieves. It was not uncommon for such criminals to steal cargo on the train, dynamite tracks, or create general mayhem in small local communities. Indian raids were also prevalent, which posed a concern for people traveling westward close to Indian lands or who had settled in newly created towns. Established local sheriffs in western towns also faced difficulties applying criminal law codes against outlaws who were rapidly mobile thanks to the use of horses. Outlaws on horseback could move back and forth through states and territories in the West, creating jurisdictional problems as to who should make arrests and prosecute criminal offenders. When an offender committed offenses in one town, but was caught in another, the town sheriff could be bought off by criminals with newly acquired wealth. In some cases, a town sheriff or local constable simply did not have the legal authority to arrest criminals or investigate criminal activity. Criminals sometimes were set free to continue committing crimes in other areas of the West.

The vulnerability of trains and people caused by the rapid expansion westward, along with the problems of jurisdiction, forced many states to pass railway police acts that allowed private railroad companies to create their own accountable police and security forces. Such railway special agents were given full arrest and investigative powers to protect goods and passengers traveling on US railways.[36] This was brought upon the West by simple necessity. The railroads and the West could not wait for law enforcement agents to volunteer to tackle the difficult and often dangerous challenges faced in the West. The railway special agent was a duly commissioned law enforcement officer that could provide extra assistance and criminal intelligence to the local sheriff for a case when the outlaw was notoriously dangerous. In some cases during this period of westward expansion, the railway special agents were the only form of law enforcement in an area. In some communities, private employees soon found themselves becoming the new public-serving law enforcement agents due to their skills as fighters and marksmen.[37]

Private Security and Policy Movies and television shows of the Wild West depict the western territories as out of control and crime ridden. Train terminals and cattle boomtowns such as Wichita and Dodge City, both in Kansas, along with Tombstone, Arizona, were raucous places filled with drunken, armed cowboys celebrating at the end of long cattle drives. Men such as Wyatt Earp worked for Wells Fargo defending their stagecoaches from outlaws when the coaches held strongboxes. Eventually Earp became a public-serving law enforcement officer in Kansas and Arizona after proving his law enforcement skills in the private security field of the Wild West.

Over time, the need for more special railway agents resulted in the hasty hiring of personnel with little experience or training, thus leading to a decline in the quality of trained railway agents. As the railways expanded throughout the West, so did the demand for security along the same lines. It was not uncommon for a young man who responded to an ad for security work in town to find himself handed just a badge and a gun along with a destination name.

In a review of this period in American history, no discussion on security would be complete without a focus on Allan Pinkerton. Born in Scotland, Pinkerton came to America and after obtaining some investigative experience he began the **Pinkerton National Detective Agency**. Pinkerton's agency reached national attention for its level of professionalism.[38] Railroad companies contracted the agency to catch train robbers, set up security systems for railroads, and assess company security. Pinkerton's services were important to his clients mainly because public enforcement agencies either were inadequate or lacked jurisdiction to arrest or bring criminals before the appropriate authorities. Pinkerton had become famous when he foiled a plot to assassinate president-elect Abraham Lincoln. Lincoln later hired Pinkerton agents for his personal security during the Civil War from 1861–1865, especially when Lincoln traveled outside of Washington, DC. At the time of Lincoln's assassination, his security detail was no longer handled by the Pinkerton National Detective Agency, but by US Army military personnel. Pinkerton's agents performed services ranging from security guards to private military contracting work. During its height, the Pinkerton National Detective Agency employed more agents than the standing army of the United States of America, causing the state of Ohio to outlaw the agency due to fears it could be hired out as a private army or militia against the interests of the state.[39] Soon the agency was being hired, like many private security personnel in England, to control dissatisfied workers. During the American labor unrest of the late 1800s, the agency was hired by American factories and industrial centers to keep an eye on workers who were striking and those suspected of organizing a worker's union. Although the Pinkerton agency acted negatively against factory workers, the agency proved to be a model for the modern corporate security firms that offer protection services today.[40]

. . . .

The Pinkerton Detective Agency is well known to historians for the famous "We Never Sleep" slogan along with the logo of an open eye. This was most likely the origin of the term *private eye* when describing private detectives hired by clients to conduct an investigation.

. . . .

■ The 1900s

During the 1930s, US industries continued to employ personnel for plant and factory security. In the face of labor unions striking and labor relation problems,

private security personnel were used to control civil unrest or as undercover infil-
trators of a union to report critical information to a company. At the same time,
public-serving law enforcement organizations such as the New York Police Department and Los Angeles Police Department were growing and becoming models
for other public-serving law enforcement agencies around the country.[41] Private
security personnel continued to grow and develop in the industrial sector, and
public-serving law enforcement agents were soon becoming more professional
on American city streets.

The federal government under President Roosevelt focused on battling the
Great Depression that kept the American economy in a tattered state. By the late
1930s, Japan and Germany had engaged in conquering vast territories despite the
outcry of European states, China, and Russia. With the possibility of America being brought into a world conflict against Germany and Japan, President Roosevelt
in the late 1930s saw military and economic aid to Europe as vital preparations
for an oncoming world war and as an opportunity for America to benefit. With
President Roosevelt steering America out of the Great Depression, it was possible
to provide American aid to Europe and other nations facing the German and Japanese onslaught. This aid became known as the Lend-Lease Program under which
the United States supplied Great Britain, the Soviet Union, China, France, and
other Allied nations with vast amounts of war material between 1941 and 1945. In
return, Britain provided the United States with military bases in Newfoundland,
Bermuda, and the British West Indies. The Lend-Lease Program began in March
1941, nine months before the December 7, 1941, attack on the US naval fleet based
at Pearl Harbor.

In this buildup to WWII, the industrial sectors and factories were tasked by
President Roosevelt to supply the bulk of military equipment and goods that were
to be shipped overseas. However, the reality of spying and sabotage taking place on
American soil created a need for a much larger security force capable of safeguarding all industrial and factory sites crucial to war preparations. It quickly became
apparent that major security breaches were possible at crucial industrial locations
in the United States. Following the Pearl Harbor attack by the Japanese military,
President Roosevelt issued an executive order giving the US War Department the
mandate to properly train security personnel to guard, patrol, protect, and respond
to any threat on US industry. For a nation still recovering from the Great Depression, the use of private security personnel was the only alternative to provide security coverage where local public-serving law enforcement agencies and federal
police agencies could not cover.[42] This federal support was a crucial moment for the
growth of the American private security profession because of the pressing need
to increase the amount of private security personnel in the country along with the
need for advanced security training for the coming world war. Almost immediately
private security forces were hired in large numbers to receive advanced training

from the local law enforcement agencies and the Federal Bureau of Investigation. In particular, besides offering advanced training, the federal government approved the status of private security guards at plants and factories to become auxiliary military police for the purpose of protecting areas of productions, goods, and their shipment.[43] By the middle of WWII, there were private security guards protecting war goods and materials at more than 10,000 factories.

■ The Private Security Field: Post-WWII

After the defeat of the Axis powers in WWII, the private security field continued to grow in size and scope. Realizing the importance of private security personnel at factories, industrial areas, and research facilities, a new standard was set by the federal government in light of the growing Cold War with the Soviet Union.[44]

Security and Police

With the need to protect locations from sabotage or theft from both criminals and Soviet personnel, the federal government made it a standard that any major company seeking to obtain a government contract to build or provide any type of manufactured product had to show proof that they had a comprehensive security plan in place. Such plans were to include a professional-level security program that used the latest developments in locks and alarms, fences, patrols, and trained personnel. In addition, the security program would have to be maintained and supervised by a full-time security officer who could coordinate changes and development of security in conjunction with the needs of the federal government. This standard made security personnel no longer optional for over 11,000 defense-related facilities.[45]

Going beyond providing security at facilities with just private security guards, defense-related facilities began the process of developing the first comprehensive security plans using advances in technology with the first generation of private security managers at the helm. At this point in American history, the fear of street crime in the post-WWII era led many retail stores, hotels, restaurants, bars, sports venues, theaters, warehouses, trucking companies, service industries, and corporate buildings to employ not just private security guards, but to develop comprehensive security plans similar to the defense contractors. A problem quickly emerged for the private security field in terms of training and development. While public-serving law enforcement agencies had developed formal police academies for the training and education of its officers, the private security field was still in its formal training infancy. Knowledge in private security matters had been passed from one person to another or learned simply through experience in a security job.

To solve this pressing need, in 1955 the American Society for Industrial Security (ASIS) was created as an association for private security professionals.[46] In addition, security companies with an organization and scale similar to the Pinkerton National Detective Agency emerged in the United States to set a standard for the level of proficiency and training of private security personnel. Companies of similar fields began to meet regularly to share specific information each company had gained on threats to security at their location or problems in their respective industry. As organized crime continued to be recognized and identified in America, information on criminal threats was relayed to different companies through these newly forming business alliances. While companies today share information via computer and through Web sites in which they have allied to help one another, this innovation also pushed companies to organize their information for purposes of training their own personnel on security matters. One of the first of these information-sharing organizations was the National Automobile Theft Bureau (NATB), which helped with discovering the trends and possible offenders in automobile theft on a national level. NATB also developed vehicle-theft databases and managed vehicle theft investigations for the insurance industry. Another was the Insurance Crime Prevention Institute (ICPI) that was created in the 1970s to investigate insurance fraud. In 1992, the NATB and ICPI merged to create the **National Insurance Crime Bureau**, the nation's premier not-for-profit organization dedicated exclusively to fighting insurance fraud and vehicle crime, which is estimated to cost the American public $30 billion annually. The organization is dedicated to stopping fraud because fraud increases costs for insurance companies, manufacturers, and customers. The increased use of credit cards by the 1980s also led to the creation of numerous information bureaus to perform credit checks and background investigations for those committing credit card fraud.[47]

Owing to rapidly increasing crime and growing social disorder in the 1960s and 1970s in the United States, there was an increased interest in private security personnel. The responsibility for preventing crime, which had formerly been the sole duty of the public police, began to shift towards more private security personnel. Attention began to focus on violence against our nation's airlines during this same time period as terrorists began implementing the new tactic of airline hijackings. From the late 1960s to 1972, there were 134 aircraft hijacking attempts that gained worldwide attention and prompted the airline industry in America to begin employing private security personnel through contract security groups. The compulsory use of security screenings soon became the normal trade practice throughout the rest of the world. As American businesses have opened operations and facilities around the globe, the threat to high-level corporate executives and their families also led to the rise of corporate executive security, corporate bodyguards, and travel security consultants as new members of the private security field.

The Hallcrest Report

With new private security personnel in different variations appearing in the United States, the National Institute of Justice (NIJ) decided in 1980 to seek a better understanding of the state of the growing private security field. In 1980, NIJ sought out Hallcrest Systems, Inc. to conduct a major 3-year national study to better gauge the state of private security in the United States by researching the growth and extent across all fields in the country. By 1985, the results of the Hallcrest Report were made public under the title of *The Hallcrest Report: Private Security and Police in the United States.* The second researched report, *Private Security Trends 1970-2000: The Hallcrest Report II,* came out in 1990. As a result of two independently conducted studies, similar results and information verified the current state of private security in the United States.[48] The following key findings from both reports overwhelmingly demonstrated the growth and heightened role compared to public-serving law enforcement organizations.

- U.S. businesses lose approximately $114 billion or more a year to criminal activity.
- Governments from federal to local municipalities have paid for private-sector security services through the increasing privatization of services. In 1975, state and local government spending for private-sector services was $27 billion; by 1982 it rose to 0. billion. Additionally, federal expenditures for private security services in 1987 were $197 billion.
- In 1990, private businesses and individuals spent $52 billion for private security.
- In 1990, 1.5 million people were employed annually by private security agencies. In contrast, only 600,000 persons were employed as sworn public law enforcement officers in 1990.
- Private security expenditures were predicted to continue to rise to $104 billion by the year 2000, when the private security industry would likely employ almost 1.9 million persons.
- The average annual rate of growth in private security employment was forecast to be 2.3% per year. This was higher than the annual 1.2% rate of growth for the entire U.S. workforce as whole.[49]

It is important to realize that the large number of personnel and expenditures was beyond what many experts believed it would be in the 1980s and 1990s, even in light of increased crime in the 1980s. Hallcrest believed that four interrelated factors largely explained the greater employment and expenditure shift from public to private protection and the increasing growth of private security. These factors were (1) an increase in crime in the workplace, (2) an increase in fear (real or perceived) of crime, (3) the limitations on public protection imposed by the "fiscal crisis of the state," and (4) an increased public and business awareness and use of the more cost-effective private security products and services.

Throughout the 1990s, private security personnel were trained and employed in much higher numbers than public-serving police officers. The reasons for the growth, even as the U.S. crime rate declined, can be explained by a number of possible reasons:

- Increasing public awareness and fear of crime
- The trend toward specialization of all services in the security field
- More sophisticated electronic surveillance devices and monitoring systems
- A lack of confidence in the ability of regular police officers to protect business interests

Private Security in the News   Even though the US housing market has experienced a slump in the past few years, during the last two decades about 25,000 new gated communities were developed and completed. Private security agencies service a larger proportion of the central burglar alarm market than do police departments. The installation of security systems in single-family homes continues to rise.

Although the crime rate in the United States as a whole began to drop in the 1990s, the 1993 World Trade Center bombing and the Oklahoma City bombing in 1995 put both American business and private citizens on alert for future attacks. American businesses began to consider more serious possibilities of future problems, which required a rethinking of security measures. In addition, the concept of business continuity practices, the ways in which a business can protect itself and continue to operate business during a crisis, began to develop and added a new subdiscipline to the ever-expanding private security field.[50]

The Columbine High School massacre in 1999, along with other school shooting events and gang violence incidents across the country, prompted the development of more initiatives and training in the area of school security. The growing American healthcare industry in the 1990s also prompted a need for more security personnel who were aware of key issues that effect hospitals and other healthcare settings.

Ultimately, effects of the 9/11 attacks on the private security field are a two-sided coin. On the negative side, the analysis from the 9/11 Commission report and other reports that later followed highlighted that improperly trained or vigilant private security personnel are a major weak link in the chain of national security. As more details about how the hijackers were able to thwart our nation's security systems and personnel has been revealed, people began doubting the capability and abilities of many private security personnel around the country. Pressure from the public has increased for the training, education, and accountability of private security employees. In a positive manner, the knowledge gained about the manner in which the 9/11 attacks were carried out also created a demand from increasing numbers of individuals and businesses to seek private security in both their planning for emergencies and providing additional security functions. More private security personnel were hired in the months following the 9/11 attacks then ever before to serve in more public settings in the interest of public safety as a whole.

■ The Professional Development of Private Security: Professional Training Groups

The period following WWII quickly prompted the private security field to develop new ways to train and educate private security personnel. In the early 1950s, Paul Hansen, serving as director of the Industrial Security Division of Reynolds Metals, met with five other private security professionals and established the beginnings of a national association of security directors. Their focus was to establish an organization based from companies with expertise in guards, security fences, safes, locks, and manual alarms. Today, that organization is known as ASIS International—American Society for Industrial Security. ASIS International has been paramount in setting industry standards for training and certification programs for private security personnel. By early 2000, ASIS membership had risen to over 30,000 private security personnel. Notably, ASIS has established one of the highest standards in security training and certification for private security professionals. Today, ASIS certifications are the most difficult to earn in the private security field. Candidates must pass stringent comprehensive written examinations, but first they must have the years of experience in the private security field to become eligible.[51]

- ASIS Certified Protection Professional (CPP): This certification designates individuals who have demonstrated competency in all areas constituting security management. Nearly 10,000 individuals have received the CPP certification since its inception in 1977.

- ASIS Professional Certified Investigator (PCI): Holders of the PCI certification have demonstrated education and/or experience in the fields of case management, evidence collection, and case presentation.

- ASIS Physical Security Professional (PSP): The PSP certification is for those whose primary responsibility is to conduct threat surveys; design integrated security systems that include equipment, procedures and people; or install, operate, and maintain those systems.[52]

Besides ASIS, a number of industry training and certification groups have developed since 9/11 specifically to provide more in-depth standards for specific areas of the private security field. All of the following organizations have set standards for membership, offer training and certification standards, hold national conferences, and in many cases have regional chapters where private security professionals can meet to advance their particular industry.

The International Foundation for Protection Officers (IFPO) is a nonprofit organization established in January 1988 to help address the training and certification needs of security and protection officers and their supervisors. The IFPO offers several distance-delivered training programs that can result in certification if completed successfully. Members of the IFPO then benefit from having an independent verification of the competence of those that obtain certification. The most widely known are Certified Protection Officer (CPO) and Certified in Security Management and Supervision (CSSM). IFPO publishes a quarterly newsletter called *Protection News*. Its circulation includes all IFPO members and candidates enrolled in either their CPO or CSSM programs. *Protection News* is designed to keep security professionals current on trends within the security industry. It contains information about physical security and life safety, as well as personal and property protection.[53]

The Academy of Security Educators and Trainers (ASET) was founded in 1980 as a nonprofit professional society. The current membership of hundreds of men and women includes academics, trainers, students, law enforcement, and government officials from national, state, and local agencies; self-employed professionals; security officers; supervisors; and security directors from major international corporations, banks, transportation companies, security service organizations, and communications, energy, retail, chemicals, insurance, petroleum, and utility companies. The purpose for the founding of the academy is to assist in the proper growth and development of security education and training. It has specific focuses of promoting the establishment of a security degree program, developing training courses, and aiding curriculum development. It also serves as a resource for legislative bodies considering regulatory action. It sponsors basic and applied research and facilitates dialogue between teachers, trainers, and practitioners.[54]

Private Security and Policy In the interest of improving the image and standards of the private security industry in light of 9/11 attacks, Congress passed the Private Security Officer Employment Authorization Act of 2004. This act gave employers the ability to request criminal background checks from the FBI for job candidates. This is important in preventing anyone from being hired for a public-serving law enforcement agency or a private security group. It also prevents someone from moving to another location to obtain a private security job.

The International Association for Healthcare Security and Safety (IAHSS) is the only organization solely dedicated to professionals involved in managing and directing security and safety programs in healthcare institutions. IAHSS was formed in 1968 by a forward-looking group of professionals in healthcare security that needed to address changes in how institutions, their patients, and healthcare providers could better promote care in a safe environment. A hallmark of IAHSS is its series of training manuals and study guides that prepare prospective healthcare security officers and others to meet the needs of their institutions and sit for one or more certification examinations of the organization. Over 20,000 individuals have successfully achieved basic certification since its inception. Three new certification exams have been added to enhance the qualifications of the security officer. Through the IHSS Foundation, seasoned professionals at the management level can sit for the Certified Healthcare Professional Administrator (CHPA) exam and earn the certification.[55]

The National Association of School Safety and Law Enforcement Officers (NASSLEO) is one the oldest security organizations of its type focused exclusively on school security. It is dedicated to providing professional information, training, and other resources to school districts and law enforcement agencies across the nation and Canada. NASSLEO's primary mission is to bring together people that are joined in a common effort to make schools safe for students and staff. NASSLEO is a nonprofit, membership-funded organization. NASSLEO membership is primarily composed of educators, law enforcement, and security officers, as well as other professionals that share the common goal of protecting students, staff, and physical assets. Joining is completed by submitting a membership application or by attending their annual 3-day training conference. Each year NASSLEO brings together top experts from around the country to address many topics of interest to their members. These items include national and international issues, programs, best practices, and recaps of major events that affect safety of children and schools. The conferences also provide a forum for vendors and exhibitors of educational and security-related programs, technology, and other materials of value. NASSLEO is organized into seven regions across the United States and Canada, each with an elected regional director. Each of these directors is a professional in his or her district and provides additional guidance on policies and training.

The Security Industry Association (SIA)[56] is a nonprofit international trade association representing electronic and physical security product manufacturers, specifiers, and service providers. SIA promotes growth and professionalism within the security industry by providing education, research, technical standards, and representation and defense of its members' interests. SIA is the sole sponsor of the International Security Conference and Exhibitions (ISC EXPOs). SIA's members include professionals from every phase of the business from manufacturing to installation, and their clients run the gamut of the economic sector: commercial, institutional, residential, and government. Technology, products, and services offered by members include, but are not limited, to notable areas such as access control, biometrics, surveillance cameras and systems, fire detection and suppression, home automation, intrusion, remote and wireless monitoring, personal security products and response systems, mobile security, lock hardware, and many specialized services.

The Association of Certified Fraud Examiners (ACFE) is a member-based global association dedicated to providing antifraud education and training for security professionals. Together with its members, the ACFE is reducing business fraud worldwide and inspiring public confidence in the integrity and objectivity of the profession by offering the certification to become a Certified Fraud Examiner (CFE). This designation denotes proven expertise in fraud prevention, detection, deterrence, and investigation. Members with the CFE credential experience professional growth and quickly position themselves as leaders in the global antifraud community. In fact, the ACFE's 2006 Compensation Guide for Anti-Fraud Professionals reveals that CFEs earn 18% more than non-CFEs in similar jobs.

■ Conclusion

From ancient times to the modern age, private security has changed and grown from inexperienced men hired during periods of turmoil to professionals with a wide background in different areas of security. Although public law enforcement agencies emerged to serve the entire general public, private security personnel have been continuously used in Asia, Europe, and America. The period before WWII and the Cold War also increased the need for private security personnel in America. The 9/11 attacks prompted a rise in private security on a national level. In the coming decades, private security personnel will continue to be sought after and used in American society in the interest of maintaining security.

■ Chapter Review

- Private security personnel were used in ancient civilizations such as Egypt, Rome, and Byzantium.
- The success of private security personnel in Europe led people to demand public-serving law enforcement agencies.
- The expansion of the railroad in the Wild West during the 1800s prompted a need for more private security personnel.
- The Pinkerton National Detective Agency served as a model for effective private security groups and a prototype for modern corporate security firms.
- American preparations for WWII resulted in federal expansion of private security forces.
- The end of WWII and the rise of the Cold War continued the need for private security personnel in America.
- The Hallcrest Reports showed the growth and effectiveness of private security personnel in America.
- Since WWII, the private security industry has worked to expand the level of training and education for private security personnel.

■ Answers to Case Study

1. In what type of business would you find private security personnel at this very moment in your town? In the modern world, you are likely to find private security personnel in a wide variety of locations: banks, schools, restaurants, movie theaters, airports, supermarkets, and residential homes.

2. What type of activities do local police perform in your community? Local police engage in prevention of criminal activity as well as responding to any criminal activity that is in progress or has taken place in an area. They also work to serve the community in public service functions such as crowd control, emergency planning, or domestic situations.

3. What do you think is the difference between local police and private security personnel? The biggest difference is that your local law enforcement agency has taken an oath to protect and serve the general public in their jurisdiction. Private security personnel are hired for specific duties on behalf of a client.

4. Think about world history, imagine hundreds of years ago: what did communities do without local police? Who protected people from harm? Communities were often on their own for security and protection. Over time, communities around the world realized that strength exists in numbers and began to develop systems in which each family could protect one another.

■ Key Terms

Assize of arms   A legal precedent developed in English common law jurisdictions guaranteeing a right to bear arms.

Bloody Code   A succession of laws enacted through the mid-1700s in which more than 200 criminal offenses carried the death penalty.

Bow Street Runners   Founded in 1749 by the novelist and magistrate Henry Fielding, they were the first paid detectives in London seeking out criminals.

Constables   These are neighborhood-appointed lawmen who had the authority to arrest criminals or summon assistance.

Feudalism   This was a general set of reciprocal, legal, and military obligations among the warrior nobility of Europe and the peasants.

Frankenpledge   A system of pledge in which kings of England and their future successors to the throne were to ensure safety and security by demanding an oath of loyalty to the rule of the king.

Gendarmerie   A military body charged with police duties among civilian populations.

Hallcrest Reports   These reports from the 1980s and 1990s highlighted the growth and expansion of private security personnel in America.

Hue-and-cry System   This was the system by which a person in medieval England could summon assistance from other people in a matter that threatens the security of an area.

Infrastructure   Infrastructure in any area is the given facilities, services, buildings, and structures needed for the community's survival.

Janitor   A slave guard posted at the entrance to a Roman building, in particular a business or the master's home.

Magna Carta   An English governing document that established a feudal system of governance during the Middle Ages and the supremacy of established law and order over the orders of the king.

Medjai   A division of ancient Egypt's police during its 18th dynasty (a part of the New Kingdom). The Medjai were also well-known in the Egyptian army.

Mercenary   A person who takes part in an armed conflict or in providing security services who is motivated by the desire for private gain.

National Insurance Crime Bureau   The nation's premier not-for-profit organization dedicated exclusively to fighting insurance fraud and vehicle fraud.

Pinkerton National Detective Agency   This was a private US security guard and detective agency established by Allan Pinkerton in 1850.

Statute of Westminster   This established the precedent that any person had a right to stop in their current activities and act affirmatively towards the apprehension and pursuit of felons when a crime was committed in front of an English citizen. Any free Englishman had royal authority to prevent crime and to act to restore security when order and peace was disturbed by others. It also established three major practical security measures for the average English person living in their local community.

Tithings   These were organized systems of 10 English families banded together for security and to provide community responsibility for law and order in a given location.

Urban cohorts   These were led by the urban prefect of ancient Rome. The cohorts were created to counterbalance the enormous power of the Praetorian Guard in the city of Rome. Their primary role was to police Rome from the roaming mobs and gangs that so often haunted its streets. Very occasionally they would take to the field of battle, but in the army they really had no more than an honorary role.

Varangian Guard   Hired security personnel used by Byzantine emperors during the height of the Byzantine Empire.

Watchman   A watchman was usually a privately and formally employed person who was paid to protect property, and/or assets, and/or people during the medieval period in England.

Watch-and-ward system   A medieval English security system that provided that local town residents were to act as watchmen; they were chosen or assigned to patrol walled cities of England during evenings keeping a lookout for criminal or unruly behavior.

■ **References**

1. Healy, M. 1992. *New kingdom Egypt*. Oxford, UK: Osprey.
2. *The Week*. 2007. Soldiers of fortune then and now. 7(332).
3. Ibid.
4. *See* note 1.
5. Kelly, M. 1988. Citizen survival in ancient Rome. *Police Studies* 11(4, Winter). *See also* Davies, R. W. 1968. Police work in ancient times. *History Today* October. *Also* Dempsey, J. 2003. *Introduction to investigations*. 2nd ed. Belmont, CA: Wardsworth. *Also* Aries, P., and G. Dulig. 1987. *A history of private life from pagan Rome to Byzantium*. Cambridge, MA: Bellnap Press of Harvard University.
6. Ibid.
7. Ibid.
8. Ibid.
9. Ibid.
10. Critchley, T. A. 1967. *A history of police in England and Wales*. Montclair, NJ: Patterson, Smith.
11. Ibid.
12. Ibid.
13. Ibid.
14. Ibid.
15. Ibid.
16. Ibid.
17. Mercenary. 2008. In *Merriam-Webster Online Dictionary*. Retrieved September 5, 2008, from http://www.merriam-webster.com/dictionary/mercenary.
18. *The Week*. 2007. Soldiers of fortune, then and now. 7(332).

19. Ibid.

20. More, T. 2001. *Utopia*. Reprint. New Haven, CT: Yale University Press.

21. *See* note 18.

22. Machiavelli, N. *The Prince*. 1984. Bantam Classics.

23. Ibid.

24. Foucault, M. 2004. *Security, territory, population*. http://www.prefecture-police-paris.interieur.gouv.fr/documentation/bicentenaire/theme_expo4.htm.

25. Ibid.

26. South, N. 1987. Law, profit, and private persons: Private and public policing in English history. In *Private Policing*. Beverly Hills, CA: Sage.

27. Ibid.

28. Tobias, J. 1979. *Crime and police in England, 1700-1900*. New York: St. Martin's Press.

29. Ibid.

30. Ibid

31. Pringle, P. 1965. *Hue and cry: The story of Henry and John Fielding and their Bow Street runners*. New York: Morrow. *See also* note 28.

32. See note 28.

33. Peel, R. 1829. *Bill for improving the police in and near the metropolis*.

34. See note 28

35. Dewhurst, H. S. 1955. *The railroad police*. Springfield, IL: Charles C. Thomas. *See also* Gough, T. W. 1977. Railroad crime: Old West train robbers to modern day cargo thieves. *FBI Law Enforcement Bulletin* February.

36. Ibid.

37. Ibid.

38. Lavine, S. A. 1963. *Allan Pinkerton: America's first private eye*. New York: Dodd, Mead, and Company. *See also* Fishel, E. C. 1996. *The secret war for the Union: The untold story of military intelligence in the civil war*. New York: Houghton Mifflin.

39. Ibid.

40. Ibid.

41. Cunningham, W.C., and T.H. Taylor. 1985. *Crime and protection in America: A study in private security and law enforcement resources and relationships*. Washington, DC: US Government Printing Office. *See also* Fischer, R.J., and G. Green. 1998. *Introduction to security*. 6th ed. Boston: Butterworth-Heinemann. *Also* Albanese, J. 1999. *Criminal justice*. Boston: Allyn & Bacon.

42. Hess, K., and H. Wrobleski. 1996. *Private security.* 4th ed. New York: West Publishing.

43. Ibid.

44. Ibid.

45. Dempsey, J. 2008. *Introduction to private security* New York: Thompson/Wadsworth.

46. About ASIS. 2008. Retrieved September 5, 2008, from http://www.asisonline.org/about/history/index.xml.

47. *See* note 45.

48. Cunningham, W.C. and T.H. Taylor. 1985. *The Hallcrest report: Private security and police in America.* Portland, OR: Chancellor. *See also* Cunningham, W.C., J.J. Stauchs, and C.W. Van Meter. 1990. *The Hallcrest report II: Private security trends: 1970-2000.* Boston: Butterworth-Heinemann. *See also* Van Meter, C. 1976. *Private security: Report of the Task Force on Private Security.* Washington, DC: National Advisory Committee on Criminal Justice Standards and Goals.

49. Ibid.

50. Weller, L. D. 2005. *Best practices for prevention and recovery.* Disaster Recover Journal. Spring 2005. Volume 18, Issue 2.

51. Davidson, M. A. 2004. Fifty remarkable years. *ASIS Dynamics* September/October 2004.

52. ASIS International Security Certifications. 2008. Retrieved September 5, 2008, from http://www.asisonline.org/certification/index.xml.

53. International Foundation for Protection of Officers. 2006. Retrieved September 5, 2008, from http://www.ifpo.org.

54. History. Academy of Security Educators and Trainers. Retrieved September 5, 2008, from http://www.asetcse.org/history.html.

55. Welcome to IAHSS. International Association for Healthcare Security and Safety. Retrieved September 5, 2008, from http://www.iahss.org/about_welcome.asp.

56. About SIA. 2008. Security Industry Association. Retrieved September 5, 2008, from http://www.siaonline.org/about/index.html.

Private Security Employment Positions

▶ ▶ OBJECTIVES

When you finish reading this chapter, you will be better prepared to:

- Understand the substantive differences between traditional public-serving law enforcement jobs and private security positions.
- Learn about the different types of private security employment opportunities in the United States.
- Understand the licensing, training, and educational requirements for certain private security positions.
- Examine some of the major US corporate security firms.

■ Introduction

As you learned in the previous chapter, the need and demand for private security personnel since WWII and 9/11 has continued to increase with each passing year. The American public now demands private security personnel to be present at various locations in the community to prevent crime and to respond to crisis situations. Even more so in the post-9/11 world, private security personnel offer the ability to prevent and handle situations in many cases without police involvement or in conjunction with traditional police activities. This means that minor incidents can be handled by a private security group without involving local police officers. This allows local police officers to respond to more pressing matters. In addition, the advanced uses of technology by individual criminals, organized criminal organizations, and terrorists have warranted a new demand by the public for more security in our everyday lives.

▶ ▶ CASE STUDY

Imagine you have recently graduated from a university and have decided to work in the law enforcement field. Upon conducting some quick research, you learn that the salary and benefits of your local police department are not very competitive and attractive. You learn from a friend that some private security positions have opened up with a major corporate security firm. The salary and benefits with this security firm are quite substantial and worthwhile. In addition, you discover in the classified ads that advertisements indicate they are hiring store security, school security, and loss prevention officer positions at different locations. You begin to wonder what other types of private security positions are available in your local neighborhood, and what it is in society that is driving the increase in new security positions opening up. Additionally, while you refer to members of your local police organization as "officers," you also wonder what your title would be as a member of the private security field.

1. What do you think are the major differences between local police and private security personnel (besides salary and benefit differences)?
2. What type of jobs are available for a person seeking an entry-level private security position?
3. What are some general requirements needed to obtain a job in the field of private security?
4. What type of work is conducted by major corporate security firms?

The general public is not the only group that has fostered a need for private security personnel. The increase in private security personnel in the United States during the past few decades stems from the rising demands of **insurance carriers**. Insurance carriers, particularly fire insurance carriers, often give substantial rate discounts to businesses that have a 24-hour security presence or a comprehensive security plan in place to prevent crime and to react to minor and major incidents. Often for business or industrial locations that have a high risk rate for an incident, such precautions are necessary. The discount from an insurance carrier can often exceed the funds being spent on a security program in its entirety for a business. For example, having security on site increases the odds that any fire will be noticed and reported to the local fire department before a complete and total loss occurs to the business. The early stages of fire can be handled in many cases by properly trained private security personnel.

Observe a variety of locations and you will see private security personnel performing different levels of tasks. In small locations, they may guard the people in the location and look for criminal threats specific to the type of organization they protect. For example, in retail outfits security guards may guard the entrance and exits of stores to deter or catch shoplifters. They are likely to work with other employees to apprehend shoplifting customers before local police arrive or work with managers when employees are suspected of illegality. Retail outfits often lose large quantities of goods and funds to theft by their own employees. Locations where large volumes of people congregate, such as shopping malls, schools, theaters, or public squares are likely to employ security personnel who have additional responsibilities. In such locations, security guards serve as deterrents to public disorder and to respond to minor incidents.

Banks, by virtue of storing money, certainly require private security personnel to guard areas where theft or robbery can occur. The transfer of funds or valuable items between banks or institutions generally involves private security personnel in armored vehicles. The general operating procedure involves an armed guard leaving the safety of an armored truck, moving to the door of a commercial bank, signing for money and returning to the armored vehicle with bags in hand. The risk lies in the movement to and from the bank when a robbery or disruption of service is likely to occur.

Medium-sized and large corporate facilities also require private security personnel to guard the movement of sensitive and important items, protect against workplace violence, be ready to handle major incidents and guard against theft. Even seemingly harmless information such as customer lists, printed data, and business transaction records can possibly be used illegally or to gain a competitive advantage over a company. Factories face theft by disgruntled employees of intellectual property or goods disappearing while in transit from one location to another. Hospitals, utility centers, industrial plants, and transportation terminals are also areas that are subject to criminal activity, including the possibility of a terrorist incident or a major theft. Certainly, government buildings can be targeted by outsiders and from within by authorized personnel.

Today, more buildings housing high-tech businesses are at increased risk as possible targets. Laboratories can contain chemicals or radioactive material that are valuable for sale or use in the development of a weapon of mass destruction. For an insider to an organization, such materials can prove tempting for someone interested in a quick profit through an illegal sale.[1]

Private security personnel now have more tools at their disposal than just experience and gut instinct to perform their guard duties. The use of electronic equipment such as cameras and metal detectors help to prevent people armed with a weapon and intent on committing a crime from entering a facility.

In America, 85% of its critical infrastructure (water, electricity, communications and transportation systems, telecommunications, Internet) is in the hands of private companies that are not under any type of 24/7 government security protection. This means that private security personnel are absolutely necessary for preventing criminal activity or terrorism from shutting down crucial systems in America. These critical infrastructures are major targets for disgruntled employees, criminals, and terrorists.

■ Private Security Contrasted with the Police

An individual interested in working in the private security field should understand the various private security jobs available. As you have learned, the local law enforcement agencies in your communities today have developed alongside private security personnel over the last few centuries. Both types of groups are concerned with security; however, for most people, understanding the nature of security is both complex and often difficult. **Security** is defined as protection or precautions taken against danger, risk, threats, and general problems. It focuses on the protection of an interest whether that interest involves goods, money, or the safety of people in a given location or place.

Government-run law enforcement agencies at the town, county, state, and federal levels operate in a specific jurisdiction and serve the people who live and work in that area. As government agencies, they serve the public and focus on protecting the general public. The focus of private security personnel is quite different from this concept. In private security, the focus is on the maintenance, protection from harm, destruction, or theft of assets. Assets of a business are tangible funds, goods, service equipment, and most importantly the employees and clients that provide a business entity with value and worth. Even public schools and universities are forms of a business entity in which the people entering and leaving are the assets that need to be protected. Additionally, government-run law enforcement personnel take an oath to protect and restore peace in a community while preventing criminal activity and act in a public service function. Such law enforcement personnel generally take an oath to defend and protect the federal **Constitution** and state constitution while they are on duty. The role played by private security personnel is not that different in terms of preventing crime and restoring order. However, the big difference is that the ultimate authority given to private security personnel comes from the **guidelines** or operating procedures of the organization that employs them. Private security personnel must function under the guidelines of their organization as well as the industry standards set by a government body for the specific private security work they provide to clients. In many cases, private security personnel ultimately derive their power not from the government, but from a contractual arrangement that gives them law enforcement powers while they work on site. Regardless whether the business is a retail store, casino, industrial plant, university, or other entity, the private security personnel must at all times keep in mind that their job is to protect and consider the assets of an organization, whether that organization employs him or her directly or whether he or she is employed by a security firm hired by the organization.

In addition, the protection of the **interests**—areas of concern such as the public image—of the business or the security firm are also the responsibility of private security personnel. While the law of a particular jurisdiction should never be violated in the interest of the business entity, above all else, the interest of the employer of a private security person comes first. The serious nature and gravity of what is at stake as a member of a private security team cannot be taken lightly. Any time a security member puts on a uniform and begins a shift, their duty is to uphold the highest level of performance to protect all assets and interests.

Private Security and Policy   The role of local police organizations is primarily reactive. They concentrate on arrests and investigations of past crimes and respond to emergencies when someone calls 9-1-1. Private security is focused on preventing crime and other incidents. It also promotes a feeling of safety before an incident occurs.

Private security has three times more employees than government-run police organizations across the nation. Private security handles close to 50% of all crimes committed on private property.[2]

It is not surprising that private security personnel are often confused or mistaken for local police officers owing to similar uniforms, badges, tools, equipment, and behaviors while on duty. Both private security personnel and public-serving police officers are likely to appear as if they are in reactive modes looking for a problem that could emerge at any second. However, the actual powers of police officers differ from private security personnel. Suppose a shoplifter was discovered in a supermarket. A police officer arriving at the scene can question the suspect, but their scope is limited under the federal, local, and state constitutions. They must honor the oath to uphold the rights and privileges guaranteed to every citizen. Police officers can only question in many cases if they have reasonable suspicion or probable cause that criminal activity has in fact taken place. If they wish to obtain a confession from a suspect, the suspect is afforded their criminal suspect rights under the Miranda doctrine that states they have a right to remain silent and the right to a lawyer.

Private security personnel have nearly unlimited power to question and detain without reasonable suspicion or probable cause. The requirement of probable cause for police officers to question and detain is more limited, and the restrictions on the police are important to understand. Additionally, legal precedents in US courts have further restrained the traditional police officers' power of "officer discretion" regarding arrests in the field. Private security personnel still enjoy much wider powers of discretion largely because of their private citizen status. Because the laws regarding the limitations of powers generally have to do with police officers interacting with criminal suspects, private security personnel are relatively free to utilize nontraditional means to protect and serve the interest of their clients.

This does not come without areas of restraint. Private security personnel do not enjoy the benefit of civil protection as do police officers; therefore, they can be sued directly for false arrests or assault if they commit such acts against suspects to the point that it is considered criminal activity or a violation of civil codes. Some private security officers with police powers, typically employed directly by governmental agencies, are called **security police**. Normally, these are private security personnel acting with specific police powers and duties primarily involved with the security and safety of a significant government installation or building.

Private police officers are private security personnel working with security agencies that have a special contract to provide patrol services in public areas. In some cases, these private security personnel are offered civil protection while limiting the scope of their ability to apprehend and question a suspect. This is accomplished by state or county jurisdictions commissioning or deputizing private security personnel. This is true particularly when private security personnel are employed in protecting public property such as mass transit stations or transportation hubs where incidents are much higher. Except in these special cases of being deputized, a private security person who misrepresents himself as a public-serving police officer is committing the crime of impersonating a police officer.

Word to the Wise   Private security personnel have to ensure they do not engage in behavior when apprehending, questioning, and interrogating a suspect that violates criminal and civil codes in their local jurisdiction. When receiving training at a new private security job, be sure to inquire about the legal restrictions regarding a private security person in your area. Many private security firms or clients have guidelines for private security personnel to follow so they do not incur legal liability.

Because both police officers and private security personnel are interested in security, they can work together for the benefit of both organizations. However, police organizations are called in by private security personnel to a location and asked to take over security when a situation warrants a higher degree of response. There are circumstances that only local law enforcement agencies can handle:

1. When the nature of activity (threat or emergency) cannot be handled by private security personnel alone
2. The situation requires a police agency to respond for the interest of the general public or victim(s)
3. When the organization decides that calling the police will solve an immediate problem
4. When the federal or state government demands that law enforcement agencies handle a situation, even when objected to by private security personnel

Based on the above criteria, there a number of high-stake situations that would require a police organization to respond. A hostage situation, a terrorist incident, a riot in progress, a potential suicide attempt by a jumper, a bank robbery, the aftermath following a natural disaster, or a four-alarm fire would all fall into this category. All of these examples are incidents that would require private security personnel to seek the assistance of public-serving agencies.

When providing security services, private security personnel are further classified by the status of who their immediate bosses are when hired. Private security personnel who were hired directly by a business organization to perform security duties are generally classified as "**in-house**" private security personnel as they perform a security function to the same organization that hired them directly. Such private security personnel are found as guards or security officers in locations such as retail stores, malls, theme parks, and casinos. A **contract employee** is a private security person that protects many different locations as per a previously negotiated agreement.[3] A private security person could find work by being hired directly by a professional private security company that performs numerous types of security duties for many different clients. Their services are generally leased or rented to another company. Contract services can be a wide range of private security activities such as private investigations, installations of alarms and cameras, armored car

TABLE 2-1. Examples of In-House and Contract Private Security Personnel Opportunities

In-house	Contract
Retail stores	Private investigations
Malls	Alarm and camera services
Theme parks	Armored car services
Casinos	Manufacturers of security equipment
Educational institutions	Locksmiths
Hospitals	Security consultants and engineers
Food services	Polygraph testing (lie detector)
Drinking establishments	Guard dog training and sales
Hotels	Drug testing
Department stores	Environmental cleanup
Manufacturing firms	Forensic analysis
Residential and nonresidential buildings	

transfers, environmental cleanup, lie detector tests, drug testing, and other activities. It is important to note that organizations continually switch from in-house to contract security groups. They may, in fact, train their own in-house security team once a contract with a private security organization has expired. The change in the use from in-house to contract employees is often dependent on the funds available for private security and the pressing need for their services (see Table 2-1).

■ What's in a Name? Public-Serving Law Enforcement Agencies versus Private Security Personnel

The private security field has created a major debate among both private security personnel and law enforcement agencies over the nature of titles. Particularly, controversy exists within the private security industry regarding the job titles of "security guard" as opposed to "security officer" and "security agent" that the private security industry currently uses. Government agencies at the state and local level heavily monitor and regulate by law the use of the title "officer" or "agent." They are concerned that the titles may give an impression to others that a security person is somehow connected to a law enforcement agency. The need to avoid confusion is important because while both security personnel and municipal police wish to protect and serve, it is important for the general public to be able to understand the different interests of an "officer" whether public or private.

Today, the watchmen of the past have been replaced by the modern term of **guards**, who are focused on preventing incidents that cause a disruption in security. Guards are one of the most visible security personnel in a stationary or patrolling

Word to the Wise   Security personnel should be careful when identifying themselves to citizens or traditional police officers as "officers," especially in a high-threat or tactical threat situation. This can result in being charged with impersonating a police officer. It can also result in serious injury or death if the police officers are led to believe that they are confronting an armed criminal committing a crime as opposed to rescuing a lawfully armed private employee. The term *guard*, however unpalatable to some, may prevent potentially lethal confusion when interacting with law enforcement agencies and dispatchers in a crisis situation. Sometimes public law enforcement officers work as private security personnel while not on duty. This is usually done for extra income, and the work is typically hazardous jobs such as bodyguards and bouncers outside high-profile nightclubs in major cities such as Las Vegas, New York City, Miami, and Los Angeles.

position.[4] Often such newly hired private security personnel for a business or private security firm have minimal training and experience. Because a guard's focus is to keep the area they guard free from incidents, they are primarily serving to prevent incidents by their presence. The range of activities in which they can adequately respond to and protect others from, therefore, is limited.

While guards are often entry-level personnel with limited training and experience, the private security position of **security officer** indicates a person with greater training, skills, and abilities. Often, security officers are highly trained through the military, law enforcement agencies, professional organizations, and general public exposure through previous employment in different fields. They may have advanced educational degrees and certifications. Such private security employees are likely to serve in a supervisory position over entry-level guards and are likely to interact with public-serving personnel (police, firemen) on a regular basis. They are also likely to serve as guards in security areas where quicker reaction and expert handling of situations are needed. It is these private security employees who tend to take more pride in their title of *officer* and despise the label of *guard*. The position of officer tends to be more sought after by people working in the security field because it allows for increased pay and faster mobility through the ranks of a security team.

Controversies in Private Security   Location, location, location! It may be a selling point in real estate, but in terms of pay equity for private security, location might not always be a feature. In searching for work in the private security field, be sure to determine where you will be working. For example, highly trained and experienced mall security officers who are often exposed to serious risks make less per hour in some parts of the country than security guards with less training and experience who are guarding industrial or transportation sites. Unfortunately, the economic reality of today is that compensation may not be significantly different in some business organizations despite different titles of private security personnel.

Private Security in Popular Television: *Dog the Bounty Hunter*   Duane Lee "Dog" Chapman is an American bounty hunter and bail bondsman who lives in Honolulu, Hawaii. He stars in *Dog the Bounty Hunter*, a weekly reality television program that is broadcast on network cable. The show chronicles Chapman and his family's business, Da Kine Bail Bonds in Honolulu, Hawaii. They also have other offices in Hawaii and Colorado. The office on the Big Island is owned and run by Duane's son, Leland Chapman. Dog Chapman claims to have captured over 6500 bail jumpers and criminals. Some of his private security colleagues do not approve of Chapman's methods or style. Penny Harding, the executive director of the California Bail Agents Association, said, "He represents all of the things that bail agents are trying to get away from—the cowboy image, the renegade, bring 'em home dead or alive." The show is aired on A&E Networks in the United States and on Bravo in Great Britain.[7]

Just as the term *officer* has brought debate in the private security industry, the term **agent** is a private security personnel title with its own controversy. The term agent can describe a legal relationship under civil law between an employer and employee or it can describe an employee of a federal law enforcement agency (FBI, ATF, DEA). Private security personnel are likely to be called *security agents* when working in the security areas of loss prevention for retail or corporate stores.[5] Such agents could be found working on the floor with members of the general public or conducting investigations while working with a computer in an office cubicle. The term *agent* can also be found among those individuals working in the realm of **personal protection/bodyguard**, in which the private security personnel are primarily focused on the lives and safety of their clients. Both of these employees often work in plain clothes without a uniform and are trained to act lawfully in the immediate defense of the life or property, which they are hired to protect. **Bail enforcement** agents or **bounty hunters** are often regulated by the same agencies in a county or state that regulate all private security personnel. A repossessor or "repo man" is now referred to as a **recovery agent**. These are private security individuals with specialized training in recovery of merchandise that must be returned to the original provider or financial lender.[6]

As you can imagine, there are many ways to categorize or define the major areas of the private security industry depending upon the specific field. Regardless of whether the title of guard, officer, or agent is used, there are continually new areas of the growing security field employing private security personnel. The following are some of the major fields in which security personnel are being employed.

Information Security

With more **hackers** (someone who illegally breaks into computer and network systems through the use of technology) attacking computer network systems and increased theft of digital information occurring more than ever before in the United States, the need for private security personnel skilled in information security is higher than ever. Such specialists can find work protecting critical information including US government classified information, people's personal information, proprietary information of businesses or entities, contractual information, project data, and **intellectual property**. Protecting intellectual property, inventions, and new creations of a company are paramount as the value of many companies lies in the intellectual property they possess. Information security deals with issues such as who should access the data and how the data is stored, controlled, disseminated, and disposed of.[8]

Personnel Security

In many cases, problems among employees can be avoided by preventing the hiring of people who are likely to pose a risk to a business organization. Therefore, personnel security works on ensuring the integrity and reliability of an organization's workforce by guaranteeing only quality employees are hired. Personnel security encompasses conducting background investigations on potential employees, drug testing of current employees, and examining employee conduct in terms of its effect on the overall business organization or entity. Background checks on prospective employees have enabled many companies to cut down on incidents of workplace violence among employees.

Educational Institution Security

American educational institutions face a number of risks from external threats such as criminals or gangs, as well internal threats from those who work, attend, or reside at an educational institution. Educational institution security personnel work to raise awareness about the campus safety issues such as crime, drugs, and emergency situations. School security personnel always place a focus on awareness, self-protection, and prevention. It is not uncommon for educational institutions to allow a government-commissioned police department on campus or contract out this responsibility to a security provider that is accountable to the educational institution itself.[9]

Financial Services Security

With the rise in white-collar crime as demonstrated by notable cases such as the Enron and Tyco scandals, financial services security personnel focus on security issues dealing with banking, stock brokerages, insurance companies, and other financial institutions where the potential for malfeasance is high. In light of some of the shocking white-collar scandals over the past few decades, federal and state governments have created regulatory agencies that guide how companies are to operate to avoid the chance of illegality. Therefore, security personnel in this area work to ensure their company is compliant with required regulations and also actively search for any financial losses or illegality occurring within the company.[10]

Gaming and Wagering Security

In the past few decades, cities such as Las Vegas and Atlantic City have introduced the new megacasino and resort hotel into our culture. Such hotels have guests checking in and out on a 24-hour basis while gambling activity takes place at a rapid pace. Millions of Americans each year flock to such locations to gamble and engage in recreational activities. In addition, new casinos and gambling establishments are opening up on a regular basis across the nation. With money flowing in and out of facilities so quickly, the potential for problems from criminals or from the patrons themselves has required the private security industry in this area to expand rapidly. Today, private security personnel are employed to secure and protect those gambling as well to prevent any activity that can jeopardize the safety or financial security of a gaming establishment.[11]

Healthcare Security

The exponential growth of the American healthcare industry has led to more healthcare facilities opening up across the nation. With healthcare facilities full of patients, staff, and visitors, the need to maintain order and control is necessary. Such private security personnel are focused on the personal protection of all people entering the facility as well the security of the facilities themselves. You are likely to find such private security personnel at nursing homes, assisted living complexes, short- and long-term care facilities, medical centers, clinics, and hospitals.

Private Investigators

The need for investigators who can provide valuable information for legal proceedings or investigations to a business that suspects its employees are conducting illegal activities has increased. The growing amount of fraud in the United States has also led many businesses to hire contract **private investigators** to examine the state of their business. Private security personnel are able to provide personal attention to the needs of a specific client that wishes to uncover sensitive information without making it known to the general public.[12]

Business Continuity Management

In the last few decades, American businesses have hired personnel with the management and security skills necessary to deal with disasters. Security personnel in the field are focused on ensuring an organization will be able to either maintain or quickly resume normal business operations when an incident occurs. Such events can range from workplace violence and criminal activity to fire, natural disasters, and terrorist incidents.[13] Business continuity management personnel are becoming an increasingly important aspect of business management and security teams. In

Tradewinds, a private contract firm located in Holtsville, New York, performs business continuity services for companies experiencing disasters or crises. Tradewinds provides teams of skilled responders and an extensive array of equipment to come in, assess the situation, and take control to safeguard and restore a firm's assets regardless of the type of emergency. They are on call nationwide for a growing list of major corporations, government agencies, and insurance companies. They also perform contracted forensic analysis. The firm was recently featured on the History Channel show *Modern Marvels*.

particular they are addressing the role of new technologies used by businesses. As devices, systems, and networks become more complex, there are simply more things that can go wrong if a business faces a natural disaster or a workplace interruption caused by crime or terrorism.

Information Systems Security

With the heavy reliance on telecommunication and computer systems in our nation, security personnel are needed to protect the physical hardware and communication networks that are necessary for businesses to operate or for the average person to communicate with the outside world. In addition, information systems security personnel focus on protecting stored information or data of an entity and ensuring it is protected. This, in some cases, calls for information to be moved for safekeeping to an outside location. Often, information systems security personnel work hand in hand with business continuity professionals.[14]

Lodging or Hospitality Security

America has built an enormous number of new hotels in the past few decades. As with any area where there is a rapid and high volume of people moving in and out of a location, hotels have had to hire security personnel focused on protecting visitors and preventing criminal activity, as well as examining the hotel for conditions that would be detrimental to the safety and appearance of a facility. Today, you can find security personnel in the major casino-hotels in Las Vegas, in resorts, motels, or even a small roadside hotel alongside any American road.

Transportation Security

American transportation hubs have been using more private security personnel to guard, patrol, and react to any threats where large amounts of people congregate for the purpose of using a form of transportation. Private security personnel in this security field can be found at regional and international airports, airplane hangers, train depots, trucking stations, seaports and land/sea transportation operations.

Manufacturing Security

Private security personnel working in the manufacturing industry are tasked with ensuring that the conditions of the production plant are such that no worker will be harmed. In addition, they are on the lookout for those individuals on the premises with illegal intentions, such as theft or sabotage. Manufacturing companies that produce any type of goods essential to the federal government also have tightened security at their plants.

Retail Store Security

America has one of the highest number of retail stores anywhere in the world. This includes the large chain retail stores found all over the country. Private security personnel working in this area are concerned with criminal activity such as theft or fraud that can take place by unwelcome visitors at a store. They also work to prevent employees from engaging in illegal activities and to ensure merchandise is properly handled at all times.[15]

■ Fast Growing Job Markets in Private Security

Security Sales, Equipment, and Services

One of the greatest demands by people, private enterprises, and government organizations, is for security cameras, alarm systems, recording devices, or any piece of technology needed by a client for security purposes. Private security personnel in this area focus on contractual installing or maintaining security devices.[16] Those trained in this area can find lucrative work with a wide variety of clients.[17]

Private Investigators

The training to become a private investigator can be accomplished at a local level in a few weeks at an educational or community institution. Openings for such positions can be found in corporate private investigative agencies, merchandise stores, insurance carriers, banks, and credit organizations.[18] Licensing and regulations for work in the private investigation field varies from state to state.

Security Guards

More than any other private security position, security guards are still the primary entry-level positions for those seeking work in the private security field. These security guard positions are generally broken down as in-house or contract positions. They can be found in urban and rural areas throughout the country. The growth of job openings for guards is to occur in corporate security firms that conduct the hiring and training of private security personnel before assigning them to work for a client.[19]

Gaming Surveillance and Gaming Investigative Officers

The need for surveillance officers in gaming establishments and personnel familiar with gaming technology will continue to grow as more states move toward legalizing gambling and the number of casinos in the nation increases. Already training courses for prospective employees in this area can be found in states where gambling is legal.

Insurance Claims Specialists

Insurance claim specialists work to determine whether an insurance company should authorize payment to an individual seeking a claim. When activity appears suspicious, they conduct investigations to uncover fraud and criminal activity. In many cases, they often uncover a ring of organized criminal groups or white-collar professionals looking to cash in through fraudulent claims. This area is likely to continue to grow in the coming decade. At the same time, the requirements for entry have become higher, often with insurance groups requiring, at a minimum, a college degree or experience in another private security field.[20]

Business Continuity Planning

As more businesses continue to prepare their organizations for emergencies that can disrupt business, the need for qualified personnel in this area is growing. As one of the younger disciplines that involves private security personnel, entry-level positions at a business organization are likely to experience rapid growth and expansion. Similar to insurance claims specialists, a minimum requirement is a college degree in a relevant business or criminal justice discipline.[21]

■ Professional Standards and Training in the Private Security Field

The private security industry suffered from a lack of uniform professional standards in the post-WWII period as specific industries set their own mandates and standards. However, prior to 9/11, some industries had begun establishing more formalized standards of training and education as a result of pressure from state governments. Generally, without a mandate from a state government agency or legislative body, many industries attempted to invest as little as possible in both the training of private security personnel and in other areas of security for their own organizations. Since the 9/11 tragedy, a number of states have begun implementing even more changes to the way that private security personnel are hired, licensed, and regulated in a jurisdiction.

Controversies in Private Security   A 1990 survey of state regulations regarding security guard licensing and training revealed some improvement, noting that 39 of the states had imposed some licensing regulations for certain private security positions in specific industries. However, it also revealed that 17 of the states had no training requirements at all for private security personnel working in their jurisdiction.[22]

Examining the general standards for obtaining an entry-level position of security guard reveals a better understanding of how little training is required; the standards are often not that vigorous. To be licensed as a guard in most states, individuals must usually meet the following requirements:[23]

- Be at least 18 years old.
- Pass a criminal background check.
- Pass a drug test.
- Successfully complete classroom instructional training in such subjects as property rights, emergency procedures, and the proper detention of suspected criminals.

The concept of minimum training hours is the most basic regulatory standard for the training of private security personnel in the United States and Canada. **Minimum training hours** means that potential employees must undergo a fixed amount of instructor-based classroom hours to develop the skills needed for the private security job being sought. The minimum training that an entry-level private security person therefore receives will depend on a number of factors. Firstly, the organization that hires him or her will set the number of instructional hours they feel appropriate. In-house private security personnel are likely to receive training that focuses on the mandates of the business entity and on the biggest concerns facing the organization. Armed guards are likely to receive more intensive training owing to the legal ramifications associated with use of deadly force.

Additionally, some private security firms require candidates take the Minnesota Multiphasic Personality Inventory (MMPI) assessment, which can reveal if a candidate has possible emotional or mental problems. Armed guard candidates undergo a more vigorous background check and examination.[24]

Private investigator positions often require no formal education. However, it is not uncommon for many entry-level private investigators to be either young people who recently completed higher educational degrees or individuals who previously worked as law enforcement agents. The private investigator position is often sought out by retirees from traditional law enforcement groups as a post-retirement position. If necessary, candidates can receive a relatively inexpensive education through a local community course or distance learning course. Many investigative firms train individuals in the field. Depending on the state, individuals who have worked in the field as an investigator for a period of time can sit for a state exam and become licensed in this field. Licensing of private investigators is done on a state basis with a few states having no licensing. The requirements ultimately vary from state to state. Although working as a private investigator in most states may require few credentials, opening up your own investigative firm may require a license from a state authority. In some states such as New York, you must complete a state exam to earn a license.[25]

Professional standards for other private security positions depend on the nature of the assets being protected and the area of security in which a person seeks employment. For example, those seeking employment in the financial services industry will be required to have a bachelor's degree in a related business or financial area. Criminal justice degrees may be required by some employers for other areas of the private security field. If a degree or any type of higher education is not required, it is likely that the prerequisite professional certificate of that industry is likely to be needed before successful employment can be obtained. For example, many private security positions require a candidate to possess one of the ASIS certifications. In many cases, higher education institutions have begun offering many of the professional certifications needed to obtain employment in various private security positions. Here are a few key things a candidate should consider before seeking employment in the private security field:

1. Learn about the specific security work of interest. This includes learning about everyday duties, average salaries, benefits, and hours for the area of interest.
2. Learn about the specific standards in terms of formal education, experience, certifications, and training for the area of interest. The standards set by the state should be understood.
3. Research online and find out how you can meet the standards required by employers in your state.
4. Ask yourself if you have the time and financial resources to meet the standards set by employers who are hiring individuals for a specific area of private security.

ASIS International has developed *Private Security Officer Selection and Training Guidelines* that set forth the suggested minimum criteria for the selection and training of private security personnel in the United States.[26]

For those seeking bodyguard positions in the United States, many candidates are now going to Israel for a short period to train as bodyguards. The town of Natanya in Israel has set up numerous bodyguard training academies that teach students a wide variety of personal protection skills (Krav Maga), shooting techniques, advanced driving, and crisis diffusion techniques. A quick search online will reveal a number of the prestigious academies that train individuals for bodyguard employment. Such training is now becoming one of the more common industry standards for bodyguards.

Training may also be unique and specific depending on the nature of the job. For example, casino surveillance security personnel are likely to receive in-depth training on gambling techniques and the cheating techniques used in the gambling field. Alarm and camera installers will need to receive hands-on training for assembling and installing various pieces of electronic equipment. The location of a private security job will also determine the level of formalized training. For example, guards at major industrial facilities, public utilities, or tourist areas may receive months of training before being put out into the field. The larger corporate security firms, such as Wackenhut, Securitas, Guardsmark, Brink's Company, and Allied-Barton, have developed their own training curriculum for entry-level and advanced personnel. In some cases, firms such as Wackenhut even have their own training facilities.

■ Employment at Major Corporate Security Firms

As previously mentioned, a large number of the entry-level job opportunities are likely to be found in some of the major corporate security firms, and there are a number of firms that lead the way in both standards and professionalism. To help you seek a position in some of these organizations, the following information is provided regarding the nature of the work they currently engage in at various locations in the United States.

Wackenhut

Wackenhut is a major provider of security guard services in the United States. A number of Fortune 500 companies are among its clients. One subsidiary is Wackenhut Services Incorporated (WSI), which is a primary contractor to US government agencies including NASA and the Army. Wackenhut provides contract security and emergency response services (fire departments) to local governments, particularly in public transport systems. Wackenhut also offers security for employers experiencing poor relations with labor unions, including strike actions. During the 1980s, Wackenhut was active in the field of airport security across the nation. After 9/11, they received criticism for not providing higher standards for airline security screeners. However, the company has stated that pressure from airports and airlines compromised the company's standards by cutting wages, which is why they only protected four airports in the United States on September 11, 2001. Today, airports in the United States are now protected by the Transportation Security Administration of the Department of Homeland Security. Wackenhut still has proven itself a leader in tough security programs such as its involvement in protecting nuclear reactors, the Trans-Alaska Pipeline System, and other high-security government installations, including those of the Department of Energy. They also are involved in providing armed security for the Area 51 military base, as well as several US military bases in and around the Balkans, such as Kosovo.[27]

Allied-Barton Security Services

Allied-Barton Security Services is a security guard company made up of the former companies of Barton Protective Services, Spectaguard, Initial Security, and Allied Security. The company, established in 1957, is headquartered in King of Prussia, Pennsylvania. Allied-Barton is the largest American-owned security service company in the United States with more than 60 offices and 38,000 employees. Many of the security employees were high-level public-serving law enforcement agents or officers before joining Allied-Barton as full-time employees. The company works with more than 100 Fortune 500 companies and is experienced in higher education security, currently serving more than 70 colleges and universities nationwide. Their list of collegiate clients includes Harvard, Columbia, and the University of Pennsylvania. Every college with whom they have contracted has given the company superb reports. In addition, Allied-Barton provides specialized training for their college officers assigned to various positions, such as foot patrol, vehicle patrol, bike patrol, housing access control, facilities security, and special events coverage. In light of the Virginia Tech tragedy, they have quickly developed some of the best protocols and training to handle school violence on college campuses. They also strive to work together with public-serving law enforcement agencies so that both groups may benefit from shared information and preparations.[28]

Guardsmark

Guardsmark is a major provider of security services in North America, Puerto Rico, and the United Kingdom. Guardsmark is the fourth largest security company in the United States and the only major security provider that doesn't have stock traded on the US stock market. As a family-run company that employs more than 18,900, they maintain a high standard for current employees as well as for newly hired entry-level private security personnel. Guardsmark claims to be one of the largest employers of former FBI agents in the United States as well as one of the most selective employers in its industry when it comes to private security personnel. Guardsmark claims to hire only 2% of the private security applicants who seek employment in their corporate security firm. The firm markets itself as offering more rigorous screening of applicants, including, in many states, the requirement that applicants submit to a polygraph examination and a drug screen for illicit and prescription drugs before hiring. The firm also seeks to enhance the image of security officers (moving away from the designation *security guard*). Among Guardsmark's distinguishing characteristics are its adoption of a formal code of ethics in 1980, and the recognition of President Ira A. Lipman and the company for leadership in the field of business ethics, including receipt of the American Business Ethics Award in 1996.

The Brink's Company

The Brink's Company was founded in 1859 to provide a new innovation in security—the armored truck. Today, the Brink's Company is a security and protection company headquartered in Richmond, Virginia. It is divided into two core businesses—Brink's Incorporated and Brink's Home Security. In 2005, the company reported a total of 54,000 employees and operations in more than 50 countries. Brink's Incorporated is popularly known for its bullet-resistant armored trucks used to carry money and priceless goods (once used to transport the Hope Diamond from an auction to the buyer's home). Brink's provides secure transportation around the world and security services to banks, retailers, governments, mints, and jewelers. Brink's Home Security, started in 1983, is a provider of monitored security services for residential and commercial properties. The home security division of Brink's has steadily risen to be ADT's top competitor.[29]

Securitas Group

The Securitas Group has 200,000 employees and operations in more than 30 countries, primarily in Europe and North America. Securitas Group entered the US market in 1999 with the acquisition of Pinkerton's, Inc. Securitas USA works with more than 80% of the Fortune 1000 companies and has annual revenues in excess of $2.5 billion. Securitas USA provides guard services, including patrols and inspections, access control, reception and badging services, security console operators, alarm response, and specialized client requested services.[30]

■ Conclusion

Although law enforcement agencies and private security groups have developed together throughout history, there are major differences between their roles in providing security in America. Entry-level private security personnel should be aware that variable titles of private security positions encompass different levels of training and salary. Private security positions within the United States include a large number of positions from guards, private investigators, alarm and camera installers, insurance claims adjusters, gaming surveillance specialists, bounty hunters, bodyguards, and business continuity professionals to name a few. Any entry-level private security person should research the required licenses, minimum training, and educational requirements for any private security position they are seeking within their state. In addition, as the private security job growth is likely to be concentrated with major U.S. corporate security firms, an entry-level private security person should be familiar with the activities of these reputable and experienced security firms.

■ Chapter Review

- Private security personnel are focused on serving their clients and the protection of assets (buildings, people, chattels) and serve a more preventive role. Police officers are reactive in nature and generally respond to crimes that have occurred along with major emergencies.
- Private security personnel are generally "in-house," meaning they were hired and trained by the organization they protect, or they are contract employees that serve multiple clients, often at the same time.
- There is debate over the use of certain titles within the private security field. The private security position of guard often denotes an entry-level position that requires beginning-level training and experience. Positions such as officer or agent in the private security field require more training and experience.

- There is a wide variety of private security positions available to those individuals interested in working in the private security field.
- Depending on the private security position sought by an entry-level person, the more training, education, and experience is required.
- A candidate for an entry-level security position should research the required licensing, training, and education in the state where they wish to work.
- America has a number of major corporate security firms that lead the way in both standards of professional and reputable private services.

■ Answers to Case Study

1. **What do you think are the major differences between local police and private security personnel (besides salary and benefit differences)?** Generally, private security personnel are paid much less than their law enforcement counterparts. This can vary depending on the location where local police and private security personnel work. Private security personnel entering the field as entry-level personnel may find that salaries will vary depending on the nature of private security employment and the location where they provide private security services.

2. **What types of jobs are available for a person seeking an entry-level private security position?** Entry-level employees to the private security field are likely to be hired as guards or in private security positions in which advanced skills and experience are not required. However, some of the more specialized private security positions can be available to entry-level personnel based on a pressing need for personnel and where on-site training is likely to occur.

3. **What are some general requirements needed to obtain a job in the private security field?** Generally, a job in the private security field requires that a person be at least 18 years old, have a clear criminal background, pass a drug test, and have a high school education.

4. **What type of work is conducted by major corporate security firms?** The major corporate security firms provide a wide variety of services. This includes basic guard work, advanced investigations, protection services, specific contract assignments for clients, alarm services, and additional varieties of security related tasks.

■ Key Terms

Agent   A title that can describe a legal relationship under civil law between an employer and employee; it can describe an employee of a federal law enforcement agency (FBI, ATF, DEA). Private security personnel are likely to be called *security agents* when working in certain areas of the security field such as loss prevention.

Bail enforcement agents/bounty hunters   Individuals who capture fugitives ("hunting") for a monetary reward ("bounty"). Other names include bail agent, bail enforcement agent, bail officer, fugitive recovery agent, fugitive recovery officer, or bail fugitive recovery specialist.

Constitution   A system, often codified as a written document, that establishes the rules and principles that govern a political entity. In the case of countries, this term refers specifically to a national constitution defining the fundamental political principles, and establishing the structure, procedures, powers, and duties of a government. Most national constitutions also guarantee certain rights to the people. In the United States, all people fall under the jurisdiction of the federal constitution and their state constitution.

Contract employee   A private security person that protects many different locations as per a previously negotiated agreement.

Gaming surveillance and gaming investigative officers   Private security personnel who work in gambling facilities. They are focused on preventing illegal gaming.

Guards   Individuals who are focused on preventing incidents that cause a disruption of security.

Guidelines   Operating procedures of an organization that establish how people and the organization will function.

Hackers   Individuals who illegally break into computer and network systems through the use of technology.

In-house   Private security personnel that perform a security function for the same organization that hired them directly. Such private security personnel are found as guards or security officers in locations such as retail stores, malls, theme parks, and casinos.

Insurance carrier   Business organizations that provide insurance to all types of organizations in case of any damage or loss to people, structures, or things.

Insurance claims specialists   Individuals who process insurance claims and conduct investigations to determine if any type of fraud or illegality is being conducted by an insurance claimant.

Intellectual property   The inventions and new creations of a company, group, or individual.

Interests   Areas of concern for a person or entity.

Mall security officers   Private security personnel who are focused on preventing crime and illegality at retail malls and on maintaining a level of safety for all guests and employees.

Minimum training hours   A fixed amount of instructor-based classroom hours of training for the skills required for a specific private security position.

Personal protection specialists/bodyguards   Private security personnel that are primarily focused on the lives and safety of their clients. Both of these positions often work in plain clothes and are trained to act lawfully in direct immediate defense of the life or property they are hired to protect.

Private investigators   People who undertake investigations, usually for a private citizen, business, insurance company, attorney, or some other entity not involved with a government or police organization.

Private police officers   Private security personnel working with security agencies that have a special contract to provide patrol services in public areas.

Recovery agent   Individuals with specialized training in recovery of merchandise that must be returned to the original provider or financial lender.

Security   Protection or precautions taken against danger, risk, threats, and general problems. It focuses on the protection of an interest whether that interest involves goods, money, or the safety of people in a given place.

Security officers   Indicates private security personnel with greater training, skills, and abilities. Such private security employees are likely to serve in a supervisory position over entry-level guards and are likely to interact with public-serving personnel (police, firemen) on a regular basis.

Security police   Private security personnel acting with specific police powers and duties primarily involved with the security and safety of a significant government installation or building.

■ References

1. Dingle, J. 1993. Back to the basics. *Security Technology and Design*. November/December. *See also* Paine, D. 1972. Basic principles of industrial security. Madison, WI: Oak Security Publications.

2. *The Economist*. 1997. Welcome to the new world of private security. April 19. *See also* Cunningham, W.C., and T.H. Taylor. 1985. *The Hallcrest report: Private security and police in America*. Portland, OR: Chancellor. *See also* Cunningham, W.C., Stauchs, J.J., and C.W. Van Meter. 1990. *The Hallcrest report II: Private security trends: 1970-2000*. Boston: Butterworth-Heinemann. *See also* Van Meter, C. 1976. *Private security: Report of the Task Force on Private Security*. Washington, DC: National Advisory Committee on Criminal Justice Standards and Goals.

3. Hess, K., and H. Wrobleski. 1996. *Private security*. 4th ed. New York: West Publishing.

4. ASIS. 1994. New roles for private patrols. *Security Management* December. *See also* Muntz, A. 1991. Contracting for the right relationship. *Security Management*, June.

5. Hayes, R. 1991. *Retail security and loss prevention*. Boston: Butterworth-Heinemann. *See also* Horan, D. J. 1996. *The retailer's guide to loss prevention and security*. Boca Raton, FL: CRC Press.

6. Clarke, R. 2003. Above the law: US bounty hunters. *BBC News* June 19. *See also Working the doors*. http://www.workingthedoors.co.uk.

7. Jablon, R. 2003. Bounty hunters assail Duane "Dog" Chapman. *Associated Press*, June 20. *See also* Dog the Bounty Hunter biography. http://www.imdb.com/name/nm1738062/bio.

8. World Intellectual Property Organization. http://www.wipo.int/about-ip/en.

9. Security Disciplines. 2008. Retrieved September 5, 2008, from http://www.asisonline.org/careercenter/careerdisc.xml.

10. Ibid.

11. Ibid.

12. Ibid.

13. Contingency Planning Exchange. http://www.cpeworld.org.

14. *See* note 9.

15. Ibid.

16. Ibid.

17. US Department of Labor, Bureau of Labor Statistics. Occupational outlook handbook, 2008-09 edition. Accessed September 5, 2008, from http://www.bls.gov/oco/.

18. Ibid.

19. Ibid.

20. Ibid.

21. *See* note 13.

22. Security Industry Authority. *Security legislation*. http://www.the-sia.org.uk.

23. *See* note 17.

24. International Association of Security and Investigative Regulators (IASIR). Homepage. http://www.iasir.org.

25. New York State Department of State. Licensing Services. Accessed September 5, 2008, from http://www.dos.state.ny.us/lcns/pifaq.html.

26. *See* note 9.

27. Minahan, J. 1994. *The quiet American: A biography of George R. Wackenhut*. Belmont, Australia: International Publishing Group. *See also* Palast, G. 2002. *The best democracy money can buy: The truth about corporate cons. globalization, and high-finance fraudsters*. London: Pluto Press.

28. History. 2008. Retrieved September 5, 2008, from http://www.alliedbarton.com/about/history.aspx.

29. Brink's Company homepage. 2008. Retrieved September 5, 2008, from http://www.brinkscompany.com/.

30. History. Retrieved September 5, 2008, from http://www.securitas.com/us/en/About-Securitas1/History/.

Entry-Level Business Techniques and Information

CHAPTER 3

▶ ▶ OBJECTIVES

When you finish reading this chapter, you will be better prepared to:

- Discuss the role of an ideal leader in the business world.
- Understand and develop business management skills.
- Know what constitutes leadership for private security personnel.
- Understand security appearances.

■ Introduction

An entry-level security employee in the United States is expected to take on a number of responsibilities. Whether he or she is hired to simply guard a location or to be proactive in other security-related activities, the level of skills required to solve problems are greater than ever. Although provided a minimum amount of training by an in-house or contract security firm, an entry-level security employee may quickly discover that security work can be challenging and in some cases unpredictable when working in the business community. This chapter will begin to provide information and best practices for an entry-level security employee on the business techniques and information necessary to handle a dynamic business environment.

▶ ▶ CASE STUDY

It is an ordinary day at the Acme Computing Corporation. As a security officer in a corporate uniform, you are finishing your morning cup of coffee and looking over the evening security reports when the fire alarms begin to sound. Examination of the fire emergency board indicates a fire on the fourth floor of

(continued)

▶ ▶ ▶ CASE STUDY CONTINUED

the building. You leave the security office on the second floor to discover people are running down the stairs from the upper floors, shouting, and apparently in a state of confusion. Some of the employees rush up to you and ask what is happening and what to do. You seem to be only person at this moment that people are looking to for guidance.

1. What responsibilities as a leader should you be demonstrating as part of your duties?
2. How should you communicate with other employees?
3. How should you act to control the situation?
4. Describe what you look like in this crisis situation; what image are you projecting?

■ Leadership in the Business World

The serious nature and gravity of what is at stake as a member of the security field cannot be understated or taken lightly. Any time a security member puts on a uniform, there is a duty to operate at the highest level of performance in protecting the **assets** and interests of the client. Security personnel serve as a dedicated and accountable group of individuals. They are expected to be a **point of information,** or source of information, for their fellow employees and visitors concerning any specific developments and notable events. As such, security personnel need to be aware of changes in the functions of the organization, staff, the business, and even the neighborhood. They should seek information on new developments or news related to their field. They are a walking symbol of the safety and security of an organization. People expect security personnel to take control during a time of **crisis** or unexpected occurrence on the physical grounds of the business. This is true whether they are working as in-house or contract employees, security at a bar, a school, a retail store, a multinational corporation, or a nuclear facility. Regardless of the nature of the organization, location, size of the client, or duties, a security officer is first and foremost expected to act as a leader and meet a standard of excellence.

Just as life can be unpredictable, so can the ever-changing problems and challenges faced by a member of the private security community. In any field, a person who is unable to lead others, command respect, and accomplish goals is ineffective. In security, such gaps in leadership among security personnel means not only that harm can happen economically to a company, but that people can possibly be harmed or even killed by the inability of a security employee to function properly as a leader. As leaders, security personnel are expected to be competent professionals capable of performing difficult and demanding jobs and tasks.

■ Business Professionals

Whether a person is a chief executive officer of a large multi-national corporation or a worker in the mailroom, business professionals are to appear and behave in a fashion different from how people act normally in society. In the military, soldiers are expected to meet a high standard of performance and execution of tasks while maintaining a focus on duty and discipline. Likewise, today's business and corporate culture requires even an entry-level security person to meet

© Christopher Ewing/ShutterStock, Inc.

the high standards of a **business professional**. A professional is an individual who exemplifies a commitment to excellence and quality in the performance of their specific duties and daily tasks. The mindset required of today's business professional is undoubtedly a high standard. It begins in the morning when a business professional must report for work. In corporate culture, to be early is to be on time and to be on time is late.

A business professional always speaks with confidence and poise when addressing an individual or a large group of people. They appear dressed in the appropriate attire for the position assigned in their workplace. They appear diligent and are committed to ensuring that their work meets a high standard at all times.[1] They are experts in time management and ensuring tasks and communication are always moving effectively. Idleness and laziness are foreign concepts to a business professional. If a specific task is finished, a business professional is busy working on a new task. They are always seeking ways to bring their particular business craft to the next level of high performance unique to their specific industry.[2] They know how to command others in accomplishing a goal whether the situation is relaxed or is during a period of stress and time constraint. This is aided by the fact that

Controversies in the Industry   There are a number of debates among private security experts on whether private security personnel should have a strong business background or a criminal justice background before being hired for a private security position. Entry-level private security personnel with a bachelor's degree in a business-related field are likely to understand business management techniques more than other candidates for a security position. Criminal justice students are more likely to understand the nature of criminal activity and the nature of crime.

© BananaStock/Alamy Images

business professionals set a high work standard in their daily duties that makes subordinate employees rise to a high level of performance. Very importantly, a business professional uses corporate and personal resources to constantly seek new information, knowledge, and training to advance their skills and job performance as part of their own personal goals.

Understanding and Developing Business Management Skills

A private security person has not only the burden of acting like a business professional, but has an additional duty. As security personnel, they are expected to be able to handle security breaches and emergency situations that may occur at a location. Before security personnel can handle security breaches and emergency situations, they must master a specific set of business management skills. Such business management skills make private security personnel individuals who work on a professional level and as individuals capable of handling heavy work tasks or difficult situations.

Word to the Wise   Go to a library, a bookstore, or take a course on business management techniques. The better a candidate for a private security position understands how a small or large business operates, the more likely they are to perform better and respond to situations in the interest of their employing company.

Time Management

In the security field, private security personnel may have numerous tasks to be completed within a given work shift. This can range from filling out reports, checking personnel entering and exiting a building, watching videotapes, attending meetings and training events, and completing any daily assigned tasks that are common to the unique security position held by an individual. However, the added stress of unforeseen events while at work can result in a security person not accomplishing all tasks in a given day. The end result is that the security person feels stressed and is likely to not perform up to the minimum standards set by the company. This can result in an individual that is denied promotions or is ultimately fired. It is therefore important for private security personnel to find a way to manage their time at work so they are effective. In addition to maintaining a daily schedule of the events or tasks to be completed every day, a **time budget** may be necessary. A time budget is a guide that can be incorporated into a daily work schedule to improve the work experience of a private security person. For example, a time budget for a security person at a computer technology firm could include the following:

- Time allowed for searching on the Internet and reading e-mail—30 minutes at the beginning and end of shift
- Time to complete an adequate facility inspection/tour—2 hours
- Time allotted for attending weekly security meeting—1 hour

Such a budget lets an employee stay on schedule while not spending too much or too little time and effort on a given task. It also allows a security person to realize when they are on or off schedule with the completion of a task and when in fact they may need assistance in completion of a task.

Backward Planning

Regardless of the type of location where a private security person is employed, long-term tasks will be assigned to security personnel for completion. Such tasks will be added on top of daily duties. In the corporate world in which a private security person operates, a key rule is that all deadlines for the completion of tasks are final. Failure to accomplish a task by deadline means termination of the employee. Therefore security personnel must determine a method of ensuring every deadline is met.

Backward planning is one such method. Backward planning is a method that involves examining a task and determining a plan of action for completion of the task. For example, if a security person is assigned in January to develop and test a new evacuation plan that is to be operational by August of the same year, a security person can quickly sit down and develop a plan.

August—Business security project due
June—Evacuation drill tested and adjusted after feedback from participants
May—Obtain participants for evacuation drill

April—Final edited draft of evacuation plan completed
March—First draft of evacuation drill completed
February—Remainder of research completed
January—Task assigned, initial research for plan conducted

In backward planning, a security person is establishing a set of checkpoints that help to mark when a task is closer to completion. It allows a security person to feel less stressed since they have a plan in place and are able to update the employer when questioned about the completion of the task. Backward planning also allows a time adjustment if an employer needs a task completed sooner. If possible, backward planning should be set up so a goal is accomplished before the deadline. In the business world, accomplishing a goal before the due date is always better.[3]

Triage

Imagine walking into the security office at a major corporate firm in a large city. Within minutes your supervisor *and* the corporate executives in the building are rapidly assigning you tasks. The sudden assignment of numerous tasks can be daunting and overwhelming to most people, even to an experienced private security person. The way to handle such situations is to conduct a **triage,** or a prioritization of tasks. When faced with numerous tasks, you should ask the following questions:

- What tasks must be accomplished immediately?
- What tasks are the most important or serious in terms of safety, security, or the organization's interests?
- What tasks have I been ordered to make a priority by my superiors?

This method provides a security person a way to ensure all tasks get completed, but also allows for a security person to not be overwhelmed and ineffective.

■ Speech and Communication Skills

Like any business professional, a security person, no matter what level or position within a business, should have a handle on the basics of public speaking and communication skills. In terms of interpersonal skills, a security person should be able to speak clearly and with authority when carrying out a task such as a greeting to a coworker in the morning or when communicating on the radio to others.[4] A security person is someone with authority and who is looked at by others as a source of safety and stability.[5] Therefore any security person must be mindful that their use of language, tone of voice, and speech patterns reflects a well-trained, confident, and educated member of the business (see Figure 3-1).

A private security person should also be able to successfully conduct a meeting and a formal presentation. Presentations are necessary as a means of training other security personnel or for training employees within a business. A security person who appears nervous, unprepared, or lacking confidence when making

Figure 3-1 Private security person in uniform, speaking with customers.
© Jupitarimages/Thinkstock/AlamyImages

a presentation is going to appear weak and therefore unable to train or inform others in an organization.

In the corporate world, everyone is judged by his or her voice and communication style. A security person must be able to speak to a group of people in either calm or heightened stress situations with a tone of voice that makes it clear that the security person is in charge of people. Speaking with confidence as a security person makes others feel confident. In responding to a security breach or an emergency situation, such language and speech patterns can be life saving. Considering a security person is in a position to protect business interests and people, the need for heightened communication is even greater.[6]

TABLE 3-1. COMMUNICATION TRANSMISSION CHOICES

Level of Importance	Transmission choice
Low importance and speed	E-mail or interoffice memo
Medium importance	Phone calls and e-mail
High importance	Phone calls and possible in-person visits to key personnel, building-wide announcements

Communication Management

The increased development of communication technology in this century has resulted in a greater reliance on e-mail and mass interoffice phone messages as reliable methods of communication of important information. Even with the latest developments in technology, a business professional skilled in ensuring information to a large group is disseminated quickly and effectively can often overlook loopholes in a communication chain. It is common for people to not receive information that is transmitted or to discover that important information is ignored or misplaced by others. Although business employees can use the excuse "I didn't get the e-mail or memo," private security personnel are held to a higher standard as the transmitter of important information. Therefore, there must be careful consideration of the method of communication chosen and the actual information being transmitted by private security personnel. Security or safety information that is not immediate or not very important can be transmitted in one manner, but time sensitive or extremely important information must be handled differently. See Table 3-1 for examples.

The constant consideration of method of transmission of information must also be followed by some form of communication receipt that the information has in fact been received by a party. So if important information is sent from the security office to a key executive via e-mail, it is important for the security person to take a few minutes and possibly make a call to ensure the information was received.

■ The Development of Good Leaders

Security personnel must be leaders. You cannot operate in the field of security without being an individual who is comfortable as a leader in the office or in the field. This is true as well with situations of heightened stress or emergency events where leadership is paramount to success. To be a good leader requires numerous **interpersonal skills** that allow success.[7] The following sections discuss guidelines necessary to be a good leader in the private security field.

Setting a Standard

Whether you are a leader of a group of security personnel or an entry-level member following orders, you are to set a high standard in everything from your conduct on the job, your ability to arrive at work early and stay later, and your interaction with others. Your actions can quickly establish your level of commitment to an employer and the ability of others to trust and consider you as a worthy security person. To set a high standard requires a key word—pride.[8] If you have pride in your job and yourself, then everything in terms of setting a high standard tends to fall into place.

Communication

As previously mentioned, to be a good leader requires the ability to speak and present information in an authoritative and confident manner. Communication as a leader also requires you to disseminate information quickly and appropriately among coworkers. This includes the ability to refrain from speech patterns or topics that may result in your personal image being tarnished. A good leader is mindful of his or her image and reputation, which can be enhanced or ruined by bad speech patterns.[9]

© RexRover/ShutterStock, Inc.

Know Your Coworkers and Subordinates

A private security worker is a people person. In dealing with other security personnel and employees, you must know the interpersonal strengths and weaknesses of employees. If one employee is better at conducting a background check while another is great with facility problems, then a security person should be aware of who can help advance your skills or who to place in an appropriate situation. More importantly, a leader builds connections with others by taking an interest in people. If a coworker is a fan of a particular sports team, ask them about it. If an individual has had a recent change in their life (marriage, birth, death), then the focus should be on building rapport with that individual. By developing a professional and friendly work relationship, your ability to conduct security matters is much easier.

Continually Seek Improvement

A leader in the private security field is constantly improving his or her skills. Security personnel should be aware of ongoing training at the business organization or at conferences, events, and seminars in the area. They should seek out local universities or training centers for educational opportunities that enhance their skill set. Knowledge is power, and in the private security field it is the fastest way to a promotion and more leadership opportunities.[10]

Delegation

Although every task in a security job must be done carefully and efficiently, it is sometimes better to delegate a particular task to someone who is better at it or who has less tasks on their daily schedule to accomplish. A good security leader is confident in his or her coworkers and subordinates. A good leader is comfortable in assigning individual tasks to be completed. The key, however, is to check at a later time to ensure any delegated task is in fact accomplished. While tasks can be delegated, responsibility when a task goes right or wrong cannot be delegated.

Appearance and Attitude

While security begins with leaders, it ends with appearance. If you were a criminal considering robbing a store, which location would you choose as a place to commit a crime?

© Steve Luker/ShutterStock, Inc.

- A retail store with a security guard that is leaning up against the wall, wearing sneakers, with an IPOD sticking out of his pants pocket and his shirt untucked. He also appears unshaven with his hair a complete mess.
- A jewelry store where the security guards are wearing dark suits or clean uniforms, polished shoes, and who are continually scanning the store. They look serious and confident in their ability to handle a criminal matter.

The reality is that not every criminal activity or act of terrorism can be prevented by even the most highly trained and qualified security personnel.

However, many problems can be avoided if the security personnel at a particular business appear as if they are prepared and ready to face a problem. Criminals and terrorists share a common pattern in that they select targets for attack based upon the opportunity of success. A security force that appears prepared and looks professional, even without advanced training, can deter a significant amount of crime. Therefore, as a private security person or a supervisor of security personnel, an individual should consider the following guidelines for appearance while at work:

- Be clean shaven and groom your hair appropriately.
- Wear a well-kept, tailored, and clean uniform or business attire.
- Avoid showing any tattoos or body piercings.
- Avoid chewing gum or eating in public while on duty.
- Avoid poor body postures (leaning against a wall, crouching, slumping).
- Do not engage in bad hygiene behavior such as spitting.
- Do not smoke or use tobacco products while on duty.
- Appear vigilant and awake.
- Wear dress shoes that are comfortable but polished.
- Avoid using any handheld devices such as PDAs, IPODS, or anything that makes you appear distracted from your security duties.
- When speaking to other employees and customers, keep it brief.

In terms of attitude, the mindset of a security person is crucial. Any security plan is only as good as its weakest link. A private security person who is disinterested in his or her position and does not care about his or her duties while at work is a serious security compromise to any organization. While a fellow security team leader should keep an eye out for fellow coworkers who are not performing to the standard of the business or industry, it is up to the individual employee to stay motivated and to stay vigilant at his or her job.[11]

Remember a private security person serves to prevent crime and incidents before they happen. If you appear as someone who is not prepared or focused, you are inviting someone to engage in criminal activity.

Private Security and Policy The expectations of private security employees in terms of the level of professionalism and standards can vary from one business to another. Keep in mind the larger the business or corporation is, and the more serious their work, the more likely the level of professionalism is expected to be higher. Research the business you are going to work for to see if it fits your lifestyle. Also keep in mind your research about the private security field, the different job opportunities, and work requirements for your particular area.

■ Conclusion

Entry-level private security personnel have a variety of business skills that they will need to develop and improve during their careers in the field. As more private security personnel are sought by businesses, clients, and organizations, entry-level security personnel should always be looking to improve their business skills regardless of the nature of the organization that employees them. They should emulate those security and business professionals who set a high standard of excellence while looking for ways to make their own unique skills a benefit to the profession. With an understanding of the basics of business management techniques, an individual working in security for the first time can quickly master the nature of working in the modern business world and become an effective leader.

- Private security personnel are to meet the high standards of business professionalism regardless of the nature of the client or organization that employs them.

- Private security personnel must understand the professional demands of the American business world.

- Time management and delegation skills are necessary for the completion of security tasks.

- Private security personnel must quickly develop a high standard in their work tasks.

- The appearance and attitude of private security personnel can result in lives being saved and property protected.

- All private security personnel are to serve as leaders in their organizations.

■ Answers to Case Study

1. What responsibilities as a leader should you be demonstrating as part of your duties? You should realize that the concern is for the employees who may be in harm's way if a fire threat is real. People will be required to move in an orderly fashion out of the building. You must immediately communicate with the security office to determine if the alarm is a drill or is in fact a real threat. If a real threat, the priority becomes one of ensuring the safety of all people in the building and contacting the local police and fire departments. The senior corporate executive will also need to be advised of the situation. During this whole time, you must appear to be calm and in control of the situation.

2. How should you communicate with other employees? You should reassure them that security personnel have control of the situation. At the same time, you should speak with an authoritative voice that commands both respect and adherence to orders given. You may have to speak in a loud voice to get and maintain control of the crowd.

3. How should you act to control the situation? You must act with authority and follow the security procedures and training of your position. It is expected that you have drilled for a situation such as a fire. Therefore you would be familiar with the objectives that need to be accomplished. You must act with the authority of a seasoned professional capable of meeting the set objectives while appearing calm and controlled. Employees might be expected to appear afraid and concerned, but you are not afforded such a luxury.

4. Describe what you look like in this crisis situation. What image are you projecting? You are in a clean, polished uniform or business attire fitting the interests of the business or corporation. You appear healthy, vigilant, and ready to handle any ordinary or out of the ordinary situations that may arise.

■ Key Terms

Assets   The parts of a business that are valuable such as tangible funds, goods, services, equipment, and most importantly the employees, which provide a business entity with value and worth.

Backward planning   A management method that involves examining a task and determining a plan of action for completion of a task.

Business   An organization that seeks to perform a service or create a product for profit.

Business professional   A business professional is an individual who exemplifies a commitment to excellence in performance of their specific duties while carrying out their daily business tasks with a high degree of professionalism or high quality.

Communication receipt   A business management technique in which a person verifies that the information has in fact been received by a party.

Crisis   An unexpected occurrence on the physical grounds of the business.

Interpersonal skills   Behavioral and business management techniques that allow an individual to communicate effectively with other people.

Point of information   Source of information concerning the specific business developments and notable events.

Time budget   A guide that can be incorporated into a daily work schedule to improve the work experience of a private security person.

Time management   A business technique for satisfactorily balancing all required tasks, work functions, and their completion deadlines.

Triage   The prioritizing of tasks based on their severity and demand.

■ References

1. Curtis, G., and R. McBride. 2005. *Proactive security administration*. Upper Saddle River, NJ: Pearson Prentice Hall.

2. Ortmeir, P. J. 2005. *Security management*. Upper Saddle River, NJ: Pearson Prentice Hall.

3. Heller, R. 1999. *Learning to lead*. New York: DK Publishing.

4. Lowndes, L. 2003. *How to talk to anyone: 92 little tricks for big success in relationships*. New York: McGraw Hill.

5. *See* note 1.

6. *See* note 1.

7. *See* note 2.

8. Brown, T. A. 2004. *Business security*. Las Vegas, NV: Crary Publications.

9. *See* note 4.

10. *See* note 4.

11. *See* note 8.

Private Security Guarding and Protection Skills

▶ ▶ OBJECTIVES

When you finish reading this chapter, you will be better prepared to:

- Understand the basics of guarding.
- Learn about body language interpretation.
- Understand interrogation techniques for private security personnel.
- Understand personal protection techniques.

■ Introduction

An entry-level security employee, regardless of their employer's location, will be expected to perform a specific variety of guarding and protection tasks. They are also expected to master a specific set of skills over time that increases their ability to protect an organization and the people. This chapter provides information regarding guarding and protection skills necessary for private security personnel.

■ Guarding

▶ ▶ CASE STUDY 1

Imagine you are a private security person at your first day on the job without a supervisor nearby. You have recently been assigned to guard the entrance to the elevators inside a corporate building. Primarily you are sitting at a desk with a metal barrier that stops people from walking straight to the elevators unless checking in with you first and showing their identification.

1. What types of behavior would you be on guard for as people enter the building? What activities would make you suspicious?
2. How do you keep alert in a job that can seem monotonous over time?
3. What techniques help make you a better guard at this assignment?

With the rise in workplace crime, terrorism, school violence, and theft, the current operating environment for organizations needs improved security more than ever in the form of guards. It should be noted that everything from the operations of an organization, activities within a building, and the image of the organization all can center on one simple private security mantra: Private security personnel who are guarding a location should be focused on crime and incidents that can be prevented, ensuring people and structures are safe, and that the operations at a location are able to continue without interruption.[1]

Guarding Basics

Private security personnel must master this first basic skill at the very heart of security protection: guard. To **guard** is to protect people and property through diligent inspection, control access and exits of a location, patrol, and observation of changes in an assigned area. Any area of business, whether an industrial plant, residence, university, or corporate office can be subject to serious incidents ranging from small thefts and vandalism to major theft, robbery, fire, and even terrorist events.[2] To be a guard in the private security field is to be proactive in maintaining an organization's policies that protect the normal operations or profit making of an organization. A focus is also placed by guards on safety and mitigation of any problems that may arise.

The security guards generally serve to "detect, deter, observe, and report."[3] Security guards are not normally required to make arrests, but they have the authority to make a citizen's arrest or otherwise act as law enforcement officers. However, as previously noted, in some jurisdictions security officers are invested with arrest powers like those of a public-serving law enforcement organization. Security guard personnel do enforce company rules and can act to protect lives and property. In fact, they frequently have a contractual obligation to provide these actions.

While guarding a location, private security personnel, to a great degree, must act with the same level of skill as any local law enforcement officer engaged in a patrol. Private security personnel are responsible for reporting and handling criminal acts that occur in a given area. They are expected to communicate any noticeable changes that are of concern and to write daily **reports**, documents that contain concise information learned during a shift that are written in a professional business style. The outgoing **shift** completing its tour (a private security team in groups of

---

Private Security and Policy   In some areas, private security personnel working as guards may not be visible in uniforms for concern it may intimidate customers and visitors to a location. Guards may be in plain clothes or professional business attire such as suits. The benefit of using security guards in uniform is that it sends an immediate message to outsiders that a security team is present and prepared to respond.

1 or more) must speak with the incoming guard shift to discuss issues of the day of importance to the security of the organization. In case of any major incident, private security personnel are expected to handle the situation as professionals and to ensure that all reports and interviews of witnesses and possible victims are able to meet the standards of evidence in a court if necessary.

Secure Guard Positions

Guarding in a business setting generally takes two forms. **Secure positions** are guard positions in which a private security person stays at a given location for a period of time. It is not uncommon for a private security person to stay present in one secure location for a few hours and then move to another secure position before finishing a shift. A secure position could include serving behind the desk in a lobby, a private booth outside a sensitive area of a company, or stationed outside at the main entrance of the physical plant of a business. A private security person assigned to a secure shift should become familiar with the alarms, cameras, and entrances and exits in the given area. The persons who also work in a given area should become familiar with the private security officer in a secure position. The private security officer should learn which employees arrive during their shift and learn their names. They should know all the administrative staff, such as cleaning and mail personnel. Since most businesses have regular drop off and pickup of parcels, the identity of those individuals should be noted. The reason comes down to one word: **patterns.** Any routine daily behavior is noted in a business setting and continuously demonstrated by people.[4] Once such persons are remembered and recognizable, any change becomes a major issue to note in a report. If Mr. Johnson always arrives and leaves on a 9–5 schedule and now suddenly begins returning to the office around 10:00 p.m., this change is one that should suddenly send a flash of concern to a security person and a need for heightened vigilance.

In a secure position, a private security person is likely to have an opportunity to observe the television monitors at a secure location that are hooked up to cameras recording areas near and outside of a secure position. Private security persons should spend some considerable time noting the placement of the cameras, the placements of objects such as garbage cans and equipment along with the status of vents, windows, and grates. Often it is the case when an incident occurs or is reported, a guard on duty may not have actually seen an incident on a monitor but must review the recorded video to see if the cameras recorded any activity. This is why when taking over a guard shift it is important to ensure that nothing blocks the view of cameras and that the cameras are in working order. Areas of shadows or hidden corners not easily picked up by the camera should also be noted with detail in a report or directly to a superior. While on duty in a secure position and looking at the monitors of the camera system, the private security officer should look for any signs of activity or change. Security personnel should also be aware of where a person or object can be hidden from the camera. This is essential when suspicion arises of illicit activity yet the camera doesn't show any direct sign of proof. If a major change in conditions occurs such as a loss of lighting in an area or the loss of a camera, an immediate response by private security personnel to the area is required. Do not assume everything is normal until you inspect the area.

It is wise to move after a period of time because anyone staying in one location for a period of time often becomes bored. Once bored, private security persons are prone to let their guard down. They often stop looking around at their environment for changes. They tend to stop scanning the environment around them for possible threats and may focus on their own personal needs or activities. They may decide to read a book or take a nap, make a cell phone call, or bide their time on the Internet. While observing monitors or the surroundings in a secure position, it is important for the private security person to continually look around in a systematic sweeping pattern that keeps their mind from being bored and also comprehensively covers all areas. Any alarms that go off are to be taken seriously unless a drill or test has been scheduled. Seemingly innocent changes in patterns such as an alarm going off cannot be underestimated at any time. To summarize, a security guard

- is generally uniformed,
- is highly visible,
- protects property and people,
- watches alarm and video camera systems,
- looks for signs of crime, fire, or disorder,
- takes notes, and
- reports incidents to clients, superiors, or emergency services.

Mobile Guard Positions

A mobile guard is a private security person who moves from location to location and checks for any signs of illegality or noncompliance with local governmental codes. They also serve a very strict **inspection** role in that they check to ensure that the conditions of facilities and the conditions of a location are maintained. The placement of garbage cans, a light that has gone out, a missing fire extinguisher, or an open vent are all important situations to be noted by a mobile guard and are all actions that require notation in a report along with an immediate response.

While on patrol, private security officers maintain movement through an assigned geographical area. This can cover the outside of a business facility, a sweep movement inside the physical plant, or a combination of both. The mobile guard is looking for[5]

- blocked emergency exits,
- vandalism, criminal mischief, graffiti,
- arson attempts,
- theft of personal and company property,

- trash, trash bins, or large dumpster fires,
- light outages,
- kingpin lock infractions and missing transport containers,
- suspicious persons or persons loitering,
- injured or intoxicated individuals,
- trash accumulation, and
- parking lot safety and security.

Mobile guarding is often done using an automobile or some form of automated vehicle such as a golf cart. The temptation with vehicles is to quickly run through an area and then stay in one position and let time pass by until the next shift takes over. Although this is a common trend in patrolling, it is a disservice to an organization or client. Movement should be methodical and slow. Even though private security officers are looking for changes in patterns, the pattern of their own movements should be constantly changing. People looking to behave illegally, whether outsiders or employees, often try to measure and plan their actions based on a consistent patrol pattern of a private security officer.[6] Therefore a change in route or timing increases the chance of observing significant events and also removes the boredom that can occur on guard duty.

It is important before a shift to take the time to walk and inspect an area where cameras record. If time permits, ensure the cameras are in working order and not obstructed by any objects.

A private security person in a particular guard position will have varied duties depending on the size, type, nature, and location of the business. The time of day and season of the year will also affect how the guarding of a location is conducted. For example, guarding locations when weather conditions are harsh may require a change in procedures for the safety or comfort of individuals on guard duty.

Layers of Security: The Onion Approach

All members of a security team, whether he or she is a rookie security guard checking ID cards in the lobby or is the head of security, comprise a multilayered approach to guarding a location. This is the "**onion concept**" of security. Just as an onion has many integrated tough layers, so do private security personnel who work together on many levels, in conjunction with security technology (alarm systems, cameras, safes, fences) to protect and prevent incidents. Translating the notion of an onion to practical terms, a facility may need to have three or more levels of guarding in place in a number of different fashions to deter crime and handle emergency situations that may arise.[7] For example, a facility can have secure guards at the building's entrance and at a desk in front of the elevators; a secure guard posted in sensitive areas where valuable items, sensitive information, or people are located; mobile guards roaming on patrol within the building itself; and mobile guards in vehicles outside the facility.

At first, the combinations of deploying secure or mobile guards are seemingly endless. However, the actual placing of personnel will depend on a number of factors, such as:

1. Which are the most important and critical areas where guards are needed at a location?

2. Is there a need to deter criminals from even approaching a business based on the nature of the location? For example, a company that makes chemicals or a school in a gang-prone area may want to show up front they have tough and ready private security personnel, whereas a medium-sized retail store may want to appear more inviting and place guards inside the business.

3. What monetary and personnel resources are available for deploying private security throughout a business?

4. Are there any circumstances that require a change in how private security is implemented (changes in seasons, weather, a recent incident, special occasion, or expectations of problems in the future)?

In 1993, J. Dingle expanded on the idea of the onion approach by creating the concept of asset protection based upon the theory of concentric zones. This idea emphasizes the onion concept even more by focusing on the placement of guards and technology based on the asset that is of primary concern.[8] The more valuable the asset that is to be protected, the more layers of security should be added. A building could be guarded by implementing the following additional security technology and personnel safeguards from the outside all the way to the heart of the building.

Layer 1:   Perimeter alarm
             Security fences
             Security patrols

Layer 2:   Secured building under camera surveillance
             Security guard patrols inside the building
             Security patrols outside of a key location in the building

Layer 3:   Security guards posted outside of key rooms in building
             Alarm system for internal rooms in building
             Locked office
             Locked and protected items in a safe or on a secure computer[9]

■ Controlling the Movement of People

Private security personnel who perform guard duties also must be able to handle crowd control situations. Public areas of special interest such as a tourist site, university during a sports event, concert area, or museum require extra attention being paid to the movement of people in and out of a location as well as the packages and bags that move with people. The **affirmative control** of people in terms of movement, seating, parking, and traffic is necessary to prevent a crowd from going out of control to the point of potentially harming people within the crowd or the site itself. In locations such as bars, adult entertainment areas, or other nightlife-based businesses, there are issues in preventing minors from entering who may cause major legal violations just by their mere presence. In addition, private security guards in nightlife settings have to protect the property and patrons from harm and to maintain a safe stable environment while festivities take place. The old notion of turning away or removing problematic patrons from a business and forgetting about them is no longer acceptable.[10] Today guards at nightlife settings are responsible by law for the criminal or disruptive activity that takes place outside of an establishment as much as they are for the unwanted nightlife activity that takes place inside.

■ Common Situations: A Day in the Life

A small business may have a single person who is responsible for guarding and all other required security tasks at a given location. Medium-sized and large private businesses are generally divided into teams and shifts based on times of the day and days of the week. Shifts can be arranged in any manner to suit the needs of the business' normal operations or to accommodate special circumstances; however, 8-hour shifts are very common unless an emergency arises. Daytime, nighttime, weekend, and holiday assignments are generally assigned based on a combination of factors such as a fairness and seniority. Generally, private security personnel can expect to eat on the job or have a set amount of time to get food from a nearby vendor instead of taking an extended break. Unless in a vehicle and mobile, being on one's feet for long hours is a normal expectation when on guard duty.

■ Checking Credentials

Security officers that are guarding a location have the task of checking credentials of people walking in and out. Checking credentials means not just going through the motion of taking an ID and handing it back to a person. Guards are expected to take a few seconds to check the ID of a person and see if the picture matches the actual person. In addition, guards should look at the ID for anything out of the ordinary. If in a secure guard location where people with appointments are allowed to proceed unattended, strict enforcement of an authorized list of guests is required at all times.

The key checking skill to develop is very simple yet often ignored: a look into the person's eyes. The eyes reflect the person's state of mind. When a person is happy, angry, confident, lying, or afraid, their emotions will be reflected in their eyes. While reading body language is another way to understand the nature of the

Word to the Wise To communicate major issues, verify information, ask a superior a question or answer one, or to hear major security updates ultimately requires a private security guard to be in constant communication through a portable radio and a cellular phone to a central security station.

person, it requires more information and training. Looking into another person's eyes, however, requires little training. A private security guard looking into a person's eyes can get a feeling from the individual. If the feeling is negative, asking some questions *while continuing to look into a person's eyes* can give a security guard better information. If a guard then does not feel satisfied for some reason with the person's response or subsequent behavior, the guard can treat the person with increased caution. All human beings are born with an instinctive feel for danger. A private security guard is in a position to develop this skill on a daily basis. In conjunction with the onion model of security, the possibility of a major incident or criminal activity decreases.

Guarding is one of the basic skills mastered by an entry-level private security employee. Regardless of the type of private security position held by a person, everyone interested in protecting the life and property of others assumes a guard role when they begin work. It is important therefore to continue to learn new information regarding the organization that needs protection as well as new techniques and technology to increase your efficiency and effectiveness when performing any type of guard duty.

■ Understanding Body Language

▸ ▸ CASE STUDY 2

Imagine you are a private security guard at a university on patrol outside, during a day shift, while many of the classes are in session. You come across a man in his late forties walking along an isolated side of an academic building. As you come closer to the man he stops in his tracks. You question him regarding his presence at this side of the building. He tells you he is lost. He doesn't appear to be a professor or student on the campus. As he speaks, you take note of his behavior to gain more insight into the possibility he is lying or is a possible threat.

1. What type of physical behavior or body posturing would make you consider that this individual is lying?

2. What additional body postures would make you concerned about this potential trespasser?

Body language is a part of the broad category of paralanguage: communication that does not involve direct verbal language. Body language is the outward appearance, expressions, movements and subtle gestures that can convey a person's emotional state in addition to verbal language, sounds, or other forms of communication. It can give private security personnel a direct edge in understanding the true intentions of people.[11] It can allow a private security person to pick out a potential risk before he or she becomes a threat to others. It is important to note that guards and security personnel should understand that knowledge about body language and human behavior is just an additional factor to take into consideration. Tone of voice, information they provide, their general appearance, location, and time of day are also major factors to consider when interacting with people.

Voluntary versus Involuntary Body Language

Before we look into how body language is interpreted and used, we must first look at the two broad categories of body movement and language. Body language can be either **voluntary** or **involuntary**. Voluntary body language is when the subject makes purposeful movements, gestures, and poses intended to communicate a direct message or feeling to another.[12] A person who is angry may throw his or her arms up to convey anger or a sad person may slump and slouch. Involuntary body language involves a person's unintentional bodily responses to a situation or environment, such as facial expressions. A private security person can use these responses to interpret the emotions of the person.

Basic Displays of Body Language

As a private security person, you are likely to be exposed to a wide variety of people, depending on your position. If you watch people talking to others, you can see that they don't just stand like motionless statues even when they are calm and relaxed. Whether people realize it or not, they express moods and intentions with physical behavior even when they do not intentionally move their bodies to convey a message to another person. Human emotions can guide our bodies in visible reactions. In some cases it is clear to people what others are doing, such as glaring at someone when they are angry. In other cases, human physical reactions seem out of someone's control, such as a lying individual whose bodily responses include increased sweating and a faster heart rate. If individuals are nervous or afraid, they can give off body language messages even when they intentionally try to hide them.[13] Here are some suggested body language interpretations private security personnel look for in evaluating a person's nonverbal communication (see Table 4-1).

One body language gesture can hold a number of meanings. For this reason, it is important to look beyond just one gesture and to examine the individual's body language in its entirety. For example, a person folding his arms might be communicating that he is defensive, upset, does not agree with the situation, or simply

TABLE 4-1. Body Language[14]

Postures

Closed-off postures	Shoulders hunched forward	Lacking interest, feeling inferior
	Rigid body posture	Anxious or uptight
	Crossed arms	Protective, upset, or cold
	Tapping fingers	Agitated, anxious, or bored
	Fidgeting with hands or objects	Has something on their mind, bored
Open postures	Leaning forward	Interested in what is going on
	Fingers interlocked behind head	Comfortable, open to ideas
	Mirroring your behaviors	They like you, want to be friendly
	Still	Their interest is in you and what you have to say

Selected specific gestures

Forehead	Wrinkled	Angry
Eyebrows	Outer edges up	Angry
Eyes	Centered	Focused
	Gazing up	Thinking
	Gazing down	Shame
	Gaze to side	Guilt
	Wandering	Disinterested, bored
Nose	Wrinkled	Disgusted, confused
	Pointed up	Arrogant
Lips	Parted, relaxed	Happy
	Together	Possibly concerned
	Wide open	Very happy or very angry
Arms	Crossed	Angry, disapproving
	Open	Honest, accepting
Hands	On top of head	Amazement
	Scratching head	Puzzled, confused
	Rubbing eyes	Tired
	Rubbing chin	Thinking
	Folded	Timid, shy
Fingers	Interlocked	Tense
	Pointing at you	Angry

is cold. If a private security person can pick out additional body language clues to support one of those possibilities, then he or she can cut the risk of misinterpreting nonverbal signals. If the individual is also portraying a facial expression that includes tight lips, a wrinkled forehead, and the outer edges of the eyebrows pointed up, it is more likely that he is angry or upset than cold. There is a major difference between considering that the person is cold or possibly hostile.[15]

Use of Body Language by Private Security Personnel: Interpreting Truthfulness

When interviewing someone suspected of criminal involvement or a security violation, the ultimate goal for a private security officer is to uncover the truth about the situation. A criminal trying to get away with a crime or a potential problem maker is not going to be truthful in their responses. Luckily, most people reach some level of discomfort when telling a lie, especially to individuals with power and authority. Their deceit is transmitted through their body language. This is where the trained eye of a private security person must tune in to the visual cues created by the lying suspect. There are several different areas in which a private security person has a greater chance of determining if a person is lying to them.

Involuntary Body Language of Liars

Often the physical expressions of a person lying to a private security person will be limited and stiff. They will have few arm and hand movements. Any hand, arm, and leg movements are likely to be towards their own body and not towards the private security person asking them tough questions. They may not realize that as they are lying to a private security person they are also frequently touching their face, throat, and mouth with their hands. They may actively touch or scratch their nose or behind their ears. A private security person should also be looking for other physical reactions. Often when a private security person begins speaking with someone, that person becomes defensive indicating they are possibly guilty of some activity or attempted activity. Innocent individuals however usually go on the offensive when questioned. A person suspected of illegal behavior may also turn their head or their entire body away or appear uncomfortable facing the private security person. They may also take it a step further and place objects such as books, cups, or bags between a private security person and themselves.[16]

Generally, it can be said that a person who is lying will not be able to look the private security person in the eye, especially in response to tough questions or during key points in the conversation. They tend to look down or away when being questioned. During a normal conversation, eye contact is maintained for about half the time on average. However, some liars will take great care to maintain constant, steady eye contact so as to make the interrogator think that they are being truthful. So, in the case of eye contact, a private security person should watch for extremes.

There is additional unusual or uncommon body language that can indicate a person is being deceitful. Tapping feet, fidgeting hands, the raising of shoulders, or any actions such as these to indicate discomfort or nervousness might mean a person is lying. A change in a person's pitch or tone of voice or the sudden stammering or throat clearing in their speech can indicate they are lying to a private security person. Other less obvious signs include blushing or paleness of the face when being questioned. Coupled with verbal cues (such as contradictory statements, sarcasm, changing subjects, and becoming defensive) are all indications of dishonesty in a person.

An understanding of body language techniques offers entry-level private security employees additional benefits. Besides focusing on suspects, private security personnel can use body language skills to gain rapport, a feeling of harmonious connection with individuals or groups who are not suspects. Building rapport helps the private security person gain intelligence about an area by making a person comfortable in sharing information. When talking in a friendly conversation with another person who is not a suspect, private security personnel should try to mimic the body language of the other person. By matching the person's volume, tone, rate of speech, and body posture, a private security person can put another individual at ease and ask questions or develop a conversation with the hope of gaining information. Think of the number of people that could supply private security personnel with information. Employees at a location, delivery personnel, mail carriers, and other individuals can be spoken to in a way that is beneficial to security through simplified body language techniques.[17]

■ Interrogation and Questioning Techniques

▶ ▶ CASE STUDY 3

Imagine working as a private security person in a supermarket. You receive word from one of the employees that they suspect a young man of stealing beer and placing it in his school knapsack. You go to the security room, which has monitors displaying what the cameras are recording in the supermarket. Upon examining one of the monitors you see a young man in a different aisle stealing candy. Based upon the description you received from the employee, it appears to be the same individual. You then proceed to the aisle slowly. You look around the corner where the young man is located. You see with your own eyes he is placing candy in his knapsack when he feels no one is watching. You now move to the aisle and put your hand on the shoulder of the young man. He turns around, seemingly afraid. You then escort him and his school knapsack to the security office.

1. What type of questions will you ask the young man?
2. How do you plan on making the young man confess to the shoplifting committed in the supermarket?

What Is an Interrogation or In-Depth Questioning?

An **interrogation** or in-depth questioning of a person is not a simple process. It goes beyond just asking a series of written questions. It is a process of obtaining information from a person reluctant to speak.[18] For private security personnel, this person will often be a criminal who is caught in the act, and the interrogation will aim to get them to admit culpability or name other criminals. While it can be seen as gathering the basic "who, what, where, when, why, and how" information similar to police detectives or investigative journalists, a good interrogation takes into account the location, nature of the suspect, and the behavior and body language patterns discussed previously. It also involves really listening to what a suspect says and being able to ask additional questions based on newly revealed material.[19] The term *interrogation* itself often brings to mind a negative image. A private security person may recall police misconduct in the news or events taking place in Iraq or Afghanistan. Private security personnel must be careful in how they perform their interrogations. For the purpose of private security, interrogations are to be conducted in a professional manner in a way that doesn't violate a person's civil liberties or results in a person being physically or psychologically harmed.

Building upon what we learned about body language, a private security person conducting an interrogation is interested in examining the body language and behavior of the individual. In a situation involving a supermarket shoplifter, it is important to note how the young man reacts when asked about shoplifting, and stealing candy and beer in particular. Interrogators would note if he avoided eye contact, placed objects so as to block the interrogator's view, tapped his foot repeatedly, or had his arms crossed. Interrogators would also note if he appeared nervous, such as appearing to tremble, sweat, or breathe heavily while denying committing a shoplifting act. The interrogator could present the knapsack with the stolen merchandise to him and note how he further reacts even when denying any illegal conduct. Ultimately, the interrogator wants to be attuned for all signs that help understand the nature of the individual being questioned.[20]

A private security person must be sure to not directly guide or influence the answers of a suspect or put words in his or her mouth. In some cases, an extremely nervous but innocent person will say things under pressure or during an overly aggressive interrogation that are not true or accurate, because they feel either guided or coerced. This can lead to possible lawsuits by people against private security personnel and their clients when interrogations are conducted improperly or without some initial evidence or proof of illegality.

Remember that private security personnel do not have to offer Miranda warnings before questioning a suspect.[21] They can even lie to a suspect to get them to admit they committed a criminal offense on private property. However a suspect is not required to remain in custody under the control of private security personnel unless they have that authority from a local or state government. Therefore,

Controversies in Private Security   You may wonder why some private security personnel conduct interrogations and later turn over suspects to public-serving law enforcement agencies. Many of the major retail outfits who apprehend a shoplifter later have their designated collection agency or law firm contact the shoplifter to seek civil damages for their actions. The information obtained and put into a report from an interrogation by a private security person can be vital in civil law.

be careful with a person wishing to leave during questioning because preventing a person from leaving for an extended period of time can be a criminal act of false imprisonment. This is why it is generally common practice for private security personnel to contact public-serving law enforcement agencies who can then arrive on the scene to handcuff and transport a person to a police station.

Questioning Techniques

The following is a guide to general approaches to interrogation used by private security personnel as well as public-serving law enforcement agencies.

Direct Approach

The direct approach is often called no approach at all, but it is the most effective of all the approaches and should always to be tried first. In the case of the shoplifter, it means asking him directly if he in fact shoplifted. The direct approach usually achieves the maximum cooperation of a suspect in the minimum amount of time.[22]

Incentive Approach

The incentive approach is a method of rewarding a suspect for his or her cooperation, but it must reinforce positive behavior. In the case of a shoplifter, a private security person can promise the suspect that if he gives the appropriate answers, he will be rewarded with anything from something to drink to not calling the police or his parents. It is important that any incentive offered must seem logical and in fact possible. A private security person should not promise anything to a suspect that they cannot deliver. If a store policy is to always call the police when a suspect is apprehended, a private security person shouldn't promise to not call the police if the suspect admits guilt. The private security person can offer that the more information the suspect offers the more likely a private security person can help them achieve some of the suspect's desired goals.[23]

Emotional Love Approach

In this approach, an interrogator focuses on the anxiety felt by suspects regarding the circumstances which they are now facing. As a private security person, you can focus on the love the suspect feels towards family and friends and get him or her to admit guilt. For example "What would your parents think? How could you shoplift?" Often with young people, discussing family and the possibility of speaking to them can result in a quick admittance of guilt and thus an end to an interrogation.[24]

Emotional Hate Approach

This approach focuses on a hate or desire for revenge suspects may feel. This is a very effective method when one or two suspects have been caught by private security personnel and the identity of other suspects is yet to be known. By using a conspiratorial tone of voice, the private security person can enhance the value of this technique. Phrases, such as "You owe them no loyalty for the way they have abandoned you," when used appropriately, can result in a suspect admitting guilt much quicker.

Fear Up Approach

In this approach, a private security person behaves in a heavy, overpowering manner, often with a loud and threatening voice. This technique works by convincing the suspects that they do indeed have something to fear (criminal sanctions, lawsuits) and that they have no option but to cooperate with private security personnel. While shouting is often used in this approach, the key is to make suspects realize that a possible way out of their situation is to admit wrongdoing.[25]

Decreased Fear Down Approach

This approach is used when suspects are in a high state of fear from being caught by private security personnel. As an approach, it is really nothing more than calming the suspects down and convincing them that they will be properly treated. A private security person can use a calm tone of voice to build a rapport with the suspects and usually nothing else is needed to get them to cooperate.[26]

Futility Technique Approach

The secret to this approach is to play on the doubts already existing in the suspects' minds. There are many different variations of the futility approach. There is the futility of the situation for the suspects in which a private security person can state "You are not finished here until you answer the questions," or futility of not talking because "Everyone talks sooner or later."

We Know All Approach

The "we know all" approach convinces the suspects that the private security person knows everything about the alleged criminal activity. It is a very successful approach for sources who are naïve or in a state of fear. For this to be effective, the private security person must organize all available data regarding the suspects. Upon initial contact with the suspects, the private security person asks questions, pertinent and nonpertinent, from their specially prepared list of questions. When the suspects hesitate, refuse to answer, or provide incomplete or incorrect responses, the private security person supplies the detailed answers to show the futility of noncooperation. In the case of the supermarket shoplifter, bringing the young man into the security room to show him the camera monitors and other security personnel are likely to make this approach easier.

Repetition Approach

The repetition approach works effectively against suspects who are very hostile. The private security person can listen to the suspects' answers to a question and then repeat both the question and answer several times. The private security person can keep this approach going until the suspects become so bored with the process that they begin to answer questions more fully, candidly, and with added information to gain relief from this monotonous questioning process.[27]

File and Dossier Approach

This approach works by the interrogator preparing a dossier file containing information. By carefully arranging the material within the file and by reading a few select pieces of information, it can give the illusion to suspects that a private security person has more information that what is actually in the file. The suspects can start to reveal information based on the feeling their activities are known to all the private security personnel.

Rapid Fire Approach

This approach plays off of the notion that everyone, including the guilty, want to be heard when they speak to another person. A private security person asks a series of questions in such a manner that the suspects do not have time to answer a question completely before the next question is asked. This tends to confuse the suspects so that they are apt to contradict themselves because they have little time to prepare their answers. The private security person then confronts the suspects with the inconsistencies of their answers, causing further contradictions. This technique may be used by an individual private security person or simultaneously by two or more private security personnel when questioning the same suspect.

Silence Approach

The silence approach may be successful when employed against either the nervous or the confident suspects. The private security person says nothing to the source, but looks him squarely in the eye, preferably with a slight smile on his or her face. It is important not to look away from the suspect, but force him to break eye contact first. The suspect will become nervous, begin to shift around in his chair, cross and recross his legs, and look away. The suspect may ask questions, but the private security person should not break the silence. The suspect may blurt out questions such as, "Come on now, what do you want with me?" When ready to break the silence, the private security person may do so with some nonchalant question such as, "You planned this crime a long time, didn't you? Was it your idea?" The private security person must be patient when employing this technique. It may appear for a while that the technique is not succeeding, but it usually will when given a reasonable chance.[28]

It must be understood that interrogation is an art that can only be practiced if given the opportunity. In reality, a private security person will not usually be in a position to practice interrogations on a regular basis. If entry-level private security personnel are in an area where they are likely to conduct interrogations, they should speak with their superiors to be aware of store policies regarding interrogations. This is a skill that can be developed, but it is also an art without a lot of room for human error.

■ Personal Protection

▶ ▶ CASE STUDY 4

Imagine you have been hired as a security officer for a residential gated community. While you are on duty one of the residents informs you that someone is following her while she is out walking the dog. She is asking you numerous questions on steps she can take to protect herself at home as well as when outside in public.

1. What advice and information would you provide to the resident?
2. What are some of the important concepts in personal protection?

Today the need for safety and protection is greater than ever. Home invasions, assaults, rapes, kidnappings, extortion, and carjackings are all too common in today's news headlines. All individuals have a powerful self-preservation drive that keeps people alive in difficult situations. As a private security employee, it is an important duty to assist clients or provide them with information to help them assist in their own safety and security.

Personal Protection Practices: Training Courses and Equipment

If a client were to ask about self-defense techniques and equipment, there are a variety of suggestions that an entry-level private security person could provide. First, it is important to make a client understand that if he or she wishes to learn a martial art, it will take money and significant commitment of time (months, years) to efficiently master many of the styles available. In the United States there are thousands of martial arts schools covering a wide variety of Korean, Chinese, Japanese, Israeli, and Brazilian martial arts. Therefore, it is important for a private security person to let a client know he or she should focus on finding a school that can provide them the in-depth training that will allow them to adequately defend themselves long enough to escape and contact authorities. Many martial arts schools offer short-term training sessions for this purpose, which can be ideal for a client who is limited due to time and budget.[29]

Word to the Wise   If a home or business becomes involved in a controversial issue to the point of being the subject of media attention or community concern, private security at that location should be aware that the potential risks to their clients or themselves has increased dramatically.

Word to the Wise   If a client tells you they intend to buy a gun, urge him or her to understand the local and state regulations for purchasing, registering, storing, possessing, and using deadly firearms. In addition, clients must understand the standards for self-defense under the criminal laws of the state in which he or she resides. These standards vary from state to state.

For a client who may wish to purchase a firearm for his or her own protection, there are also additional concerns that must be made clear. Guns are the ultimate in personal protection weaponry, which may be attractive to clients who feel they are currently under threat or who have been victims of crime on a previous occasion. As a private security employee, it is important to tell a client they have a right under the Second Amendment to own a firearm for self-defense. He or she should do some research on their own and attend training sessions at local gun ranges, gun courses, hunting camps, and home self-defense classes that teach individuals to become proficient in the use of guns for their safety and those around them.

Additionally, clients can also purchase items such as tasers, stun guns, mace, pepper spray, swords, knives, and a host of other personal protection items. A client should understand the legality of using and carrying such items as each state has restrictions on specific uses of items. Some states have strong restrictions on using taser weapons on other people or even possessing such items. Such items should never be carried on planes and none of the above listed items should ever be used except for self-defense. Clients should always be informed that items already on their person such as keys can be used to defend against an attacker.[30]

Residential Security Techniques

When speaking to a client, private security personnel are expected to be honest about the nature of home protection. Although a client may have hired private security personnel to prevent and respond to any incident, the client needs to look for signs of possible trouble as well as take steps to make their residence a secure place. Private security personnel should inform a client that he or she should develop their own security safeguards. For example, to prevent sexual assaults at a residence, clients should never give the impression that they are home alone if strangers telephone or come to the door. If a stranger asks to use a client's phone, they should be made to wait outside while the client calls private security personnel or other people. In the age of widespread cell phone usage, someone asking to use your home phone should be considered with caution. If a client comes home and finds a door or window open or signs of forced entry, he or she should not go in but alert private security at their location or call the local police.[31]

The Big Four

A client should know four important concepts regarding their residence. In the long run, these can make a huge difference in safety and security:

1. While at home, a client and family should rehearse safety drills and be aware of procedures to escape danger and get help from private security personnel and public-serving agencies (police and fire).

2. Vary daily routines; avoid predictable patterns that can lead the client to become a victim of a crime.

3. Know where all family members are at all times.

4. A residence is a castle; keep as many windows and doors locked whether home with family or home alone.

Clients should continually check the following:[32]

- Front door
- Rear door
- Garage door(s)
- Service door(s)
- Patio door
- Sliding glass door
- Gate

Clients should also do the following:[33]

- Make sure there are two window locks installed on all windows.
- Lock windows, especially on the ground floor.
- Have locks installed on fuse boxes and external power sources.
- Check and use burglar alarms.
- Keep at least one fire extinguisher on each floor, and be sure to keep one in the kitchen. Remind the client to show family members how to use them.
- Periodically check smoke detectors and replace batteries when necessary.
- Keep flashlights in several areas of the house and check the batteries often, especially if they have children in the home.
- Know their neighbors by developing a rapport with them and offer to keep an eye on each other's homes.

Letter and Parcel Bombs

It is not unheard of for a client to receive an explosive piece of mail, depending on the nature of their work or personal life. Additionally, private security personnel signing or receiving letters and parcels are possible victims of a criminal looking to harm a client. Letter and parcel bombs generally are "victim activated," meaning that a victim or intended target must activate the device by opening it. Such bombs do not normally contain timing devices. These types of bombs can range from the size of a cigarette package to a large parcel. Letter and package bombs have been disguised as letters, books, candy, and figurines. Delivery methods have included mail systems, express package delivery services such as FedEx and UPS, personal delivery messengers, or placement at the recipient's site.[34]

Indicators of Letter or Parcel Bombs

- Suspicious origin
- Name of sender is unusual or unknown
- An honorific title is appended to the name of the addressee
- Excessive or inadequate postage
- Off-balance or lopsided letter or package
- Unusual weight for the size of the letter or package
- Letters may be unusually thick
- Stiffness or springiness of contents
- Protruding wires or components
- Unusual grease or oil stains on the envelope
- Strange smell, particularly almond or other suspicious odors
- Handwriting of sender is not familiar
- Foreign style not normally received by recipient
- Common words or names are misspelled
- Restrictive markings such as "confidential" or "personal"
- Small hole in the envelope or package wrapping
- Rattling inside the envelope or package, possibly loose components of a device

---

As a private security guard or officer it is important to inform a client and other private security personnel what to do if they come across a suspected letter or parcel bomb. The following is a general guideline in handling such suspicious mail items:

- Don't let anyone near it.
- Don't submerge it in water.
- Don't bend the envelop excessively.

- Notify local authorities immediately.
- Leave the letter or package in an open area, such as a yard.

Vehicle Protection Techniques

Many clients under the protection of private security personnel may be attacked while driving, entering, or exiting a vehicle. A client may even be attacked while using a vehicle inside a location protected by private security or inside a gated community. In particular, carjacking is a major threat to anyone in any type of community. The client's own alertness during an attack in or near a vehicle is the key to safety. The following provides a list of recommended actions that a client should know for their own protection:[35]

- Drive with doors locked.
- In stop-and-go traffic, never have windows all the way down.
- Keep enough maneuvering distance away from the car in front to go around the vehicle with the steering wheel cut hard to one side.
- If someone is exiting their vehicle to come after a client, the client should kick the attacker's door near the rear edge when they are 1/3 of the way out of the vehicle.
- If someone approaches the driver's side of the car, a client should only open the window a crack. They should never open the window wide enough for the perpetrator to have personal access to them or their vehicle.
- If someone grabs a client through the window, the client should use his or her left hand to close the window on the arm, drive away at a speed of 10 MPH and after about 30 seconds lower the window.

Let a client know that if he or she is being followed or harassed by another driver, he or she should try to find the nearest police station, hotel, or other public facility. Once he or she finds a place of safety, the client should quickly park anywhere (legal or not) and run into the location. If another driver tries to force the client to pull over or to cut him or her off, the client should keep driving and try to get away. The client can try to note the license plate number of the car and a description of the car and driver, unless this effort places the client in danger. The information is not as important as his or her safety.

If clients are being followed, they should never lead the person back to their home or stop and get out. When the client parks, he or she should look for a spot that offers good lighting and is close to a location where there are a lot of people. Remind clients to lock valuables in the trunk, and lock all doors. If you are security person at a shopping complex and asked for advice, you may want to let people know to take extra precautions when shopping. If they take packages out to lock them in their trunk, and then plan to return to the stores to do more shopping, it may be a good idea for them to move their car to another section of the parking lot or street. This is a good tip for thwarting criminals, especially during holiday seasons. A criminal watching people will know that a client will be coming back and can wait to ambush them. By moving their car, a client gives the impression they are leaving the shopping venue.[36]

Walkers and Joggers

Many victims of crime are people who are walking and jogging. If you are a guard at a residential location or gated community, remind clients to do the following:

- Be wary of automobile passengers.
- Don't wear headphones or ear buds when walking in isolated areas at any time.
- Regularly change routines.
- Mark out houses or shops at intervals on each route that are known to be occupied by a friend or acquaintance that may be used as "safe houses" in the event of an attack.
- Be alert at all times.
- Don't presume that because your area has been "safe" thus far, that it will continue to be so.

Private security personnel in the area of personal security should always strive to let clients know that with simple changes and attention to detail they can help prevent a problem in the future. It is important for entry-level private security personnel to develop a relationship with clients. The clients should feel comfortable approaching private security personnel to seek current information on how they can help assist with their own safety in different settings.[37]

Key Indicators of Possible Threats to Private Security Clients

The Secret Service uses a process it calls the "threat assessment approach" to evaluate potential threats to an individual. This approach is based on government research that identified three fundamental factors in violent acts targeting individuals.

1. Acts of targeted violence are neither impulsive nor spontaneous. Targeted violence is the result of patterns of thoughts and behavior, which security professionals can use to understand and identify threats.
2. Violence stems from an interaction between the potential attacker, a current situation, and the target. Many attackers wish to become famous and choose their potential targets with that goal in mind.
3. Those who commit acts of targeted violence often engage in telltale behaviors that precede and are linked to their attacks, including planning and logistical preparations.

■ Conclusion

Entry-level private security personnel are likely to be employed as guards at a location. It is important therefore to master the basic skills required to be effective guards. Understanding the body language of people allows a private security employee an advantage when determining the veracity of a person's statements. The ability to perform a lawful interrogation of a suspect can yield a successful gain of information necessary to protect an organization. The ability to provide personal protection information to people is necessary for private security employees to assist others in their efforts to avoid being victims of crime.

■ Chapter Review

- Serving as a guard is one of the most basic skills to be mastered by an entry-level private security employee.
- Guarding a location requires a variety of tasks and responsibilities regardless of the institution being protected.
- Understanding body language techniques allows a private security employee to have the increased ability to assess people as possible threats as well as the veracity of statements made by people.
- Interrogation techniques can be employed by private security employees in a way that does not violate the law but yields important information from a suspect in custody.
- Corporate espionage activity is present in most major businesses. Understanding the nature of this criminal activity will afford a private security employee the ability to protect the organization.
- Entry-level private security employees should know basic personal protection techniques for the safety of their clients.

■ Answers to Case Studies

Case Study 1

1. What types of behavior would you be on guard for as people enter the building? What activities would make you suspicious? A security guard should look for anyone who appears nervous or engages in activity inconsistent with the nature of the organization. You should look for anything that is unusual, such as a person wearing a winter coat in July. You should be familiar with the normal personnel who enter and leave a location on a regular basis and give extra attention to strangers. Any person who appears to be in a heightened emotional state should also be viewed with concern.

In addition, information from local police or superiors regarding possible threats to the organization can also help a guard focus on the people who may be a possible threat.

2. How do you keep alert in a job that can seem monotonous over time? A security guard should consistently scan the environment closely and change routines. If you patrol the same location regularly, alter your patrol routes. You should seek to work in pairs or with other security people to stay focused while on duty. Also you can ask your superiors for additional work duties related to guarding that can assist the organization as well as break up the monotony.

3. What techniques help make a person a better guard in the private security field? Your ability to interact with people and your ability to stay aware of how current news developments may affect your location will make you a better guard. Your desire to seek out new skills and training are also important both for your professional growth and promotion opportunities.

Case Study 2

1. What type of physical behavior or body posturing would make you consider that this individual is lying? Not making eye contact, fidgeting, tapping their foot can be considered suspicious. The appearance of a person in terms of dress can also indicate possibly lying.

2. What additional body postures would make you concerned about this potential trespasser? A person who keeps reaching into their pocket, slowly moving their hand to a location on their person, or who has their arms crossed could indicate possible anger marking the individual as a threat to a private security employee.

Case Study 3

1. What type of questions will you ask the young man? In dealing with shoplifting suspects, it is important to attempt to get admission of guilt. You should also seek information as to whether the shoplifting suspects have engaged in this criminal activity on previous occasions and in what manner. This allows you to learn of possible shortcomings in the location's security. In addition you should question the suspects whether they had any accomplices or people who assisted their criminal activity. You can also question the suspects about personal information and the motivations for their criminal activity.

2. In terms of his behavior, how do you plan on making the young man confess to the shoplifting committed in the supermarket? The method for interrogation chosen will depend on the nature of the suspect. Suspects who are young and appear to be afraid are more likely to be interrogated successfully through an approach that involves fear or a promise of allowing them to

speak to family. Suspects who are hardened and resistant to questioning may require an approach that puts you in a more adversarial role.

Case Study 4

1. What advice and information would you provide to the resident? It is important to be realistic with the resident and inform her that there are limits on what private employees can do to prevent criminal activity and victimization. Security on a personal level therefore begins with the individual person. Residents should engage in activities in their daily life that decrease the possibility of becoming victims. This would include locking doors and changing patterns in their daily routines, along with being vigilant of possible criminal activity.

2. What are some of the important concepts in personal protection? Personal protection is something that doesn't occur overnight or on a whim. It should involve serious thought as to how to improve human techniques and security at a location. People should consider technology such as alarms or items that can be used for protection in case they are attacked. Self-defense courses and training opportunities should also be considered for one's own safety. The more steps on numerous levels that are taken by an individual, the less likely they are to become a victim in the future.

■ Key Terms

Affirmative control Controlling the movement of people in terms of seating, parking, and traffic to the extent necessary to prevent a crowd from going out of control and potentially harming the people themselves or the business.

Guard To protect people and property through diligent inspection, controlled right of entry and exit of a location, patrol, and observation of changes in an assigned area.

Inspection An examination of physical and environmental conditions, organizational standards, people, and objects as required by an organization, government demand, or public interest.

Interrogation A form of in-depth questioning usually done under difficult or heightened emotional circumstances for the purpose of eliciting sensitive information.

Involuntary body language Involves bodily responses to a situation or environment that are not intentionally made by the subject.

Onion concept The concept in security of employing multiple levels or layers of security through the use of personnel and technology to ensure a location is adequately protected from internal or external threats.

Patterns   Consistent and repeated behavior by human beings in everyday life or generally when engaging in specific behavior.

Reports   Documents that provide detailed accounts of any activity completed, observed, or suggestions on ways for an organization to improve.

Secure positions   A stationary position from which private security guards can guard a location while providing additional services. They may also be able to monitor cameras and serve as a center for private security communications.

Shift   A period of time, usually around 8 hours, in which a private security person at a location is on duty performing a specific private security function.

Voluntary body language   When a person makes purposeful movements, gestures, and poses.

■ References

1. Dingle, J. 1993. Back to the basics. *Security Technology and Design* November/December.

2. Ibid.

3. Ibid.

4. Ibid.

5. Ortmeier, P. J. 2005. *Security management.* Upper Saddle River, NJ: Pearson Prentice Hall.

6. Ibid.

7. Hess, K., and H. Wrobleski. 1996. *Introduction to private security.* Stamford, CT: Wadsworth.

8. *See* note 1.

9. *See* note 1.

10. Muntz, A. 1991. New roles for private patrols. *Security Management* December.

11. *See* note 1.

12. Coleman, K. 2006. *Body language. Spy-Ops Training Brief* 13, TB 62.

13. Ibid.

14. Ibid. Table printed with permission of Spy-Ops.

15. *See* note 12.

16. *See* note 12.

17. *See* note 12.

18. Lewis, J. 2001. *The SAS combat handbook.* Guildford, CT: Lyons Press. *See also* McNab, C. 2002. *The SAS mental endurance handbook.* Guildford, CT: Lyons Press. *Also* McNab, C. 2005. *How to survive anything, anywhere.* New York: McGraw Hill.

19. Ibid.

20. Ibid.

21. *See* note 1.

22. *See* note 1.

23. *See* note 1.

24. *See* note 1.

25. *See* note 1.

26. *See* note 1.

27. *See* note 1.

28. *See* note 1.

29. *Spy-Ops.* Personal protection brief *8, TB 39. http://www.Spy-Ops.com. See also* Brown, T. A. 2004. *Business security.* Las Vegas, NV: Crary Publications.

30. Ibid.

31. Ibid.

32. Ibid.

33. Ibid.

34. Ibid.

35. Ibid. *See also* McNab, C. 2005. *How to survive anything, anywhere.* New York: McGraw Hill.

36. Ibid.

37. Ibid.

Advanced Business Security Issues

CHAPTER 5

▶ ▶ OBJECTIVES

- Understand the basics of business continuity management.
- Begin to know how to handle emergency public relations.
- Become familiar with the field of private investigators.

■ Introduction

Private security employees may find themselves during their careers being challenged to know and demonstrate their proficiency with advanced business security techniques. From being involved with the business continuity planning and management of an organization to understanding the basic function of investigators, private security personnel should be aware of the advanced business security issues they will face.

■ Business Continuity Management (BCM)

▶ ▶ CASE STUDY 1

Imagine as a private security officer for a corporation you receive a promotion to a supervisory position after a short period. You quickly receive word that you are to attend a meeting with some of the upper-level management. The meeting concerns business continuity planning. You are filling in for your superior who is ill. Based on the activities of the company, the head of the corporation has called this meeting out of concerns about fires or criminal acts taking place inside the main corporate headquarters and research lab. You are not familiar with business continuity planning.

1. What types of information and assistance can a private security officer contribute to business continuity planning?
2. What makes business continuity a growing security field?

Business continuity planning methodology is scalable for an organization of any size and complexity. Arguably every organization should have a business continuity plan to ensure the organization's longevity. Private security is involved in the BCP process.

Since 2001, the private security field has seen a growth in the area of business continuity management. **Business continuity management** (BCM) or business continuity planning (BCP) is not a new concept; plans for handling disasters, like Noah's Ark, are evidenced from the beginning of human history. In the years prior to January 1, 2000, governments anticipated computer failures, called the Y2K problem, in important social infrastructure like power, telecommunication, health, and financial industries. Today BCM is a vital activity for every type of business regardless of the size and nature of a business. BCM activities have as their goal making a business operate and recover no matter what disruptions occur. Such disruptions can be anything from a small fire, flood, information network shutdown, to major criminal events and terrorism. At any time, any business can experience a serious incident that can prevent it from continuing normal business operations. Business continuity management requires complex strategic planning (manuals), training, and management to keep businesses operational in the worst-case scenarios and should cover all essential and critical business activities. Executives and management therefore have a responsibility to recover from such incidents in the minimum amount of time possible. For private security personnel, a key understanding of this growing field is essential as more private security personnel are on the forefront of planning for businesses. The following section introduces an entry-level learner to the field of business continuity management.

Creating a Business Continuity Management Plan

There are five steps to creating a successful business continuity management plan:

1. Business impact analysis
2. Risk assessment
3. Risk management
4. Risk monitoring
5. Contingency management and planning (data protection)

This framework is useable regardless of the size of the institution. Business continuity management should focus on all critical business functions and activities that need to be recovered to resume operations.

Step 1—Business Impact Analysis

A business impact analysis (BIA) is the first step in developing a solid BCM plan. It is a methodical approach to ensure that all areas of concern or threat have been covered in great detail. It should include the following:

- Identification of the potential impact of uncontrolled, nonspecific events on the institution's business processes and its customers
- Consideration of all departments and business functions, not just data processing; and an estimation of maximum allowable downtime and acceptable levels of data, operations, and financial losses
- Focus is on the recovery priorities for business processes that identify essential personnel, technologies, facilities, communications systems, vital records, and data.

Step 2—Risk Assessment

Performing a risk assessment is a major step in the risk management process. Generally, **risk assessment** measures two quantifiable areas of the risk for a business entity: the magnitude of the potential loss, and the probability that the loss will occur. When going through the risk assessment portion of a BCM plan, you should ask yourself "What risk(s) exist in and near your company and how severe are they relative to operational capability, and what do we do (fix or mitigate)?" You should also learn about past incidents in the building. Each year you need to create a checklist, review everything, and test and drill. A common example of a risk would be a building near a power plant or in the path of a hurricane. A preventative measure would be to install cement or steel stanchions in front of or around the building or facility to keep a vehicle containing bombs as far away as possible from the building to lessen blast damage.

There are a number of common scenarios that need to be explored for a proper risk assessment under a BCM plan. The following is a list of difficult situations in which a plan and a preparation plan must exist; otherwise, a business is vulnerable.

- Every building of a business entity is out of service.
- The data center is gone.
- People are gone or killed.
- All electricity or power sources are gone.
- Telecommunications are gone.
- No water is available.

It requires a lot of work to go from department to department and discover what problems they would face if confronted with the above scenarios. Because six out of ten people aren't motivated at work nor committed to the survival of the business, you need to pick the right people to be involved in risk assessment.

Structural Integrity of the Physical Building and Plant. The integrity of any building needs to be examined in detail in preparation for a natural disaster, terrorist event, or a negative change in the environment. Architectural design and structural concepts can be used to make the location less attractive for terrorist targets or crime. Existing structures can be retrofitted and incorporated easily into new construction. For example, buildings designed with a large amount of glass can cause injuries when an explosion or other force send shards of broken glass far beyond the area of a blast. Laminated or hardened glass can withstand a degree of blast damage.

Internal Security. Many threats to a business entity can be avoided by preventing the threat from entering in the first place. A risk assessment plan should therefore examine the following:

- Is access to heating and air-conditioning systems controlled to diminish or defeat an attack intent on the distribution of toxic or insidious microorganisms throughout a facility?
- Are visitor movements controlled in areas not open to the public? Are visitor's logs used, dated visitor's passes issued, and possibly security or personal escorts to the visitor's destination employed?
- Is access to sensitive areas or those areas not open to the public discouraged and challenged?
- Is access to underground parking, particularly for truck delivery, strictly monitored and controlled?
- Is public and visitor parking near the building prohibited? Are parking areas closest to the building reserved for trusted employees?

Step 3—Risk Management

Risk management in itself has grown to become a new field servicing American businesses. Risk management as the third step in a BCM plan involves one simple question: If you discover a potential risk during a complete assessment of a business, do you fix the problem or mitigate it? In some cases a risk can be something that cannot financially be prevented based on the finances of the business or the nature of the risk. Also the halting of business activities to replace infrastructure inside a building may not be a wise idea in all cases. When a problem or risk is discovered as part of the assessment process, it is up to a team of professionals to meet and discuss the pros and cons of fixing a problem or just mitigating it and planning to fix the problem at a later date.

Step 4—Risk Monitoring

This portion of a BCM plan involves a constant review of a risk area if no immediate action is taken. The review of constant risks to an organization is normally determined by the nature of the business and also the amount of time, personnel, and funds that a business desires to allocate to risk monitoring. Major companies may have weekly meetings and annual testing of equipment while smaller businesses may not be as stringent in their monitoring. If a risk exists and no steps are taken to remedy it, regular assessments must be made to determine if the risk is the same or has grown to a point that action is required.

Step 5—Contingency Management, Planning, and Data Protection

Every business big or small should ask, "How are we ensuring our data is protected and can be retrieved in a crisis situation?" The final step of protecting a business is an examination of how to prevent damage of the informational data of a business and, if damage does occur, how the data is to be recovered. Data recovery is the process of salvaging data from damaged, failed, corrupted, or inaccessible primary storage media when it cannot be accessed normally. Often the data is being salvaged from storage media formats such as hard drives, storage tapes, CDs, DVDs, RAID, and other electronics. This can be due to physical damage to the storage device or logical damage to the file system that prevents it from being mounted by the host operating system.[1]

Data recovery is also the term used to describe the process of retrieving and securing deleted information from a storage media for forensic purposes. Today many businesses use outside firms to move data to a distant location or use new technologies to protect the integrity of computer data from fire, flood, or natural disasters.

As a person involved in the BCM process, you must focus your attention in different ways. In terms of people, you will have to address terrorism, hostage situations, lack of trained personnel, nonessential people, sabotage, workplace violence, kidnapping, and embezzlement. With buildings you will have to pursue alternate sites, infrastructure (from soup to nuts), possible maintenance and equipment failure, and physical security. The company's procedures and arrangements with business vendors must be explored for possible weaknesses and potential for disruptions.

The business' financial systems are vulnerable during a time of crisis. It is possible in emergency situations for personnel to seize or misappropriate funds, or commit fraud. Measures of protection need to be in place no matter how dire a situation becomes for the business. Data centers, networks, data-communication, outsourcing issues, Internet business, and PayPal and wire transfers need special attention. Vital records such as original papers, legal documents, and electronic information need to be copied, backed up, or moved to a secure location, preferably in a separate facility. Storage sites for company data should be geographically dispersed: 30–40 miles away for tape backups, and anywhere from 30 to 300 miles away for a **hot site**. A hot site has all the equipment needed for the enterprise to continue operation, including office space and furniture, telephone jacks, and computer equipment.

All personnel are potential assets. It is up to you to discover what assets they have and how they can be employed for the benefit of your organization. Document personnel with special skills.

When making any plans or drills always construct timelines. It must be carefully determined how long an exercise will last, and whether it is successful or not in the event a situation in fact does arise in the immediate future. Ultimately the BCM process is essential for a business to survive a difficult and possible catastrophic event. Why all the fuss? *No plan equals chaos.*

Incident Command System (ICS)

To assist in emergency planning, the **incident command system** (ICS) is a management system used within the United States by local and federal agencies to organize emergency response. It was designed to offer a scalable response to incidents of any magnitude. As part of FEMA's National Response Plan (NRP), the system was expanded and has become the National Incident Management System (NIMS). The system is designed to grow and shrink along with the incident, allowing more resources to be smoothly added into the system when required, and also the smooth release of resources when no longer needed.[2]

Any organization or business entity can adopt an ICS-NIMS framework. A business entity should appoint a person to be the commanding officer or person in charge when a crisis or emergency arises. The commanding officer within a business organization should have the ability to control teams headed by competent personnel trained in operations, planning, logistics, finance, safety, information and public liaisons, and legal affairs.

When a crisis emerges, the commanding officer can quickly organize the teams to work together to protect the safety of people, safeguard business assets, discover financial issues and funds that need to be recovered, manage public image and media relations, handle liability issues and employee relations, implement plans to recover the physical infrastructure of a business, and handle any other issues that arise.

Such a model can be used by any business for any crisis. However, it is important to note that to ensure such an organizational method works requires training, drills, and after-action reviews with the commanding officer and subordinate teams to learn what went right and wrong. A mock drill or roundtable discussion can also allow team leaders and their commanding officer to discuss problems that were not foreseeable by all parties involved in such planning.

Word to the Wise Emergency planning is important for getting people out of buildings and ensuring their safety. You need to train and designate leaders who constantly drill. Also you must ensure reception personnel and those who protect data always leave with information/log books for accountability purposes. Additionally, you must always coordinate with the police and fire department and have connections to vital emergency personnel in every building.

Resilient Enterprise

Resilient enterprise, a term coined by Yossi Sheffi, professor of engineering systems at MIT, is the ability and capacity to withstand systemic discontinuities within a business and to adapt to new risk environments. An effective organization aligns its strategy, operations, management systems, governance structure, and decision-support capabilities so that it can uncover and adjust to continually changing risks, endure disruptions to its primary earnings drivers, and create advantages over less adaptive competitors.[3]

A resilient organization establishes transparency and puts in place controls for CEOs and boards to address risks across the extended enterprise. It can withstand improper or fraudulent employee behavior, IT infrastructure failures, disruptions of interdependent supply chains or customer channels, intellectual property theft, adverse economic conditions across markets, and myriad other discontinuities companies face.

Establishing greater resilience is especially necessary in the current economic and security environment, which poses a new set of challenges to executives and boards. The openness and complexity of today's extended enterprise increases a firm's dependence on global financial, operational, and trade infrastructure. Although that provides for greater efficiency and effectiveness, it also exposes most companies to risks that were unfamiliar during the era of national markets and the vertically integrated enterprise, and compounds the effect of conventional business risks. The availability of communications technology is important, but companies must also have a culture of communications (horizontal and vertical). At computer maker Dell, every two hours managers get a report on their phone about the latest status of PC manufacturing. This is done so everyone can jump in to fix things when they go wrong. Added to a culture of communications is urgency. When things go wrong, the entire company must participate in the solution. This urgency yields a flexibility that mitigates the need for excess redundancy.

What's more, the legal and regulatory landscape has undergone significant change since the September 11, 2001, terrorist attacks. The accounting and governance scandals in the United States have raised the level of diligence stakeholders expect from senior executives, boards of directors, private security personnel, and corporate board audit committees in ensuring the safety and continuity of the enterprise. The July 2002 United States *National Strategy for Homeland Security* recommends that industry sectors and corresponding government agencies responsible for critical infrastructure protection develop national infrastructure assurance plans that bridge the public and private sectors. The Sarbanes-Oxley Act of 2002 has tightened boards of directors' audit committee responsibilities, imposed new CEO and CFO certification requirements, and raised the "standard of care" obligations on management dramatically. The Basel II Accord commits financial services institutions to set aside larger capital reserves against possible future operational disruptions.[4]

It is important for the survival of personnel, the existence of a business, and national security for business executives to take steps to prepare and train their personnel for the worst-case scenarios that could disrupt business for a few hours to a few days. The failure to plan for the future is tantamount to negligence in today's business world. Business continuity management is the lifeline that will save most businesses from ruin during a crisis or natural disaster. Company executives and boards of directors are being held accountable by their shareholders and customers alike to implement plans and procedures, such as an incident command system, to manage the physical and virtual assets of a company during times of crisis or disaster. Responsible organizations will have a BCM plan in place before the need arises. Businesses that ensure good BCM practices are those that take their responsibilities seriously for safe and secure work environments. BCM planning and implementation are going to be part of the duties for many entry-level private security employees.

Emergency Public Relations

▶ ▶ CASE STUDY 2

You are a private security employee that works at a local restaurant. Last night while no one was in the restaurant, a drunk driver drove through the front of the restaurant. Now local media reporters are swarming outside the restaurant along with law enforcement personnel. The owner has informed you that the restaurant is still functioning and will be open for business. However, there are a number of concerns from reporters regarding the safety of restaurant patrons and the reporters want more information on how this incident occurred. The owner, who is camera shy, has asked you to speak to the reporters and to calm their concerns and let the general public know that the restaurant will not be closed. He has also asked you to prepare the staff for any media inquiries.

1. How would you plan on talking to local reporters?
2. How would you prepare the staff for questions from reporters?
3. What are some of the major issues with conducting a public relations session?

In the communication age, the need for information is rapid and intense. Any incident of significance at a business, school, or organization is likely to gain statewide and national attention. While major corporations are likely to have formalized experts in the field of dealing with the public and media groups, it is important for private security personnel to understand this process along with its unique difficulties. It would not be uncommon for private security personnel or any person with authority in an organization to be tasked with dealing with the public and media representatives such as reporters. For an entry-level private security person given such a task, the pressure and public spotlight could seem daunting. Therefore examining the manner in which any organization should properly handle communications in light of an incident or disaster is paramount. Imagine you are a private security person tasked with providing overall security in a location. You would have to consider that not only certain incidents at your organization would gain the attention of the general public but the attention of the media as well.

Understanding a Crisis

Regardless of the size of an organization or the nature of an activity, the possibility that a crisis can occur at some point in time is almost guaranteed. A **crisis** is defined as anything that disturbs the natural flow of business or normal operations and jeopardizes an organization's existence if recognized too late or addressed improperly. A crisis is a situation that if not handled properly can turn into a disaster. Imagine a situation in which a restaurant was found to have roaches in the basement or a private school in which a teacher is caught having sexual relations with students; such activity if not properly discussed and explained to the public and media can lead to the end of those organizations. Generally the types of crisis situations that can be faced by any organization are broken down into three major forms:

- Financial (profit failure, takeover)
- Reputation (failed products, corruption, mismanagement)
- Outside forces (boycott, labor, regulatory action, force of nature)

Of the criteria listed above, any of those three forms of a crisis can lead to permanent damage to an organization or the demise of the organization by people being fired or the organization as a whole being destroyed.

In dealing with a crisis as a private security employee, it is important to realize that not every crisis situation is a blazing red alert causing every possible employee to panic and for every reporter in an area to arrive on the scene. Many crisis situations begin as simply issues categorized by the following conditions:

- Known inside company or organization
- Not yet public
- Not disruptive completely to the business or organization

It is possible for a crisis in its early stages to be handled and maintained as a private affair known only to the business or organization. This requires a combination of teamwork from business owners and management, private security personnel, attorneys, communication experts, and any effected parties. In some cases however, a crisis situation arises so fast within an organization that it is not possible to contain the public and media awareness. When a situation has reached a major crisis point, everyone working for a business or organization should do what is needed to

- Make the crisis go away as soon as possible.
- Keep the crisis low profile or no profile in the eye of the public and media.
- Keep on doing business as usual.
- Avoid any damage to reputation.
- Keep the crisis from affecting the finances of the organization.

On the Front Line

Imagine you get a call at three in the morning that the organization or client you work for has experienced a possible crisis. Regardless of the nature of the crisis at this point, if you are involved with emergency public relations you must immediately ask questions based upon the three Ws to ascertain the current state of a crisis.

- What do we know?
- When did we first know it?
- What did we do about it?

When you hear of a crisis that has emerged in an organization, an invisible timer has already begun. It is the start of a race between the general public and reporters and those working on covering that crisis. With an organization or client, the elapsed time between the question that needs to be solved and the answer is key since the sooner the answers to the three Ws, the more likely a positive result can be achieved when gathering information concerning a crisis.

Once the three Ws are known, private security personnel can begin to gather the correct information. Once the information of an incident is known to the appropriate personnel for a business or organization, a position can be formulated in light of the crisis. A position is the expression of how the organization feels about the crisis. In dealing with the general public and media reporters, there are four major positions (The Four Rs) that should be considered before speaking on behalf of an organization.

- Regret
- Reform
- Restitution
- Recovery

These positions send a clear message to the public and to reporters regarding the feelings of the organization in terms of the crisis.

With an understanding of the company's position, a person is now ready to communicate with the general public and media representatives. Any communication,

> **Word to the Wise**   Dealing with the public and media is a lot different from dealing with questions in a court of law. Inside a courtroom, a business or organization is innocent until proven guilty. However in the courtroom of public opinion, a business or organization is guilty unless proven innocent.

whether done in a scheduled press conference, Web site, mass e-mail, or radio interview, must follow a key set of guidelines. The person representing an organization should be the first to speak before others can make negative comments in the public arena. Any statements made should be factual based on available information. It should be made as soon as possible, and it should be an honest and frank expression of the state of a crisis and the views of the organization. If done correctly, an organization can be seen as the victim of a crisis. If not done correctly, it can be seen as a villain for not responding in time, providing enough information, or providing the wrong information to the public and reporters.

Preparing for a Crisis

As mentioned in the section on business continuity planning, it is important to discover possible problems or vulnerabilities that an organization may face. For example, a mining company should examine the possibility of dealing with the public and media when there is a cave-in at a site. An airline company should consider handling communications if there is a crash of an airplane. Examining the possible worst-case scenarios allows any person tasked with handling crisis communications to come up with written statements, speeches, or guidelines to employees before a crisis emerges. It also allows time to find out who has the best public speaking skills, as well as providing opportunities and times to rehearse dealing with tough questions from reporters. As a private security person who may be put in front of an emotionally charged crowd when a crisis emerges in an organization, the more preparation and practice the better.

Handling the Media During a Crisis

Besides providing security and carrying out possible crisis communication tasks for an organization, it is also important to manage outside influences that inevitably surface when a crisis or disaster strikes. For example, when things go wrong with a business, it is not uncommon for executives to be ambushed by members of the press. An incorrect statement by any employee or private security person can lead to a misrepresentation of the status of an organization and make the organization look foolish. The following is a guide on how to handle a surprise media interview. This is useful both as a guide for private security personnel as well as instructions that a security team can offer to employees or members of an organization.

1. Remain calm: The sudden appearance of a reporter and/or microphone is startling. Think of yourself as having been stopped by a stranger asking directions: you may not be able to help them, but you're going to tell them to whom they should talk to get the latest information.

2. Be courteous: Stop. Face the reporter. Identify yourself and, if the person has not told you who they are, ask. Beyond your name, you do not have to give additional information about your position or affiliation. You may reply to further questions by asking, "What can I do for you?"

3. Set ground rules: Inform the reporter that you are on your way to an appointment, and have only a moment. If they are overly aggressive or the camera, lights, and microphone are thrust at you, pause for a moment to collect your thoughts.

4. Be helpful: Advise the reporter that you can put them in direct contact with the senior member of the company who is able to provide information on the subject. Offer a name and a phone number. You should also ask for their business card.

5. Leave: Without responding to further questions, thank them for their interest and get into your car or walk away. They will probably continue to talk to you or even follow you. Don't run away. Merely go about your business in an orderly fashion. If you were about to enter a facility, you may wish to change your mind to avoid being followed inside.

6. Beware of "off the record" comments. A reporter may tell you that they will turn off the cameras and microphones if you will speak to them privately. They are probably lying. Anything you say is on the record despite what you have been led to believe.

7. Don't be goaded or intimidated: A reporter may ask a question such as, "How do you feel about the people that are now hurt or have been killed in your organization?" If you have already started to leave, keep going. If you have not yet left, and wish to say anything, you may certainly explain the company position. But be aware that the reporter will then seek to draw you into a discussion.

8. Reporters and activists also pose as customers or colleagues at industry meetings or on the telephone. If a person to whom you are speaking suddenly seems to be asking probing questions about sensitive issues, ask them for more information about themselves and offer to refer them to someone who can provide answers.

While crisis communication seems to be a daunting task, it is one that entry-level private security personnel should embrace and not fear. With some guidelines, instructions from superiors and a little common sense, a private security employee can successfully conduct crisis communications for the benefit of an organization or a client facing a difficult situation.

■ Private Investigators

▶ ▶ CASE STUDY 3

You have been hired as an entry-level private security person working in an investigative firm. You've been asked to conduct a private investigation on behalf of an attorney that is representing a client in a divorce case. The attorney has hired the investigative firm to find out if the other party in the case has in fact been engaged in an extramarital affair. Your boss has asked you to conduct surveillance and gather information that supports or negates this allegation.

1. What concerns would you have in conducting such a private investigation?
2. What are some necessary tasks needed to complete such an objective?

With more organizations and people seeking investigative services, there is no better time to learn the skills and techniques of private investigators. Illegal activity or information that needs to be determined as rapidly as possible has continued to increase the demand for investigative services in the United States. Before an entry-level private security employee can find employment in such a dynamic and growing field, it is important to know the basics of private investigators and their work duties along with the requirements for work in a particular location.

What Is a Private Investigator?

By general definition, a private investigator is a person privately hired to perform investigative or detective work by a client. The client may be a person, a small business or a large corporation, an insurance company, a retail establishment, an attorney, a private organization, or even a government. Generally speaking, a private investigator is hired to obtain information regarding the identity, habits, conduct, movements, whereabouts, affiliations, associations, reputation, or character of any person or group of persons. A private investigator may also conduct investigations regarding the credibility of witnesses; the whereabouts of missing persons; the location or recovery of lost or stolen property; and the causes and origin of—or responsibility for—fires, libels, or losses.[5]

Requirements

Although a formal state license is not required to conduct private investigations, it is beneficial to work towards obtaining a formal license that affords a private investigator legal and insurance protection as well the opportunity to work in more diverse investigative positions. Generally, entry-level private investigators work with licensed investigation firms to gain the necessary experience required for a license. Private investigators can also gain experience by working for insurance companies

Private Investigator License Requirements   Standards for licensing vary from state to state, but generally have similar criteria. A few states having no licensing. The general requirements include

- At least 25 years of age
- High school diploma or GED equivalency
- Pass a state-administered examination
- Three years of full-time work as
  - A proprietary investigator
  - An employee of a licensed private investigator
  - An investigator in a government investigative agency or police agency
- Or three years in an equivalent position and experience
  -where the primary duties were to conduct investigations
  - supervising and reviewing the work of at least three persons performing investigations
- Proof of Insurance
- Fingerprints on file with local law enforcement agency

that are frequently investigating fraudulent claims of insurance policy holders. Each state has different requirements to become a "licensed" private investigator.

In addition, private investigators must renew their licenses periodically, and have the financial resources to be begin self-employment.

Different Types of Investigators

Although there are similar techniques and skills used by any private investigators, the area of investigations is always specific to a certain field. **General investigators** are those private security employees hired for a variety of jobs by multiple clients. They can provide a wide range of services for businesses or individuals. The location of missing persons, preemployment background checks, undercover operations, surveillance, and internal theft investigations are common tasks carried out by general investigators.[6]

Legal investigators focus on conducting private investigations for attorneys or parties that need assistance in a case. They are usually employed by law firms handling mostly personal injury cases or divorce cases. Their responsibilities involve accumulating and assembling facts so attorneys can apply the law in the best interest of their clients. They conduct interviews of prospective witnesses and may testify as experts during litigation. They search out testimonial information along with documentary and physical evidence.[7]

Insurance investigators focus on investigating false claims of injury by those clients seeking insurance coverage and payment. They are generally employed directly by insurance companies or subcontracted by them. They perform the same basic function as legal investigators, but their goal is to defend the insurance

> **Word to the Wise** Learn the laws regarding admissibility of recorded film and audio footage in your state. Learn the process for getting a formal license in your state.
>
> Specialized related fields of investigation often refers to individuals who engage in private investigations but are focused on other activities not of an investigative nature. The techniques used in these specialized fields are the same as those in primary investigation. However, the range of skills and actual fact-finding tasks are limited. Private investigators usually work in these specialized related fields as a secondary business through their main business. For example, **repossessors** focus on finding and returning vehicles and other property that has been repossessed by a bank or monetary lender. Bounty hunting, as previously mentioned, uses investigative skills to search out individuals to be returned to the custody of the criminal justice system. Bodyguard and security work for private clients, especially high-profile celebrities, may also involve some investigative work depending upon the requests of the client.[9]

companies against fraudulent claims. They investigate cases involving arson, product liability, workmen's compensation, and personal injury as well as medical malpractice.[8]

Corporate investigators are employed by large corporations and businesses. They are often hired from within the company's own security forces to investigate internal matters. They engage in preemployment checks of prospective employees to ensure quality workers are hired who do not pose a threat to the company in the future. Corporate investigators focus on discovering white-collar crime as well as investigating any employees of a corporation who may be engaged in illegal acts or activities that may embarrass the company. Internal theft, falsifying records, accidents, workmen's compensation cases, and lawsuits are also activities performed by corporate investigators.

Power and Responsibility of Being a Private Investigator

New private investigators learn certain confidential techniques that give them power and ability over the average citizen. Therefore individuals entering the field of investigations must adhere to a higher level of responsibility and ethics. Some of the skills a new investigator learns could result in a misuse of power. These include determining the following:

- A person's true identity
- A person's background
- A person's current employment
- Someone's personal or professional reputation
- A person's financial background
- A person's unlisted telephone number

Danger and Risks in Private Investigation

Risk is the voluntary taking of a dangerous chance. Some aspects of private investigation have no inherent danger or risk. These include activities such as searching public records, pretrial preparation for civil actions, or computer crime investigations. However the nature of investigations does often involve risk. Generally danger and risk can be broken down into two forms, **expected** or **unexpected danger or risk.** When an investigator can expect a high probability of danger, then the danger is expected risk. Unexpected danger is unforeseeable and uncontrollable, such as an ambush or assault when you least expect it. Examples of expected danger include

Criminal investigation
Employee theft
Undercover investigation
Process serving
Marital investigation
Surveillance
Bodyguard work

Qualities Necessary for Private Investigators

The days of the tough, ex-cop working as a private detective in a small office are over. Investigators who can put people at ease and are sensitive to their feelings are more likely to obtain information. Investigators must be able to recognize and control their own bias and prejudices. Investigators must be intelligent and possess good reasoning abilities. Good investigators are observant and have excellent memory. Being curious and imaginative is very important as is a good knowledge of human nature. Honesty and the ability to withstand corruption are expected. Communication skills are a must. Investigators have to be able to testify in court. They also need technical know-how. Today, "data detectives" who can do an exceptional job in data gathering and computer research are in high demand as private investigators.[10] Finally, an investigator needs perseverance, passion and purpose.

An Example of Expected Risk   An investigator doing surveillance on a subject driving a vehicle risks the hazard of running a red light because he does not want to lose the subject. Risk in this case is taken under condition of uncertainty that exposes the investigator to possible loss in order to reach a desired outcome.

Tools of Private Investigators

An investigator needs a car that is practical for both surveillance and transporting clients to lunch or various locations. In some cases, a vehicle can become an investigator's kitchen and bathroom. The three important tools of the trade are a digital still camera, a digital video camera, and a 35-mm single lens reflex camera. Important factors for digital cameras are the optical zoom and the number of viewable pixels. Additionally, private investigators need a computer, with a very large hard drive, and as much RAM as can be afforded. A fast color printer and a CD/DVD burner should also be obtained before beginning investigatory work. Private investigators should have a good pair of 7×50 binoculars for long-range observations. A good quality microcassette recorder can also be used for taping information or people. Additionally, office materials are needed for recording your findings and creating the formal portfolios or reports you will provide your client.

Basic Private Investigator Techniques

Finding a Missing Person

One of the core duties a private investigator performs is locating a missing person. Missing people can include employees who have stolen corporate funds and have disappeared, an upset family member, or anyone who has a reason to disconnect themselves from their established family, friends, and work contacts. Also known as a **skip trace**, the focus in finding a missing person is to find as much information that can help narrow down the possible area where the person is located. In the beginning stages of a skip trace, the following sources of information should be examined. These sources can also be used to find out information regarding a person if a client or organization requests such information.[11]

1. Person-to-person contact is a good start. Investigators should always speak to people who knew the missing person.

2. Investigators should search the correct last name online or in local records (keep in mind women marry and change names).

3. Investigators should find out the state and city of the last known whereabouts of the missing person.

4. Knowing a person's occupation can help narrow a search. For example, a marine biologist is likely to relocate near the ocean.

5. Use search engines such as Google or Lycos. Investigators can complete a cache search, which involves searching online and viewing where specific search terms appear. Investigators should try variations of terms and use other Web sites. Pay attention to the "WhosWhere" white pages on Lycos and "Superpages" with reverse searches and when lists were last updated.

6. If necessary, investigators can use pay sites such as quickinfo.net and searchamerica.com's Address Checker™. However, they should ensure that their contract with a client allows billing for this activity.[12]

7. To locate a person's e-mail address, investigators can use pay sites such as www.iaf.net, www.theultimates.com/email, www.bigfoot.com, www.411locate.com, www.emailfinder.com, or www.world.email.com.

8. The Social Security Administration has a master death list. Checking this information lets an investigator know if a person is deceased.

Private investigators can contact the secretary of state of each state and determine from public records if a person has started or is involved with any new business ventures. Many of the officers and directors of corporations or businesses are listed publicly along with the location of the business.

Check driver's licenses and driving records. Every state has public records for anyone with a license. Investigators first need a birth date and social security number of the person they are searching for. The Driver's Privacy Protection Act prevents this information from being released, but there are exceptions that include licensed private investigators in some states. Additional Web sites charge for the information, but ultimately it can be obtained by an investigator through diligence. Many states in the United States sell this information in bulk to large resellers to generate state revenue.

Utilities companies are frequently owned by a municipality, and their records are public for an investigator to search.

Check the jails to determine if a person is in any type of correctional institution.

If an investigator has an old number or address on a person, they can ask to speak to a reference librarian in the area where a person may be located, and ask "politely" for them to do a reverse or cross-search of records.

Real property transactions such as sales and mortgages are recorded in the official records of the county and are public records that can be viewed by investigators or the general public.

At the federal level, investigators can go to the PACER Service Center, part of the Administrative Office of the U.S Courts, to find out if a person has been or is currently involved in a federal case.[13]

Investigators can contact credit bureaus (Transunion, Experian, and Equifax), and can either pretend they are the missing person or get a court judgment (shows bills, business transactions, and locations of businesses). A person's credit information is invaluable in finding a person's location because it contains the following:

- Name (and previous names)
- Date of birth
- Social Security number

Word to the Wise Exploit habits—they are behavioral fingerprints. Everyone has habits of behavior they engage in no matter where they are located. If a person is a major collector of rare comics, they are likely to continue such behavior in a new location. Such behavioral information can help locate anyone who is attempting to stay missing and undiscovered.

- Telephone number
- Current and previous addresses
- Current and previous employers

Credit bureau searches must be done with caution. Many states have restrictions on such searches. Therefore, investigators must be mindful of the laws and have a valid purpose for getting this information. Otherwise individuals face violating state and possibly federal law based on their activities.

Investigators starting out at the entry-level of a private investigative firm may also subscribe to a private investigator database service. Private investigator databases provide information such as: credit header data, magazine subscription lists, telephone directory information, postal changes, marriage and divorces, book club lists, and registered vehicles.[14] Two of the best database services are AutoTrackXP with access to 13 billion records and the Flat Rate Info Web site that also covers public records.

Performing Background Investigations

Private investigators are very likely to be requested by their client or employer to conduct a **background check** or **preemployment screening** of a person. Before they can begin a check, the investigator must have the name, date of birth, Social Security number, current address, and contact information of personal references. Generally this information is provided up front, especially in the case of a business that will ask prospective employees for the information and later notify them that their background will be checked as a condition of a job offer. Once this information is obtained, the investigator can put together the five ingredients to a good background/preemployment screening.

1. Criminal arrest/conviction search: Investigators should check public records via the Internet and check with the police department and ask for a field report/field identification report.
2. Civil records: Investigators can search online or visit the clerk of the court that has what they specifically need for their client.
3. Previous employer: When investigators call to verify, they generally get an administrative or human resource employee who can only say (by law) that

a person worked at the place and from what dates. For further information, investigators should be sure to get a person's last supervisor's contact information. They then can call the supervisor, develop a rapport to the point that it seems like a social call, and then use language such as "Between you and me, what was this person like at work?"

4. Educational verification: Ninety percent of the time, if investigators call the registrar's office at a school about a job applicant, the registrar will tell the investigator if a person has in fact attended the institution along with the dates and the degree obtained by the person. The other 10% of the time the registrar will ask for a release. Private investigators for businesses therefore must make sure the job applicant provides a release form to allow verification of their education.

5. Personal references: When investigators call, they should ask the following:[15]

    a. In what ways has the applicant demonstrated to you they were dependable?

    b. Can you give examples when the person was not dependable?

    c. Can you give me an example of the person's honesty?

    d. Did the person ever do anything strange or criminal?

    e. What are the applicant's strengths and weaknesses?

Neighborhood Investigation: The Basics

When an investigator wants to check out a neighborhood, is looking for someone, is handling a personal injury case, dealing with a runaway or kidnapped child, or wants to find out what happened when a client was burglarized, an investigation of a neighborhood can yield tremendous information. As an entry-level private security investigator, such an assigned task during the early part of an employment period is not uncommon. The following information is designed for a new private investigator to become familiar with investigating a neighborhood in detail.[16]

1. Dress for success, and keep in mind the environment you are going into for a case.

2. Knock on doors (talk not just to neighbors but to everyone who lives in a specific location.) Don't forget children or teenagers who may be witnesses to any activity in an area. However, parental permission is needed before you obtain a statement from a minor.

3. Check out vehicles. Record license plates in neighborhoods, especially on the same day or time when an offense occurred and contact people.

4. Consider the getaway car used in the crime. If dealing with a burglary or kidnapping, certain vehicles work and others are not ideal for an offender.

5. Find the nosy neighbor. Every block has a neighbor who keeps watch of all activities.
6. Listen carefully to people for important information, which may require you to ask additional questions.
7. Tell people you talk to what is at stake and be truthful.
8. Neighbors who take care of their yards tend to be good witnesses.
9. Check your details and notes later.

Surveillance Investigations

A private investigator under the guidance of a licensed and experienced investigator at some point will be required to perform or assist in surveillance. Surveillance is a way for private investigators to obtain information through a close monitoring of a location or a person for any activity of significance within the assigned mission of the client. In watching a home or building, the potential of danger and risk increases. Following people as they walk or drive away always creates a problem for private investigators if they are caught by their target. Therefore the key with surveillance, whether using a van, a car, or while on foot is not be discovered by the person being observed. It is important therefore for the basics to be understood as well as the nature of surveillance. An entry-level beginner to surveillance techniques should note carefully the following section before conducting any type of surveillance activity.[17]

Stationary Surveillance

There are two types of stationary surveillances: Fixed and fixed mobile. Both are designed to obtain information from one specific point. Fixed surveillance requires capturing images and video of a subject from a well-hidden vantage point. This can include spots on a residential street or a high area like an apartment.

The fixed mobile may be a van that can be brought in and out as needed, but the surveillance should be conducted from as far away as possible while still capturing good quality video or photographs that are clear enough to recognize the faces of people. Surveillance vans should be insulated for sound and temperature. Circulating fans and a 12-volt television monitor should be installed. The vans should look like work vans and be painted white or blue. One method for setting up surveillance in residential neighborhoods is to have the driver pretend the van is broken down and walk away, leaving a second private investigator in the back to get the video recording of a target. Pesky neighbors are best dealt with directly. Introducing and identifying yourself solves most trespassing or police reporting problems. To avoid being stopped by the police, a licensed investigator can check in with a local police station so patrol officers are aware of the situation. You must be constantly alert; there can be no book reading or leaving the site. Be prepared for a long haul. If you don't have access to a van, be sure to have a sedan in which you can drop a seat back and hide if necessary.

If Checking Out a Stationary Vehicle
- Look in vehicle for pieces of mail and get license number.
- Look on vehicle itself for bumper stickers.
- Motor vehicle records have addresses: vehicle identification numbers (VINs) can be run through public records.
- New York State driving records have address, number, photo, date of birth, traffic convictions, and accidents available from services online or you can just go in person to the DMV office.
- License plates lead to home addresses.
- Most states sell their databases.

Moving Surveillance

Moving surveillances are conducted in a vehicle or on foot, Generally if you are conducting a one-man surveillance, you should know in advance where the subject is going, if possible. Plan your exit; know every way the subject can go and where you can go. You should always try to put some distance between the suspect and yourself, and keep something between you. However, if you are right behind the subject, do not play follow the leader, especially into a parking lot or a large public area. Go in a different direction, but keep an eye on the suspect. If you are on foot, change your appearance (hats, coats, sunglasses, scarves). Finally, don't get in front of your subject.[18] If working in a two-person team put one person in the search area and have the other individual run a search on a suspect or a suspect's vehicle via cell phone, personal digital assistant, or laptop computer.

Additional Techniques

Investigating Infidelity

As a general investigator or legal investigator, the possibility of being hired to determine if **infidelity** or activity that is a violation of the mutually agreed upon rules or boundaries of a relationship is likely. If approached by a client that seeks an investigation of this type, ask the client if he or she has noticed any of the following behaviors that could be indications of infidelity or an extramarital affair taking place:

1. Has the partner suddenly starting working out or gone on a diet? All women and men make an effort to improve body image when a new love interest enters their life.
2. Has the partner avoided picking up the phone, and if they do, they say very little and cut it short?
3. Has the client experienced hang-up telephone calls?
4. Has the partner started seeking more private time?
5. Has the client noticed unusual charges/bills?
6. Is the partner is missing in action?

7. Has the client heard people talking?

8. Has the client become infected recently with a sexually transmitted disease (STD)?

Speaking to a client confidentially regarding the possibility of such signs can help you determine if surveillance or an investigation is necessary along with providing you with additional starting points for an investigation.

Runaway Teenager

When teenagers run away private investigators are often called in to find the runaway. A young person runs away for a wide variety of reasons, including anxiety over divorce, estrangement, or as a way to rebel against parents, to escape abuse, or in response to a perceived injustice. Before beginning a skip trace on a teenager, there are ten major pieces of information that must be collected before any productive search can be conducted, regardless of the investigator level of experience.

1. Obtain the most recent photo of the person. What did he or she look like at the time he or she ran away?

2. What was the person wearing when he or she left? The person probably has had the same clothes on for days.

3. Does the person have any tattoos, piercing, or identifying marks?

4. If the teenager ran away before, where did the person run to?

5. Is a friend or lover involved? Get their information.

6. How did the person make their escape? If a driving accomplice is involved, find the driver.

7. What is the person driving? Get a description and the make of the car and license.

8. Does the person have a cell phone or pager? What is the number? Get a copy of the bill.

9. Get account numbers for any ATM or credit cards. When did the person last use them?

10. Make a list of friends of the person and get addresses and phone numbers. Who do they speak to on a regular basis?

When dealing with parents in an emotional state, it is important to advise them that providing the information is necessary for you to complete this task properly. Additionally, have the family keep you updated with any changes. Contact local police agencies for their assistance.[19]

Word to the Wise   When it comes to missing children or teenagers, consider a surveillance of friends or relatives. Additionally, ex-spouses tend to take children when a custody battle or divorce is taking place. Always report a disappearance to the police.

■ Report Writing as a Private Investigator

Every type of private investigator must be proficient in writing reports. Each investigative application you use to solve a client's problem or develop information will at some point require that you write a report. On average, over 50% of people are comfortable with report writing, but while many have the skills necessary they unfortunately lack the confidence in writing good investigative reports. Imagine if you were out in the field observing the activity of a person on behalf of a client. The key to writing is simple. If a person can go out and see something, then they have the ability to write down a conceptualization of what is important in what has been seen and ultimately transfer those pieces of evidence onto paper. While many private investigators consider writing reports their least favorite activity, it is the most important. A good investigator has to be a good report writer. A report is the only way your employer or client understands the results of your investigation. A report is a product to your employer or client and is the agency's proof of work completed on behalf of the client. A report is also a reflection of the person who completed it, since it has the investigator's name on the report and will be seen by many people (e.g., boss, client, DA, defense attorney). Keep in mind that if you can produce a well-written report, you are more likely to be assigned better types of cases and advance in your career.

Preparation of the Report

A private investigator's report should provide a mission statement or scope so a client can review once again what the ultimate mandate of understanding was in engaging in investigative activity. The report should note the investigation in terms of what activity was requested along with the limits. Every report should work towards setting the stage and presenting the information about what activity was completed when private security investigation was conducted. A report should note time frames from when an investigator entered or left a location as well as a time breakdown of all activity observed or completed while on duty, in chronological order. A chronological pattern also helps prevent writer's block and reduce anxiety. When you are writing your report, always use facts and not inferences. A fact is something that can be proven; an inference is a conclusion based on reasoning.

Be objective and never subjective. A subjective report presents what you think the client would want to hear. An objective report presents *everything* you observed or learned that is relevant to the case—no emotions, no emotionally charged words.

The report must be able to answer who, what, where, when, why, and how. Toward that end, the report should be broken down into the five standard paragraphs format shown in the following box.

Sample Guidelines on Investigative Report Writing[20]   First, identify yourself and provide a log of your time. Indicate where you started from, what time you arrived at the scene, and what time you left.

I, investigator Smith, am employed by Such and Such Company. I arrived at the vantage point at 7:00 AM, March 12, and left at 5:45 PM of the same day.

1. Describe the Mission or Scope of the Investigation—Limit the descriptions to what you were hired to determine. Is it a child custody case? Focus on what might endanger the child. Is it a worker's compensation case? Focus on injuries.

Client reports subject (spouse of client) is a heavy drinker. Client is seeking confirmation that subject drinks and drives while client's 12-year-old daughter is present in car.

2. Arrival at scene—Provide a description of the location, and a description of vehicles involved.

10 Maple Street is a 2-story, single-family residence with an unmaintained yard. The subject's white, four-door Ford Focus SE, license plate #2VWX487, was parked in the driveway.

3. Establish vantage point—Identify your point of observation

I took up surveillance on Maple approximately 100 yards south of the residence.

4. Describe individuals under surveillance.

Subject: John Jones—white male, 35 yrs of age, approximately 6'1" tall, medium build, brown hair, and mustache, unemployed.

5. Subject/Claimant Activity—This is the body of the report. Be specific, and describe activity in detail. Remember that you've already seen what you're reporting on. Don't include information that does not have possible value. Whenever possible, report addresses, stores traveled to, streets, vehicles entered, etc.

It is important to note that a client is hiring a private investigator for their best efforts, not for buying the results that may not be possible. For example, a client may hire a private investigator to discover if a spouse has been involved in an extramarital affair. However, if no affair is taking place, the private investigator must note that no evidence was found to support that notion. Therefore a report must report the facts and not merely what the client wants. It should always be objective and note what the investigator has seen and discovered. Investigative reports should be submitted to a customer at such a time and in such a manner that has been agreed upon by the licensee and customer. Remember this report is your product, the "meat and potatoes"—what your client purchased from you. Therefore a private investigator is legally contracted to give the report. The report is part of a contract and really what the client is buying because often a client needs it down on paper for use in some manner, such as an attorney using it as bargaining power.[21]

Principles of Clear Report Writing
1. Write concise and clear sentences.
2. If you're struggling where to punctuate, chances are that it is a run-on sentence. Use a period and start a new sentence.
3. Keep it simple and direct.
4. Use active voice, not passive voice. A sentence written in an active voice would be: "The claimant mowed the lawn without any visible sign of pain or restriction." A sentence written in the passive voice would be: "The lawn was mowed by the claimant without any visible sign of pain or restriction."
5. Write in the past tense.

For entry-level security personnel looking for experience and exciting work, private investigations offer an opportunity to learn a variety of skills. It requires a strong attention to detail and a deep commitment to the completion of tasks for a client or organization. It also requires an in-depth understanding of the techniques, applicable technology, report writing, and the possible dangers that accompany certain forms of investigations. Like other areas mentioned in this chapter, private investigation skills are necessary for the development of entry-level private security employees to more advanced security professionals.

■ Conclusion

Understanding the advanced skills required of a seasoned and experienced private security person can help an entry level security employee prepare for future expectations during their career. As more demands are made upon security personnel, a working knowledge concerning private investigations will prove invaluable. Business continuity management and emergency public relations are also skills that a private security employee should strive to understand and master.

■ Chapter Review

- Understanding business continuity management and the role security plays in such plans is essential for a business organization's survival when an incident occurs.
- With American media and public reactions to news moving at such a rapid pace, private security employees should know the basics of emergency public relations to protect the image and existence of an organization when faced with a crisis.
- Private investigations are a necessary part of the security field and an area where private security employees can gain some exciting experience.

■ Answers to Case Studies

Case Study 1

1. What types of information and assistance can a private security person contribute to business continuity planning? As part of the business continuity process, a private security person is the best person who can offer information regarding the state of security at a location as well as any problems that require immediate attention. They can inform superiors regarding the status of the physical structure and security integrity of the location. They are likely to be aware of the relationship with local public service law enforcement agencies and fire departments. They will be familiar with evacuation and fire drills as well as the need to improve, or increase in frequency, such drills. Any particular dangers or concerns seen through the eyes of a security person can be brought to the attention of the upper management of a business who can prioritize and fund immediate changes as part of the future planning process.

2. What makes business continuity a growing security field? The increased amount of workplace violence, natural disasters, and possible terrorist attacks in recent times have all prompted the business community in the United States to invest more time, money, and personnel in business continuity planning.

Case Study 2

1. How would you plan on talking to local reporters? Be cordial and respectful, address reporters, and inform them of the appropriate time and place in the near future in which you can offer information and address questions. Provide only accurate information that is authorized for release by superiors or a client. Do not provide more information than necessary. When answering reporters' questions, appear confident and relaxed. Avoid answering questions that are leading questions, questions with a slant, or when possible answers are already supplied in the questions. Ensure that the position of the client or organization regarding the crisis is properly and completely told to the reporters and members of the public who seek that information. Consider also using other areas of communication such as the radio and Internet.

2. How would you prepare the staff for questions from reporters? Inform staff or employees not to speak to reporters unless they have permission and clearance from the person in charge of public relations or their superiors. If ambushed by reporters, they should remain calm and refer them to another who can provide the information they are seeking.

3. What are some of the major issues with conducting a public relations session? The key to dealing with the public and reporters at a public relations session is to ensure that the company or client is properly protected as well as to ensure that you control the group of people who are asking questions.

Case Study 3

1. What concerns would you have in conducting such a private investigation? The nature of a divorce case brings to light the possibility that the client or the opposing party may become hostile at any point. There is a possibility of danger in conducting such an investigation against the other party. Caution therefore is required. As a private investigator you must report only the facts obtained during the investigation, even if the investigator does not confirm the client's suspicions. A complete and professional report documenting the activity that took place during the investigation is also required.

2. What are some necessary tasks needed to complete such an objective? A surveillance of the opposing party along with a possible background search of the individual will be necessary for this assignment. The client will need to provide as much personal information regarding the opposing party as possible to assist the investigation. The mission will be completed once the investigation is finished and a final report is drafted.

■ Key Terms ▬▬▬▬▬▬▬▬▬▬▬▬▬▬▬▬▬▬▬▬▬

Background check (preemployment screening)   An investigation conducted by an investigator to verify information provided by a person as well as to search for information of concern to a client or organization.

Business continuity management   The management processes and procedures that identify potential impacts that threaten an organization and provide a framework for building resilience with the capability for an effective response that safeguards the interests of the organization's key stakeholders, reputation, and value-creating activities. Ultimately, it concerns survival of people and the business entity itself.

Corporate investigators   Investigators that engage in preemployment checks of prospective employees to ensure quality workers are hired who will not pose a threat to the company in the future. Corporate investigators focus on discovering white-collar crime as well as investigating any employees of the corporation who may be engaged in illegality or activity that may embarrass the company.

Crisis   An unexpected occurrence on the physical grounds of the business.

Expected danger   A high probability of danger during an investigation that is expected by those conducting an investigation.

General investigators   Investigators that can provide a wide range of services for a business or individuals. The location of missing persons, preemployment background checks, undercover operations, surveillance, and internal theft investigations are common tasks carried out by general investigators.

Hot site   A commercial disaster recovery service that allows a business to continue computer and network operations in the event of a computer or equipment disaster. For example, if an enterprise's data processing center becomes inoperable, that enterprise can move all data processing operations to a hot site. A hot site has all the equipment needed for the enterprise to continue operation, including office space and furniture, telephone jacks, and computer equipment.

Incident command system (ICS)   A management system used within the United States, parts of Canada, the United Kingdom, and other countries to organize emergency response and that was designed to offer a scalable response to incidents of any magnitude.

Infidelity   Activity that is a violation of the mutually agreed-upon rules or boundaries of a relationship.

Insurance investigators   Investigators that work to defend insurance companies against fraudulent claims. They investigate cases involving arson, product liability, workmen's compensation, and personal injury, as well as medical malpractice.

Legal investigators   Investigators with responsibilities that involve accumulating and assembling facts so attorneys can apply the law in the best interest of their clients. They conduct interviews of prospective witnesses and may testify as experts used in litigation. They search out testimonial along with documentary and physical evidence.

Reposessors   Investigators who seek out and find vehicles or property or focus on finding property that is to be repossessed by a bank or monetary lender.

Resilient enterprise   Resilient enterprise is the ability and capacity to withstand systemic discontinuities within a business and to adapt to new risk environments.

Risk assessment   The determination of the potential impact of an individual risk by measuring or otherwise assessing both the likelihood that it will occur and the impact if it should occur, and then combining the result according to an agreed rule to give a single measure of potential impact.

Skip trace   A search for missing people or information on missing people by private investigators.

Unexpected risk   When there is high probability of danger during an investigation that is unknown by those conducting the investigation.

■ **References**

1. Spy-Ops. 2007. *Business continuity planning and risk assessment.* http://www.Spy-Ops.com.
2. Ibid.

3. Sheffi, Y. 2005. *Resilient enterprise.* Cambridge, MA: MIT Press.

4. Contingency Planning Exchange. http://www.cpeworld.org. *See also* note 1.

5. McKeown, K. 2000. *Your secrets are my business.* New York: Plume. *See also* Brown, S. 2003. *Private investigating.* Upper Saddle River, NJ: Pearson Education. Brown, T. A. 2004. *Business security.* Las Vegas, NV: Crary Publications.

6. Ibid.

7. Ibid.

8. Ibid.

9. Ibid.

10. Ibid.

11. Ibid.

12. Ibid.

13. Ibid.

14. Ibid.

15. Ibid.

16. Ibid.

17. Ibid.

18. Ibid.

19. Ibid.

20. Ibid.

21. Ibid.

Loss Prevention, Gaming, and Security Systems

- Learn the basic techniques of loss prevention and security.
- Be aware of gaming and casino security techniques.
- Have knowledge concerning alarm security systems.

■ Introduction

During their careers, private security employees may find themselves being challenged to know and demonstrate their proficiency in thwarting those individuals that seek to invade and perform criminal activity at a business location. Understanding the types of criminal activity at retail and casino institutions along with the nature of alarm systems found at any business location is no longer optional for private security personnel.

■ Loss Prevention

▶ ▶ CASE STUDY 1

You are working as a retail and loss prevention officer at a local electronics store. The owner has recently informed you that he suspects that his employees are stealing some of the merchandise and shipping it out of the back of the store. There are over 80 employees at the store, all who have access to the rooms, entrances, and exits. The owner has made it clear that he wants an investigation completed, but he doesn't want the employees to be aware they are being monitored.

1. What steps would you take to begin investigating the employees?
2. What are some of the ways you can improve the security at this electronics store?

Retail prevention officers, store detectives, or loss prevention personnel are common names for the private security employees focused on private investigation into larceny and theft. The focus of such investigations generally includes shoplifting, embezzlement, credit fraud, and check fraud. *Loss prevention* or "LP" is a term used to describe a number of methods used to reduce the amount of all losses or **shrinkage** often related to retail trade. Shrinkage is the lost profits or merchandise as a result of employee theft, shoplifting, vender fraud, administrative errors, bad checks and credit cards, fraud, and vandalism. According to the 2001 National Retail Security Survey conducted by the University of Florida, retail operations suffered an average annual shrinkage percentage of 1.75% in 2000. Although most retailers' shrinkage is less than 2%, some smaller retailers often experience monthly and annual average shrinkage percentages as high as 20%. According to the National Retail Security Survey, 30.6% of shrinkage comes from shoplifting, 46% from employee embezzlement, 17.6% from administrative error, and 5.8% from vendor fraud.[1] In 2001, of the $1.845 trillion annual sales in the United States, $33.21 billion was lost to shrinkage.

The need for extensive retail security personnel and measures was not always high. Years ago the rate of theft and crime committed by employees was much lower. Stores usually had only one security person known as a **floor walker**, an individual who served as a deterrent to theft by walking around the retail location. Over time the floor walker acquired the title of *store detective* as stores employed more security personnel, which led to more people making careers in the massive retail industry. In the past decade, nearly every major retail store chain developed more extensive store security measures, which led to a change of job title from store detective to retail security. As the number of retail stores continues to grow in the United States, the current title for private security personnel in retail locations is **loss prevention agent**.[2]

Duties of a Loss Prevention Agent

While a private security employee in this area is focused on many possible situations that can disrupt a business, the primary duty is to protect the business against shrinkage. Even when loss prevention tasks are part of a security guard's duties at a location, the focus is on preventing any activity that could decrease profit during a given business day. Additionally, loss prevention officers may be tasked with[3]

- possible criminal incidents at a location
- handling fire and alarm response systems and maintaining these systems
- building security
- workplace safety
- workplace violence
- disgruntled customers and employees
- strikes or pickets

- crowd and traffic control
- disaster planning and response
- cash, check, and credit card controls

When you take a retail/loss prevention position or any private security position that involves a retail business, you must consider a number of possible areas where the shrinkage may occur. Every business organization experiences some form of shrinkage. It is unavoidable and cannot be prevented 100% at even the most sophisticated and expensive business locations. As a private security person in this role, the focus is on keeping shrinkage from growing to a point that disrupts the ability of the business to exist. Walking into this position for the first time may result in a business owner asking for a plan to lower the rate of shrinkage. Any entry-level security person in this role should always focus on the following five areas when beginning work at a new retail location:

1. Clearly identify security problems in the store.
2. Determine how significant the losses are.
3. Determine where and when the losses occur.
4. Look at current security procedures.
5. Determine how to make improvements.

For loss prevention agents newly arrived at a retail location, it is important to note that setting the standard operating procedures regarding loss prevention is not up to security personnel but is up to the management of the retail outfit that may want areas of diminished security for the sake of enticing a customer to examine, touch, and purchase retail items. As a loss prevention agent, the focus is on enforcing the standard operation procedures that have been initiated by a security manager based on the input and orders from the management of the retail outfit.[4] However, retail stores can employ a variety of measures to prevent theft of shrinkage, and as a loss prevention officer, you can advise and work with the management to implement these measures if you don't see them already in place. For example, you can suggest that small valuables such as jewelry and small crystal pieces be kept in a glass case, small merchandise is not displayed near exits, and clothing near exits is hung on locking security fixtures or tied down. Signs can placed at various spots around the store that state the store uses undercover security personnel or that cameras are used in the store.

As the management reviews the accounts and ledgers of a retail organization on a regular basis, eventually they will quickly discover if the amount of goods sold doesn't add up to the profit that should have been earned by the business. When there is a loss, management of a retail location will take shrinkage very seriously since lost profit means a lowered ability to pay employees as well as maintaining operations. In other words, an increasing amount of shrinkage (lost profits) means that the business is heading towards the inability to continue. Before a business reaches a critical point in losses, private security personnel will be asked to investigate specific claims of shrinkage or to be in a constant state of investigation. The investigation of shrinkage at a location can take one of two forms, overt and covert.

In a retail store, private security personnel following an overt style of investigation make it apparently clear they are investigating shrinkage. It can mean speaking to employees and customers as well as constantly observing people at a retail location. Such an investigation is likely to lower the amount of shrinkage; however, any internal and external culprits are likely to disappear or stay under the radar.

In a covert type of retail investigation, employees and customers are not aware that an investigation is taking place at the retail location. A covert investigation disrupts business operations of a store very minimally and allows normal operation of a business while the investigator seeks out external and internal sources for loss. However, for private security personnel new to investigations, finding possible culprits at a location can be difficult.[5]

Regardless of the manner of retail investigation chosen, private security personnel at a retail store will have to respond to a shrinkage problem in the following manner:[6]

1. Determine the size of shrinkage and loss to the business or store.
2. Determine place, time, and time period of shrinkage.
3. Evaluate all information from the store or business.
4. Interview workers and take notes.
5. Check if stolen property is on the premises.
6. Be observant of strange or nervous customers or employees starting to flash wealth.
7. Seek out suspects who have motives.
8. Listen to people.
9. Use polygraphs (lie detectors) if it is a standard store policy.
10. Complete a report and deliver to management and indicate if an investigation is still ongoing or should continue in a different direction.

Observing

As a loss prevention specialist, a special focus is placed on observing the retail location and being able to report on people and activity in detail. The key in a retail location is to pay attention to everything occurring in the store. Many private security personnel in the loss prevention field consistently check their watch while working to ensure they remember not just details while on duty but the time an incident takes place. When suspects are being observed, it is important for loss prevention agents to communicate descriptions effectively to other security or management employees. Security descriptions should always be given in a law enforcement form of communication that focuses on:[7]

1. Race
2. Gender
3. Height
4. Weight
5. Clothing
6. Age
7. Any distinguishing features (tattoos, piercings)
8. Location in retail store

As noted previously in the section on body language, it is important to observe people and note their behavior while in a store. If they appear nervous or suspicious, they are most likely involved in activity that is questionable or criminal. A loss prevention agent should always keep a focus on the clothing, facial expression, body gestures, and vocabulary of individuals in the store, especially if they are suspects. Gang members and possible drug addicts observed in a retail store should be noted with caution since stopping them when they are caught shoplifting or engaging in a disruptive incident can lead to a possible violent confrontation.

Employee Theft

Employees raise a major security concern for the retail industry. In some cases they can account for as much as 80% of the theft at a retail store location. Employees who get into the habit of pocketing money from a cash register or helping themselves to small electronic goods can result in thousands of dollars missing over time. In perspective, one employee can steal more, and more often, without being scrutinized compared to a person who shoplifts occasionally in a retail store. A general guideline for loss prevention agents is that catching one employee engaging in illegal activity is equal to 10 shoplifters.[8]

The reasons employees steal or engage in criminal activity can be explained in a number of simple self-interested explanations. An employee may have outside expenses or major debts that require extra funds. The easy and sometimes unprotected access to money and goods is a major temptation. Pressure from friends and family to bring items or money home can also be a major factor in a decision to engage in criminal activity. Employees may view themselves as being entitled to extra benefits or privileges that may have been denied them by their superior. Employees may rationalize to themselves that stealing a few retail goods or some money doesn't hurt a major retail store chain that is profitable.

At many retail locations, there are more inside jobs done by groups of employees than thefts by individuals. For private security personnel, the focus should be on the receiving, shipping, and warehouse areas, which are most vulnerable to theft by employees.

It is important for security to speak with newly hired personnel. They are likely to be told gossip about employees as well provided information about other problems including vandalism and the morale of employees.

As a retail prevention agent who is undercover, you are likely to be in a position to act as a customer who can truly test employees for honesty. In testing employees, there are a number of current methods being used by private security personnel.

Employee Theft: Where Do They Steal?
- Receiving and shipping departments
- Cash and credit card sales
- Merchandise returns or exchanges
- Employee sales
- Customer sales
- Accounts payable and accounts receivable
- General accounting and record keeping
- Payroll funds
- Inventory records
- High-end merchandise taken from display cases

Based on the numerous areas of employee theft, it is important to review sales and accounting documents on a regular basis to determine if any losses are apparent. In addition, keeping an eye on employees in locations where they can engage in criminal activity is paramount. Often the presence of a private security employee can deter criminal activity when employees perceive they are being watched.

How Employees Steal at a Retail Store

Employees have a variety of ways in which to steal from customers or a retail store location itself. They may under-ring merchandise or sales and pocket the cash difference between the totals. They may bag merchandise and put it in a trash bag to steal at the end of the day from the store. They may wear clothing or items on their person and walk out of a store. They can hand off cash and merchandise to friends and family leaving a retail location. Regardless of the tagged price, an item can be rung up at a lower amount than the original stated price. In particular an item being rung up can be voided and money pocketed by an employee. Ultimately, a person working a cash register can always just steal a little bit of money right out of the cash register.

Credit cards also provide employees an opportunity to engage in criminal activity. With a customer's credit card account number, they can order products online or over the telephone with the bill for such items going directly to the victimized customer. An employee can also save a slip from a credit transaction with the customer and use the information to charge merchandise for themselves while in the store. In addition customer credit information and data can be sold to criminals. Criminals in turn can manufacture fake credit cards that appear to be authentic except they are missing the card holder's name or account number. The criminals gather as many customer credit card account numbers as possible from retail store employees so they can print them on the fake credit cards and then sell them to dishonest people.[9]

In the shipping and receiving area, employees can steal items by manipulating the system. They can put additional merchandise in a package to be delivered, gift wrap items without receipts, note that items did not arrive when in fact they have been delivered, or alter delivery manifests to hide stolen merchandise.[10]

Testing Employees at the Register

One of the biggest areas where employees can engage in illegal activity is at the register. When a store is full of people, management are often unable to watch their employees, which opens up an opportunity for employees to engage in illegal activity. The following are ways in which a private security employee at a retail location can catch an employee engaging in illegal activity at the register.

1. The "hurry up" customer: In this employee test, an undercover detective acting as a customer (or a person selected to act as a customer by the retail/loss prevention officer) hands over the exact amount for an item and leaves before the receipt can be given to the customer. The employee is left holding the money and the item in their hand, which they can either address with the manager or keep in their pocket.

2. Checking receipts or employee ID codes: Employees are usually required to punch in their ID code whenever they use a register. These codes, or access numbers, record and store which employee was using the register at the time of a specific retail transaction. Over time, employees get to know each others' access numbers. Employees looking to engage in criminality may use the access number of another employee, thus diverting any suspicion of criminal activity towards another person. A retail/loss prevention agent should periodically check if the receipts with the employee ID match the employee actually at the register as well as checking to see that correct change is handed out to customers. Have a policy of automatic termination when a cash register is short over $100.

3. Integrity shop: A common example of this technique is marking a large denomination bill such as $100 and placing it in a cashier's drawer. The goal is to see if the bill disappears from the drawer or doesn't make it to its appropriate location such as a cash office once it is in the employee's register. The information gained from an integrity shop can be used to initiate investigations or conduct interviews that could possibly reveal dishonest activity or outright theft.[11]

Almost every large retail institution has some form of **electronic journal** that records all its transactions. Information such as credit card numbers, gift card numbers, refunds, and merchandise voids is gathered at the point of sale. These journals can then be used to view and print facsimiles of receipts or checks. Loss prevention agents also focus on audits. Another common method for preventing illegal activity, the **cash office audit,** or counting of money earned during the operating hours of a retail location, compares cash earned to the record of goods sold to determine if any shortages or discrepancies exist. It is usually conducted by a common retail employee who counts up the cash from transactions at the retailer's registers. A shortage occurs when the dollar amount contained in the register does not match what the cash audit says it should be. Shortages are used to begin cash embezzlement cases that are investigated by loss prevention departments. Cash office audits include information pertaining to which employees used a particular register during the day. Loss prevention investigators narrow the field of suspected employees using this information.

Shoplifters

Shoplifting is one of the most common property crimes in the United States today. Regardless of whether the shoplifter is committing the act for the first time or is experienced, the cost to a store is still staggering. On a given Saturday at a retail mall location, a retail store can lose over $5000 worth of merchandise. On the same day during a holiday season, the amount can be double or triple.

Anyone can be a shoplifter, an important fact for loss prevention investigators to understand. Those who focus on stereotypes such as race and age generally have a difficult time detecting shoplifting. Generally shoplifters come in three types: spur of the moment habitual type (often elderly people), shopping shoplifter (common with juveniles), and professional shoplifter. The reasons for shoplifting can be a lack of money, personal need, peer pressure among juveniles (or as a dare), or to support a drug habit or any form of addiction. Retail stores in areas with a high drug or crime rate can be prone to a higher rate of shoplifting.

Characteristic Signs and Behavior of Shoplifters

For loss prevention agents, recognizing a shoplifter is one of the most important skills that must be developed as soon as possible. It is important to note that most amateur shoplifters tend to spend too much time selecting merchandise and looking for investigators, thus making them much more likely to be detected. Professional shoplifters on the other hand tend to already know what merchandise they wish to steal and move quickly to get it. When observing people in a retail location, a private security person must develop the habit of going through a mental checklist that covers a number of the behaviors usually found in shoplifters.

Hands. A loss prevention officer should watch the hands of a possible shoplifter closely because the hands of a suspect are what are used in the act of stealing.

Size. Generally when people shop for clothes they check the tag or hanger for the appropriate size and fit. A person who is going to shoplift will steal an article of clothing without noting the size. In addition, watching the physical size of a person once he or she enters a store for indications of "sudden" growth could be an indication he or she is hiding objects on his or her person.

Eyes. The eyes of shoplifters often give away that they are engaged in suspicious activity. A person who is planning to steal will often look at customers and sales representatives and not at the retail items at a store location.

Appropriate clothing. An individual wearing clothing that is unusual for the season or current weather conditions or clothes that are oversized can be indications that shoplifting is going to occur.[12]

Red Flag for Shoplifting

- A subject enters a store, picks up, touches and inspects items but appears not to purchase.
- A person avoids sales personnel and tries not to talk to individuals.
- The person has swivel head syndrome (constant looking left and right for others).
- The person is sweating during normal temperatures.
- The person wears baggy clothing and walks in an unusual manner.
- A person suddenly becomes pregnant.
- A person enters a store with a large bag or box.
- A person has a baby carriage and objects are dropped in the carriage.
- A person leaves an area hastily after casually strolling in the store.
- You catch the person with shoplifting tools.
- One person talks to a salesperson while another steals.
- A person is poorly dressed and doesn't fit the regular clientele of the retail location, a high-end jewelry store for example.
- A group of teenagers enter in a hurried fashion and immediately split up.
- A person enters a store wearing heavy, loose-fitting clothing not in keeping with the weather or temperature of the day.
- A person enters a dressing room to try on clothing and when leaving appears to have gained considerable weight.
- A person enters a store and appears to immediately look about for CCTV cameras, mirrors, and other surveillance.
- A person who seems suspicious of anyone nearby or following.

Shoplifting Techniques

Shoplifting by individuals also involves a number of theft techniques and equipment. A common technique used by professional shoplifters is called a "grab and run" in which the shoplifter quickly enters the store, grabs an item, and runs out of the store. Due to the quickness of this technique, professional shoplifters are difficult to catch. A "turn" is an additional method for a more experienced shop-lifter. The scam involves two people, one who serves to distract others while the other engages in the actual shoplifting. Generally, the distractor person serves to create a situation for the purpose of getting the attention of any retail salesperson or customer who comes near long enough for the shoplifter to steal the selected item. The **shield technique** involves a person who blocks the view of the shoplifter from cameras or security personnel. Professional female shoplifters may also use a technique known as **crotching** which involves rolling items into a ball and quickly placing it between their legs while they are wearing a dress.

A paper bag can be used by bringing it into a retail location inside a pocket, purse, or parcel. The bag is then removed from hiding and filled with stolen retail items. Once filled, the bag no longer has to be concealed since it looks inconspicuous. Shoplifters can line a bag with silver duct tape to defeat an electronic article surveillance alarm. Shopping bags can also be used to steal thousands of dollars of merchandise from a retail location. Shoplifters can walk into a retail store with a shopping bag from an-other retail store and then begin to fill their bag with items as if they were purchased earlier in the day. Female shoplifters often use purses because almost every woman has a purse that can be used to hide small retail items along with the clutter of other personal items. Winter coats with large pockets offer a great way to steal since they tend to hang below the hips and bulge inward towards the thighs and knees of a person. A coat over a person's arm can serve as a drape to cover up any items grabbed from a counter or shelf. In recent years, shoplifters have increasingly used "booster boxes," a box with a hinged trap door on the bottom that conceals additional space. The trap door is hidden when other items are placed over it.

Ultimately, there are always shoplifters who create new methods for stealing retail merchandise. As a new loss prevention agent, the key is to understand the nature of the differences between the techniques used by the different classes of shoplifters. Amateur shoplifters tend to use only small bags, shopping bags, or a day pack while professional shoplifters steal in much larger volume with more advanced techniques designed for more valuable merchandise.

Apprehending Shoplifters and Other Criminals

As previously mentioned, apprehending a suspect requires a great deal of train-ing and skill. There are certain types of shoplifters that can usually be expected to "come along quietly" when apprehended. They are children, elderly people, some women, and some people who steal while with companions who are unaware of the theft activity. If a shoplifter or criminal is a drug user or gang member, it could lead to violence and harm to the loss prevention agent or other people. Once ap-prehended, focus should be on moving the suspect to the security office as fast as possible and without a scene that draws attention to the shoplifter or that causes violence for the loss prevention agent. If the person being apprehended is a differ-ent gender, have a fellow employee of that suspect's gender be present and serve as a witness. Handcuffing is generally not necessary unless the suspect becomes violent or hostile.

Generally loss prevention agents use a number of tactics to handle a shoplifter in a way that detains the suspect but doesn't overly disrupt the retail store environment for customers.

1. Loss prevention agents usually apprehend individuals in a low-key manner without creating a scene and with immediate activity that displays their authority.

2. When speaking to a suspect, the agent is firm and confident and never appears confused or afraid.

3. The agent uses only the amount of force necessary to move and detain a resisting suspect.

4. The agent responds with similar words if the shoplifter or criminal is verbally abusive. The agent says very little and removes the suspect from the public's eye as soon as possible.

5. The agent is polite, firm, and professional with the suspect at all times.

6. The agent uses handcuffs only when the suspect acts in such a way that physically securing them is the only way to prevent an escape or harm.

7. If other persons who accompany a shoplifter were not aware or not a part of the criminal activity, the agent should advise them that they are not under arrest and can wait quietly outside of the security office if they wish. If they become disruptive, the agent should have them escorted off the store property.

8. While walking a suspect to the security office, the agent always walks on one side and slightly to the rear.

9. Once in the security office, the agent maintains a position between the shoplifter and the door while in the security office.

If a loss prevention agent is working alone at a retail store location and a shoplifter drops merchandise while running away, the priority should always be on the recovery of the stolen merchandise rather than pursuing the suspect. The local authorities should be notified once the suspect has left the store. If a loss prevention agent leaves the store to make an apprehension and the suspect pulls a weapon, the apprehension process should be interrupted. The information on the suspect should be relayed to the local police.[13]

The Legal Implications of Apprehending Shoplifers

Apprehending people also has legal implications. If done incorrectly, a loss prevention agent and the retail store could be sued by a customer. Before apprehending a suspect, a loss prevention agent must ensure a number of criteria are met and followed:[14]

1. The suspect must be observed stealing; a loss prevention agent must see the suspect steal and know that the item in their possession is stolen retail merchandise.

2. See the suspect conceal the item. If the suspect conceals the item it is a plus for a case of shoplifting because concealment shows the person did not have the intent to pay for the item as a law-abiding customer.

3. Maintained uninterrupted surveillance of the suspect at all times. If at any point a loss prevention agent loses sight of a suspect, they should consider not apprehending the suspect. During the break in surveillance, the suspect may have dropped or ditched the stolen merchandise to successfully leave the store.

4. See the suspect not pay anything at the cash register for the item. As the loss prevention expert in a retail store, you are going to have to provide an affidavit to the police and to your superiors that the item was the property of the retail store and that the suspect bypassed a cash register.

5. Apprehend the suspect outside of the retail location, preferably just outside the door of the store.

6. Immediately identify yourself as a security professional. You should identify your name, title, and purpose for stopping a suspect.

7. Recover the stolen retail merchandise as you apprehend the suspect. The retail merchandise must be recovered by the loss prevention agent. It is the evidence that the suspect has in fact shoplifted the retail merchandise and it is a loss to the store unless returned.

The retail store management has the discretion whether or not to release the suspect with a warning or to turn a suspect over to the police. If a suspect is going to be turned over, a report as well as the observations will have to be relayed to the police officer that arrives on the scene. Without the firsthand knowledge and observation of the shoplifting, a police officer may not arrest the suspect. If the private security person does plan on detaining the suspect for a period of time, he or she must contact the police without unnecessary delay. In addition, the private security person should write down everything the detained person says and pass it to the officer who arrives at the retail store.[15] However, one method of bypassing the steps that are commonly employed is establishing the selection of merchandise. This is usually done by noting what a suspect had when first observed entering a store.[16] If seen later with several items he or she did not have before, especially on his or her person, it may be reasonable to assume that the merchandise belongs to the retailer. Generally, common sense and good judgment are key to making successful apprehensions. At times not all conditions can or will be met to make an apprehension. However, it is still possible to prevent the loss by letting the suspect go once they remove the objects from their person.

Loss Prevention Reports

As with private investigation, loss prevention agents must create reports to be viewed by the management at a retail store as well as local authorities if a suspect is turned over to the police. In general, the focus is on covering essential information. In particular, a shoplifting report should provide the following information:[17]

1. The shoplifter's name
2. Location where the loss prevention agent observed the shoplifter
3. The loss prevention agent's reason for surveillance
4. What was stolen and how it was stolen
5. A statement that the shoplifter had an opportunity to pay for the item
6. The exit the shoplifter used to leave the retail store
7. The distance the shoplifter went outside of the store before apprehension
8. How you identified yourself as a security employee
9. A description of where stolen retail merchandise was recovered
10. A statement indicating if shoplifter was released or turned over to the police

Methods for Detecting and Preventing Shoplifting

Generally, loss prevention agents focus on four major ways to prevent shoplifting or to discover additional criminal activity: Surveillance by loss prevention agents on the floor, security observation booths (or vents), closed-circuit television cameras (CCTV), or two-way mirrors.

CCTV systems are common to almost all loss prevention departments, and many loss prevention agents consider the systems indispensible. The benefits of CCTV cameras are that the agent can gain a better view of a suspect or employee, and record incidents and not reveal their identity to criminals or employees. Cameras can view and record different areas of a store, which can be viewed by an employee while activity is suspected or reviewed at a later date when criminal activity is discovered. Some retail store locations use a secure position where one person watches the CCTV camera system to detect shoplifters and a floor person to follow the suspects and apprehend them. Some related benefits of the CCTV system included protection from employee theft.

Two-way mirrors allow a shoplifter or criminal to be caught off guard as a loss prevention agent or employee watches them from a different location. Observation booths are areas to watch for criminal activity that, to a customer, are not readily apparent. From the position of a merchandise display, small fitting room, or corner, a loss prevention agent can have a good field from which to watch a store. Air vents that lead from stockrooms to the retail-selling floor can be used for the same purpose. Through a stockroom air vent, a loss prevention officer can view shoplifters or other criminals and then respond immediately by reentering the store floor, an advantage over some observation booths.

Where to Put CCTV Cameras[18]   In placing CCTV cameras, there are a number of locations to consider.

- Areas where loss can occur
- Areas selling high-end merchandise
- Receiving and shipping docks
- Warehouse and storage areas
- Elevators and escalators
- Garbage areas
- Entrances and exits
- High-traffic areas
- Sensitive rooms
- Parking garage and fields
- Areas important for an investigation based on past crime

Almost all loss prevention personnel use some form of two-way radio communication while on duty. Loss prevention teams often use the two-way radio system in a particular manner. Communicating and moving in two-person teams, one person often follows a shoplifting suspect and summons assistance from the other team member when ready to apprehend a shoplifter or anyone else who is disrupting security at a retail location.[19] With regard to communication, even making frequent announcements regarding security, "Security to area 30, please" can have a positive effect.

One of the most widely used advances in technology for retail locations has been the use of **electronic article surveillance** (EAS) equipment. EAS involves the use of electronic security towers and electronic security tags. Hard tags or label tags are placed on items throughout the store. The tags are disabled when the cashier either removes the hard tag using a detacher or scans label tags over a magnetized strip or label deactivator. If the tag is not disabled it will activate the alarm tower located at the exit of the store. EAS tags and labels are extremely effective in deterring amateur shoplifting, but most professionals require a combination of hard tags, labels, and ink tags to keep them in check. Even with the most elaborate antishoplifting systems, some goods will be lost; this is possible with booster bags or simply a "grab and run."[20]

Store Actions that Encourage Shoplifting[21]
1. Employees appear disinterested and too busy to help customers
2. No evidence of security precautions
3. No EAS devices attached to devices
4. Secluded or dark areas are available
5. Employees fail to react to alarms
6. Security guard at a door is not being attentive
7. Employee fails to follow proper procedures
8. No antishoplifting signs are visible

Customer Credit Card Fraud

As noted previously, credit cards can be used to commit a number of fraudulent activities. One of the most common methods of fraud besides shoplifting is credit card fraud. Criminals use a number of simple techniques in retail stores. With a stolen credit card they may directly charge retail items and leave never to return. They may purchase items at a retail store and then return them soon afterwards to receive cash before the real holder of the credit card discovers fraudulent charges. Loss prevention agents can train and work together with employees in many cases to prevent credit card fraud. A number of practices are currently used in the industry to prevent this form of retail criminal activity. Here are a few that should be considered:

- Check opposite sex usage: If a woman or man is using a credit card with the name of someone of the opposite gender, an ID and explanation should be sought before the transaction continues.
- Check signature: The signature on the card should be examined to see if it matches the signature on the charge slip.
- Underage use of a credit card: If a person appears too young to be using a credit card, ID and an explanation should be sought.[22]

Customer Accidents

As a loss prevention agent in a retail location, the possibility of responding to an accident requiring your assistance is likely. Even when accidents are not listed as a job task, often a sales clerk or employee will call the security department to report an accident. When a customer accident occurs, a loss prevention agent should do the following:[23]

1. Notify his or her supervisor or store manager as soon as an accident occurs.
2. Take care of the customer in a polite and helpful manner. The customer should decide if they want to go to the hospital or home.
3. Ask how the accident happened.
4. Get the names of witnesses immediately, before people start leaving the location. The names and addresses of customers along with the names of employees should be recorded.
5. Inspect the unaltered scene of the accident with another employee as soon as the victim has been moved.
6. Take a picture of the unaltered accident scene before it is cleaned up by other personnel.

While these are important steps that should be taken, a loss prevention agent handling an accident situation should also avoid some specific activity. At no time should the loss prevention agent admit that the store or an employee is responsible for the accident. There should be no offer to pay the victim any of their medical bills. The insurance coverage of the store should never be mentioned to a victim or their family. A loss prevention agent should not engage in an argument as to who or what caused the accident with or in front of the victim. An employee should not be reprimanded or disciplined at the scene of the accident. The focus must be on preventing a negligence-based lawsuit against the retail store.

Word to the Wise   There are a number of individuals who fake injuries at retail or store locations to receive compensation. Conduct investigations and create a report on people who get injured in the store and seek compensation for $5000 or less. Usually such criminals are looking to settle quickly.

Emergency Planning

Working in a retail location, it would not be uncommon to be asked by the owners to participate in the emergency planning of the retail outfit. Emergency planning involves creating a plan that is precise and specific on how to handle emergencies when they occur. It exists to saves lives and property and reduces the exposure to being shut down and supports the restoration of normal business. If selected to create an emergency planning document for a retail store, a private security employee should describe in detail the following areas of concern:

1. The company's policy
2. Risk assessment
3. A description of each emergency or serious incident that could occur and detailed procedures for each

4. The evacuation and shutdown procedures

5. A list of all emergency equipment available on site

6. A list of all employees with first aid or first responder training

7. A list of all mutual aid agreements or procedures with police, fire, ambulance, electric, gas, and telephone emergency responses

8. A list of pre-approved repair services such as elevator repair, glass replacement, plumbing, and alarm maintenance

9. A list of all management and administrative personnel of concern who are to be notified depending on the incident, including their emergency telephone and pager numbers, with these suggested people on the contact list:

   - Store manager
   - Operations manager/assistant store manager
   - Duty managers
   - All security personnel
   - Maintenance/engineering staff

Such emergency planning documents should also include specific guidelines as to what employees should be doing in case of an emergency. Such a document should be used to answer such questions as:

1. Who should respond to what emergency or serious incident, when, where, and how?

2. What duties or responsibilities are assigned and to whom?

3. Who becomes "in charge" of the scene or the incident?

4. What decisions and notifications are to be made and by whom?

5. Who will make public announcements or act as the spokesperson if and when the media becomes involved?

For such emergency planning documents to be useful for a retail store, the emergency planning procedures and personnel should be tested, evaluated, and trained on a regular basis. In particular, fire, robbery, burglary, and evacuation drills should be conducted with employees on an annual or biannual basis.[24]

If an emergency situation arises, a loss prevention agent can successfully navigate a difficult situation to save and protect the lives of customers and employees even without previous planning. When an emergency occurs, a loss prevention agent should get to the emergency or accident promptly after being notified. As previously noted for all private security positions, they should remain calm and act as a leader. They should notify their superior so they can make upper-level decisions as to the appropriate response, such as closing a store, calling local police, or evacuating an area. No matter how difficult the situation is, it should always be viewed objectively.

Missing Children

To a parent, a missing child is an emergency, but to private security personnel working at a retail location it is one of the most common events. Nevertheless, it is a heightened event that must be taken seriously, and the situation can be handled in a thorough and systematic manner for the benefit of the child's guardians. When handling a missing child report in a retail store, do the following:[25]

1. Get a description (body, clothes, languages spoken, height, weight, etc.).
2. Create a plan to cover all exits quickly.
3. Have an employee stay with the guardian.
4. Search all rooms and areas (including hidden areas).
5. Stop a child if he or she matches the description, if with an unknown adult, stall and communicate with child to determine if child is being coerced.
6. If no child is found after 10–15 minutes, contact police.
7. File a report.

Fire

When a fire occurs at a retail location, specific steps should always be rehearsed and drilled to protect people and property. If a fire does break out, a loss prevention agent needs to know specific steps to respond quickly and effectively.

1. Find and use extinguishers and other fire equipment.
2. Know the fastest way to contact the fire department and alert them.
3. Be aware of the location of the sprinkler shutoff valve in the store.
4. Instruct or lead customers to safety.

Blackouts

A blackout, a complete loss of power at a location leaving people in the dark, is a possibility due to energy shortages, disrupted electrical power lines, or any other activity that can disrupt electrical power. Blackouts in a retail store present an opportunity for shoplifting and theft by customers and employees. When a blackout occurs, loss prevention agents should focus on the following:

1. Getting the customers out of restrooms, elevators, and other confined spaces
2. Positioning employees at the entrances to prevent more customers from entering the store
3. Ensuring all cash is stored in a safe and is secure
4. Instructing all high-ranking employees to lock all cash registers until power is restored
5. Alerting the company's corporate director or security chief, if the store is part of a major chain

Evacuations

In a crisis situation, a retail store may have to be evacuated. In such a case, the private security personnel will be at the forefront leading personnel and customers to safety. Evacuation may be required for a fire or report of fire, a bomb threat or actual detonation of a device, a gas leak, a blackout, or any other emergency that might place the occupants of a building in jeopardy.

Guidelines to Evacuation by Loss Prevention Agents

1. Agents should become aware of their location. This should include an approximate head count of customers in the department.
2. Once an evacuation is announced, the agent should direct all customers to and through the closest fire exit.
3. The agent must instruct people not to use an elevator.
4. The agent should ensure all safes, cash boxes, and specific merchandise are as secure as possible given the likely time constraint.
5. The agent should prevent panic.
6. Before leaving, the agent should make sure everyone is out.
7. Once out of the building, the agent should instruct the employees to meet and line up with other coworkers from the same department so that their manager or supervisor, who should have all work schedules, can take a head count. If someone is not accounted for, it should be reported immediately.

Robbery

A robbery at a retail outfit is also another risk that a store faces. Depending on the area where the store is located, the possibility of a robbery taking place varies. For private security personnel who may be unarmed, an armed robbery puts the private security guard at a disadvantage. Although unarmed, a number of steps can be taken to assist with the criminal being caught and in everyone staying safe during the actual robbery.[26]

1. Remain calm.
2. Obey commands.
3. Engage in a three-portion analysis: (1) glance at the upper portion of the robber's body, (2) make a note of the middle portion, and (3) as they depart, observe their lower portion, noting in all cases clothes, height, weight, gender, race, and other identifying factors.

Workplace Violence

The threat of violence at work has increased in the United States. At any time, employees and customers at a location could be victimized by someone who is disgruntled or mentally unstable. In the United States, workplace violence can be statistically broken down into three categories based on the nature of the offenders: stranger violence (60%), customer or client violence (30%), and employee violence (10%).

Stranger violence and customer or client violence are hard to predict even for an expert in private security. For preventing employee violence, the key is to complete a thorough background search on every employee before they are hired by a retail organization. A focus should be placed on a migratory work history, and history of domestic abuse, sex crimes, and assault crimes. If the person has a reputation for being a loner or you learn of other eye-raising personality quirks during your background search, consider such factors before hiring the employee.[27]

For entry-level security employees, working in a retail location in a security position offers a chance for experience. For many college students, working in a retail location in a loss prevention position is the first security job and begins a career towards more advanced security positions. Retail stores face situations that involve criminal activity and danger, thereby needing competent personnel who have the ability to make split-second decisions when the retail store environment changes.

■ Gaming Security

▶ ▶ CASE STUDY 2

Imagine you are working as a newly hired gaming security officer at a recently opened gaming establishment. After going through 72 hours of training, you are now busy working on the casino floor each shift and searching for any illegality or improper conduct by both employees and patrons. You receive word before starting your shift that the accounts of casino patrons and their personal information are being accessed and possibly downloaded. Such information in the wrong hands can lead to identity theft or additional criminal activity. The casino is now on high alert for anyone who may be involved with such activity.

1. How would people be able to steal the information about casino patrons and gamers in a casino?
2. What other criminal activity or schemes can take place within the casino?

As previously mentioned, the gaming industry is going to continue to grow in the United States, and so will the need for private security to work in gaming establishments or casino–hotel resorts. Casinos are locations where money is constantly flowing in and out of peoples' pockets and accounts. With gambling revenues increasing in the United States, it is more likely criminal activity will take place. In terms of private security, the nature of gaming establishments and casino–hotels are themselves unique institutions. Working in some locations may require additional professional training or schooling before even an experienced private security officer can successfully obtain employment. The nature of slot machines, computer systems, banking, card games, surveillance technology, and cheating are all areas requiring special knowledge. Whatever the case may be, an entry-level security person who wishes to seek work in such a location in the future should understand the basic nature of gaming and casino–hotel security issues. By examining some of the unique security problems in casinos, a learner can acquire an advanced skill set that will be useful later in his or her professional career.

Patrolling the Location

A gaming or casino security officer should always begin a shift by checking physical security. If on patrol within a gaming institution, walk through the public spaces in the casino. A public space is an area in the casino designated for general access by the public or noncorporate groups (lobbies, customer areas, parking lots). Such locations must be examined to ensure that they prevent unauthorized access after normal business hours or during a normal work shift. Secondly, the interior spaces of the casino such as the hallways, office areas, and common areas, must be monitored and controlled, especially when large crowds begin to appear in a casino. Restricted space areas such as offices, data centers, executive briefing centers, infant and child care centers, mechanical areas, and vaults, are restricted areas that also need to be examined even though the center of activity is the casino main public area.[28] Outside of the casino, security officers should be noting the nature of perimeter security. All gaming institutions rely on private security personnel to check that adequate lighting is provided in parking lots, loading docks, ramps—all for the safety of everyone.

Employee Parking Garages

It is important for security personnel to ensure that the following conditions are met in employee parking garage areas.[29]

1. Working electronically operated gates
2. Working intercom systems
3. Adequate and working lighting/CCTV systems
4. Unobstructed camera views of vehicles entering and exiting
5. Signs posted around the property for visitors and unauthorized persons

Completing a Patrol of a Hotel–Casino

Once the internal and external sections of a casino are known to be secure, gaming officers on patrol should be observing conditions of the casino or employee activity that warrant immediate action as follows:[30]

1. Poor safety practices, violations of safety rules, or hazardous conditions not specifically noted in the officer's instructions
2. Poor fire prevention practices or obstructions to any area that would prevent swift access to fire equipment or fire evacuation
3. Improper storage or handling of private documents or products
4. Defective motors, fans, or other electrical equipment
5. Open doors that should be locked and locks that may be open
6. Defective, misplaced, or missing fire or emergency equipment, including fire extinguishers and first aid kits
7. Any evidence of insects or rodent pests in any area, or even animals inside the complex

An officer on building patrol at a gaming institution should be particularly careful for his or her own safety.

1. Use a flashlight if lighting conditions are not adequate.
2. Never assume perceived fumes are harmless.
3. Make note of open doors.
4. Make note of all burned out lights.
5. Make note of anything unusual.

If a gaming officer is patrolling in a vehicle, he or she should drive slowly enough to be thorough and complete when searching for any changes or significant events. As a standard practice in the private security field, gaming officers should complete a report on everything they observe and note after a patrol.[31]

Gaming Criminals' Theft Techniques

The other factor for gaming security personnel is the protection of patrons. Patrons entering a casino are often focused on having a good time and not on criminals who are present to victimize them while they gamble, eat, drink, or stay at a casino–hotel. Thieves often converge on the casino during holiday weekends and conferences. Foreign nationals are preferred targets of thieves and scam artists. A trained gaming officer soon learns to pick out people who are not at a casino–hotel for fun. Gaming criminals use some of the same methods as shoplifters, but they also have their own techniques and equipment unique to gaming locations. Gaming security should therefore always be vigilant for the following:[32]

1. The groups—People who enter a casino together and then split up, moving in the same direction but parallel to one another or one behind the other.
2. The watchers—People who are watching the patrons playing the games.
3. The roamers—Individuals who roam the slot areas without playing (alone or in a team). They drop a coin near a player, who turns one way while the

criminal grabs the bucket of coins—distract and grab. A variation of this involves a team of two; one engages a victim in conversation while another grabs something of value. Hotel check-in areas, bell desks, and valet areas where people are distracted are major target areas. Surveillance can't catch all of this going on so you need to train floor people very well and must always review tapes.

4. The impersonator—Keep watch of exit and entrance areas for people pretending to be employees to make change and then take money and dash. Stop anyone who looks like they are wearing an outfit similar to the employee uniform.

5. The short-change artists—A short change artist may have five $20 bills with a $10 bill concealed in the other hand. He asks for a $100 bill. When he is given the $100 bill he turns around immediately and says, "I'm sorry, you gave me a $10 bill." When the cashier or change person gives the individual the other $90, of course, the bank will be $90 short.

6. The pickpockets—Follow the large crowds, and patrol areas near the pickpocket signs and ATMs. Pickpockets may have a large bag or something over one arm such as a heavy jacket or sweater so they can conceal a purse or wallet. They usually work in teams to hand off stolen merchandise. When a purse or wallet is missing, always check wastebaskets and restrooms first; most thieves just want the cash.

7. The cheaters—When it appears that a person seems to be unbeatable while gambling, they should be monitored carefully for possible cheating activity.

Security Management in Gaming Institutions

As part of the entry-level private security personnel in a gaming institution, you are likely to begin your work as both a guard and someone who handles protecting patrons. Patrons in a gaming institution are looking for a good time and not considering opportunistic criminals. In particular, alcohol consumed by gaming patrons makes people forget to safeguard their valuables. Request the help of gaming pit personnel to protect guests from their own carelessness. When a patron has had too much to drink, you should tactfully step in and try to get the person to his or her room, or put them in a taxi to wherever they reside. Even when the patrons become aggressive and threatening, security should try and take a quiet approach.[33]

Casino–Hotel Guest Protection

In protecting guests staying on site, security should begin with examining the points of access in a casino–hotel. Security should be present on the main level and lobby of an area with checkpoints at the elevators or hallways leading to guest accommodations. Guards can then request guests show room keys and vouch for any nonguests in tow before proceeding to hotel rooms. There should also be a continuous crisscrossing of officer patrols inside the hotel complex. All officers create an electronic record of their tours by swiping a magnetic stripe card through readers mounted at various locations along the route. The guest room door locks can aid security by using electronic systems in which computers can offer a printout of the times of any room entry. The electronic key systems also store a record of the times and a location of any key's use in a lock.[34] Maids, bellmen, and other people with access to rooms may be thieves. If a guest reports something stolen from a room, you should promptly check maid carts and areas where maid carts are stored. In addition, all guest rooms are equipped with an in-room safe specifically designed for the laptop computers that are the prime pickings of today's hotel room burglars. As a private security employee, you can provide a briefing sheet to every patron entering a hotel–casino who asks for suggestions on security.

When celebrities reside at the hotel–casino, security will consult with the VIP staff to create an effective, comfortable level of security. Security escorts can be assigned to accompany the celebrity when he or she is on the property. If needed, hotel floors or sections of floors can be blocked off, or security officers can be stationed at elevators to make sure that no one who is not a key-carrying guest for that level arrives on that floor. Security personnel can also be posted at the door to the VIP's suite. Security personnel should regularly check bookings to find out if there is anyone coming who has any type of status that might be of concern to security. Often, however, celebrities want to remain anonymous. If so, security can provide plainclothes escorts or any other low-key security services that the VIP might request.[35]

Protection of Guests Outside of the Hotel–Casino Complex

Gaming and casino–hotels often have thousands of people entering and leaving in a given day. Criminals will often follow customers outside of a casino to victimize them. As a private security officer it is possible to diminish the ability of criminals to engage in activity near the gaming location. First, high rollers, gamblers who spend large amounts of money at a casino, are possible targets for criminals. If a high roller has a significant amount of money on his or her person, he or she should be offered an electronic transfer or a security escort to his or her vehicle or to a taxi (or even to his or her room).[36] The protection of the names and address of hotel–casino guests must be a major priority at all times. As mentioned earlier, the increased traffic of people in and out of a gaming location on holidays or major conference days requires increased security outside as well. Patrons can be victimized in self-parking areas, in particular.

Be aware that in high-traffic areas, or new construction or renovation projects, cleaning and landscaping crews at work can all disrupt the lighting, access, and camera views in key spots. Therefore as changes outside of the gaming institution occur, security must check and determine if there any new threats to the security of people entering or leaving a gaming location.[37]

Prostitutes

The nature of cash flowing in and out of a gaming institution also brings the problem of prostitution. Prostitutes looking for potential patrons are likely to enter gaming institutions. Prostitutes also work as thieves. Gaming institutions should be very concerned about prostitution because prostitutes that are allowed to solicit on the casino floor are likely to continue to operate for an extended period. This encourages additional prostitutes, drug dealers, and other criminals who engage in vice activity to appear in a casino. All of these activities affects the reputation of the casino (especially family-friendly hotel-casinos), threatens patrons, and can lead to local authorities disciplining a gaming institution. Therefore, all gaming institutions should have a zero tolerance policy towards prostitutes.

The harder aspect is conducting a quick investigation to determine if someone is in fact a prostitution suspect. Prostitution raises the problem of attempting to protect the corporate reputation while preventing private security personnel from being charged with harassment.[38] Women are often able to recognize a prostitute before a male officer does; therefore, female private security officers are essential members of a gaming security team. Typically, a prostitute is a single female or male who orders a drink and walks from man to man carrying on a conversation. The prostitute will leave with a patron and then is often back at the bar in less than an hour. Prostitutes are very friendly with bartenders and waitresses who help them set up their Johns and tip well in return. As a rule, prostitutes do not carry identification; if they are arrested, they can give a phony name.

In the event you suspect a potential prostitute, stop him or her, inquire as to what the person is up to, and arrest the individual if you have the authority and probable cause to do so, or give a trespass warning followed by a detailed report. If necessary, contact the local law enforcement vice unit for assistance. The prostitute will know you are the security force, but they may not know the vice cops.[39]

Documenting Suspicious Activity in a Gaming Institution

As a new gaming security officer, you are not likely to be a master of all card games or cheating techniques. It is likely that an entry-level person will be on the floor of the casino looking for suspicious activity. Above the casino in a special location, experts on cheating and illegal activities watch monitors and can be directed by security personnel to scrutinize individuals in the casino. You should check that all monitor have a time-date stamp that is synchronized. For a security officer on the casino floor, there are key steps that should always be taken. By communicating with those individuals who work in casino surveillance rooms, activity can be recorded and analyzed quickly.[40]

When Something Suspicious Is Occurring When you believe there is suspicious activity, do the following:[41]

1. Communicate to those in the surveillance room about your suspicions. Be specific.
2. Ensure surveillance officers get good camera coverage from at least three different camera angles if possible.
3. Identify the table number or the slot bank number or other location on video.
4. Ensure cameras get clean coverage of suspects, dealers, and pit or other personnel by preventing any obstructions from occurring.
5. Log the tapes by number in a daily shift report (DSR) and any other reports. The original recording tapes may be called for by the criminal justice system or private security team at a later date.

If you are the individual working in the surveillance room, the focus is on recording and preserving video of activity within the casino. Without the proper recording of footage along with its storage, any criminal who is later apprehended and turned over to the local police may escape prosecution. The rules of evidence obtained are very strict in most states. Newly hired surveillance specialists working with other security personnel must operate at a high standard. Such high standards include the following:[42]

1. It is of vital importance to know the layout of the casino floor and all the possible camera angles available to record a questionable act.
2. Tapes must clearly show the full sequence of what has occurred. You have to practice watching behaviors: when somebody does something different, it shows; rubbernecking, hesitations in acting, people paying attention to other people, and so on.
3. Keep in mind that if you show a videotape in court, you will not be showing it to other gaming professionals.
4. Make sure you get a clear face shot of the individual in question. The tape must clearly show who has committed the action or crime.
5. Make sure you get the number of the particular area, game, or slot machine on video and associate the person or incident with that area.
6. The tape must clearly show when the incident occurred.
7. Make sure the tape shows security personnel detaining the person.
8. Make sure the tape is of excellent quality throughout its entire length—protect it.
9. Make two copies of any recorded criminal activity.

10. Maintain a record of all times the tape is removed from a locker, copied, or viewed.

11. Write a good report of the incident.

Internal Crimes by Employees

As with retail stores, the potential for employees to pocket the profits of a gambler or the casino itself are highly possible. Theft and security violations will always take place within a gaming institution because of the simple fact that the temptation to steal money or information for high personal gain will always be present. As a new gaming security employee who is most likely trained by the gaming establishment itself, it is important that you remember to scrutinize all employees when on duty. For example, employees working in bartending and gift shop areas are sometimes not closely watched (cameras on these employees will deter thefts).

The constant movement of money can lead to some employees being tempted to steal. Coins and money are constantly counted with machines known as hoppers, and then placed in or removed from fill bags. The counting and movement of money always involves the signature of those supervising the process. When gaming security officers are inspecting a hopper being used to count money, there a number of signs of possible employee illegality.[43]

- Fill slip is not signed at the location of the hopper fill.
- Coin for fill is not placed directly into the hopper.
- The correct signature of verifying personnel may not be legible or identifiable on the slip.
- The fill is not located at the machine listed on the slot machine or paper trail.
- The required number of personnel are not present at the fill.
- Fill bag has been opened prior to arriving at the machine.

Besides the hopper, employees can steal money from slot machines. Reporting false jackpots enables employees to create paperwork that they handed out money to a lucky customer when, in fact, they embezzled money. Gaming security personnel should examine jackpots in the following manner for these signs of illegality: [44]

- The jackpot form is not signed at the location of the jackpot.
- Jackpot is not located at the machine listed on the slot monitoring system or your paper trail.
- The required number of personnel are not present at the jackpot for all appropriate paperwork.
- Signatures of verifying personnel are not legible or are unidentifiable.

Cashier or Change Person Theft

Cashier and moneychanger personnel can also be tempted to engage in illegal activities. If not watched closely by gaming security, customers and the casino can lose money. Gaming security officers should look for these signs of possible wrongdoing in a casino by cashier or money change personnel:[45]

- An employee goes to the body or the pockets or other areas without clearing their hands.
- An incoming cashier discovers short straps of currency positioned in the back of the drawer.
- The relieving cashier doesn't count the bank and accepts the number that the outgoing cashier gives him or her.
- An employee counts down the bank numerous times.
- An employee is constantly counting or manipulating the funds in the bank and possibly misplacing bills, like a $20 bill under a stack of $5 bills.
- Rolls of coins are missing out of the cans, but are then later discovered placed behind other cans.
- The change person is constantly looking around or appears very aware of where the surveillance cameras are and tries to block the views.
- A customer complains they were shorted (they asked for $10.00 in coins and got $9.50).

Slot Technicians

Although slot machines are the best employees of a gaming location because they do not require food, water, or a break, they do in fact need maintenance. Although many slot machines today have computers that print vouchers with any money won by a gambler, a technician can alter them to pay out illegal wins. Gaming security therefore should watch for technicians working on machines for no apparent reason without a player present. Watch their hands and make sure they fill out a report. Alert the camera people if you suspect a technician is altering a machine.[46]

Employee and Computerized Accounts

There are a number of key areas to watch and actions to take if you suspect employees are using the computers to engage in criminal activity.[47]

1. Observe employees who have computer access (especially those with account-editing privileges) to sensitive information on a routine basis for suspicious or unusual activity.
2. Ensure employees use computer logins and passwords to prevent unauthorized access. If left on and unattended, computers should be equipped with a screensaver requiring a password.

3. Ensure that sensitive transactions such as changes to accounts and access into dormant accounts generate exception reports to the auditing department.

4. Ensure that someone is responsible and held accountable for reviewing daily security reports or reports of any money being short in an area.

5. Watch for employee-clerks writing down the information of players and changing account information or establishing accounts for friends and family to receive complimentary bonuses from the casinos.

6. Ensure that cameras are working in bartending and gift shop areas where employers are sometimes not being watched.

Although gaming security requires a large amount of expertise about the nature of gambling, it is still centered on some of the basic techniques of guarding, vigilance, and common sense used by all private security personnel. For entry-level security personnel, gaming institutions and casino–hotels offer an opportunity to work in a fast-paced environment and to learn a special skill set in the private security field.

■ Alarm Security Systems

▶ ▶ CASE STUDY 3

While working as a newly hired private security guard for a private security company, you have been assigned to guard and respond to calls at a residential location. A few days on the job, you receive word from your superior to report to the home of a client. It appears someone has broken into the home and set off the alarm system that was installed and monitored by your security firm. Your security company also has a report on its alarm computer system of an unauthorized entry into a home and that local police authorities have been contacted as part of the alarm system.

1. What are some of the immediate concerns for a private security guard responding to an alarm/security situation?

2. What are some of the explanations for an alarm/security system to activate?

Alarm Security Systems

Alarm security systems have proven in the past few decades to be one of the major areas of the security field in which the technology continues to make major advances. With the increasing speed of microprocessors in the computerized components and advances in computer software, modern alarm security systems have become extremely sophisticated. Modern alarm security systems offer a myriad of new technology features such as, optional sensors, signaling devices, and control options that were not available just a few years ago. Most systems offer the capability to communicate with a remote monitoring station, where operators are on duty twenty-four hours a day to dispatch the appropriate authorities when an alarm system has identified a breach in security at a location.[48]

It is important to understand how the typical alarm security system works to become familiar with the strengths and weaknesses of the systems. As in the past, an alarm security system alerts people when someone has entered a restricted area. An alarm system could be as simple as a rope and a bell to sound an alarm. The focus of any alarm system is to detect and monitor a zone for a possible breach, and to report in some manner the nature of a breach when it immediately occurs.

Returning to the rope and bell example, a person entering a restricted area that trips a rope surrounding a protected zone would result in a metal bell ringing and alerting people of an intrusion into a zone. Today any alarm security system may be activated and triggered by a wide range of detection devices including motion sensors, door and window contacts, glass breakage detectors, and more. At this time there are three general types of alarm security systems in use: hardwired, wireless, and hybrid systems that can use both wireless and hardwired sensors.[49]

All alarm security systems operate by providing a zone of security in which entry and access are protected. A single zone can have multiple sensors connected to it. The zones allow the system to determine where or what type of alarm has occurred. For example, in a multiple zone system, zone 1 could be the main door, zone 2 the 1st floor front windows, zone 3 the first floor rear windows, zone 4 the smoke detectors, zone 5 a motion sensor, and so on. By segregating areas of the facility and alarm types into different zones, the alarm can alert the occupants, security personnel, or a monitoring station to exactly what type of problem has occurred. This is done through a keypad, by a different sounding siren, or in the case of the monitoring station, different digital data.

Hardwired systems are considered the traditional alarm system. These systems have a main panel that contains all of the basic electronics, which is directly wired to various sensors, sirens, and remote keypads around the facility. Hardwired systems are generally considered to be the most reliable, but wireless systems are catching up. Hardwired systems are more difficult and expensive to install in an existing facility, because wires need to be run throughout the facility to support all of the sensors and other devices. The best time to install an alarm security system is when a facility is being built. Because of the extensive wiring involved, hardwired systems are more labor intensive to install than wireless. However, wiring a facility under construction may be less expensive than installing a wireless system after the building is completed.[50]

Wireless systems consist of a main control panel that contains the electronics necessary to receive signals from various transmitters placed at doors and windows around the facility. The transmitters are battery operated (meaning you must replace them periodically), but most systems use "supervised" transmitters, which means the transmitters report their status to the main panel every few hours, so the panel can let private security personnel know if a battery is low or a transmitter didn't report in. Wireless systems are often a cost-effective, easy-to-install option for existing facilities. Such systems often use wireless key chain transmitters to arm and disarm (like a car alarm), which gives them added flexibility.

The hybrid systems offer the best of both worlds. They have a panel that accepts hardwired sensors as well as wireless signals. These panels are more expensive, but offer the most flexibility. They give private security personnel the option of adding new devices at any time with or without wiring, and will enable you to use items like key chain remotes.[51]

Major Components of an Alarm Security System

Today, modern security systems feature a number of commonly used alarm components regardless of the type of system installed or the security firm that installed the system for a client.

Keypads

The management of any alarm security system is done through a keypad interface. The keypad is usually installed near a popular main entryway. Keypads for an alarm system allow the system to be activated and deactivated (armed and disarmed) by pushing codes on the keypad buttons. The best keypads are easy to use and understand, even for visitors; many have emergency buttons that will notify the monitoring center if a client needs police, fire, or emergency medical assistance immediately.

Card Access

Card access systems can provide two types of security. First they contain microchips utilizing a unique code. When the card is held up against the reader, the code is read and checked against a list of codes that have access. If the code is on one of the lists then access is granted. Second, access cards are often also a portrait card, meaning they show a picture or portrait of the user. This prevents users from switching detection devices, which are critical elements of security systems.

Control Panel

The brain of a security system is the control panel, which is typically installed deep within the facility to prevent tampering. All components of the security system are wired to the control panel, or communicate via a radio transmitter (wireless) that sends data back to the monitoring center. The better control panels have battery backups for continuous operation in the event of a power failure.[52]

Heat, Smoke, Temperature, and Carbon Monoxide Sensors

Besides monitoring for physical intrusion, most alarm security systems can include sensors that detect smoke or heat, carbon monoxide, or temperature. These sensors will trigger the alarm in the event of fire, carbon monoxide, or if the temperature in the facility rises above or falls below a certain desired range (for example, the furnace quits working in the winter).

Notification Devices

Sirens are installed in the facility to issue a loud noise in the event that the alarm has been triggered. Some security systems can include strobe lights, which will light up and go off when the alarm is triggered. The better security systems will allow private security personnel to customize and program which events will trigger and activate the siren and/or strobe lights.[53]

Physical Sensors

Sensors are installed throughout the facility (and the perimeter if desired) and wired back to the control panel to detect any unwanted activity. Many physical sensors are now wireless, and hybrid systems are becoming the norm. Perimeter (window and door) sensors detect if a secured window or door is opened. If a security system consists only of door and window contacts, it may not provide adequate protection. Thieves have been known to enter buildings without being detected by breaking holes in concrete block walls. Once inside they can "shop" at a leisurely pace and take what they want. A good system includes interior motion sensors, which detect movement within the facility and glass breakage sensors, which detect the sound of broken glass. Infrared or photoelectric beams along docks or overhead doors are also a good investment.[54]

Driveway Sensors

A facility can also benefit from a driveway sensor by alerting the company of arriving customers while automatically opening the gates to the business. The driveway sensor can also turn on outside and inside lights when a vehicle is approaching.

> **Word to the Wise**   To assist in the protection of a facility, many private security personnel ensure that a sign or sticker of an alarm security system is in place at a location and is visible to those entering. This assists private security personnel in deterring criminals by making it clear that an operating alarm security system is in use.

Other Alarm System Features

Alarm security systems can also offer a wide range of additional features, such as: [55]

- Voice prompt—The keypad provides audible voice instructions.
- One-button arming—This system can be armed by pushing a single button.
- Door chime—The system will chime if the door is opened.

- Pager—If the system is not shut off by a given time the system will page individuals.
- Additional user codes—Coupled with voice and/or picture recognition, these codes allow cleaning people and other contracted services to use the system without knowing the main codes.
- Self-testing—If one component of the system fails, the system will notify private security personnel with a status light.

The Role of Alarm Security Systems in Security Programs

An alarm security system is only one part of the overall security planning at a location. As mentioned in the earlier discussion on guarding, an alarm system works in conjunction with other private security activities as part of the onion system of multiple security levels. An alarm security system in and of itself is not enough. Essentially, private security efforts will be a state of mind as much as the application of technology countermeasures. Every member of a private security team at a location has an important role to play in safeguarding company assets, especially those that process information that are particularly sensitive and critical.[56]

A full security program must be developed and implemented to ensure the proper safeguards against crime and other emergency situations are in place. The primary objective in developing a security program is to render trial espionage or other criminal activity ineffective by implementing appropriate security measures. A well-planned security program using alarm security systems will encompass a number of efforts. Background checks on employees or newly hired private security personnel prevent individuals who may engage in criminal activities from thwarting an alarm security system from the inside. In addition, private security employees should consider the following key areas when implementing an alarm security system as part of the overall security planning:[57]

- Lock and key control program
- Security system design and operation
- Facility/property vulnerability/risk analysis
- Security equipment evaluation, placement, and operation
- Development of integrated security programs
- Business continuity planning
- Preventing unauthorized entry and controlling access to a location where an alarm security system is in effect
- Classifying sensitive and critical materials and information
- Safeguarding and protecting sensitive materials actively and effectively
- Inspecting security controls and conducting audits periodically
- Establishing levels of accountability, enforcement, and authorization

- Controlling disposal efforts
- Developing access restrictions and controlling movement in the facility
- Evaluating and monitoring personnel continuously in sensitive areas
- Developing education programs in information security
- Applying security techniques, devices, procedures, and policies

While guarding a location, private security personnel must consider whether the alarm security systems have been examined as part of the patrol activities. The following is a list of key areas that should be checked while on patrol.

1. Check that all unoccupied buildings are always locked and alarms set.
2. Check that all fire and smoke alarms provided within all building structures are operational.
3. Ensure that there are not any new conditions at a location that may interrupt security measures or the successful operation of alarm and fire security systems.
4. Check that, "Authorized Personnel Only" signs are posted at entrances to all facilities.
5. Ensure important telephone numbers are posted on the outside of each building and/or on the inside of fences, and readily visible for emergency use by the public.
6. Check that all facility grounds are randomly and frequently patrolled.
7. Ensure that daily security sweeps are adequately conducted.
8. Check that environmental conditions are inspected, including those portions not readily visible to the public or other staff.
9. Ensure that parking is designated or otherwise controlled at the facility.
10. Check that access to sensitive areas are in fact controlled, locked, and/or fenced.
11. Ensure that entrance gates are adequately protected and that security personnel control access.

In today's security-sensitive world, businesses, government buildings and other public facilities increasingly demand technologically advanced security and safety systems for protecting employees, confidential data, and equipment. Ultimately, the need for security systems has never been greater. Individuals who can install and monitor alarm security systems will continue to be in demand in the coming decades. In addition new advances in technology will make alarm security systems more advanced and efficient in alerting private security personnel when an intrusion has occurred at a location.[58] Although technology is important in providing security in this century, it is people using alarm security systems that are able to provide adequate security at a location.[59]

■ Conclusion

As more demands are made upon security personnel, a working knowledge concerning retail and gaming issues will prove invaluable. The gaming industry and retail stores also require a specific advanced skill set to be successful security personnel for long term employment. As technology changes at a rapid pace, knowledge of alarm security is also needed for developing effective security programs.

■ Chapter Review

- Retail locations require private security employees, known as loss prevention agents, who can respond to criminal activity and emergency situations.

- Gaming security requires private security employees to have a specialized skill set regarding the nature of gaming locations and casino–hotels.

- Knowledge of alarm security systems is essential in developing comprehensive security programs and in assisting private security personnel guarding at a location.

■ Answers to Case Studies

Case Study 1

1. What steps would you take to begin investigating the employees? An investigator can engage in a covert investigation in which people are formally questioned for indications about criminal activity. A covert investigation, however, may yield successful results. Cameras can be examined to ensure they cover entrances and exits where merchandise can disappear from the store. Store records and electronic logs can be analyzed without employees realizing they are under investigation for stealing merchandise. Notification to local police who may recover missing merchandise would also be a positive step in stopping illegal activity.

2. What are some of the ways you can improve the security at this electronics store? A security employee should examine the current manner in which merchandise is cataloged, stored, and moved throughout the store. Current alarm or camera systems should also be reviewed for possible areas of improvement. Employees can be tested to determine any propensity for illegal activity. All records and logs should be examined on a regular basis. Security guards can also be posted in key locations to deter criminal activity.

Case Study 2

1. How would people be able to steal the information about casino patrons and gamers in a casino? It is important to watch for outside criminals who may take advantage of unsuspecting patrons who are not paying attention to their belongings. In terms of employees, it is important to observe employees who have computer access and account-editing privileges regarding casino patrons. Employee clerks if tempted, can also write down the information of players and later change the account information to their own account. They can also establish accounts for friends and family to receive complimentary bonuses from the casinos.

2. What other criminal activity or schemes can take place within the casino? Based on the nature of money flowing very fast through a casino or gaming location, employees may be tempted to steal money from customers or from the casino directly. Casino patrons may also be victims of crime in areas outside the casino. High rollers or wealthy clients may be subject to crime or fraud at any given point. Prostitution is also a major concern inside gaming institutions.

Case Study 3

1. What are some of the immediate concerns for a private security personnel responding to an alarm/security situation? A private security employee should consider that the alarm/security system has now alerted them of a possible breach at a location. Such a breach in a security system should be addressed with speed and with caution in case an intruder is armed or dangerous. Additional private security personnel at the location should be alerted. In addition, there is the possibility that a system has notified of a breach as part of an employee error or a misuse of the arming or disarming of an alarm system. However, until a noncriminal act can be determined as the cause of an alarm/security system notifying others of a breach, all protective measures should be addressed immediately to the location where a breach has possibly occurred.

2. What are some of the explanations for an alarm/security system to activate? A working alarm system, depending on the zone designated, may activate when an intruder has entered a room, broken a window, opened a safe, or trespassed onto the property. All activations of an alarm security system can occur through various types of technology connected to the system, which notes and reports when a change in the environment of the zone has taken place indicating a possible breach at a location.

■ Key Terms

Cash office audit   A counting of money earned during the operating hours of a retail location that is compared to the record of goods sold to determine any shortages or discrepancies.

Crotching   A shoplifting technique that involves a woman rolling retail items into a ball and quickly placing it between her legs while wearing a dress.

Electronic article surveillance (EAS)   A tagging system on retail articles used by stores to deter shoplifting.

Electronic journals   Electronic computerized record-keeping system that records the transactions that take place at a retail location.

Floor walker   An individual who serves as a deterrent by walking around the retail location.

Loss prevention agent   The current title for private security personnel who work in the U.S. retail industry.

Shield technique   A shoplifting technique that involves a person who blocks the view of a shoplifter from cameras or security personnel.

Shrinkage   The lost profits or merchandise as a result of employee theft, shoplifting, vender fraud, administrative errors, bad checks and credit cards, fraud, and vandalism.

■ References

1. Hayes, R. 1991. *Retail security and loss prevention*. Boston: Butterworth-Heinemann. *See also* Horan, D. J. 1996. *The retailer's guide to loss prevention and security*. Boca Raton, FL: CRC Press. *See also* Curtis, G., and McBride, R. 2005. *Proactive security administration*. Upper Saddle River, NJ: Pearson Prentice Hall.
2. Ibid.
3. Ibid.
4. Ibid.
5. Ibid.
6. Ibid.
7. Ibid.
8. Ibid.
9. Ibid.

10. Ibid.

11. Ibid.

12. Ibid.

13. Ibid.

14. Ibid.

15. Ibid.

16. Ibid.

17. Ibid.

18. Ibid.

19. Ibid.

20. Ibid.

21. Ibid.

22. Ibid.

23. Ibid. *See also* Ortmeier, P. J. 2005. *Security management.* Upper Saddle River, NJ: Pearson Prentice Hall.

24. Ibid.

25. Ibid.

26. Ibid.

27. Ibid.

28. Powell, G., Tyska, L., and Fennelly, L. 2003. *Casino surveillance and security: 150 things you should know.* ASIS International. *See also* Ortmeir, P. J. 2005. *Security management.* Upper Saddle River, NJ: Pearson Prentice Hall. *See also* Curtis, G., and McBride, R. 2005. *Proactive security administration.* Upper Saddle River, NJ: Pearson Prentice Hall.

29. Ibid.

30. Ibid.

31. Ibid.

32. Ibid.

33. Ibid.

34. Ibid.

35. Ibid.

36. Ibid.

37. Ibid.

38. Ibid.

39. Ibid.

40. Ibid.

41. Ibid.

42. Ibid.

43. Ibid.

44. Ibid.

45. Ibid.

46. Ibid.

47. Ibid.

48. Coleman, K. 2005. *Security systems*. Spy-Ops Training Brief—Security Systems. Vol 4. TB 16. *See also* Hess, K. and Wrobleski, H. 1996. *Introduction to private security*. Stamford, CT: Wadsworth. *See also* Curtis, G., and McBride, R. 2005. *Proactive security administration*. Upper Saddle River, NJ: Pearson Prentice Hall. *See also* Dempsey, J. 2008. *Introduction to private security*. Stamford, CT: Wadsworth.

49. Ibid.

50. Ibid.

51. Ibid.

52. Ibid.

53. Ibid.

54. Ibid.

55. Ibid.

56. Ibid.

57. Ibid.

58. Ibid.

59. Ibid.

Financial Security Issues

▶ ▶ OBJECTIVES

- Understand the nature of corporate and white-collar crime.
- Understand corporate espionage.
- Become familiar with money laundering.
- Understand the nature of mortgage fraud.

■ Introduction

Private security personnel are on the front line regarding economic and financial security issues. Corporations and major businesses face criminal activity occurring from within their own organization in the form of theft and espionage. Money laundering through financial centers and businesses is likely to increase in the coming years. As the American real estate market faces a major crisis in terms of available mortgage loans to purchase a location, mortgage fraud is likely to become a major area of criminal activity in the coming years. To prevent and mitigate the damage of criminals in these areas, private security personnel must now strive to investigate and prevent new forms of theft and fraud that threaten the American economy.

■ Corporate and White-Collar Crime

▶ ▶ CASE STUDY 1

You begin your shift as a security officer at a major corporation as usual. At 10:00 a.m. you are called into a meeting with a number of head managers of the corporation. The purpose of the meeting is to confidentially discuss the possibility that a fellow employee may have engaged in some form of corporate criminal activity while at work.

1. What are the major differences between street criminal activity and corporate and white-collar crime?

2. What type of corporate and white-collar criminal activity takes place in the United States?

For private security personnel, there is an additional concern that jeopardizes business security: Corporate crime is at an all time high in the United States. Corporate, or white-collar, crime does not involve your typical, off-the-street criminal. This is the crime of the business world where the stakes are high and the financial reward goes to those at the top. Edwin Sutherland first introduced the idea of white-collar crime in 1939. Sutherland, a well-known author who wrote the definitive work on corporate crime in America, defined white-collar crime as any crime committed by a person of respectability and high social status in the course of his occupation. Today, **corporate crime** or **white-collar crime** can be defined as the offenses committed by corporate officials, and the offenses of the corporation itself. Occupational crime, on the other hand, consists of offenses committed by individuals for themselves in the course of their occupation. Such a person can be someone high on the socioeconomic scale, but does not always have to be.

Whatever the status, the criminal in general keeps a professional persona in public while using his position to secretly gain access to whatever is needed to obtain his desired end results. It is not, however, a straightforward type of crime. It involves a number of possible schemes and manipulated situations controlled by one or more people for personal gain. It includes, but is not limited to antitrust violations, credit card fraud, phone and telemarketing fraud, bankruptcy fraud, healthcare fraud, environmental law violations, insurance fraud, mail fraud, government fraud, tax evasion, financial fraud, securities fraud, insider trading, bribery, kickbacks, counterfeiting, public corruption, money laundering, embezzlement, economic espionage, and trade secret theft. As in many other areas, computers and computer hacking abilities have opened up a whole new world to white-collar criminals.

Prosecution of Corporate Crime

Corporate crime is criminalized, investigated, and policed quite differently than traditional crimes. Corporate crimes are viewed predominantly as wrongdoings and violations that should be corrected by the continual use of regulatory agreements with state agents, out-of-court settlements, and nonpunitive sanctions from the state. By contrast, traditional street crimes are defined legally as offenses and are subject to strict punitive control by the state.

Several sanctions have been put into place and are imposed when offenders are apprehended. Penalties may be brought on individuals or corporations as a whole depending on the situation. Where an individual may bear the weight of confinement and/or monetary sanctions, a corporation receives mainly financial penalties, forced closings, forfeitures, or the like (these penalties are more feasible at the corporate level and are shared by all who have a stake in the company).The available legal restraints can be evaded to a large degree. For example, directors and managers, through the use of corporate charters and governance documents, can be given limited liability and exemptions for poor business decisions and irregular business conduct. For environmental, health, and safety violations, fines imposed against the corporation as a business organization are usually just regarded as little more than a minor tax or operating fee in the course of doing business. Moreover, when being investigated or prosecuted by the state, a corporation that is of a large size and scope has greater means of defense than a private individual. It has its own legal department and ample resources to cover its tracks, delay proceedings, construct elaborate defenses, and it can counterattack by complaining of oppressive state regulation. This makes it extremely difficult to root out the source of illegal corporate activity.

Statistics show that the persons of lower rank are more apt to get caught since upper management usually has the ability to insulate themselves from scrutiny. In addition, persons of lower rank are frequently used as pawns in white-collar crime; much of the time they are not even aware that they are involved. Frequently, those persons responsible for the deception are not uncovered and held responsible. However, when upper management is implicated, statistics show that they are more likely to get stiffer penalties from juries.

On an individual basis, options for lesser sanctions than those appropriate for the alleged offense are sometimes offered if the offender takes responsibility for what was done and assists the authorities in their investigations. Penalties include fines, home detention, community confinement, prosecution costs, forfeitures, restitution, supervised release, and imprisonment. Most of the time, the crime has not been committed by only that person. In fact, in many cases, claims of entrapment by the defense portray the fact that webs of deceit exist in such situations, although the claims are not always true. Many juries render a lighter sentence on low-level offenders because the defense is usually successful in portraying an upstanding and respectable citizen caught in a web of deceit and deception. Or, they convince juries that upper management used them as a pawn in a higher scheme, and they often had no choice but to play along. Given the hierarchical and interdependent nature of a corporation, it is extremely unlikely that the necessary criminal liability will ever be identifiable in a single individual corporate offender.

It should be noted that a successful prosecution does not always completely destroy a white-collar crime web. There is almost always a diffusion of responsibility that makes it nearly impossible to find all of the individuals involved. The focus on individual offenders when a crime is committed causes problems when it comes to large corporations because of the way that a corporate body distributes power and responsibilities throughout its organization. Although a piece, or even several pieces, of a puzzle may be removed from a crime ring, residual pieces can still remain. The individuals left behind learn from the mistakes of their partners and often carry on the deception. Unfortunately, even when someone is caught, penalties are often not harsh enough to keep him or her from returning to their ways or to deter others from continuing on the same path.

Economic Costs of Corporate Crime

The differences in punishment are not attributable to the supposed lesser harm caused by corporate crime to victims. It is certain that the effects of white-collar crime greatly exceed conventional crime. Depending on the source, the costs of corporate crime vary. It had previously been estimated that the costs of white-collar crime in the United States alone are in the region of $415 billion, with trade violation estimates at nearly $250 billion annually, compared to the annual estimated cost of street crime of $13 billion. Corporate crime just in the healthcare industry is estimated to cost $100 billion annually. The Federal Bureau of Investigation estimates that white-collar crime costs this country about $300 billion annually. The problem of corporate crime appears to be growing at an exponential rate. Crimes such as consumer fraud, antitrust, commercial bribery, tax violations, and others make the financial costs of conventional property crimes such as robbery, burglary, and larceny seem almost trivial. As seen with the recent Enron scandal, the growing economic costs can be devastating. Ultimately, it ends up being the public who pays the cost of white-collar crime.

Private Security in the News   Where was the security? The Enron scandal resulted in thousands of workers and their families losing jobs, pensions, and retirement packages, without any hope of compensation. The increasing amounts of harm being committed can be staggering. Recently the $3.9 billion account fraud at WorldCom and the $1.9 billion in phony revenue at Xerox show the levels of damage that can be done.

Physical Costs

The impact of corporate crime is not just limited to economic costs. Corporate crime has the potential to kill many people due to the actions of a few offenders. The actions of groups such as gangs, organized crime, and terrorist groups have been recognized traditionally as sources of mass killing and violent assaults. What has not been focused on historically or in great detail is how corporations and their agents through the years have, on a large scale, killed and maimed more than any organized or terror group, and they have been more violent at times than any other lower-level socioeconomic group. There is an astronomical toll in deaths, physical health, emotional suffering, and fiscal costs that will certainly overshadow any of the losses from street crime. Thousands of workers are injured or killed annually by the criminal actions of corporate offenders, and millions of consumers are hurt by corporate decisions or improperly released products. Corporations are now being sanctioned by governments for the illegal dumping of defective medical devices, lethal drugs, carcinogens, and toxic chemicals, along with continual dumping and offloading of products and materials to developing nations after such materials have been banned elsewhere. More importantly, Sutherland pointed out as far back as 1939 that corporate criminal acts have a destructive impact on public confidence in the economy and in the commercial world. Every time a corporate scandal is discovered, the public has less faith in business and financial institutions. Interest rates are affected and stock prices drop. This has lead to a widespread concern about the collapse of corporate ethics and how business rules should operate.

The Roots of Corporate Crime

It is important to consider exactly how a corporation works and what theories of liability have traditionally been available for a corporation and its leadership. A corporation is made up of itself—with its own legal personality, shareholders who can buy or sell stakes in the company and receive profits, its directors who are legally responsible for determining the actions and business of the corporation, and officers with their lower-level employees that act on behalf of the corporation and who can create vicarious liability for their employer and themselves. The corporation and its corporate members can also be defined another way. They can be described as an organization for the accumulation of capital in order to maximize profits.

The culture of competition in the corporate world exerts great pressure on corporate directors and high-ranking officers to achieve high profit and investment margins and obtain high-profile market evaluations of the corporation's performance because their careers are linked with the company's stock and earnings. Therefore, this leads corporate officers to do everything possible to maximize output while minimizing costs and external constraints, which in turn can lead to questionable, unethical and, at times, criminal business practices. They rationalize or justify these practices as necessary to achieve vital economic goals or just to survive in the competitive and global business economy. This appeal to necessity is especially common among those employees who participate in illegal activities because their employer expects results. Sutherland cites the case of an idealistic young college graduate who reported losing two previous jobs because he refused to be involved in illegal corporate activities.

Malfeasance in the corporate setting is defended by claims that the laws of the state that are being violated are unnecessary or even unjust in a contemporary business world. Corporate businessmen who are facing tough global competition and trying economic times are constantly lobbying the state and federal governments to remove unnecessary regulations and legal impediments, or they are seeking help from various agencies in avoiding the constraints of the law. Another related and often problematic feature of corporate crime is that major banks, insurance companies, and law firms can be a party to ignoring or covering up crimes because they hold large amounts of stock in corporations.

In theory, a corporation is a legal human being for purposes of a contract with the state and governmental authorization. Although corporations may be treated as if they are human for legal purposes, the reality is that corporations only share some of the attributes of human beings, and lack many others necessary to prevent crime.

Corporate Fraud

If the American economy is currently considered a precarious or fickle institution, it could be due to what has been called a new brand of capitalism: paper entrepreneurism. **Paper entrepreneurism** is a focus by American companies on the status of numbers and computer-generated models that produce false information on the financial status of a company. This information is usually an indication of the financial success of a company by many financial and corporate analysts. However when the information of a company turns out to be a result of fraud or false information, the public's confidence in a company can be affected drastically. Since the 1980s, the public confidence in US companies has continued to decrease with each rising scandal. The less confidence Americans have in their economic institutions and corporate entities, the less likely it will be that they will invest in these institutions for the benefit of society. The recent Enron and WorldCom scandals have demonstrated the potential security and economic effect that corporate fraud can have on American society. In these cases each company lost their entire value when it was proven their practices were fraudulent. For private security personnel, the focus is on catching such corporate criminals before their activity can affect not just a company but the entire US economy.

In simple terms, corporate fraud occurs when greed among corporate leaders is allowed to go unchecked, and oversight by security or truthful accounting services is nonexistent. Corporate fraud problems arise in a variety of ways.

Embezzlement

Embezzlement is when someone who has been entrusted with money or property appropriates it for their own use and benefit. For major corporate executives, the temptation to siphon off some profits of a corporate deal to their private bank account instead of back to their employees is very high. Crimes of this nature generally have involved a relationship of trust and confidence, such as an agent, fiduciary, trustee, treasurer, or attorney. Corporate officials, especially those who are at the top of a corporation have the potential to rob a company and its investors from within their organization. Nonrepayable loans can be given out to corporate executives as in the recent Tyco corporate scandal, which are tantamount to stealing. Assets of a corporation or profits from a company can be siphoned directly into the bank accounts of corporate leaders who are free to act without any oversight to transfer company wealth to personal wealth. With vast sums of money coming into a corporation, the temptation to take a little off the top becomes overwhelming. While accounting or security measures should discover irregularities indicating embezzlement, it is likely that a corporate embezzler has brought associates into a scheme to transfer and hide embezzlement activities. It is therefore paramount to have accounting and security investigations conducted by outside groups that are not controlled by potential corporate embezzlers.

Limited Partnerships

Limited partnerships are set up as a legal way to raise venture capital. They also provide a vehicle to shift corporate debts or to cover up a company's financial picture when corporate officials engage in risky financial gambles. This intricate web of partnerships allowed Enron to wipe out huge tax obligations and to hide their true corporate financial picture.

Insider Trading

Insider trading was made a criminal offense with the passage of the Security Exchange Act of 1934. **Insider traders** are any business personnel such as stockholders, directors, officers, or any recipients of information not publicly available who take advantage of such limited disclosure for their own benefit. Whenever an insider uses information to their advantage, there is always a legitimate investor or stockholder who pays the price. In simple terms, for most businesses, the use of insider information is the same equivalent as stealing directly from that organization. Arguably, small trades conducted on the basis of insider information seem trivial. However, the constant nibbling away at the corporate block of cheese by traders with insider information results in a company's annual return slowly, over time, being reduced by a critical amount. The numerous examples of insider trading in the past few decades have demonstrated a continued threat to the financial stability of corporations and the US market. Insider trading is an equal opportunity corruptor. The temptation to profit from privileged information has seduced and corrupted politicians from both US political parties. The use of the Internet to obtain secure company information that may benefit only a few individuals has also risen to giant proportions.

Stock Manipulations

Stock manipulation is the criminal practice of getting investors to buy or sell a publicly traded stock through false and deceptive practices. In the 1990s, Americans began to invest, sometimes for the first time, as the boom of dot.com companies reached a new frenzy. They were unaware of the role analysts would play in tricking naïve investors. Analysts for a brokerage company can trick potential investors by hyping up the prospects of companies they represent while privately dismissing them and generating large fees for their brokerage firm. The routine practice of brokerage firms hyping stocks for companies that are paying huge fees for their investment banking services can happen if oversight is not taking place. In just one 12-month period, Morgan Stanley earned $517 million in fees through initial public offerings (IPOs), while investors suffered losses on these IPOs averaging almost 55%. In 2003, the Securities and Exchange Commission rocked Wall Street when it announced it had imposed $1.4 billion in fines and disgorged profits on some of the biggest brokerage firms in the nation. Citibank's Salomon Smith Barney and

Credit Suisse First Boston were given the heaviest fines for publishing fraudulent research reports that hyped up companies and their profit projections.

Today con artists all over the nation with a computer and telephone can lure potential investors into giving away money to a brokerage firm that will never be returned. Shutting down basement or "boiler room" firms that commit fraud against US investors is difficult even with ongoing investigations and multiple operations being shut down. According to a report by the New York State attorney general, regulators can close a firm one day only to find the same operation reopened the next day in the same building under a different name. With the Internet offering mass audiences, low operating costs, and anonymity, a computer-literate stock hustler can send out an e-mail that can reach a million people and trick some honest Americans into handing over their life savings. Investment scams from the Internet are now at an all time high in this country. Internet financial bulletin boards and chat rooms have created a particularly growing environment for criminals to engage in securities fraud. Microcap companies who offer "penny stocks" or "over-the-counter" stocks are not even required to file periodic reports with the SEC, making information about such companies very limited.

Online Extortion

Corporations or business can themselves be victims. **Online extortion** is the use of computers to force a company to pay a ransom or suffer a possible consequence. Online extortion is quietly affecting thousands of businesses, for a very simple reason: it works. This arises when a large commercial organization receives credible information that it will suffer loss or damage in a particular way unless money is transferred to an unknown criminal. One major area of threat includes a *denial of service,* which targets corporations that have a major presence on the Internet. Online gambling institutions have been targets in this realm. However, more legitimate businesses are increasingly at risk for being targeted for attack through service disruption. Disrupting the portal through which online sales are made could seriously affect the corporation's revenue flow. Hackers use DDoS (distributed denial-of-service) attacks with botnets. Then they say, "Pay us $40,000, or we'll do it again." Another example is the introduction of poisons or other dangerous chemicals into the products offered for sale in a supermarket or other large store. Such activities could significantly damage retail sales or influence a manufacturer or national distributor to pay extortion money. For example, a blackmailer threatened Masterfoods Corporation, the company that manufactures Mars Bars in Australia, claiming to have poisoned seven Mars and Snickers bars at random in New South Wales. How bad is online extortion getting? Alan Paller, a speaker at a London SANS Institute conference, claims that, "Six or seven thousand organizations are paying online extortion demands."

Additional Corporate Crime and White-Collar Activities

For many entry-level security employees newly hired by a corporation, the chances of later uncovering a major scandal by a multinational corporation are unlikely. However anyone working in the private security field or as a private investigator for a business or client, should know and be able to detect a number of criminal activities. The list that follows includes fraud committed by individuals and businesses.

- Advanced fee schemes—An actor induces a victim to give him or her some type of advanced fee in return for a future benefit. The future benefit never occurs, and the victim never receives the advanced fee back.

- Airport scam—An actor approaches a victim in an airport stating that the newspaper stand cannot change his $100 bill, which he claims to have left with the cashier, and asks the victim for change. The victim provides the actor with the change, the actor returns to the store to get the $100 bill back, and never returns to the victim.

- Check kiting—A bank account is opened with good funds and a rapport is developed with the bank. The perpetrator then deposits a series of bad checks but prior to their discovery, withdraws funds from the bank.

- Coupon redemption—Grocery stores amass large amounts of coupons and redeem them to manufacturers when in fact merchandise was never sold.

- Directory advertising—An actor either impersonates a sales person from a directory company like the Yellow Pages or fraudulently sells advertising that the victim never receives.

- Home improvement—An actor approaches a home owner with a very low estimate for a repair or improvement. Inferior or incomplete work is performed. Once the repairs are completed, the perpetrator intimidates the victim to pay a price much greater than the original estimate.

- Pyramid—An investment fraud in which an individual is offered a distributorship or franchise to market a particular product. The promoter of the pyramid represents that although marketing of the product will result in profits, larger profits will be earned by the sale of franchises. For example, if a franchise price is $10,000 the seller receives $3500 for every franchise sold. Each new franchise purchaser is presented with the same proposal so that each franchise owner is attempting to sell franchises. Once the supply of potential investors is exhausted, the pyramid collapses. Many times, there are no products involved in the franchise, simply just the exchange of money.

- Land fraud—An actor induces a victim to purchase tracts of land in some type of retirement development that does not exist.

- Ponzi—An investment scheme where the actor solicits investors in a business venture, promising extremely high financial returns or dividends in a very short period of time. The actor never invests the money; however, he or she does pay dividends. The dividends consist of the newest investors funds. The first investors, pleased to receive dividends, encourage new investors to invest. This scheme falls apart when the actor no longer has sufficient new investors to distribute dividends to the old investors or the actor simply takes all the funds and leaves the area.
- Antitrust violations—Infractions of the Sherman Act (15 U.S.C. 1-7) and the Clayton Act (15 U.S.C. 12-27) constitute antitrust violations. The goal of antitrust laws is to shelter trade and commerce from price fixing, monopolies, and so on, and to foster competition.
- Bankruptcy fraud—Committed by individuals and corporations who conceal and misstate assets, who mislead creditors, and who illegally pressure bankruptcy petitioners.
- Blackmail—A demand for money or other consideration under threat to do bodily harm, to injure property, to accuse of a crime, or to expose secrets.
- Corruption—The practice of unlawful or improper use of influence, power, and other means. Political offices have been susceptible to corruption throughout history. Grant's presidency was marred by the corruption of some of his officers.
- Self-Dealing—This refers to transactions between a financial institution and persons who are in positions of influence over, or in control of, the institution. A key part of the 1992 financial sector reform was the implementation of comprehensive controls on such transactions.
- Bribery—The offer of money, goods, services, information, or anything else of value that is presented with the intent of influencing the actions, opinions, or decisions of the taker.
- Computer and Internet fraud—Fraud of this type includes using or applying for credit cards online under false names, unauthorized use of a computer, manipulation of a computer's files, computer sabotage, and so on.
- Credit card fraud—The unauthorized use of a credit card to obtain merchandise.
- Counterfeiting—Occurs when someone copies or imitates an item without having been authorized to do so and passes the copy off for the genuine or original item. While counterfeiting is most often associated with money, it can also be applied to designer clothing, handbags, and watches.
- Economic espionage and trade secret theft—Economic espionage involves the theft or misappropriation of proprietary economic information (trade secrets) from an individual, a business, or an industry.

- Environmental law violations—Discharge of a toxic substance into the air, water, or soil that poses a significant threat of harm to people, property, or the environment. This can include air pollution, water pollution, and illegal dumping, and is in violation of federal environmental law.
- Extortion—This occurs when one person illegally obtains property from another by actual or threatened force, fear, or violence, or under cover of official right.
- Financial institution fraud (FIF)—Involves fraud or embezzlement occurring within or against financial institutions that are insured or regulated by the US government. Financial institutions are threatened by a wide array of frauds, including commercial loan fraud, check fraud, counterfeit negotiable instruments, mortgage fraud, check kiting, false applications, and a variety of traditional and nontraditional FIF scams.
- Government fraud—Fraud against the federal, state, or local government may involve government contracting or publicly-funded entitlement programs. As it relates to federal government contracting, fraud schemes can target public housing, agricultural programs, defense procurement, educational programs, and corporate frauds. Investigations often involve bribery in contracts or procurement, collusion among contractors, and false or double billing.
- Healthcare fraud—These types of fraud include kickbacks, billing for services not rendered, billing for unnecessary equipment, and billing for services performed by a less-qualified person. The healthcare providers who commit these fraud schemes encompass all areas of health care, including hospitals, home health care, ambulance services, doctors, chiropractors, psychiatric hospitals, laboratories, pharmacies, and nursing homes.
- Insurance fraud—A variety of fraudulent activities committed by applicants for insurance, policy holders, third-party claimants, or professionals who provide insurance services to claimants. Such fraudulent activities include inflating or "padding" actual claims and fraudulent inducements to issue policies and/or establish a lower premium rate.
- Kickbacks—The return of a certain amount of money from seller to buyer as a result of a collusive agreement.
- Mail fraud—Mail fraud occurs when the US mail is used in furtherance of a criminal act.
- Money laundering—A process or series of actions through which income of illegal origin is concealed, disguised, or made to appear legitimate to evade detection, prosecution, seizure, and taxation. Illicit proceeds must be laundered to make it appear as though the funds were generated through some legitimate means. This allows criminals to enjoy the "fruits" of their criminal activity without raising suspicion.

- Public corruption—Involves a breach of public trust and abuse of position by federal, state, or local officials and their private-sector accomplices. By broad definition, a government official, whether elected, appointed, or hired, may violate federal law when he or she asks, demands, solicits, accepts, or agrees to receive anything of value in return for being influenced in the performance of their official duties.
- Racketeering—The operation of an illegal business for personal profit, common with organized crime groups such as the Mafia.
- Securities fraud—This includes theft from manipulation of the market, theft from securities accounts, and wire fraud.
- Tax evasion—Fraud committed by filing false tax returns, or not filing tax returns at all.
- Telemarketing fraud—According to the US Department of Justice, telemarketing fraud is any scheme to defraud in which the perpetrators use the telephone as the primary means of communicating with the potential victims of the scheme. Typical fraudulent telemarketers use multiple aliases, telephone numbers, and locations. They frequently change their product line, sales pitch, and recently many have moved their operations to Canada in response to effective US law enforcement efforts.

There are nearly 5 million known white-collar crime offenders. Technological advances such as the Internet have contributed substantively to the rate of financial crime cases. The threat of corporate crime to the economic and physical stability of the United States is paramount. Corporate fraud, embezzlement, insider trading, and other methods of engaging in corporate crime can destabilize a business and destroy a community that depends on a business for their livelihood. Business professionals such as management consultants, accountants, lawyers, and others are at the front of the battle against corporate crime. Such professionals are now required to examine the possibilities of fraud, theft, espionage, and other serious activities such as computer crime and identity theft with their clients and within their organizations. Proactive enforcement and vigilance by security professionals is necessary to ensure that corporate officials make legal business decisions, and that people engaging in corporate business are acting legally and not as criminals that victimize the general public.

■ Corporate Espionage

▸ ▸ CASE STUDY 2

Imagine as a security officer you receive a call to respond to a theft in the corporate building where you work. You quickly arrive at a cubicle of an employee. The employee informs you that a flash drive storage device with saved information was in the computer before the employee went to lunch, but upon their return it is now missing from the USB port of the computer. In addition, the employee tells you that their computer was password protected, yet appears that someone logged on and accessed information in the computer related to specific corporate projects.

1. What type of information could have been stolen from the cubicle?
2. What other types of corporate espionage activity may have taken place in this company?

The area of corporate espionage is likely a new realm of criminal activity for individuals just entering the private security field. While corporate espionage has received more attention in the past few years, it is a criminal activity that grew exponentially over the last two decades of the 1900s. Many corporations and businesses now employ private security employees to guard against theft or transfers of information. Covert spying on employees who are under suspicion for corporate espionage is also at an all time high. Over 85% of the Fortune 1000 companies in the United States have regular private security covert investigators who focus on the movements and communications (phone and e-mails) of their employees.[1] Although it may seem that companies are using private security in a more draconian fashion, the reality is that information from a company is worth millions of dollars when put in the hands of a competitor. This has led to increases in computer hardware and software security. Companies are also investing more time training employees in the methods criminals use to commit corporate espionage.

Corporate espionage is the use of illegal means or deceptive practices to gather information or intellectual property. As a criminal act, corporate espionage is considered a direct theft.[2] It is also commonly referred to as industrial or economic espionage based on the area being targeted by criminals. In 1999, Fortune 1000 companies reported a total of $45 billion in losses from corporate espionage (See Figure 7-1). The financial losses have increased over the years; currently, it is believed that theft of trade secrets exceeds $100 billion annually in the United States.[3] Additionally many of today's most successful enterprises have been hit hard by electronic espionage incidents with the number of incidents climbing steadily. **Industrial espionage** (or economic espionage) is the clandestine collection of sensitive, restricted, or classified information. This information by its very nature is not openly accessible and can only be obtained through covert collection means.[4]

Private Security in the News   In March 2006, two former Coca-Cola employees were sentenced to serve federal prison terms for conspiring to steal and sell trade secrets to rival Pepsi. When Pepsi was presented an opportunity to buy trade secrets obtained through corporate espionage, Pepsi contacted the FBI and Coca-Cola. The criminals received an 8- and 5-year prison term, respectively.

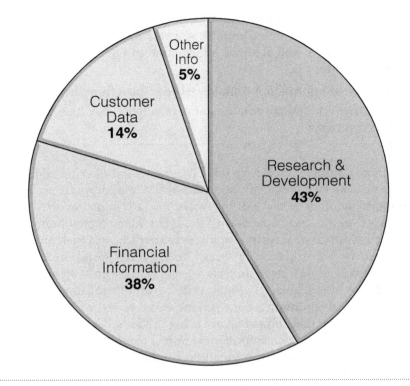

Figure 7-1   Percentage of corporate espionage losses by information type.

It is important to understand that every business that makes a profit in America has valuable assets in the form of data or information. Any unique manufacturing process, pending patents, secret recipes for a product, or any research and development material for a business are known collectively as forms of intellectual property. Such intellectual property can equal 70% or more of a business organization's value.[5] Additionally, information about future corporate takeovers or mergers, purchases of land, expansions, or any change in the company are material information that can be stolen and sold to others.

As a world superpower, it is not surprising that American businesses are the usual targets of corporate espionage activities. With the **globalization** of the world economy and increased competition among businesses, the pressure to stay ahead of the competition in the world marketplace has pushed the procurement of information.[6] Many companies do not openly report theft of information or intellectual property to protect their reputations and to save on court costs. Over 95% of corporate espionage attacks go unreported. On average it takes two to three years for a corporate espionage investigation to be brought to court.[7] Additionally, there are no regulatory requirements to report corporate espionage incidents, and many of them go undetected. However, under the Economic Espionage Act of 1996 (EEA), businesses can request investigation by the FBI and criminal prosecution by the US Attorney's Office.[8]

People and Organizations Who Engage in Corporate Espionage Activities[9]
- Disgruntled employees
- Foreign or multinational corporations
- Foreign government-sponsored educational and scientific institutions
- Freelance agents (some of whom are unemployed former intelligence officers)
- Computer hackers
- Terrorist organizations
- Revolutionary groups
- Extremist ethnic or religious organizations
- Drug syndicates
- Organized crime groups

Corporate Espionage Techniques

There are a number of techniques that can be used to obtain information or intellectual property from a business. An understanding of these techniques will help a private security employee be on the lookout for possible corporate espionage activities.[10]

- Bribery—Employees may be approached directly by outside corporate intelligence agents offering cash to provide them with proprietary or confidential data.
- Social engineering—The manipulation of a network administrator or other IT personnel (by insiders or outsiders) to divulge information, such as a person's login information or other authentication information, which can be used to obtain access to sensitive information.
- Group collusion—When several employees band together to use their collective knowledge and privileges to gain access to information.
- Employee access privileges—Using the employee's own access privileges to enable them to access proprietary or confidential information. Also important, but often overlooked, is the disgruntled employee. A disgruntled employee is more likely to sell proprietary information for profit than a satisfied employee.
- Social engineering—A nontechnical approach to obtaining information stored on a computer network. It may include contacting employees in an attempt to receive sensitive documents by e-mail. As an example, help desk employees are often targeted by social engineers in an attempt to learn about

the network structure and to gain access. At the very least, employees should understand varying techniques that are used to gain network access or to obtain sensitive information. Protecting documents with file passwords and encryption can also minimize the threat of social engineers.

- Dumpster diving—This is the most basic form of corporate espionage and simply means looking through a corporation's trash for valuable information. Organizations who do not shred and destroy CDs, DVDs, papers, disks, and tapes contribute to the problem and often make corporate espionage very easy. Other techniques require more elaborate preparation and technical knowledge. One example is gaining access to cache chips on certain fax and photocopying machines that have the capacity to digitally store hundreds of pages of documents. Another example is the frequent targeting of laptop computers for theft or intrusion because of the vast amount of information they hold. These and other techniques can provide spies and terrorist organizations with information about an organization that may be used to its detriment.

- Password cracking—Several password cracking programs, freely available online, including BO2K and SATAN, help hackers gain access to networks. Most password analyzers are limited to simple combinations of dictionary words and numerical combinations.

- Trojan horses—Computer programs available online can be obtained and executed on a victim's computer to enable an outsider to gain control of that computer and gain further network access. Hackers can use programs such as Net Bus, Back Orifice, and BO2K to capture data from the victim's computer and send it to a remote location. BO2K has been enhanced so that it can disguise itself once it has been installed on the user's computer. Generally, backdoors are e-mailed to the user, downloaded from a Web site, or disguised as a benign e-mail attachment or program. Once the attached file is opened, it installs itself on the user's computer without their knowledge or consent. Some programs enable criminals to record all keystrokes input on a victim's computer, allowing the criminal to capture username and password information, which will provide access to more valuable information or intellectual property.

In beginning a search for possible suspects who have committed corporate espionage at a business, it is important to first ask two questions: (1) who has access to sensitive information or intellectual property, and (2) who has a motive to sell the information or intellectual property? Finding the answers to these two questions will likely help private security personnel focus and find the suspect at hand, especially if the criminal is an insider to the business organization.

Businesses with a High Risk for Corporate Espionage Attacks[11]
- Manufacturing and fabrication
- Advanced materials and coatings
- Advanced transportation and engine technology
- Aeronautics systems
- Aerospace
- Armaments and energetic materials
- Biotechnology
- Chemical and biological systems
- Computer software and hardware
- Defense and armaments technology
- Directed and kinetic energy systems
- Electronics
- Energy research
- Guidance, navigation, and vehicle control
- Signature control
- Space systems
- Telecommunications
- Weapons effects and countermeasures
- Manufacturing processes
- Marine systems
- Materials
- Nuclear systems
- Semiconductors
- Sensors and lasers

Looking at these two questions, it easy to imagine that an employee who has suddenly been noticed entering or leaving in a different time pattern, who is known to be going through a bitter divorce, or is known in the office for having a gambling problem would be a possible suspect. Add an additional fact such as that he or she has access to the research and development office of a business and the individual becomes a prime suspect.

Recruiting as a Tool of Corporate Espionage

One of the new methods for committing corporate espionage is the use of false recruiting. Using fake job postings and targeting specific individuals for fake job interviews has become a way to obtain information or intellectual property. The victim is lured into a job interview by a person claiming to be a representative of another business organization (a possible business competitor) that can offer a high salary, benefits, or other enticements. Once the interview is underway and all parties become relaxed, the employee is less guarded about the details of the work they are doing for their current employer. Answering seemingly harmless questions about strategies, plans, programs, practices, people, or even technologies in a job interview can lead to derivative intelligence. **Derivative intelligence** is the information synthesized out of the lower-level data, facts, timelines, and events that may be disclosed during a job interview or on a professional's resume.[12]

> **Word to the Wise**   All corporations or businesses should take the time to reconsider the effectiveness of their overall security programs, given the current threat of corporate espionage. Comprehensive security programs should address this threat based on the onion approach to security. Though corporate espionage cannot be eliminated, implementing multilayer safeguards can at least minimize losses.

As more business fields become competitive on the international market, corporate espionage will continue to rise. Private security personnel will continue to serve as specialists involved in the safeguarding of information crucial to the existence of a company. Therefore entry-level security employees should continue to learn about the new techniques of corporate espionage that are constantly being used against businesses and clients. Since criminals are always one step ahead of those who protect others, private security personnel must do their best in terms of training and knowledge to close this gap.

■ Money Laundering

▶ ▶ CASE STUDY 3

As an investigator for a major banking firm, you are tasked with reviewing any financial transaction that appears out of the ordinary. Recently your supervisor has asked you to review some transactions in which a local carpenter has been depositing tens of thousands of dollars in cash in a very short period.

1. Why is depositing tens of thousands of dollars a suspected activity?
2. What are some of the ways in which money is laundered without using a bank or financial institution?

The crime of money laundering has been around throughout our history; however, since the start of the 21st century there has been a dramatic increase in this practice. Terrorism financing, white-collar crime, increased sales of illegal drugs, smuggling, organized crime activities, and the resurgence of gangs have all contributed to the increase in money laundering. Government regulations require organizations to report suspicious activities and the US Patriot Act extended the suspicious activity reporting requirements. As a result, many business and financial centers have begun to review very closely the manner in which money is deposited and transferred. Private security personnel in many locations are tasked with reviewing, investigating, and tracing the movement of money for illicit and criminal purposes. By understanding the nature of money laundering, private security personnel can help protect innocent businesses as well as help with the fight against funding terrorist and criminal organizations.

Money Laundering Basics

Money laundering ranges from the very simple to the very complex. Rather than being a crime in itself, it is actually a necessary means to other crimes. Criminal activity in general has a variety of goals. Much of the time criminal activities have a primary objective of financial gain. When funds are accrued, criminals cannot reveal the origin of their profits since they are, in fact, illegal. This in turn creates the need for money laundering. **Money laundering**, simply stated, is the hiding of the origin of such money. The end result is that money gained through illegal activities can be used or invested without the criminals involved having to divulge the true source of their income.

From start to finish, money laundering can be a lengthy process. Criminal activities such as bribery, computer fraud schemes, embezzlement, insider trading, drug dealing, and numerous other areas generate substantial amounts of cash that would attract unwanted attention from authorities. Criminals involved in money laundering want to control their funds so they do not attract attention that might lead to the uncovering of the sources of their wealth. This is done by disguising sources of funds, changing the form of funds (cash to gold or physical property), and transferring funds. Tracking the laundering of money, therefore, can lead to the capture of criminals and the break up of criminal rings, drug cartels, and organized crime.

The general process followed in money laundering involves three steps: placement, layering, and integration. In **placement**, the initial amounts of money are broken down into smaller sums. Smaller amounts of money attract less, if any, attention. In most cases, this simply involves depositing fractions of the total amount into various bank accounts locally and around the world. It is common practice to limit transaction dollars to under $8000 USD. This is done to avoid regulatory thresholds for reporting of high-cash value transactions. **Layering** is where more significant distancing from the original sources of the money takes place. In this stage, the goal is to create a larger gap between the money and where or how it was made. This is done through transforms, or converting currency to other types of financial assets, and reconverting them to cash. Finally, during the **integration** stage, the money is put back into the economy. It is in this stage that the funds are spent or invested further through things such as real estate or business expenditures.

Private security personnel should be aware of a number of the common tactics used during the money laundering process.

Postal money orders—Exchanging cash for money orders, then shipping them out of the country for deposit.

Telegraphic transfer of funds—Wiring money from one city or country to another without physically carrying the money.

Structuring or "smurfing"—This is possibly the most commonly used money laundering method. It involves disseminating a large amount of cash received in an illegal activity to many individuals who deposit cash or buy bank drafts in amounts under $10,000. These individuals then turn the bank drafts over to other individuals and the cash is recompiled and is considered to be laundered. This method is common in both Canada and the United States.

To give an entry-level private security person a better understanding of the scale of money laundering taking place, it has been estimated that money laundering funds total somewhere between $590 billion and $1.5 trillion internationally. As money laundering has now become an international criminal activity, geographic locations are key in how funds are placed, and they often cross international lines during the stages of processing. In the placement stage, they mostly stay close to the source for a convenient and quick assignment to an account. It is in layering, where the attempt to avoid traceability of the funds occurs, that international boundaries are often crossed. Here, some criminals transfer funds to offshore financial centers, large regional business centers, or world bank centers until there is no trace back to the source and no trace implied to the destination. Where the integration stage takes place depends on where the original funds were made. If they were made in a stable area with increased investment opportunities, they may return to that area. If not, the criminals will find someplace else to invest.

Money launderers seek out locations that have specific characteristics. Namely, they look for places where they are obviously at low risk for detection. Such places have weak enforcement programs and therefore do not track these criminals well. Ideally, money launderers will look for such a situation within a stable financial system. One key characteristic of a good location for money laundering is limited oversight and regulations of the financial services sector.

Private security personnel should be aware of countries that are commonly used for money laundering. These countries do not have any effective legislation or governing bodies to regulate this form of illegal activity. As of September 2008, the list included the following:

- Cook Islands
- Egypt
- Guatemala

- Indonesia
- Myanmar
- Nauru
- Nigeria
- Philippines
- St. Vincent and the Grenadines
- Ukraine

Therefore private security should be wary if transactions at a business or bank begin to occur between an individual and locations in these nations.

Another good location for money laundering is any business that deals in large sums of cash. It is easy to hide cash among funds that are received through legitimate businesses. Offshore gambling would be a very good example of a cash business that could be easily used for money laundering. The last two years have seen a rise in money laundering through the following methods.

High-Price Purchases with Low Denominations

In purchasing expensive items such as cars or jewelry, a person paying cash is not unusual. However, paying for an expensive item worth $25,000 in $20 and $50 bills is highly unusual behavior. Although this method of payment is out of the ordinary and the salesperson's suspicions are instantly aroused, an opportunity for a quick close and a hefty commission silences any questions that the salesperson should be asking. By ignoring key indicators, an individual may have directly participated in the scheme through willful blindness.

Professional Advisors (Accountants, Attorneys, and Stockbrokers)

A professional advisor can be caught up in money laundering indirectly when the advisor doesn't realize the source of money being handed over by a client is tainted. It is not uncommon for a criminal to conduct legitimate business with a professional advisor for a period of time before slowly turning over "dirty" funds for the advisor to invest, safeguard, or transfer. It is important, therefore, for professionals in this area to inquire the source of funds handed over and to be familiar with the regulations in relation to safeguarding, transferring, and investing the money of clients.

Financial Lending Institutions and Construction Groups

The rising boom in construction in the United States and around the world along with a new boom in financial lending institutions has also added an increase in money laundering. Money deposits of large amounts are not uncommon for a construction project or for someone paying back a loan. It is important for employees in the construction or financial lending industry to note any unusual change in the depositing habits of customers. Lenders in particular should be aware that money laundering techniques can also involve paying off a debt faster than income would support.

Financial Transmitters

Currency exchange locations and check cashing businesses offer an easy place for someone to change the form of money or transmit to another location. Also such locations offer a great deal of customer anonymity.

Word to the Wise   If you are investigating a money-laundering suspect, watch for frequent visits to 7-11 stores. With 7-11 now tied to Western Union and Citigroup Banking, a person can walk into any 7-11 and change money into money orders and transfer money through money wires or the Citibank system. By doing this in small amounts at numerous 7-11 locations, the chance of being caught diminishes greatly.

Casinos

With more casinos and gambling institutions opening in the United States and around the world, cash can now be deposited with a casino in exchange for chips or tokens. After a few turns at the table the player can cash in the remainder for a cashier's check that can be deposited in their account with ease and no suspicion. Without strict governmental oversight, Indian casinos in the United States offer a chance for individuals to commit money laundering outside the eyes of state and federal agencies.

Money laundering has several effects on numerous levels of society. For financial institutions, it can be devastating. If a money laundering scheme is uncovered, it lowers or eliminates trust and integrity, which are both vital to the successful operation of financial institutions. If illegal money moves freely through the system due to bribery or the blind eye of officials or management, the financial institution can be considered a part of the crime ring. Financially, money laundering in the bigger picture leads to significant economic downfall and consequences on international trade and relations. Money laundering fosters a vicious cycle in society in general. When successfully processed through the system, laundered money comes out to fund further criminal activity. As a result, it enables the original criminal activity to continue. As the illegal money makes its way through the system, it can infiltrate financial institutions, take over large parts of economies in investments and can be used to bribe public officials and governments. All in all, money laundering activities can weaken society by lowering ethical standards and compromising democratic institutions. It is up to governments to set the standards and punishments to control this criminal activity, but this is difficult and involves international cooperation.

Private Security and Policy In preventing money laundering, many US businesses do not even know they are required to comply with regulations like the Bank Secrecy Act and the US Patriot Act. The complexity of legislative acts has created confusion about who has to comply and what constitutes compliance. Currency transactions above $3000 are required to be reported by federal law. Any suspicious activity can be filed as a suspicious activity report with the Financial Crimes Enforcement Network (FinCEN) at www.fincen.gov. Add to that the technology that enables financial transactions like eBay and PayPal and the challenge to combat money laundering continues to become more and more difficult.

Private security personnel working at any location should note anyone engaging in unusual practices such as transferring money on a regular basis or making unusual deposits and transfers. In addition, learning about the nature of new money laundering techniques can keep a security person on par with those who engage in criminal activity. Awareness of local and federal regulations regarding the transfer or deposit of money can help to find anyone engaging in money laundering activity. Cooperation with local law enforcement personnel can also help in investigating any money laundering occurring at a location. If suspected, it is important to contact local authorities for additional instructions as well as reexamine security protocols to prevent any future money laundering. For private security personnel, the key is working and developing processes and procedures to detect money laundering as well as direct observations of such behavior.

■ Mortgage Fraud

▶ ▶ CASE STUDY 3

As a private investigator you are hired by a newly formed mortgage company. They have hired you regarding a recent transaction with one of their clients. After completing the deal, the mortgage company realized it had apparently given a mortgage loan to an individual who hid a number of liens and debts. The mortgage company wants to know if such activity is commonplace and seeks assistance in preventing such fraudulent activity on other deals.

1. What type of fraud did the mortgage company fall victim to through the transaction with their client?
2. What are some of the ways of committing mortgage fraud?

For private security professionals involved with investigations of fraud or criminal activity, the rise in mortgage fraud in the United States requires a more complete understanding of how criminals are able to engage in victimization of people and financial institutions. **Mortgages** involve the loans people receive from financial institutions in order to purchase a home. The current state of mortgage fraud is staggering. In 2005, the US Mortgage Brokers Association mortgage origination estimation topped $2.7 trillion. With the 2008 financial crisis on Wall Street which has forced financial institutions to look closely at mortgages it is likely to double the 2005 estimate. Experts estimate that 10–15% of mortgage loans involves some kind of fraud. This means that between 2 to 3 million home loans originated this year could be fraudulent; that equates to over 7500 new fraudulent loans every business day. As the mortgage market grows, new and innovative ways to defraud financial institutions will appear. This will require more private security personnel to rise to the challenge of investigating and catching individuals involved in such activity.

What Is Mortgage Fraud?

Fraud has generally been defined as an intentional perversion of truth, or a misrepresentation of a matter of fact, that induces another person to part with some valuable thing belonging to them, or to surrender a legal right. **Mortgage fraud** describes a broad variety of methods where the intent is to materially misrepresent information on a mortgage loan application to obtain the loan or tangible financial asset. It is further defined as a material misstatement, a misrepresentation, or an omission relied upon by an underwriter or lender to fund, purchase, or insure a loan. Mortgage fraud occurs when one or more individuals defraud a financial institution. Additionally, predatory lending is when a dishonest financial institution willfully misleads or deceives the consumer. With nearly $2.5 trillion in mortgage loans being made in 2005, there are plenty of opportunities for abuse and illegal activities. For the most part, a significant portion of the mortgage industry is void of any mandatory fraud reporting, thus making accurate losses due to fraud unattainable. However, an assessment released in November 2006 by the Financial Crimes Enforcement Network (FinCEN) revealed that suspected mortgage fraud in the United States continued to rise and had risen 35% in 2005. The results are based on the analysis of suspicious activity reports filed regarding suspected mortgage loan fraud. This analysis identified trends and patterns that are useful to security professionals.

Mortgage fraud can be perpetrated in multiple ways in this country and private security personnel should be aware of the major methods. Keep in mind, however, that techniques used to commit mortgage loan fraud evolve and change as technology and regulations change.

Credit fraud—The mortgage applicant's identity, credit score and history, and/or liabilities are misrepresented and, in some cases, fabricated for the purpose of obtaining a better interest rate.

Social Security number fraud—There are significant discrepancies in the Social Security numbers (SSN) used by the applicants. In some cases multiple SSNs are given, and the one with the best credit rating is used. It is important to note that identity thieves sell stolen SSN information online for about $100. Identity theft remains the number one concern among consumers contacting the Federal Trade Commission.

Fake buyers—The identity of the buyer is concealed through the use of a front person who allows the buyer to use the front person's name and credit history to apply for a loan.

Property value—The property value gets inflated, and there may be misrepresentations in other areas of the loan application or associated documents. In some cases, appraisal companies are persuaded to change the appraised value for their own financial gains and/or the promise of sending business their way.

Property fraud—Material facts about the property or the comparable sales are hidden or misrepresented, failing to provide an accurate impression of the property and its value.

Assets fraud—The information about the applicant's funds is artificially inflated or completely fabricated. The assets, things of value to a person, are misstated or fraudulently misrepresented on a loan application.

Side loans—The borrowers obtain cash from a nonofficial lending source for deposit in their savings account to inflate their net worth and obtain a more favorable interest rate. Once the savings account value has been verified, the applicant returns the money with a hefty interest payment to the nonofficial lending source.

Liability hiding—Applicants work to conceal financial obligations, such as loans on other properties or newly acquired credit card debt, in order to reduce the amount of monthly debt declared on the loan application.

Shotgunning—Shotgunning is the practice of taking out multiple loans for the same property simultaneously.

Silent second—The buyer of a property borrows the down payment from the seller through the issuance of a nondisclosed and unrecorded second mortgage. The primary lender believes the borrower has invested his own money in the down payment, when in fact it is borrowed.

Income fraud—The applicant's income or employment information is inflated or fabricated. In some cases, a second income from a sideline that is typically a cash business is used to increase the loan applicant's total annual income. Another variation of this is when the applicant claims they are an independent contractor (1099-type worker) and use their bank accounts to prove their ability to pay. Their bank accounts are artificially inflated by fund transfers from friends and family enabling them to inflate their individual asset value.

Occupancy fraud—The applicant's intent to occupy the property was materially misrepresented. In many cases, the applicant may intend to purchase the property as an investment and rent it out.

Equity skimming—An investor may use a front person as the buyer, and use false income documents and false credit reports to obtain a mortgage loan in the front person's name. Subsequent to closing, the front person signs the property over to the investor, transfers all rights to the property, and provides no guaranty to a clear title. The investor fails to make any mortgage payments and rents the property until foreclosure takes place several months later. This often nets several thousands of dollars in profit.

Quick flip—This occurs when a buyer is purchasing a property or properties and artificially inflating their value through false appraisals or other means. The inflated properties are then repurchased several times at a higher price.

Money laundering—The sale of real estate can be an effective means to launder money. The buyer of the property convinces the seller to accept a lower contract price and a side cash payment. This can benefit the seller financially, and the property can be resold at the full price thus obscuring the real source of some of the money.

Affinity fraud—Affinity fraud is a situation where a trusted member of a social group or organization preys upon and/or takes advantage of other members of the group for financial gain. This has occurred in social and even church groups.

Title fraud—Title fraud occurs when someone impersonates the property owner, and then sells a piece of property out from under the rightful owner. The rightful owner is still liable for the mortgage, but cannot get in his former house or cannot get a clear title. While this type of fraud is rare, it should be noted that there are over a dozen variations to this criminal act.

Willful blindness—Willful blindness occurs when a person or organization becomes aware of the need for some inquiry and declines to make the inquiry because they do not wish to know the truth. They would prefer to remain ignorant.

Signs of Mortgage Fraud

Once the techniques used in mortgage fraud are understood, one should also understand what apparent indicators to look for to avoid mortgage fraud. While no one indicator can definitively be used to determine if a mortgage application is fraudulent or not, it is the knowledge of the indicators, combined with the knowledge of the client, the lender, and the lender's professional experience, that provides the best foundation for determining if the application is legitimate or fraudulent. Any investigation should focus first on determining if the following possible issues were present during a mortgage application process.

- Information missing on the loan application, including signatures, or any other important line item(s) on any form left blank
- Numerous corrections on the loan application
- Changes made by the lender or broker after data was entered on the loan application
- Any documents purposely left out of the loan file that are pertinent to the lending decision
- A loan amount obtained higher than the value of the home
- The property has been refinanced several times and in each instance either the amount of the monthly payment or the total amount owed on the property increased
- Attempts to contact employers of the applicant were unanswered, but after the fact the employers contacted the lender
- Proof of identity documents of applicant appear fake or altered
- Any pieces of information on forms or cards that do not match such as Social Security number
- An application has credit reports that did not come from one of the three main credit bureaus

If any suspicious activity is determined by private security personnel, they should alert their superiors as well as the authorities. Any suspicious mortgage activity can also be filed as a suspicious activity report with the Financial Crimes Enforcement Network (FinCEN) at www.fincen.gov. In addition, private security personnel should always advise individuals who handle mortgage applications to maintain a strict set of security standards. One way even entry-level security personnel working as investigators or financial security professionals can assist those employees who handle mortgage applications is to ensure that when handling mortgage applications they do the following:

1. Verify the identity of any person seeking to open a bank account for the purpose of seeking a mortgage.
2. Check for altered or counterfeit documents.
3. Call a borrower's employment reference; do not accept them calling back.
4. Do a Google search on both the borrower and their employers to verify that the information provided is accurate.

5. Maintain records of the information used to verify the borrower's identity. It should be noted here that both borrowers and lenders should conduct a verification check. There are as many fraudulent lenders as there are borrowers. Loan participants should securely store all the documents collected throughout the process.

6. Lenders should determine whether the borrower appears on any known or suspected terrorist or criminal watch lists.

While the above-mentioned guidelines and checklists are important steps for private security personnel handling mortgage fraud situations, it is important to focus on instinct. If a loan application or a borrower makes a security person feel that something is not right, chances are there is a problem somewhere that warrants further investigation or clarification. In addition, private security personnel should be aware of the many professional organizations that work towards educating security and financial employees regarding this form of criminal activity.

■ Conclusion

Economic and financial security crimes pose major a threat to the American economy and to individual business organizations. In particular, fraud and corporate espionage will continue to increase as the United States faces more economic difficulties. For private security personnel it requires an advanced skill set to perform financial investigations along with recognizing signs of criminality. Private security personnel seeking employment in these areas will require additional schooling and training before successful employment. However, as the criminal threat increases, so will the demand for individuals seeking a career investigating and mitigating the damage done to undermine the economic and financial security of American businesses.

■ Chapter Review

- Corporate and white-collar crime is continuing to grow in the United States.
- The physical costs of criminal activity at the corporate level are also growing in the United States.
- Corporate crime and white-collar crime come in a number of forms at different levels.
- Corporate espionage will continue to rise as more globalization occurs in the business world.
- Corporate espionage can be done by both employees and outsiders through a variety of methods.
- Money laundering is major form of economic crime occurring in the United States.

- Money laundering gives criminals and terrorists the ability to store money for later criminal and terrorist activity.
- The change in the real estate market has lead to a rise in mortgage fraud committed by individuals seeking mortgage loans.

■ Answers to Case Studies

Case Study 1

1. What are the major differences between street criminal activity and corporate crime and white-collar crime? Street crime generally involves violence and victimization that occur against a single victim or group. Corporate and white-collar crime often involves fraud or stealing from many people. It can involve millions of dollars and result in a company going out of business, thus affecting the US economy and the lives of the employees of the affected business. It is also criminal activity that be may committed without the need for violence or threats. With a few adjustments on a computer or with a pen, a person in the right position can defraud or steal large sources of money.

2. What type of corporate and white-collar criminal activity takes place in the United States? Criminal activity at the corporate level can be conducted in a number of ways. The financial books and information of a company can be manipulated to show profit where it doesn't exist or be manipulated to cover up theft. Businesses can also be involved in bribery of government personnel, stock manipulation, insider fraud, or a variety of criminal activity depending on the nature or size of the organization.

Case Study 2

1. What type of information could have been stolen from the cubicle? A criminal committing corporate espionage may have taken a variety of information. Intellectual property may be the number one choice for thieves because it can be sold for a large amount of money to rival companies. This can include technical plans, research materials, or planning documents. Customer data and information is another target for criminals since it can be used to commit identify theft or sold to those individuals who can profit from such information.

2. What other types of corporate espionage activity may have taken place in this company? Direct theft of physical items such as computers or equipment that can be sold at a later date are common things stolen. Employees can also be a source of providing invaluable information about a business without realizing they are divulging major secrets.

Case Study 3

1. Why is depositing tens of thousands of dollars a suspected activity? Most people walking into banks or financial centers generally try to avoid carrying large amounts of cash. To bring cash into a business on a regular basis without a specific nonsuspicious reason known to security should warrant further inquiry and close scrutiny for possible money laundering.

2. What are some of the ways in which money is laundered without using a bank or financial institution? Money can be laundered by purchasing expensive items such as diamonds to later be converted back into cash. Real estate or construction projects offer a similar way to convert cash into nonsuspicious forms. Wiring money is also a way to send small portions to various locations around the world. Casinos can also be used by an individual savvy enough to gamble then convert the money and transfer it to another location or to another form.

Case Study 4

1. What type of fraud did the mortgage company fall victim to through the transaction with the client? The mortgage company failed to thoroughly check out their client and fell victim to fraud in the form of the client failing to disclose additional information regarding his or her debts and liens. The mortgage company should have examined the application with closer scrutiny as well as completed a more complete and comprehensive examination of the client when they were applying for the mortgage.

2. What are some of the ways of committing mortgage fraud? Mortgage fraud can be committed by using the mortgage process for a number of illegal purposes. This process can gain personal information about an individual such as Social Security number and other information for identity theft. Other ways of committing mortgage fraud can include altering the value of a piece of property, credit fraud, and shot-gunning just to mention a few.

■ Key Terms

Corporate crime or white-collar crime   The offenses committed by corporate officials for the corporation, and the offenses of the corporation itself, whereas occupational crime consists of offenses committed by individuals for themselves in the course of their occupation.

Derivative intelligence   Information synthesized out of lower-level data, facts, timelines, and events that may be disclosed during a job interview or on a professional's resume.

Embezzlement   The fraudulent conversion of property of another by a person in lawful possession of that property. Crimes of this nature generally have involved a relationship of trust and confidence, such as an agent, fiduciary, trustee, treasurer, or attorney.

Fraud   An intentional perversion of truth, or a misrepresentation of a matter of fact, that induces another person to part with some valuable thing belonging to them, or to surrender a legal right.

Globalization   Globalization can be defined as the integration of economic, cultural, political, religious, and social systems reaching the whole world and practically all human beings. In economics, globalization is the convergence of prices, products, wages, rates of interest, and profits towards developed country norms. Globalization of the economy depends on the role of human migration, international trade, movement of capital, and integration of financial markets.

Industrial espionage (or economic espionage)   This is the clandestine collection of sensitive, restricted, or classified information. This information by its very nature is not openly accessible and can only be obtained through covert collection means.

Insider traders   Any business personnel such as stockholders, directors, officers, or any recipients of information not publicly available who take advantage of such limited disclosure for their own benefit.

Integration   The stage in money laundering when money is put back into the economy. It is in this stage that the funds are spent or invested through things such as real estate or business expenditures

Layering   The stage in money laundering where more significant distancing from the original sources of the money takes place. In this stage, the goal is to create a larger gap between the money and where or how it was made.

Limited partnerships   A legal way to raise venture capital, it also provides a vehicle to shift corporate debts or to cover up a company's financial picture when corporate officials engage in risky financial gambles.

Money laundering   The process of hiding the origin of money for criminal purposes.

Mortgages   The loans people receive from a financial institution in order to purchase a home.

Mortgage fraud   A term used to describe a broad variety of methods where the intent is to materially misrepresent information on a mortgage loan application in order to obtain a loan.

Placement   The stage in money laundering when initial amounts of money are broken down into smaller sums.

Online extortion   The use of computers to force a company to pay a ransom or suffer a possible consequence.

Paper entrepreneurism   This is the focus by American companies on the status of numbers and computer-generated models that produce false information on the financial status of a company.

Stock manipulation   The criminal practice of getting investors to buy or sell a publicly traded stock through false and deceptive practices.

Structuring or "smurfing"   A money laundering method that involves disseminating a large amount of cash received in an illegal activity to many individuals who deposit cash or buy bank drafts in amounts under $10,000.

■ References

1. Corporate espionage. Spy-Ops Training Brief. http://www.Spy-Ops.com. *See also* George Smiley joins the firm. 1988, May 2. *Newsweek.*

2. Ibid. *See also* World Intellectual Property Organization. http://www.wipo. int/about-ip/en/.

3. Ibid. *See also* Dempsey, J. 2008. *Introduction to private security.* Stamford, CT: Wadsworth.

4. Notable industrial espionage cases. http://www.dss.mil./search-dir/training/ csg/security/Spystory/industry.htm.

5. Ibid. *See also* World Intellectual Property Organization. http://www.wipo. int/about-ip/en/.

6. Shefi, Y. 2005. *Resilient enterprise.* Cambridge, MA: MIT Press.

7. Corporate espionage. Spy-Ops Training Brief. http://www.Spy-Ops.com. *See also* Dempsey, J. 2008. *Introduction to private security.* Stamford, CT: Wadsworth.

8. *Economic Espionage Act of 1996.* http://rf-web.tamu.edu/security/secguide/ T1threat/legal.htm.

9. *See* note 7.

10. Ibid.

11. Ibid.

12. Ibid.

Current Private Security Threats: Issues and Information

- Be able to recognize terrorists.
- Become familiar with bombs.
- Understand the importance of protecting critical infrastructure.

■ Introduction

The last decade has seen a rise in the level of threats that can affect the lives of millions of citizens. Various forms of terrorism, threats to vital areas of the nation, along with the use of technology to violate the safeguards of our critical infrastructure facilities are no longer beyond the realm of possibility. Private security personnel, in turn, are now working at a time when heightened risks require them to have advanced knowledge and training to protect their clients when it comes to major security threats.

■ Terrorist Recognition

▶ ▶ CASE STUDY 1

You are working as a guard at a major banking center in a metropolitan city. Recent Homeland Security alerts as well as news updates on local news channels indicate an elevated possibility of a terrorist attack in the area near the banking center where you work.

1. How would you be able to recognize a terrorist approaching the banking center?
2. What is the means of operation for a terrorist?

Private security personnel are now expected to recognize possible terrorists as well as understand their means of operating in order to stop a catastrophe. Just as security experts note that "It takes a thief to catch a thief" you must think like a terrorist to catch terrorists before they strike against a target.

Terrorist Means of Operation

Most terrorist organizations operating in the United States and around the globe follow a general pattern of behavior when planning and executing a terrorist attack. Noted security expert Dan Sommer said this pattern of behavior for terrorist organizations can be viewed as a "wheel of terror" in which terrorist organizational planning ultimately comes to fruition. This wheel of terror notion can be expanded further as a more reoccurring process an organization can continually repeat until disrupted.[1]

Examining the Origin of a Terrorist Organization

Every terrorist organization must be examined by private security personnel in terms of what prompted the organization to form in the first place. Every terrorist organization has a declared enemy that they seek to dominate or destroy whether it is a government, corporation, individual, facility, ethnic group, social group, or business connection. When private security persons learns of a news alert or news story concerning a terrorist organization, they should quickly assess which possible targets would be considered by a particular terrorist organization.[2]

Surveillance

Before terrorists can begin planning an attack, they must conduct some form of surveillance of their intended target. Often terrorists pose as tourists, laborers, or visitors to a site. By scouting a site, terrorists can gain the following information about their chosen target: routes, routines, procedures, methods of transportation, security measures, protection measures, residences, facilities, and workplaces. It is important to note that private security guards can make it difficult for terrorists to conduct a successful surveillance, therefore possibly preventing an attack in the first place. The important factor to remember is that if the terrorists can see the target, then the target can also see the terrorists. Therefore the work of stationary and mobile private security guards becomes important. Later the terrorist group will conduct a preattack surveillance to gather specific target-related information about route options, target habits, accessibility, operations hours, and structural strength of a building.

Planning and Execution

Continuing through the cycle, terrorist organizations will engage in planning an attack once they have successfully completed their surveillance of a target. They will finalize the particular method of attack and the personnel who will attack the chosen target. As Sommers has noted, to gain tactical superiority the terrorists generally will plan a surprise attack on the target and the target's defense forces. If they plan on using a firearms attack they will need to have open fields of fire. They must be able to have control of the target, control of time and conditions, and have support positions, diversions, or secondary attack sites and options. Therefore as part of security drilling, private security personnel should consider training in a manner consistent with this pattern. Often terrorists use a "point man" who will decide whether to abort an attack or to go ahead and engage in the planned terrorist activity. The difficulty is that if terrorists get as far as the execution phase of a terrorist operation, then they are very likely to succeed in attacking their chosen target. Whether it is an assassination attempt, a bombing, a kidnapping, a hostage and barricade, a hijacking, or a safe-distance attack, the reality is the same. If terrorists can surprise private security, the terrorists are likely to succeed in causing damage, injury, or death to innocent people.[3]

Escape and Exploitation

For the most part, terrorists generally wish to escape and evade capture following the completion of a terrorist attack (The exceptions to this norm are fanatical or religiously motivated terrorist organizations.). Terrorists are interested in spreading a message of fear to their intended target as well as the community. Often additional terrorists are near their target for the purpose of filming or taking pictures of the attack or the immediate aftermath. Such recorded materials are then sent to media groups who might show the materials, thus further motivating the terrorist organization as well as spreading fear to innocent people in an area. If an attack is publicized by media sources, it encourages terrorists to work on selecting another target and executing a new attack. Private security personnel must continually assess if an attack is likely to occur by taking into account their location, current news information, and information from local police organizations. You must set aside time as you start work every day to make this assessment. Whether a site is a possible target can depend on the following criteria used by terrorists:

- The attack must be strategic.
- The attack must be symbolic.
- The attack must be catastrophic.

Terrorist Profiling

Terrorist profiling is an art and science and requires the use of intuitive analysis to find potential terrorists. It is a methodical process that is used to uncover common terrorist behavior, based on information collected from previous interviews with captured terrorists, evidence at the scenes of attacks, and attack victims. Patterns of known behaviors and emotions suggested by historical activity, scenes, and victims are then used to create templates from which we can infer characteristics about current activities and individuals. These patterns are inferred from reasoning about statistical data on specific terrorist behavior. While in-depth data on terrorists and their techniques is not in abundance, there is enough data to derive some critical intelligence and create a base profile for most terrorists.

Terrorist Personnel Profile[4]
- Male
- Between the ages of 21 and 35
- Unmarried
- Fundamentalist
- Has some university education
- Comes from an upper-middle class family
- Has a revolutionary ideology
- Lives an average lifestyle
- Has a dysfunctional family background
- Is a joiner (a person who seeks out participation in groups)
- Seeks self-deindividuation (seeks to replace his own self-identity with a terrorist group's identity)
- Difficulty forming group identities outside the home and in social settings
- Not obviously or consistently mentally ill
- Slightly less socially interactive (not loners though)
- Active lifestyle, not a recluse

It is important to note that private security personnel should be focused not just on Middle Eastern terrorism but all forms of terrorism from any organization. In America today, domestic-based groups such as racial hate groups, environmental extremist organizations, and political revolutionary groups that exist in the United States all can fit the above listed criteria. It is also important to understand that most terrorists do not start out as psychopaths.

Word to the Wise   Terrorists strike where they see a weakness in security so that their strike has a better chance of being successful. While working in the private security field, try to think how terrorists would infiltrate, survey, and destroy the location where you are employed. While no area can be 100% protected against the activities of terrorists, the more difficult you make it for terrorists the less likely an attack will occur. [5]

Suicide Attacks

Terrorist organizations have been using suicide attacks since the 1980s as a way to invoke massive casualties, gain the attention of their enemies, and provoke a reaction from the international community. The use of suicide attacks has increased, especially in areas where major conflicts are occurring. The possibility of a future suicide attack within the continental United States is a real and frightening reality. By definition a suicide attack is an attack on a chosen military or civilian target in which an attacker intends to kill others and damage a site by committing suicide through a devastating and destructive act. The means of the suicide act can include vehicles filled with explosives, passenger planes carrying large amounts of fuel, and individuals wearing vests filled with explosives. Additional descriptors for suicide attacks include suicide-homicide bombing, martyrdom operations, and predatory martyrdom.

The first modern suicide bombing involving explosives deliberately carried to a chosen target was perpetrated by Hezbollah during the 1981 Lebanese civil war. The terrorist tactic continued to spread to additional armed groups like the Tamil Tigers of Sri Lanka, Palestinian groups, al Qaeda, and, by 2005, to dozens of countries where a weaker power is fighting a stronger one. Targeted sites include Israeli targets such as public areas and buses in Israel since 1994 and Iraqis since the US-led invasion began in 2003.

With terrorist groups such as Hezbollah and al Qaeda calling for suicide bombers to attack American businesses or areas of strategic interest, entry-level private security personnel should understand the nature of suicide bombers. Suicide bombers are the ultimate smart weapon in the sense the terrorists themselves choose the time and place of action, according to the prevailing circumstances. They can abort an attack at the last minute or change targets when the original target appears too difficult to penetrate. Suicide attacks themselves are simple and low-cost operations requiring no escape routes or complicated rescue operations. Remember, for a suicide bomber, there is little risk of being captured and giving away important information. In terms of the message of terror being spread, suicide bombings have an immense impact on the public and the media. For private security personnel, it is important to look at suspicious people as potential suicide bombers.[6]

In recent years, Western security experts have begun to learn more about the nature of Islam and the individual. Individuals decide to engage in suicide attacks as an act of faith. Suicide bombers are often seeking a religious salvation for themselves and their family. A suicide bombing itself often leads to celebration and memorialization by a local community in the Middle East because it is believed a suicide bomber will join the heavenly ranks of past martyrs and combatants for their cause. Individuals are also engaging in suicide bombing for financial security that is often provided to their families from terrorist organizations or through their belief in heavenly blessings. In addition, the rise of female suicide bombers has shown that women may engage in suicide bombing to seek heavenly blessings and salvation for their family or to sacrifice themselves to correct a dishonor to their family.[7]

How to Recognize a Suicide Bomber[8]

- Repeated attempts to steer clear of private security
- Walking slowly while glancing side to side, or running in a suspicious manner
- Nervous, hesitant, profusely sweating, or mumbling
- Keeps one or both hands in pockets at all times
- Clothes unsuitable for place or climate
- Clothes significantly bigger than the person's body
- Suitcase, handbag, or backpack that a person keeps a tight grip on at all times
- Electrical wires, switches, metal, or electronic apparatus protruding from bag or clothing
- Obvious disguise

Contrary to belief by many, suicide bombers are usually not mentally depraved individuals who come from low socioeconomic backgrounds. They are often educated, with college or university experience, and come from middle class homes. Most suicide bombers do not show signs of psychopathology. Indeed, leaders of the groups who perpetrate these attacks search for individuals who can be trusted to carry out the mission because persons with mental illnesses are not ideal candidates.[9]

The US military has made a substantial effort towards understanding the connection between Islam and suicide attacks. A Pentagon intelligence group, the Counterintelligence Field Activity Unit (CIFA) has focused on understanding the sections of the Koran where terms such as *Jihad* and *martyrdom* appear, partly to understand the justification for the attacks and partly because suicide bombers may recite these passages prior to a suicide attack. An additional justification for suicide attacks can also be found outside of religion. Noted academic Robert Pape of the University of Chicago has written extensively that suicide attacks may be a response to foreign occupation rather than a result of Islamic religious fervor and fundamentalism.

You must understand that terrorist methodology and terrorist profiling by themselves are not an effective means of complete protection against terrorist threats. Any profile of terrorists provides guidelines of the most basic characteristics, but terrorists can easily get around this by recruiting outsiders or individuals who can operate without raising any suspicion. Additionally, terrorists are constantly exploring new ways to engage in terrorist activity in ways never imagined by security professionals. It is important therefore for entry-level security personnel to continually seek new information and stay up-to-date on developments in the world as well as training opportunities in counterterrorism. Also private security personnel will have to continue to work and cooperate with public-serving law enforcement agencies in terms of sharing information and conducting joint drills and training sessions for the benefit of society.

■ Bombs

▶ ▶ CASE STUDY 2

While on duty as a private security guard, you receive word from a superior that a bomb may have been placed somewhere in the office building where you are employed. The bomb is suspected to have been placed by a disgruntled former employee. Your supervisor informs you that an anonymous caller claiming to have planted the bomb states that C-4 was used and that a remote detonator has been set up.

1. Why is it important to know the different types of explosives and switches in bombs?
2. What steps should a private security team consider in dealing with a possible bomb threat?
3. What steps can a private security team take to prevent future incidents?

Bombs are still the most important strategic attack method of modern terrorism. Criminals, employees, students, and terrorist organizations have all used or threatened to use bombs in the United States and abroad. Slightly more than half of all the recorded international terrorist incidents in 2001 were bombings. Between 1977 and 2001, bombings accounted for 63.5% of all recorded incidents.[10] This estimate has risen closer to 75% of all recorded incidents in newer estimates. These individuals or groups are likely to use homemade bombs made from a variety of materials, also known as **improvised explosive devices (IEDs)**. By understanding the nature of bombs, a private security employee can successfully respond faster when a threat emerges, develop techniques to detect their presence, and develop methods to prevent future threats.

Historically, terrorist and criminal bombing was made much easier after the invention of nitroglycerine and dynamite. Alfred Nobel made nitroglycerin safer to handle by adding a blasting cap and absorbent material, which, in turn, ushered in a new era of high-powered, cheaper explosives. (Nobel became a pacifist late in his life and saw to it in his will that a part of his fortune was set aside for the famous Nobel prizes and to the establishment of the Peace Prize.) Today, explosives and bomb technology are easily accessible to terrorist groups or criminals at low cost. In the United States, the majority of bombings that are carried out are pipe bombings. These simple devices use black powder inside a container combined with materials that can easily be acquired at a hardware retailer.

What Is a Bomb?

A **bomb** is a device that generates and releases its energy very rapidly in the form of an explosion with a violent and destructive shock wave. An **explosion** is further defined as the sudden and rapid release of gases to a confined space.

Photo Courtesy PDphoto.org

While IEDs come in many variations, they all consist of the same basic components including a fuse or initiation system, a detonator, a power supply for the detonator, explosives, and a container. These components are consistent whether the IED is a truck or car bomb, letter bomb, nail bomb, pipe bomb, or even a radiological or "dirty" bomb.[11] To understand how a bomb works, you must think of a fire. To create a fire, you need a combustible material, oxygen for the fire to grow, and a source of ignition. An explosion that follows the detonation of a bomb happens the same way except that the oxygen and combustible material are bound together so the process occurs at an extremely fast rate.[12]

Detonators

Bombs ultimately require a detonation. The "fire" must be started by something. While some detonators are commercially available with proper documentation and licenses, many detonators can be improvised. The **detonator** is essentially a mini-explosive device that sets off the larger explosion process. Most terrorist organizations use a "booster," a chemical or organic compound needed to increase the power of an explosive material or compound, for the improvised mix. Without the booster, there is a very good chance that the homemade explosive will not detonate due to the crude method of construction.[13] Detonators can be either electrical or nonelectrical. In an electrical detonator, the actual electric charge from the device sets off the detonator substance. Many nonelectrical detonators are chemical detonators.

Private Security in the News Private security personnel were unable to prevent the 1993 World Trade Center bombing that was carried out with a bomb made of urea pellets, sulfuric acid, aluminum azide, magnesium azide, and bottled hydrogen with surgical tubes as a fuse and nitroglycerin as the detonator.

Types of Explosives

A bomb is not a bomb without the use of explosive material as one of its components. The following are some of the most common explosives used in bombs today:

- Black powder is fine to course black powder, and black to rusty brown in color.
- Smokeless powder is slate grey to black, and is available in tiny cylinders, rods, or wafers.
- TNT and dynamite are used for commercial and military purposes, and are available in paper, cardboard, or plastic wrappings. It is a common misconception that TNT and dynamite are the same, but this is not the case. TNT is the specific chemical compound trinitrotoluene; dynamite is a type of wood pulp or other absorbent mixture soaked in nitroglycerin, compressed into a cylindrical shape, and wrapped in paper. Straight dynamite is a mixture of liquid nitroglycerin, sodium nitrate (which supplies the oxygen for complete combustion), and wood pulp or ground meal that absorbs the shock of the nitroglycerine. The strength of straight commercial dynamite is determined by the percentage of nitroglycerine by weight in the dynamite formula.
- **Nitroglycerin** is a heavy, oily liquid that is clear to amber in color; brown streaks may appear as the liquid turns brown over time.
- **Ammonium nitrate** is available in white or grey pellets. Most fertilizers have a high content. It can also be mixed with different chemicals to create the following explosive mixtures:
  - Anfo—Mixed with fuel oil
  - Anal—Mixed with aluminum powder
  - Anic—Mixed with icing sugar
  - Annie—Mixed with nitrobenzine
  - Ans—Mixed with sugar

- **Composition 4** or **C-4** was discovered during WWII. It is a yellow substance that resembles modeling clay and can be molded into a variety of shapes. C-4 has no odor, has a greater shattering effect than TNT, and detonates at a much higher rate. It is resistant to heat, shock, and friction.

- **PETN** (pentaerythritol tetranitrate) is mixed with different materials to create sheet plastics. It is available in thin sheets allowing it to be easily hidden in electrical devices, such as laptops. Pure PETN closely resembles ordinary clothesline and is also referred to as datachord, primex, or primacord. It is resistant to heat, shock, and friction.

- **Semtex** looks like orange putty and is very common in terrorist attacks as a high-velocity plastic explosive. It has trace elements that can be traced back to the manufacturer.

- **Acetone peroxide** (also known peroxyacetone, TATP for triacetone triperoxide, or TCAP for tricyclic acetone) is an organic peroxide and a primary high explosive. It takes the form of a white crystalline powder with a distinctive acrid smell. It is highly susceptible to heat, friction, and shock. Because of its instability, it has been called the "Mother of Satan." Experts say it is made by mixing common household items, such as drain cleaner and bleach. Triacetone triperoxide (TATP) is relatively difficult to detect so it is a common explosive used by terrorists, particularly suicide bombers. Transportation Security agents check routinely for this explosive material at US airports.[14]

- Gasoline is the low-tech approach to making a bomb. Gasoline is always accessible and one gallon of gasoline has the blast power of seven pounds of high explosives when detonated.

The most widely used system for classifying these explosives is based on the rate of **velocity** or detonation of explosion. There are two categories: low-velocity explosives and high-velocity explosives. Low-velocity explosives have rates of detonation below 3000 feet per second. Black powder averages 1312 feet per second whereas dynamite has a velocity range of 7000–18,000 feet per second.

> **Low velocity:** Black powder, smokeless powder, gun powder
> **High velocity:** Dynamite, TNT, C-4, ammonium nitrate and fertilizer bombs, PETN

The Components of a Bomb: P.I.E.S.

Today most bombs, whether sent in a letter bomb form to a company or constructed by a terrorist organization, all follow an easy to remember structure.

Power supply—Various batteries: two 9-volt, two AAs, or one D cell; a cordless phone battery, camcorder battery, or 2-meter handheld ham radio battery; or a button battery or one C cell and two AAAs, are commonly used for power in the explosive device.

Initiator/detonator—Detonators are used for initiating high explosives and contain small amounts of a sensitive primary explosive. Although they are manufactured to absorb a reasonable amount of shock during handling and transportation, they are normally treated with caution.

Explosive—Explosives are any chemical compound, mixture, or device in which the primary or common purpose is to cause an explosion with a substantial instantaneous release of gas and heat.

Switch—This can include any toggle, timer, trigger, remote, cell phone, or other device used to set off the explosive. Cell phones and garage door openers are the most common ways to detonate an IED.

Blast Effects

When an explosive is detonated, the black powder, stick of dynamite, block of TNT, or chunk of C-4 is instantaneously converted from a solid into a rapidly expanding mass of gas. The detonation will produce several secondary effects, but the following three primary effects produce the greatest amount of damage: fragmentation, blast pressure, and secondary fires.

Fragmentation

In a pipe bomb, a quantity of explosive filler is placed inside the length of a pipe at each end with a piece of time-fuse used for detonation. Once detonated, the explosive will shatter the pipe and propel pipe fragments outward from the point of detonation at rates possibly up to 2700 feet per second. The pipe can also be filled with nails, razor blades, staples, and glass to cause more damage. In addition, dynamite can be covered in a plastic bag filled with two inches of nails and staples.[15]

Blast Pressure

The detonation of an explosive charge produces very hot expanding gases. These gases exert pressures of approximately 700 tons per square inch and rush away from the point of detonation at speeds of up to 7000 miles per hour. There are two distinct phases to the blast pressure effect: the positive pressure phase and the negative pressure phase.

The positive pressure is formed at the moment of detonation with the leading edge of the positive pressure wave known as a shock front. A bomb therefore gives a one-two punch, the shock front followed by the positive pressure wave. The shock front can shatter the walls of a building while the positive pressure waves pushes the walls outward in a radiating pattern from the source of detonation.

Also of concern is the negative pressure that is present when a bomb is detonated. This is the vacuum that forms in the gap of air due to the detonation. As air moves towards the source of detonation it will crush and topple anything in its path, including other parts of a building or people.[16]

Secondary Fires

This effect is produced by an explosion. When a bomb goes off, there is a bright flash or fireball that causes a fire. Any combustible materials near the source of a detonation will ignite. In a building or site there can be hundreds of items that can catch fire or explode.

Detecting a Bomb

Private security personnel, regardless of the nature of the setting, are responsible for protecting people and property from a bomb attack. Whether it is a retail store, gaming institution, or corporate office, security personnel can take steps to detect possible activity. The presence of a number of signs and indicators should warrant heightened security and possibly more extensive searches by private security personnel.

1. Containers, gas balloons, fuses, explosive fillers, shrapnel, or contaminants, such as rat poison, are to be viewed with caution.

2. An unusual number of cellular phones in a location; these may be used as remote devices to activate detonators.

3. Bomb accessories such as:
   - Absorbents
   - Alcohol
   - Aluminum foil
   - Heat resistant containers
   - Petroleum jelly
   - Protective gloves
   - Scales
   - Tubing
   - Wires

4. Household items such as vinegar, aluminum powder, fuel, oil, sugar, nitric acid, potassium chlorate, nitrate, vehicle batteries, thermometers, and hydrogen peroxide in unusually high quantities.[17]

Word to the Wise   Any suspicious object, an abandoned bag with or without wires, gas canister, knapsack, or even a shopping bag, may require an immediate evacuation of the area by private security personnel along with intervention by public law enforcement agencies.

Suicide Bomb Vests

As previously noted, suicide bombers are likely to engage in suspicious behavior and have apparent signs of a bomb on their person. Generally, a suicide bomber carries an explosive device that ranges from 10–30 lbs. in a vest or bag along with ball bearings, nails, razors, or metal fragments packed tightly around the bomb to maximize damage in a target area. A suicide vest is typically constructed by making a wooden mold in which shrapnel content is placed. The explosive is then rolled over the shrapnel like a layer of baking dough. This content is then placed into a vest and is usually detonated electrically with a remote arming mechanism or with a wire connection to the bomb.

Vehicle-Borne Improvised Explosive Device (VBIED)

Private security personnel now face a deadly new innovation in bomb attack. Criminals and terrorists now also use **vehicle-borne improvised explosive devices** (**VBIEDs**), which involve the packing and detonating of explosives into a car or truck for increased mobility and lethality. Typically, cars and vans are the preferred vehicles used for bombings. However, more recent trends include the use of railway cars, buses, and large trucks to increase casualties. In most vehicle bomb deliveries where suicide is not part of the plan, the bomb device is armed only after the vehicle has been parked and the driver is ready to escape from the area. If the arming switch is located near the driver's seat, the driver may be seen manipulating it before exiting. Private security personnel have to be extremely vigilant in order to spot a driver who appears hurried or nervous while exiting a vehicle, or who is looking around to see if he or she is being watched. If the arming switch is located with the main charge, the driver may be observed opening the trunk or cargo doors to manipulate the device. In most legitimate, nonthreatening situations, a driver opening the trunk or cargo doors will either be removing something or placing a package inside. Security personnel should always be suspicious if the driver opens the vehicle and then closes it again without removing anything. FBI analysts advising the Homeland Security Program believe that truck bombing by terrorists may be preempted if the general public is educated about and remains alert for certain indicators. While the existence of one or more of these indicators does not guarantee that such an attack is being contemplated, the FBI advises that law enforcement be notified to enable prompt further investigation. Attack methodologies with VBIEDs include the following:[18]

1. Placing explosive materials on or in a car in order to kill the occupants
2. The use of a vehicle as a launching system for rocket-propelled grenades (RPG)
3. The use of a vehicle as a booby trap or antipersonnel device to ambush law enforcement, military, or bomb disposal personnel

4. The use of a hostage for the transportation and delivery of explosives
5. The use of a vehicle as a fragmentation device when a large amount of explosives are used
6. The use of multiple vehicle bombs in a coordinated terrorist strike
7. The use of a vehicle in a suicide attack

Private security personnel should consider any security alerts or information provided by public law enforcement agencies as an indicator that heightened security is required. In particular, private security personnel should regularly engage in the following activities to prevent a VBIED from occurring at a location:

1. Check for improvised or mismatched vehicle tags and license plates that are inconsistent with vehicle registration.
2. Look for vehicles that appear to be carrying a heavy load, especially in the trunk area.
3. Be aware of modified trucks or vans with heavy-duty springs for heavier loads.
4. Report any contact with drivers of rental vans with false papers.
5. Notice and note the rental of storage space for chemicals or mixing devices.
6. Be aware of the delivery of chemicals from the manufacturer to storage facilities or unusual deliveries of chemicals to residential or rural addresses.
7. Examine vehicles coming into a parking lot, especially underground parking areas in certain facilities.
8. Vehicles parked for an excessive period in a central location, loading, or no-parking zone.
9. The trunk or rear of a vehicle is leaking fluid.[19]
10. Change traffic patterns near a site through exterior vehicle barriers and roadblocks.
11. Private security personnel in patrol cars should be parked randomly near entrances and exits.[20]

Private security personnel should also take note of commercial vehicles that appear out of place in high-risk locations and report these to their security team and to local police. Trucks bearing hazardous material placards that are outside established trucking routes or parked in nonindustrial areas are also cause for suspicion. Studies of previous incidents have revealed several types of suspicious behavior, which when observed may indicate a possible vehicle bomb delivery.[21]

- Rental trucks with hazardous cargo placards
- Parked in nonindustrial settings
- Moving outside usual trucking routes

- Unattended and driver cannot be located
- Unattended passenger vehicle or van with apparent heavy load
- Driver manipulates something near driver's seat before exiting the vehicle
- Driver opens vehicle trunk or cargo doors before leaving the vehicle area
- Second person exiting the back of a truck or van
- Parking suspect vehicle and departing the area in another vehicle
- Smoke, unusual odors

In some terrorist bombing situations, a second person will ride in the back of the van or truck so that they can connect and arm the device after the vehicle is in place, and then that person exits from the back of the vehicle. This scenario is common if the vehicle cab is separate from the cargo box or trailer. Private security personnel should watch where a driver goes immediately after parking. In some cases, a second vehicle may be used for a quick escape after delivery of the device. This second vehicle may follow the suspect vehicle into the location. The vehicle bombs used in Oklahoma City and the 1993 attack on the World Trade Center used burning fuse delays.[22] These produce a gray, acrid smoke. If private security personnel note any unusual odors or smoke or leakage from an unattended vehicle, they should consider an evacuation of the area and a call to 911.

Bomb Threats

Telephone bomb threats are the most common. Any public employee or volunteer who may answer a telephone capable of receiving outside calls should receive basic orientation on how to deal with telephone bomb threats. The call taker is in the best position to obtain information needed to enable private security personnel and law enforcement to assess the credibility of the threat and act promptly upon it.

Private security personnel should remind the call taker that all calls mentioning bomb threats, suspicious objects, suspected explosives, incendiaries, or biological devices should be considered real. Instruct the call taker to keep calm, use a hand signal to summon help, keep the caller on the line, and carefully note what the caller says. The call taker should write the information down on a Bomb Threat Checklist, which should be part of a company's emergency procedures.

- *Where* is the bomb?
- *When* will it explode?
- *What* does it look like?
- *What type* of bomb is it?
- *What can be done* to stop it?
- *Who* are you? (Usually prompts a hang-up by person offering a bomb threat.)

It is frightening to contemplate that most bombs almost always work as designed. It is also important to realize that only 4% of bombings are preceded by a threat. It is vital that any bomb threat be taken seriously! Therefore, you should never assume that a threatening call is a hoax or that the caller is merely a crackpot. There is also the possibility that bomb threats or suspicious items may be used to disrupt an event, consume human resources, or used as a distraction from other criminal activity.[23] Private security personnel should always trust their intuition regarding the possibility that something is wrong. In addition, fire marshals and law enforcement agencies can provide additional guidelines in responding in the most appropriate manner.

A bomb threat delivered through e-mail is always a possibilty. E-mail threats are more difficult to trace, but the the recipient should be instructed to save the e-mail message, print the message, and copy it to a floppy disc or USB, and contact the security personnel.[24]

Searching for a Bomb

It is important to note that most private security personnel are not likely to engage in an active search for finding and removing a bomb. Depending on the location, private security personnel are likely to call public police organizations and request instructions and assistance if they believe a bomb is present while they are on duty. However, where there is a great possibility of a bomb detonating, the private security personnel may actually be forced to respond. This would require the organization of the private security personnel into a **search team**, a designated private security team trained and authorized to search for a bomb. Generally, a private security team requires more than one individual to search any area or room, regardless of the size of the location. One individual can often miss even the most apparent signs of a bomb. One way to deploy a search team is to conduct a quick and rapid search that does not alert people of a possible threat. This approach is favorable because there is no loss of profit or of employee working time.[25] However, if a bomb is found, a problem with employee morale may develop if the employees find out that they were not initially made aware of the threat.

Using experienced private security personnel on a search team is likely to yield more positive results because they are likely to be more familiar with the site. These individuals are likely to notice if doors, windows, or objects are out of place or appear altered. Additionally, a search team can notify fellow employees of the possibility of a bomb and direct them to search their areas for a possible bomb. Such a search is often comprehensive and completed only after significant training and continual practice. Ideally, it is optimal to have private security personnel train employees to search for and report abnormal conditions in their workplace on a regular basis. If a crisis situation develops, having employees that are able to search their own areas can yield a much faster search. However, a drawback to this search technique is the increased danger to nonsecurity employees. Ultimately, the decision to use a search team in a specific manner requires a decision and investment by management.[26]

Bomb Searching Techniques

The basic technique for searching for a bomb is a room search conducted by two members of the security team. When the two-person search team enters the room, they should first move to various parts of the room and stand quietly with their eyes closed and listen for any sounds coming from an explosive device. They should also identify perceived background noises, such as traffic sounds, rain, and wind, that can disrupt or distract private security personnel during a search. The private security person in charge of the searching team should examine the room and determine how the specific room is to be divided. A search of a room will consist of a low sweep followed by a high sweep, focusing searches at different heights with extra scrutiny. The first search sweep will cover all items and spaces located from the floor up to a designated height, usually at the same level as a person's hip. The division of the room should be based on its specifics, such as the number of spaces and objects, and not on the size of the room because all rooms should be divided in the same manner regardless of size. To begin the first sweep, private security personnel should examine the furniture, objects, and spaces in the room to determine the average height of the majority of items resting on the floor. In an average room, this will usually include tables, desk tops, and chair backs. After the room has been divided and a search height has been selected, both private security personnel then go to one end of the room and start from a back-to-back position along the room's division line. Each private security person then begins a search in their direction around the room working towards the other private security person. The focus is on examining all items resting on the floor and the areas around the room including the walls. The walls, in particular, should be checked in great detail, especially the structures embedded in the walls including air conditioning ducts, baseboard heaters, built-in wall cupboards, and other fixtures.

A second sweep takes place in the room following the first search. The focus of this search is from the height of the search leader's hip to the top of their head. The two private security personnel then repeat the same process focusing on higher objects like pictures, bookcases, and table lamps. A third sweep can also be completed by conducting the same process from the top of the private security officer's head to the ceiling. This includes a focus on air-conditioning ducts and light fixtures. Once a room has been satisfactorily searched, private security personnel can then move on to another area.[27]

If you find a suspicious package, object, or an actual bomb, it is important that you report it immediately. There should be no attempt to move or disarm an explosive device. The local police should be called in and given all available information.

Summary of a Bomb Search in a Room

1. Private security personnel divide the room and select a search height.
2. Start from the floor and work up to the general hip level.
3. Private security personnel then start searching back to back and work toward each other while searching all objects and spaces.
4. Walls are searched while moving towards the center of the room.

Evacuation and Scene Control

Bomb threats, fires, explosions, and the release of hazardous materials are always dangerous, whether caused by criminals, terrorists, or natural or technological disasters. Evacuating a building requires extensive planning and coordination by the public safety and law enforcement incident commander. The use of qualified personnel with the proper training and the implementation of safety equipment is essential. Additional resources may also be brought in as needed. Private security employees must focus on assisting others in an orderly evacuation and should use their communication skills to help create a safe public refuge.[28] Public safety in an evacuation should be coordinated by qualified private security personnel that can do the following:

- Assist individuals in harm's way to safety.
- Deny entry to unauthorized personnel.
- Establish perimeters and operational zones.
- Establish an incident command system.
- Establish a safe refuge for the public.

The area should be identified as a danger area and blocked off with a clear zone of at least 300 feet. The clear zone includes the floors above and below the position of the suspicious object or bomb in a multistory building. Windows and doors should be opened to minimize primary damage from a possible blast and the following secondary fragmentation damage that will occur. The area should also be evacuated and reentry should be restricted until the device has been removed and the local police have given authorization to return to the area. As per the previous section on public relations, any media representatives or news reporters should be directed to one appointed spokesperson that has been designated to answer questions and provide information.[29]

The minimum evacuation distance is the range at which life-threatening injury from the blast or fragments is unlikely. According to the Bureau of Alcohol, Tobacco, and Firearms, detonating a passenger car carrying 500 lbs. of explosives produces a lethal blast of air up to 100 feet and propels fragments over 1000 feet. A van with 2 tons of explosives produces a lethal blast up to 200 feet and throws debris as far as half a mile away. A box truck with 15 tons of explosives produces a lethal blast to

500 feet and hurls debris over a mile. When evacuating, stay as far as possible from the location and take advantage of substantial barriers and terrain for protection. Avoidance of windows and overhead glass is also important. As a knowledgeable civilian, the most important thing you can do is to recognize potential threats, help others get *far* away to safety, and notify the appropriate public safety authorities.[30]

Evacuation criteria for private security personnel include the following:[31]

- Have a planned evacuation area and assembly area.
- Prior to use, check evacuation area for suspicious items or vehicles.
- Have an alternate assembly point.
- Use terrain features or solid objects as protective shielding.
- If stuck inside a building, evacuate the area by going to the farthest lateral point from and at least several floors below the device.
- Avoid areas with flammable or hazardous materials, windows, and any overhead glass.
- Take a roll call and account for absentees.
- Stay at least 300 feet from small devices or at least 1000 feet from larger devices in the open.
- If a very large device or vehicle bomb is suspected, get as far away as possible.

A bomb scenario is one of the scariest and most tension-filled moments for a private security person to face. However, with continual training and experience, a private security person can handle a bomb crisis with professionalism and maintain a focus on safety. It is important for private security employees to remember that they have no special governmental privilege or authority. Incident management must be left to public safety professionals, including fire and police organizations. The focus of private security, therefore, should be on prevention, detection, and assistance of public safety agencies and the safety of bystanders.

■ Critical Infrastructure

▶ ▶ CASE STUDY 3

You are a private security employee responsible for supervising other private security employees at a major power plant. Information has just been released that there is a heightened alert that terrorists or environmental activists may attempt to shut down all power plants in the state.

1. Why do power plants and other utility centers require heightened security?
2. What are some considerations when protecting critical infrastructure facilities?

With blackouts, terrorist threats, and cyberattacks threatening key utility centers in the United States, private security personnel currently face the daunting task of protecting the vital underbelly of the nation. Since WWII, private security personnel have focused on developing security measures to protect American resources and utilities. Because terrorist threats against notable infrastructure are constantly surfacing, private security personnel are likely to continue to serve on the front line of our nation's defense.

Critical infrastructure refers to assets, systems, and functions that are vital to the survival of the nation. The Department of Homeland Security has classified 1700 of the 33,000 entities in the national asset database as nationally critical. Critical infrastructure assets include transportation (land, water, and air modes), energy systems, defense installations, banking and financial facilities and networks, water supplies, chemical plants, food and agricultural resources, police and fire departments, hospitals and public health systems, government offices, and national symbols. An event that disrupts or destroys critical infrastructure would have a debilitating effect on our national security, economy, government, public health and safety, and morale. Landmarks such as the Statue of Liberty and the Golden Gate Bridge are included in this area. Communication and computer network systems are also vital to our daily lives. Critical infrastructure requires significant protection because any disruption or destruction of these critical locations through natural or man-made actions would completely disrupt the normal day-to-day lives of many Americans.[32] Consider the vast number of locations in the United States that fall into this category.

- A single natural gas supplier has over 35,000 miles of distribution pipeline.
- The electricity industry's capacity is 1089807 megawatts as of December 2007.
- A single electrical utility has over 21,000 miles of distribution lines.
- There are nearly 10,000 airports in the United States.
- There are approximately 1.5 million miles of gas pipe in the United States.
- There are nearly 7000 bridges in the National Highway System inventory.
- There are nearly 10,000 high-hazard dams in the United States.[33]

Protection of critical infrastructure has traditionally been provided and maintained by the federal and local government. Today, large numbers of critical infrastructure locations are widely distributed, which makes protection very difficult and costly. The reality in the post-9/11 world is that it is up to private industries to provide for their own security. Currently, about 80–85% of our critical infrastructure is privately owned in the United States.[34]

Critical Infrastructure Asset Classifications[35]
- Information technology centers
- Telecommunication sites
- Chemical plants and transport routes
- Transportation systems
- Emergency services headquarters
- Postal and shipping services
- Agriculture and food sites
- Public health and healthcare facilities
- Drinking water and water treatment facilities
- Energy facilities
- Banking and finance centers
- National monuments and icons
- Defense industrial bases
- Key industry and technology sites
- Large gathering areas

All of these critical infrastructure categories listed in the box are of vital importance for the normal functions of every person in the United States. With so many different areas of critical infrastructure, it is apparent to an entry-level private security person that it is a huge task to protect so many different locations.

Private security personnel are likely to find employment in many of the 15 areas listed above. In particular, the areas of critical infrastructure involving energy, chemicals, and computers offer private security personnel an opportunity to work in a number of exciting areas.

Energy and Chemicals

Electricity is an integral part of life in the United States. It is unimaginable for most people to consider a day, a week, or a month without electricity. The economic impact to a nation that has no power could be in the billions of dollars due to all commerce and financial activity grinding to a halt. **The Northeast Blackout of 2003** revealed how a lack of power can cripple a nation . The massive power outage that occurred throughout parts of the northeastern and midwestern United States and Ontario, Canada, on August 14, 2003, left millions without power. Although not a terrorist attack, it demonstrated how vulnerable our nation is if a hostile group were to attack and shut down a vital piece of our infrastructure. Unlike the 2003 blackout, a terrorist attack on our current infrastructure could not only damage transmission and distribution lines, but also generators and safety and switching equipment that take days or weeks to repair and recover. The impact of a terrorist attack that would disrupt our flow of electricity makes this area a high-value target for terrorists and thus requires private security personnel to be on site.[36]

Private Security in the News   The last installment of the *Die Hard* movie series focuses on criminals who were able to disrupt the entire Northeast by attacking the critical infrastructure of the nation.

There are nearly 3200 electrical utilities in the United States. The national power grid is the interconnection of electricity produced across the 48 contiguous states. Comprising high-voltage electrical transmission lines running across the United States, the network is divided into three separate grids:

1. The Eastern Interconnected System
2. The Western Interconnected System
3. The Texas Interconnected System

These three grids consist of extra high-voltage connections between individual utilities designed to permit the transfer of electrical energy from one part of the network to another. The system's automatic transfer switch monitors incoming voltage from the grid or utility line. Any major disruption from a man-made or natural source can jeopardize the electricity for entire communities or regions.

In addition to energy, chemicals are also of vital importance to our nation. Chemicals are used on a large industrial scale for the production of many of the common goods that we use daily. Chemicals are also an integral part of our existence on a much smaller scale. They are used in various ways, including preserving food sources, medical treatments and medications, and as disinfectants in both commercial buildings and residential homes. However, terrorists, extremists, and saboteurs can use common chemicals found in communities in industrialized nations to create improvised explosives, incendiaries, and chemical agents. Private security personnel, therefore, are often on high alert to ensure that chemicals are not released, exploded, or stolen by hostile people. For example, a train carrying chlorine gas can be targeted by a criminal or terrorist organization because its contents could kill or harm hundreds of people. An industrial plant that is attacked could release chemicals into the air, which could poison an entire region. Likewise, chemicals such as those found in fertilizers can be used in explosives. Chemicals manufactured in and stored throughout the nation are much too accessible. Some of the more common types of chemicals that could be used in improvised chemical weapons include acids, ammonia, benzene, chlorine, propane, and numerous other chemicals and gases.

Locations Where Chemicals Need Private Security Protection[37]
- Chemical manufacturing plants
- Industrial facilities
- Food-processing and storage facilities
- Chemical transportation assets
- Gasoline and jet fuel storage tanks at distribution centers
- Compressed gases in tanks, pipelines, and pumping stations
- Pesticide manufacturing and supply distributors
- Educational, medical, and research laboratories

The accessibility of industrial chemicals means that protecting these potentially lethal but necessary entities is a daunting challenge. For example, chemicals are routinely transported using other parts of our critical infrastructure—rail, water, roads, and air—making them easy targets for sabotage and even more difficult to protect. Air transportation of chemicals may seem surprising, but in 2005 the US Department of Transportation hazardous materials information system identified over 1600 incidents in air transportation. As with other areas of infrastructure, many state and local enforcement agencies do not have policies that address the specific problems that can occur if chemicals are released in dangerous quantities, even though federal law requires chemical emergency response plans. The focus in recent years has been on terrorist use of **weapons of mass destruction** (WMD), which can be chemical, biological, or nuclear.[38]

The size of the chemical industry itself warrants an increased need for private security personnel. There are currently about 600,000 workers in the chemical manufacturing industry. It is unclear how many employees have gone through background checks. In addition, people who support the facilities and who are involved in the transportation of chemicals add another uncontrollable dimension. When you combine the number of facilities and the number of tankers, trucks, and barges with the number of locations where large quantities of these chemicals are stored, you begin to realize how many large gaps in security are possible.

Computer Security and Cyberthreats to Critical Infrastructure

While the energy and chemical sectors of critical infrastructure of the United State are crucial, there is a common concern that connects all of the 15 mentioned areas of critical infrastructure: computers. All sectors of critical infrastructure rely on computers and networks that can be hacked, stolen, tampered with, and destroyed, thus affecting the lives of millions. Currently the computer systems of critical infrastructure sites as well as major business organizations are now being targeted by individuals who have the ability and training to disrupt critical infrastructure sites.

Attacking computer networks to disrupt the critical areas of our country can be classified as **cyberterrorism**. Cyberterrorism is any premeditated, politically motivated attack against information, computer systems, computer programs, networks, and data that results in violence, disruption of, or damage to noncombatant targets by subnational groups or clandestine agents.

Cyberterrorism is a current and real threat to US businesses. However, most Americans do not realize the threat or fully understand the nature of such computer attacks. IT (information technology) specialists and private security personnel fight and defend thousands of daily attacks upon computers and computer networks while working to recover lost data. The Internet has become a means for organized criminals and terrorists to shut down critical systems, relay information, recruit personnel, and to attack computer networks.[39] According to the US Commission of Critical Infrastructure Protection, possible targets include the banking industry, military installations, power plants, air traffic control centers, and water systems.[40]

It is important to make the clear differentiation between those engaged in cyberterrorism and hacktivists. Hacktivists have political agendas and generally engage in e-mail attacks, hacking and computer break-ins, and the design of computer viruses and worms. A cyberterrorist, on the other hand, engages in computer attacks that result in violence against persons or property, or at least that cause enough harm to generate fear. Attacks that lead to death or bodily injury, explosions, plane crashes, water contamination, or severe economic loss would be examples. In addition, there are Web sites vandalized, services disrupted, data systems sabotaged, viruses and worms launched, and companies harassed and threatened on a regular basis. These cyberattacks are facilitated with easy-to-use and easily available software tools, which are often found free of charge from Web sites on the Internet.[41]

One of the first recorded cyberterrorist attacks was in 1996 when a computer hacker allegedly associated with the white supremacist movement temporarily disabled a Massachusetts ISP and damaged part of the ISP's record-keeping system. The ISP had attempted to stop the hacker from sending out worldwide racist messages under the ISP's name. The hacker signed off with the threat, "You have yet to see true electronic terrorism. This is a promise." Since 1996, attacks have continued with increasing severity.[42]

- In 1998, Spanish protestors bombarded the Institute for Global Communications (IGC) with thousands of bogus e-mail messages. E-mail was tied up and undeliverable to the ISP's users, and support lines were tied up with people who couldn't get their e-mail. The protestors also spammed IGC staff and member accounts, clogged their Web page with bogus credit card orders, and threatened to employ the same tactics against organizations using IGC services. They demanded that IGC stop hosting the Web site for the *Euskal Herria Journal,* a New York-based publication supporting Basque independence. Protestors said IGC supported terrorism because a section on their Web page contained materials on the terrorist group ETA, which claimed responsibility for assassinations of Spanish political and security officials and attacks on military installations. The IGC finally relented and pulled the site because of the "mail bombings."[43]

- In 1998, ethnic Tamil guerrillas swamped Sri Lankan embassies with 800 e-mails a day over a two-week period. The messages read "We are the Internet Black Tigers, and we're doing this to disrupt your communications." Intelligence authorities characterized it as the first known attack by terrorists against a country's computer systems.[44]

- During the Kosovo conflict in 1999, NATO computers were blasted with e-mail bombs and hit with denial-of-service attacks by hacktivists protesting the NATO bombings. In addition, businesses, public organizations, and academic institutes received highly politicized virus-laden e-mails from a range of Eastern European countries, according to reports. Web defacements were also common. After the Chinese Embassy was accidentally bombed in Belgrade, Chinese hacktivists posted messages such as "We won't stop attacking until the war stops!" on US government Web sites.[45]

- Since December 1997, the Electronic Disturbance Theater (EDT) has been conducting Web sit-ins against various sites in support of the Mexican Zapatistas. At a designated time, thousands of protestors point their browsers to a target site using software that floods the target with rapid and repeated download requests. EDT's software has also been used by animal rights groups against organizations said to abuse animals. Electro-hippies, another group of hacktivists, conducted Web sit-ins against the WTO when they met in Seattle in late 1999. These sit-ins all require mass participation to have much effect, and thus are more suited for activists than terrorists.[46]

In financial terms, cyberterrorism can devastate the nation's economy. The February 2000 denial-of-service attacks against Yahoo, CNN, eBay, and other e-commerce Web sites was estimated to have caused over a billion dollars in losses and caused a panic in the e-commerce community, especially for regular customers and clients.[47] Furthermore, cyberterrorists can create chaos and fear in business operations by attacking banking and other financial computer networks. They can also steal information or disrupt the data recovery processes of businesses in order to cause panic or for financial gain.

The greater danger, however, lies in the fear that terrorists and other criminals could attack and penetrate our nation's critical infrastructure computer systems and endanger human lives by disrupting emergency medical services, land and air transportation systems, telecommunications, and utilities. Shutting down a local 9-1-1 emergency response system, military communication system, or electrical power plant would cost businesses billions of dollars and endanger the lives of many in a given area.[48]

In 1998, the Center for Strategic and International Studies issued a report that revealed that cyberterrorists are plotting a number of heinous attacks that if successful could "destabilize and eventually destroy targeted states and societies."[49] The National Strategy to Secure Cyberspace should be part of our overall effort to protect the nation. However, today there are no early detection systems in place to warn of an attack in the United States besides the military and government. In 2007, cyber-terrorists effectively shut down the nation of Estonia in one of the largest cyber attacks ever witnessed. Therefore, it is up to American businesses themselves to begin preparations for cyberattacks.

Why Cyberterrorism?

It is important to understand the complex nature of cyberterrorism in order to put in place measures to prevent future attacks. Cyberterrorism is a cheap method of attack compared to traditional terrorist methods, it requires less physical training, and can be conducted remotely. With a computer and online connection, a computer-savvy terrorist can cause fear among millions and cost American businesses billions It is also an anonymous form of terrorism, with terrorists using created usernames and online nicknames. This makes it very difficult for law enforcement personnel to track these terrorists. Unlike the real physical world, the online world has no physical checkpoints, metal detectors, or body searches. Cyberterrorists are always one step ahead of law enforcement personnel. The diversity and large number of targets make cyberterrorism attractive. Disruption of airlines, government networks, and public utilities can cause major problems. Emergency services and electrical power grids are highly vulnerable because such areas use computer systems that make it impossible to eliminate all potential weaknesses. In the case of the I LOVE YOU virus, cyberterrorism can arguably affect more people than traditional terrorist modalities and generate even more media coverage desired by terrorists. In other words, cyberterrorism is an effective method of attack that produces the desired results.[50]

Criminals and terrorists use cyberspace to facilitate the more traditional methods of terrorism such as bombings or spreading messages of hate. For example, the Web sites of Islamic fundamentalist groups are used to present messages, coordinate members, and recruit young supporters.[51] US troops in Afghanistan have recovered al Qaeda laptops with structural and engineering software containing information on computerized water systems, nuclear power plants, and US and European stadiums.[52] It should be noted that cyberterrorism also has its drawbacks. Unless people are injured, there is less drama and emotional reaction by society, which terrorists are looking to achieve. In terms of danger to human life, the improvised explosive device (IED) truck bomb is arguably much more dangerous than a computer virus. This doesn't mean that the threat of cyberterrorism should be ignored. Currently, more than 120 countries or foreign organizations have or are developing formal programs to create information weapons that can be used to attack and disrupt critical information systems used by the United States.[53]

Attack Methods of Cyberterrorism

There are many types of attacks that all fall under the heading of cyberterrorism. They include computer viruses, denial-of-service attacks, and software vulnerability exploitation.

Computer Viruses

A **computer virus** is a self-replicating computer program that spreads by inserting copies of itself into other executable codes or documents. A computer virus behaves similarly to a biological virus, which spreads by inserting itself into living cells. Extending the analogy, the insertion of a virus into the program is termed an "infection," and the infected file, or executable code that is not part of a file, is called a "host." Viruses are one of the several types of malicious software or malware. In common parlance, the term *virus* is often extended to refer to worms, Trojan horses, and other sorts of malware. Viruses in the literal sense of the word are less common than they used to be, compared to other forms of malware.[54]

While viruses can be intentionally destructive, for example, by destroying data, many other viruses are fairly benign or merely annoying. Some viruses have a delayed payload, often referred to as a bomb. For example, a virus might display a message on a specific day or wait until it has infected a certain number of hosts. A **time bomb** occurs during a particular date or time, and a **logic bomb** occurs when the user of a computer takes an action that triggers the bomb. The predominant negative effect of viruses is their uncontrolled self-reproduction, which wastes or overwhelms computer resources.

Today there are over 60,000 computer viruses in existence, many of which have multiple mutant strains. The rate of virus creation and release has accelerated over the past few years with nearly 250 new and mutated viruses appearing each month. In 2005, we saw the first hacking and virus attacks on cell phones and smart phones with PDAs built in. The most notable occurrence was when a celebrity phone was hacked and the contents of the contact list were taken and used. The year 2006 got off to a bad start with four massive virus attacks in January, including a multiwave attack of seven variants. In February of 2008, we saw the second virus that affected Apple computers running the Mac OS X operating system, further eroding the long-held belief that Mac machines are more impervious to attacks than Microsoft's Windows-based personal computers. Viruses, as with all cyberattacks, are becoming more complex, damaging, and difficult to detect. The frequency of viruses being released is also increasing.[55]

Denial-of-Service (DoS) Attacks

A **denial-of-service attack** is an assault on a computer network that floods it with so many requests or transactions that regular traffic is either slowed or completely interrupted or halted. A distributed denial-of-service (DDoS) attack simultaneously uses multiple preinfected computers to flood a network. Unlike a virus or worm, which can cause severe damage to databases, a denial-of-service attack interrupts network service for some period. The *Washington Post* reported that on October 22, 2002, a DoS attack struck the 13 "root servers" that provide the primary road map for almost all Internet communications worldwide.[56] It caused no slowdowns or outages because of safeguards built into the system, but a longer and more extensive attack could have inflicted serious damage.[57]

Software Vulnerabilities

Cyberattacks have caused billions of dollars in damage and have affected the lives of millions. Recent data indicate several troubling trends. First of all, the numbers of software vulnerabilities that can be exploited are increasing as the demands for more software to be released early rises. **Software vulnerability** refers to the area of software that contains codes that can allow the cyberterrorist to use the software in a malicious fashion. The increasing availability of these information weapons is partially related to certain groups who create attack kits that are sold via the Internet to anyone willing to pay the price. Within the information security industry, there is the widespread belief that an organization in South America has been created and funded with the sole purpose of developing malicious code that takes advantage of vulnerabilities recently uncovered in commercial software. The time from when vulnerability is reported and announced until the first malicious code is discovered is shrinking. The last few announcements of commercial software vulnerability saw the exploitation code released in less than 24 hours—one taking only 17 hours. The time required for the software vendor to create a patch was 8 days.[58]

Controversies in Private Security   In March 2000, Japan's Metropolitan Police Department reported that a software system they had procured to track 150 police vehicles, including unmarked cars, had been developed by the Aum Shinrikyo cult, the same group that gassed the Tokyo subway in 1995, which killed 12 people and injured 6000 more. At the time of the discovery, the cult had received classified tracking data on 115 vehicles. Furthermore, the cult had developed software for at least 80 Japanese firms and 10 government agencies. They had worked as subcontractors to other firms, making it almost impossible for the organizations to know who had developed the software. As subcontractors, the cult could have installed Trojan horses to launch or facilitate cyberterrorist attacks at a later date.[59]

Software companies are highly concerned about their products. A survey of almost four hundred IT professionals conducted for the Business Software Alliance during June 2002 revealed that about half (49%) felt that an attack is likely, and more than half (55%) said the risk of a major cyberattack on the United States has increased since 9/11. The figure jumped to 59% among those respondents who are in charge of their company's computer and Internet security. Seventy-two percent agreed with the statement "There is a gap between the threat of a major cyberattack and the government's ability to defend against it," and the agreement rate rose to 84% among respondents who are most knowledgeable about security.[60]

The book *Black Ice: The Invisible Threat of Cyber-Terror*, published in 2003 and written by *Computerworld* journalist and former intelligence officer Dan Verton, describes the 1997 exercise code-named "Eligible Receiver," conducted by the National Security Agency (NSA). The exercise began when NSA officials instructed a "Red Team" of 35 hackers to attempt to hack into and disrupt US national security systems. They were told to play the part of hackers hired by the North Korean intelligence service, and their primary target was to be the US Pacific Command in Hawaii. They were allowed to penetrate any Pentagon network but were prohibited from breaking any US laws, and they could only use hacking software that could be downloaded freely from the Internet.[61] They started mapping networks and obtaining passwords gained through "brute-force cracking" (a trial-and-error method of decoding encrypted data such as passwords or encryption keys by trying all possible combinations). Often they used simpler tactics such as calling somebody on the telephone, pretending to be a technician or high-ranking official, and asking for the password. The hackers managed to gain access to dozens of critical Pentagon computer systems. Once they entered the systems, they could easily create user accounts, delete existing accounts, reformat hard drives, scramble stored data, or shut systems down. They broke the network defenses with relative ease and did so without being traced or identified by the authorities.[62]

These results shocked the organizers. First, the Red Team had shown that it was possible to break into the US military's command-and-control system in the Pacific and potentially cripple it. Second, the NSA officials who examined the experiment's results found that much of the private business sector infrastructure in the United States could easily be invaded and abused in the same way.[63]

A separate study conducted by the House Government Reform Subcommittee on Technology that reviewed preparedness and vulnerability showed some alarming results. More than half of the federal agencies surveyed received a grade of D or F. The Department of Homeland Security, which has a division devoted to monitoring cybersecurity, received the lowest overall score of the 24 agencies surveyed. Also earning an F was the Justice Department, the agency charged with investigating and prosecuting cases of hacking and other forms of cybercrime. Commenting on these results, Rep. Adam H. Putnam (R-FL), chairman of the House Government Reform Subcommittee on Technology, declared "The threat of cyber-attack is real....The damage that could be inflicted both in terms of financial loss and, potentially, loss of life, is considerable."[64]

According to Symantec, one of the world's corporate leaders in the field of cybersecurity, new vulnerabilities to a cyberattack are being discovered all the time. The company reported that the number of "software holes" (software security flaws that allow malicious hackers to exploit the system) grew by 80% in 2002.[65]

Preparations by Private Business Firms and Critical Infrastructure Points

The increase in the number of attacks continues to climb in the United States. In one minute, there are approximately 54,000 serious computer attacks reported to hackerwatch.org. that computer experts and private security personnel have had to address. Five percent of businesses estimate the cost of systems disruption can be over $5 million an hour, and 60% of businesses do not know how much computer attacks cost them. Only 1% of business continuity plans address cyberattacks, and only 3% address computer viruses. In a recent study conducted by the Computer Crime Research Center, 90% of respondents detected computer security breaches within the last 12 months. For private security employees in the 21st century, the focus ultimately is to learn the continually evolving nature of types of attacks and methods by criminal groups and terrorist organizations. This requires private security personnel to seek continual training on techniques for protecting critical infrastructures' computer systems and for recognizing and disrupting a cyberattack when it occurs.

Private Security in the News   According to the FBI, terrorist groups are increasingly adopting the power of modern communications technology for planning, recruiting, propaganda purposes, enhancing communications, command and control, fund-raising and funds transfer, information gathering, and the like. Computers are used in more than 50% of the crimes committed today.

Experts believe that a significant cyberattack will occur following the 2008 elections. Protecting the United States against cyberbased attacks and high-technology crimes is the number three priority of the FBI.

Ultimately, whether addressing energy, chemicals, or the computer systems that connect to all areas of critical infrastructure, the answer for solving such major security threats requires more than just continual responses by federal and state agencies. The reality is that governmental abilities to click on any part of our nation's critical infrastructure and instantly know its status, any known or suspected threats, and other critical data is still years away. For now, private security personnel must remain on the front line of protecting people. Today, private security guards, alarm systems, gates, video surveillance, and diligent patrolling are the primary methods for protecting critical infrastructure sites. Computers are also now monitored by computer and private security experts for possible cyberattacks and intrusions into computer networks. Any critical infrastructure site must now maintain an alert, well-trained security force that can recognize and react to suspicious activities.

As previously noted, there are currently nearly 1.5 million private security guards working in the United States. Over 28% of this workforce is assigned to protect our critical infrastructure. There are currently no federal requirements to train these private security guards other than at airports and nuclear plants.

A recent report to Congress identified 22 states that do require basic training for licensed security guards, but few specifically require counterterrorism training. State regulations regarding criminal background checks for security guards vary. Despite the recent terrorist attacks on public facilities around the world, 16 states still have no background check regulations for those working at critical infrastructure locations.

Systems for Private Security Personnel to Protect Critical Infrastructure Locations

The task of protecting critical infrastructure locations is extremely daunting. Noted security expert, Kevin Coleman, has offered one of the most sophisticated and advanced methodologies for protecting critical infrastructure locations and computer networks. Known as **scenario-based intelligence analysis** (SBIA), it is a system in which private security personnel can create possible scenarios that could destabilize the security of a location. By developing and creating possible ways for a location to be breached or attacked by criminals or terrorists, private security personnel can then begin an analysis on how such activity could be prevented. Private security personnel are also able to examine the level of sophistication of a possible attack, the costs involved, and most importantly, the overall impact to a critical infrastructure location as well as the impact to society on a larger scale.[66]

Sample Scenario-Based Intelligence Analysis

Scenario Name: Delivery truck infiltration

Sophistication: Low to moderate

Skill Required: Limited

Cost of Attack: Low to moderate

Overall Impact: Moderate to high

Access to Materials: Fairly open

Attack Method: Bomb

Secondary Method: Chemical release (choking agent)

Sample Scenario Abstract for Creation and Use by Private Security Personnel

Terrorist cells plan to attack an industrial facility near a moderately sized city in the United States. The industrial complex selected has two midsized chlorine storage tanks. The terrorists observe the facility and record common deliveries made regularly by multiple vendors. The terrorists plan to hijack one of the delivery vehicles as a mechanism for delivering a bomb inside the plant. Because no one would consider it unusual to see a regular delivery truck or tool supplier truck at an industrial plant, this would create an opportunity to deliver the threat in plain sight.

The terrorists select the tool vendor and lay in wait for the opportunity to take over the vehicle and capture the driver. The terrorists drive the delivery truck to a warehouse where they load the explosive device. They have created a bomb from materials that were easy to obtain.

Once the device is loaded, a terrorist puts on the truck driver's uniform and drives the truck back to the industrial complex. Many delivery companies do not have company photo IDs (counterfeiting an ID is not a difficult task either).

The security guard at the industrial complex sees the vehicle and thinks nothing of it. He or she may even inquire where the normal driver is; however, they would not think anything out of the norm is happening given that the tool vendor's vehicle routinely enters the plant and proceeds to the maintenance building to deliver orders, pick up tools for repair, and present new tools to the maintenance workers.

The truck is driven near the two chlorine storage tanks, the terrorist driver exits and heads upwind via a previously planned escape route, and then, after a few minutes and at a safe distance, he remotely detonates the explosive device via a cell phone. The resulting explosion breaches the tank releasing a toxic cloud of chlorine gas. The operation was simple, quick, and inexpensive with a huge potential for injuries and death. These are all trademarks of a terrorist attack.

Countermeasures

Private security employees can then consider ways in which the specific industrial complex can be guarded and protected. For example, based on the above scenario, planning could be done to equip each truck or vehicle entering or leaving the industrial complex with **GPS or telemetric devices** that provide vehicle location and other operational data. Any deviation from a preauthorized route would automatically trigger an alarm to private security personnel at the industrial complex. The use of this system could provide an almost immediate benefit and reduction in the risk at critical infrastructure locations. In addition, detailed, methodical planning is required if a countermeasure against ideas generated by this system are to be implemented successfully. It would also require a huge increase in communication between the private security personnel and the law enforcement agencies. While not impossible to accomplish, currently there are huge policy and legal issues that impede this from happening. As common citizens, we can only hope that our nation takes the necessary steps to begin implementing widescale protection systems for our critical infrastructure before another terrorist attack occurs.

Thus far, there have been no successful terrorist attacks launched against our critical infrastructure. However, such vital areas ultimately require private security personnel to provide a heightened vigilance and seek new security methods and technology to safeguard our nation's critical infrastructure.

■ Conclusion

The number of new security threats that private security personnel must face in modern times is astounding. Learning specific knowledge regarding the source and nature of such terrorist threats is crucial for private security personnel to perform at a high standard for the sake of their organization or client. Terrorist recognition skills allow private security personnel to be aware of possible attacks before they occur. Understanding the contemporary construction and use of bombs can save lives when an attack or threat is imminent. A thorough understanding of critical US infrastructure helps remind entry-level security employees that they are on the front line of protecting the operating assets of the nation, such as energy, chemicals, and computer systems.

■ Chapter Review

- Private security personnel are on the front line of recognizing terrorist activity at locations in the United States.
- Understanding the nature of bombs gives private security personnel a major advantage when dealing with such a threat.
- Understanding the various types of explosives can help a private security person understand the possible threat they may face in the future.
- Modern bombs can be assembled in a very simple, yet effective manner.
- Private security guards today must be aware of the nature of suicide bomb vests and their destructive power.
- Vehicle-borne improvised explosive devices require private security personnel to engage in a number of key steps to prevent an explosive attack.
- Searching for a bomb at a location is a time-consuming and organized process.
- Critical infrastructure involves 15 vital areas that every person depends on for survival.
- Energy, chemical, and computer sources are vulnerable to damage, theft, or destruction by criminals and terrorists.
- Scenario-based intelligence analysis offer a way for private security personnel to train, prevent, and prepare for attacks on critical infrastructure.

■ Answers to Case Studies

Case Study 1

1. How would you be able to recognize a terrorist approaching the banking center? Private security employees should look for a number of key signs. They should look for repeated attempts to steer clear of private security, walking slowly while glancing side to side, or running in a suspicious manner. They should look for people who are nervous, hesitant, profusely sweating, or mumbling. Suspicious persons may keep one or both hands in their pockets at all times. Notice if they are wearing clothes unsuitable for place or climate. Their clothes may also be significantly bigger than their body.

Detonator   A mini-explosion device that will set off the larger explosion process.

Explosion   The sudden and rapid release of gases into a confined space.

Fragmentation   A quantity of explosive filler placed inside a length of pipe at each end with a piece of time fuse used for detonation.

GPS/Telemetric devices   Devices that provide vehicle location and other operational data.

Improvised Explosive Devices   Homemade bombs made from a variety of materials that are used by criminal and terrorist organizations against a target.

Logic bomb   A type of computer virus that occurs when the user of a computer takes an action that triggers the bomb.

Nitroglycerin   A heavy, oily explosive liquid that is clear to amber in color; brown streaks may appear as the liquid turns brown in time.

Northeast Blackout of 2003   The massive power outage that occurred throughout parts of the northeastern and midwestern United States, and Ontario, Canada on August 14, 2003, which left millions without power.

PETN   Explosive material mixed with different materials to create sheet plastics, which are easily hidden in electrical devices like laptops.

Scenario-Based Intelligence Analysis (SBIA)   A system in which private security personnel can create possible scenarios which could destabilize the security at a location.

Search Team   A designated private security team trained and authorized to search for a bomb.

Secondary Fires   The effect produced by an explosion in which any combustible materials near a source ignite.

Semtex   Explosive material that looks like orange putty that is very common in terrorist attacks as a high velocity plastic explosive.

Software vulnerability   Areas of software that contain code that allows the software to be used in a malicious fashion.

Time bomb   A type of computer virus that occurs during a particular date or time.

Vehicle Borne Improvised Explosive Devices (VBIEDs)   The packing and detonating of explosives into a car or truck for increased mobility and lethality.

Velocity   The most widely acclaimed system for the classification of explosives based on the velocity of explosive material.

Weapons of Mass Destruction (WMD)   Highly destructive and dangerous weapons including chemical, biological, and nuclear weapons.

■ **References**

1. Sommer, D. 2006. *The wheel of terror.* http://www.SurveillanceDetection.biz.

2. Ibid.

3. Ibid.

4. Nacos, B. 2006. *Terrorism and counter-terrorism.* Pearson/Longman. *See also* Spy-Ops, Terrorist recognition training brief. Vol 5. TB 22. http://www.Spy-Ops.com. Griest, P., and S. Mahan. 2003. *Terrorism in perspective.* Thousand Oaks, CA: Sage.

5. Ibid.

6. Ibid.

7. Ibid.

8. Ibid.

9. Ibid.

10. Fay, J. 1994. Getting ready for the bomb in your building. *Security Management,* April. *See also* Jenkins, A. 1991. Bomb threat preparation: Defusing an explosive situation. *Security Management,* November. McCarthy, W., and R. Quigley. 1992. Don't blow it. *Security Management,* March. Seuter, E. 1991. Are you ready? *Security Management,* July. *Learning for life: Law enforcement study on bomb threats.* http://www.learning-for-life.org/exploring/lawenforcement/study/bomb.pdf. Ortmeier, P. J. 2005. *Security management.* Upper Saddle River, NJ: Pearson Prentice Hall.

11. Ibid.

12. Ibid.

13. Ibid.

14. Thurman, J. 2006. *Practical bomb scene investigation.* London: Taylor & Francis Group.

15. *See* note 10.

16. *See* note 10.

17. *See* note 10.

18. *See* note 10.

19. *See* note 4.

20. *See* note 10.

21. *See* note 10.

22. *See* note 10.

23. *See* note 10.

24. *See* note 10.

25. *See* note 10.

26. *See* note 10.

27. *See* note 10.

28. *See* note 10.

29. *See* note 10.

30. *See* note 10.

31. *See* note 10.

32. Spy-Ops. 2006. *Critical infrastructure training brief.* Vol. 10. TB 49. http://www.Spy-Ops.com.

33. Ibid.

34. *The president's critical infrastructure protection board.* http://www.whitehouse.gov/pcipb. *See also* Critical infrastructure protection program. http://cipp.gmu.edu. *Critical infrastructure protection.* http://www.epic.org/security/CIP.

35. Ibid.

36. Ibid.

37. Ibid.

38. Ibid.

39. Coleman, K. 2006. *Cyber-Terrorism* 11(54). http://www.Spy-Ops.com. *See also* Brandon, K. 2002. Hactivists help human rights, bit by byte. *Chicago Tribune.* Nov 21. Hess, P. 2002. *Cyber-terrorism and information war.* New Delhi, India: Anmol. Weimann, G. 2004. *Cyberterrorism: How real is the threat?* Special Report No. 119. United States Institute of Peace.

40. Ibid.

41. Brandon, K. 2002. Hactivists help humans rights, bit by byte. *Chicago Tribune.* Nov 21.

42. Hess, P. 2002. *Cyber-terrorism and information war.* New Delhi, India: Anmol.

43. Ibid.

44. Ibid.

45. Ibid.

46. Ibid.

47. Weimann, G. 2004. *Cyberterrorism: How real is the threat?* Special Report No.119. United States Institute of Peace.

48. Ibid.

49. Center for Strategic and International Studies. Cyber-terrorism. http://www.csis.org/goc/rc/cyber.html.

50. *See* note 47.

51. Denning, D.E. 2000. Cyberterrorism. Testimony before Committee on Armed Services, U.S. House of Representatives. http://www.cs.georgetown.edu/~denning/infosec/cyberterror.html.

52. Ibid.

53. Lewis. Assessing the risks of cyberterrorism, cyber war, and other cyber threats. Center for Strategic and International Studies – Cyber-Terrorism. http://www.csis.org/goc/rc/cyber.html.

54. Institute for the Advanced Study of Information Warfare. http://www.psycom.net/iwar.1.html.

55. Coleman, K. 2006. *Cyber-Terrorism* 11(54). http://www.Spy-Ops.com.

56. *See* note 47.

57. *See* note 47.

58. *See* note 55.

59. *See* note 51.

60. Greenspan, R. 2002. Cyberterrorism concerns IT pros. *Internetnews.com.* August 16.

61. Verton, D. 2003. Black ice. *Computerworld.* August 13.

62. *See* note 47.

63. *See* note 47.

64. *See* note 47.

65. *See* note 55.

66. *See* note 32.

Riots, Domestic Terrorism, and Maritime Security Issues

CHAPTER

9

▶ ▶ OBJECTIVES

- Be aware of private security actions when dealing with demonstrations or riots.
- Become familiar with domestic terrorism.
- Understand the nature of maritime piracy and terrorism.

■ Introduction

As the US faces difficult political and economic times, the potential for an increase in civil insurrection and domestic terrorism is a real and frightening possibility. Likewise the potential for America to be caught off guard during difficult periods can result in a successful attack by an outside group against a vulnerable area of American infrastructure; our domestic port and maritime operations. Private security personnel should be aware of such situations and the nature of handling such matters.

■ Riots and Demonstrations

▶ ▶ CASE STUDY 1

As a private security employee working at a retail location, you are working a shift during the holiday season. A brand new gaming system is being released at the store that very morning. You haven't even finished your cup of coffee when already over a hundred people are lined up at the entrance at 5:00 a.m. After 30 minutes, the crowd appears to become restless. After speaking with the manager of the store, you discover that there are only 45 gaming systems in the entire store.

1. What possible unusual situation may occur at this retail store?
2. What are some common occurrences that could occur at a store?

Private security personnel working at a small or large location may experience a riot or demonstration based upon a number of various causes. The right and freedom of assembly is guaranteed as a matter of constitutional law. However, many localities have placed restrictions and laws in place that require people to seek permits and hearings before gathering in large numbers. In addition, heightened emotions over a product at a retail store, a criminal act that was committed in the area, political activism near a site, a concert, or a sporting event are just some of the flash points that can lead to people assembled in large numbers to demonstrate or riot. As a private security employee, the focus is not on guaranteeing people their assembling rights. Protecting the people, profits, and property of a location is the paramount concern. When large groups of people begin to gather outside and near a location, private security personnel should immediately consider steps to mitigate possible harm and destruction of property. While contacting law enforcement agencies is necessary the minute mass assemblies of people begin to form, private security personnel are still responsible for protecting their client or organization.

> **Word to the Wise**   Retail stores are usually the hardest hit locations during riots or civil disturbances. Hospitals and universities can also suffer major financial losses or injured personnel.

Riots and demonstrations have been a part of human civilization from the beginning. They can occur in difficult political and economic times when large amounts of people are dissatisfied about a matter, or during times when socioeconomic and racial tensions are high. While public-serving law enforcement agencies are the main agents responsible for handling a demonstration, private security personnel must act promptly when appropriate.

Riots and demonstrations are different in substantial ways. A **demonstration** is a gathering of people wishing to express a concern over a particular topic or issue. Demonstrations can take many different forms that don't necessarily involve anger or agitated personnel. However, demonstrations outside of a location can disrupt the normal business of a location and can be escalated towards a more hostile, openly loud, and disruptive event. Depending on the topic, the demonstration can become angry or pose a threat to those near the demonstration. If a demonstration is unexpected, private security should quickly determine what type of group or organization is involved. Local law enforcement agencies should be contacted and a plan should be formulated. If a demonstration has been sought with government approval and licenses, local police may already be in place prior to the demonstration starting.

Private security should first consider the location of the demonstration along with the placement of local law enforcement agencies. The distance and placement of public-serving law enforcement agencies can help determine what possible risks or concerns there will be for private security personnel. A demonstration close to a location may require private security personnel to alert employees of the nature of the demonstration along with possible concerns.[1] The safety and convenience of those entering or leaving a location should be evaluated. Private security personnel should also consider if the location of the demonstration is likely to disrupt normal business operations. For example, if a demonstration is located right across the street from a retail outfit or industrial plant, a meeting between private security personnel and management should take place to discuss a plan to avoid disruptions.[2]

If a location protected by private security employees is being directly demonstrated against by a group, heightened security will be needed. Private security personnel should work directly with management to discuss possible attacks or difficulties that could occur during the normal workday. Sending a representative to speak with the demonstration's leader in order to seek an alternative resolution to the conflict should be considered. As always in this type of situation, law enforcement agencies should be contacted immediately for added assistance and protection.

Compared to a demonstration, a **riot** is a much more dangerous gathering of people. Riots can be characterized as a form of civil disorder in which disorganized groups lash out in a sudden and intense rash of violence, vandalism, or other crime. While individuals may attempt to lead or control a riot, riots are typically chaotic and exhibit herdlike behavior. Riots often occur in reaction to a perceived grievance or from dissent over a situation and may not have originated from a demonstration. It is important for private security personnel to recognize when a situation is moving from an angry demonstration towards a possible riot. Generally, there are three main stages in the development of a riot:[3]

1. Formation—A conglomeration of people with the same common feeling of impending activity forms.
2. Progression—Crowd members lose their individuality and start to function as one unit, united by the actions of leading aggressors. The mob/riot has developed, and the leading aggressors are fueling the crowd into a frenzy and attracting more people.
3. Outbreak—The riot is now engaged in criminal and potentially deadly behavior.

At concerts, sporting events, or any other event in which beer and alcohol have been consumed, the three stages of a riot can occur very quickly. Therefore, it is important for private security personnel to attempt to control the agitators or organizers of a riot and to separate them from the rest of the crowd. A private security officer can often prevent any escalation by enforcing restrictions and removing those individuals engaged in minor infractions if it appears the crowd is swelling towards the formation stage of mob/riot development. In addition, law enforcement officers coming to the scene can be directed by private security personnel to those individuals attempting to stoke the fires of riot.[4] If possible, a private security officer must first try to use persuasion to make an unlawful crowd dissipate before force is used. When force is used, it must be only the degree of force necessary to restore peace and order within the limits of the law and the operating procedures of a client or private security company. [5]

> **Demonstrations vs. Riots**   Demonstrations generally involve groups that have cleared with a government agency the date and time of their protest, their intent, and have secured permits. Although the demonstration or protest is approved by law and protected by the Constitution, it still needs to be monitored in order to prevent the situation from getting out of hand.

For private security personnel working in urban settings, the likelihood of facing a protest or demonstration is much higher based on more people working and living in a much more confined location. As previous riots have demonstrated in American history, it is important for private security personnel to work with law enforcement agencies as well as to be aware of steps that need to be taken when a given situation arises.

■ Domestic Terrorism

▸ ▸ CASE STUDY 2

> As a contract security guard for a major private security company, you are assigned to work at a university patrolling and responding to events on the main university campus. The university has recently invited a controversial speaker to present at a conference regarding the nature of minorities and different religious groups. Law enforcement personnel meet with private security personnel a few days later to inform them that a possible domestic terrorism organization may be planning to protest on campus or commit a violent criminal act.
>
> 1. What is the nature of domestic terrorism in the United States?
> 2. What scenarios would warrant a private security guard to be on heightened alert for a possible domestic terror attack?

Domestic terrorism is a concept that threatens American business and private citizens on a regular basis in the United States. While not always receiving media attention, it is a major focus for security professionals and public-serving law enforcement agencies. The **Oklahoma City Bombing** in 1995 was a major wake-up call that made us realize that attacks by American citizens, as opposed to foreign nationals, are possible. It is now up to private security professionals to lead the way in protecting American lives and property from possible attacks. However, it is important to first learn about the nature of domestic terrorism in the United States.

Oklahoma City Bombing   The Oklahoma City Bombing on April 19, 1995, was aimed at the Alfred P. Murrah Federal Building, which was a major US government office complex in downtown Oklahoma City, Oklahoma. The bombing resulted in 168 lives lost and left over 800 people injured. Until the 9/11 attacks in New York, it was the deadliest act of terrorism on US soil.

Domestic terrorism is loosely defined as terrorist actions originating from persons and influences within a country. It involves the unlawful use, or threatened use, of violence by a group or individual, operating entirely within the United States (or its territories) without foreign direction.[6] The violence is committed against persons or property to intimidate or coerce a government, the civilian population, or any segment thereof, in furtherance of political or social objectives. Throughout the Clinton administration, domestic terrorism was erroneously seen as a greater threat than Islamic terrorism. Counterterrorism and law enforcement professionals agree that it is only a matter of time before another domestic terrorist group eventually exceeds the death and destruction caused by Timothy McVeigh with the Oklahoma City Bombing.

Domestic terrorism has existed since the birth of the United States, although it has been labeled as *terrorism* only in recent years. Unlike Islamic militant terrorism, which is globally focused, well-organized, and well-funded, domestic US terrorist groups are dispersed and fragmented. Of the four most notorious domestic terrorists of recent times, two were lone individuals engaging in terrorism on their own—the Unabomber, Ted Kaczynski, and the antiabortionist, Eric Rudolph, the Olympic Park Bomber. The Oklahoma City bombers Timothy McVeigh and Terry Nichols, however, operated as a team in their terrorist attack.

Right Wing Versus Left Wing Domestic Terrorism Groups

Domestic terrorism has traditionally been broken into two groups, right-wing terror groups and left-wing terror groups. **Right-wing terrorists** are usually driven by mainstream and nonmainstream Christian beliefs, antigovernment ideology, antiabortion beliefs, race, and end-of-time and world-order conspiracy beliefs. There is growing evidence that right-wing **Aryan race groups**, white power organizations often based in Nazi ideology, along with Mexican groups who advocate violence to reclaim Arizona, New Mexico, and California, are now more active than ever before.

Many other militia and cult practices and beliefs also drive right-wing groups. **Left-wing terrorists** are usually driven by anti-Christian beliefs, antigovernment ideals, race, proabortion beliefs, right-wing and other conspiracy beliefs, and are cult practitioners as well. Viewed cynically, the category that most of these groups fall under depends on the political persuasion of the viewer. During the Nixon administration, left-wing groups like the Communist Party, Black Panthers, and various antiwar groups were labeled and investigated. During President Clinton's administration, right-wing groups and militias were targeted for infiltration and investigation.[7]

It is important for private security professionals to realize that there is potential for destruction far greater than the Oklahoma City bombing. The potential for acquiring and using weapons of mass destruction (WMD), attacking a chemical plant or reactor, or bombing a department store is certainly a possibility for domestic terror groups. Without a source of financial support, domestic terror groups are limited in their attack strategies. It is nearly impossible for a domestic group to build a nuclear weapon or obtain high-tech weaponry. However, biological or chemical warfare and mass killing and destruction through shootings or bombings are possible for those committed to waging such actions against targets in the United States. In addition, the Internet has made information sharing easy for those individuals or groups seeking manuals, bombs, and poisons, as well as information for those planning assassinations. Weapons can be purchased online or negotiated between individuals in the US using the Internet. Biological warfare is within the realm of most college science majors.

During the 1980s, Americans living in Wasco County, Oregon, experienced a biological attack from followers of Bhagwan Shree Rajneesh. The Rajneeshees were a religiously motivated commune who believed in beauty, love, and guiltless sex. They moved into Wasco County, Oregon, in 1981 and began a bid to take over political and economic control of the county. Political correctness in the FBI and other government agencies had begun by then, and just like with the Islamists today, the FBI failed to investigate a growing number of complaints and suspicions concerning the Rajneeshees and some of their methods. When hundreds of the county's residents came down with severe food poisoning, the Rajneeshees' compound was raided, and a full-blown biological weapons lab was found. There were numerous strains of virulent bacteria found along with sophisticated lab equipment and detailed records of tests used to make weapons out of various biological agents.[8] Further investigation found the cult had bugged city government offices, local hotels, and had carried out surveillance on local citizens. They had a "hit list" of political leaders and citizens to eliminate. In short, a group had waged warfare on a county.

In 1995, when followers of Aum Shinrikyo launched a sarin gas attack on a Tokyo subway, the FBI found that the group had offices in downtown Manhattan and that law enforcement at all levels were completely unaware of their presence.

Special Interest Terrorism

Special interest terrorism differs from traditional right-wing and left-wing terrorism in that extremist special interest groups seek to resolve specific issues through **activism**, involvement in action to bring about change; be it social, political, environmental, or other change. This action is in support of or opposition to one side of a controversial argument and is not designed to effect widespread political change. Generally, activist groups engage in activities that are protected by constitutional guarantees of free speech and assembly. They become special interest terrorist groups, and law enforcement becomes involved, when the groups conduct acts of politically motivated violence to force segments of society, including the general public, to change attitudes about issues considered important to their causes. These groups occupy the extreme fringes of animal rights, prolife, environmental, antinuclear, and other movements.

One of the first of these forms of domestic terror groups is the **Earth First** movement, which began in 1979. Formed as a disaffected radical environmental group, the group began perpertrating more militant acts by 1984, such as the insertion of metal or ceramic spikes in trees in an effort to damage saws used by logging companies.

Earth Liberation Front and the Animal Liberation Front

Among the active terror groups operating within the United States today, the **Earth Liberation Front (ELF)** and the **Animal Liberation Front (ALF)** are possibly the most dangerous. The ELF is the name for anonymous and autonomous individuals or groups that, according to the now defunct *Earth Liberation Front Press* office, use "economic sabotage and guerrilla warfare to stop the exploitation and destruction of the natural environment in the United States, Canada, and the United Kingdom." Founded in the United Kingdom, ELF members say their organization is an eco-defense group dedicated to taking the profit motive out of environmental destruction by targeting and causing economic damage to businesses through the use of direct action. The ELF was classified as the top domestic terror threat in the United States by the FBI in March 2001. The ELF's guidelines for members require that individuals or groups acting on its behalf "take all necessary precautions against harming any animal including humans." Their techniques involve destruction of property that they believe is being used to injure animals, people, or the environment. These activities are sometimes called *ecotage*, and there are marked differences between their actions in the United States and in the United Kingdom.[9]

The Animal Liberation Front (ALF) is a name used internationally by members of the organization who oppose any group or business that abuses, destroys, or experiments on animals for profit. The ALF is considered a terrorist group whose purpose is to bring about social and political change through the use of force and violence. This includes stealing animals from laboratories or fur farms, and destroying facilities involved in animal testing and other animal-based industries. The ALF activists have engaged in a steadily growing campaign of illegal activity against fur companies, mink farms, restaurants, and animal research laboratories. Estimates of damage and destruction in the United States claimed by the ALF during the past ten years, as compiled by national organizations such as the Fur Commission and the National Association for Biomedical Research (NABR), are more than $45 million.[10]

In 1993, the ELF was listed for the first time along with the ALF in a communiqué declaring solidarity in actions between the two groups in committing criminal activity for their causes. The ALF and the ELF have jointly claimed credit for several raids including a November 1997 attack on the Bureau of Land Management wild horse corrals near Burns, Oregon, where arson destroyed the entire complex resulting in damages in excess of $450,000. The June 1998 arson attack of a US Department of Agriculture Animal Damage Control building near Olympia, Washington, resulted in damages exceeding $2 million. The ELF claimed sole credit for the October 1998 arson attack of a Vail, Colorado, ski facility in which four ski lifts, a restaurant, a picnic facility, and a utility building were destroyed. Damage exceeded $12 million. Other arsons in Oregon, New York, Washington, Michigan, and Indiana have also been claimed by the ELF. Recently, the ELF has claimed responsibility for attacks on genetically engineered crops and trees.

The FBI estimates that the ALF and ELF have committed more than 600 criminal acts in the United States since 1996, resulting in damages in excess of $43 million to the business community. In light of recent pollution scandals and dog fighting cases surfacing in American news media, there are likely to be an increase in the number of attacks by these two organizations.

Countermeasures for Private Security Personnel

Private security personnel have to consistently be aware of the activities of their organization or their client that may incur a response by domestic terror organizations. In addition, being aware of the presence of any organizations on a local level that may engage in criminal activity is important in developing and implementing security plans to protect specific facilities, especially those that involve critical infrastructure. In addition, private security personnel should engage in the practice of domestic terrorism awareness by noting possible signs of domestic terrorist activity. Such signs of domestic terror activity in a given area include the following:

1. Someone bragging or talking about plans to harm citizens using violent attacks, or who claims membership in a terrorist organization that espouses killing innocent people

2. Suspicious packages, luggage, or mail that has been abandoned in a crowded place, such as an office building, airport, school, or shopping center

3. A suspicious letter or package that arrives in the mail or by UPS or FedEx

4. Someone suspiciously entering or exiting a secured, nonpublic area near a train or a bus depot, airport, tunnel, bridge, government building, or tourist attraction

5. Any type of activity or circumstance that seems frightening or unusual within the normal routines of your neighborhood, community, and workplace

6. Someone unfamiliar loitering in a parking lot, government building, or around a school or playground

7. Someone using or threatening to use a gun or other weapon, place a bomb, or release a poisonous substance into the air, water, or food supply

8. Strange odors, smoke, fire, or an explosion

9. Someone who is relentless in searching for information about bombs, weapons, biological agents, or tactics of war

10. Anything that looks out of place including abandoned vehicles

It is also important that any signs or possible indications of domestic terror activity should immediately be communicated to law enforcement agencies as soon as possible.[11]

As many private security personnel are realizing today, the threat of violence or harm to people and property can occur from US citizens who are engaging in their own private war. It is therefore paramount for private security personnel to stay aware of news developments about such organizations, cooperate and share information with law enforcement agencies, and seek continual advanced training in protecting locations from possible domestic terror attacks.

■ Maritime Piracy and Terrorism

▶ ▶ CASE STUDY 3

You are a private security employee assigned to protect a major shipping vessel that is transporting millions of dollars of merchandise from Southeast Asia to California. While at sea off the coast of Indonesia, you receive word from the captain to report to the bridge. Once arriving at the bridge, you are informed that the ship is under attack from maritime pirates or possibly maritime terrorists who are firing on the vessel from their own small water craft.

1. What steps should be taken to protect the ship and its crew?

2. What criminal activity will maritime pirates or terrorists engage in if they can board the vessel?

One of the oldest criminal professions has made a deadly comeback in recent years. Since the fall of the USSR and the end of the Cold War, piracy has gotten out of control. Both the US and Russian navies, which used to control the high seas, have reduced their naval forces by 50% and the rate of maritime piracy has skyrocketed. Three centuries after pirates such as Blackbeard terrorized shipping and domestic security, new bands of modern marauders have begun to terrorize the high seas both for profit and for terrorist objectives. Modern maritime pirates operate beyond the reach of the law in key locations that can affect the security of nations around the world as well as the world economy. For private security, it is now one of the most demanding positions.

What Is Maritime Piracy?

Maritime piracy, according to the United Nations Convention on the Law of the Sea (UNCLOS) of 1982, consists of any criminal acts of violence, detention, or depredation committed for private ends by the crew or the passengers of a private ship that is directed on the high seas against another ship, aircraft, or against persons or property aboard a ship. Piracy can also be committed against a ship, aircraft, persons, or property in a place outside the jurisdiction of any state.[12]

Through modern technology, many of the traditional hazards of shipping have been neutralized. Ships today are bigger, safer, faster, and all but impervious to most storms. International waters have been charted and well traveled, and satellite communications are used to locate ships. However, the threat of piracy still remains and is growing.

Because of its vast size, the ocean allows a large area for pirates to be kings of their own domain. Supertankers, commercial cruise lines, yachts, and personal crafts face daily attacks. If such attacks occurred on land on a daily basis, the public outcry would be deafening.[13]

In particular, merchant shipping, the lowest hanging fruit of world commerce, is at the mercy of the wild frontier of the sea, which offers almost no defenses. Only 10% of maritime piracy cases are ever reported by companies when a ship has been attacked. Therefore an annual report of over 300 attacks could reflect over 3000 attacks at sea. If pirates rob a merchant vessel, steal $1,000,000 in cargo, and kill the entire crew, it is likely that the public will never hear about it. Merchant ships that avoid one pirate attack but fear additional attacks are forced to reroute, use more fuel, and face increased insurance and security costs, which, in turn, will result in higher costs for goods to be purchased by consumers. Add to this equation that most merchant and transport ships, which are the size of the Chrysler building in New York, often have no armed guards and little security. An insider working on the ship can also diminish any security protocols that are in place on a merchant ship.[14]

At Sea You Are Alone

Smaller developing nations can't defend against pirate attacks occurring within their jurisdiction. Local authorities in areas such as Malaysia and Indonesia are not equipped with the technology and resources to combat maritime pirates. While Singapore and Malaysia have increased their forces, other countries like Indonesia need help in curtailing pirate activities. Indonesia has a navy with 170 vessels, one-third of which are not operable and cannot be used to combat maritime piracy. Pirates in contrast are armed to the teeth with the latest and best weaponry and equipment.[15]

Issues of jurisdiction and response also play a major role. When a ship is attacked, confusion arises as to who is responsible for fighting the pirates. The country of origin of the vessel, the nationality of the owners of the vessel, and the nationality of the nearby waters are all complicating issues that lead to a stagnant response when ships come under attack. Only 1% of maritime pirates ever get caught. and even when they are the result is likely to yield few results. It has taken over thirty years for neighboring countries at risk for pirate attacks to allow one another entry into sovereign waters to chase pirates. Therefore if Malaysia catches pirates that committed attacks in Indonesia, it is questionable whether they will be extradited or held accountable for their activities.[16]

Pirate Centers

World geography has allowed pirates to influence the security and economics of world powers. Pirate attacks occur frequently in the Strait of Malacca, which is the shortest route from Southeast Asia to Europe, the Gulf of Hormuz, Gibraltar, the Panama Canal, and the Gulf of Suez. The following is a list of major pirate centers:[17]

- Philippines
- Indonesia
- Somalia
- Nigeria
- Brazil
- Columbia

At any given moment, there are some 500 vessels pushing through these areas. Parts of these areas are no more than half a mile from one shore to another. In the Strait of Malacca, in particular, 25% of all commercial sea trade and 50% of oil shipments move through this area. The Gulf of Hormuz has over 25% of the world's oil moving through its waters. A major pirate attack in such areas can affect the availability of resources to foreign nations, even if it is not reported.[18] Piracy and hijackings of ships costs world shipping and industry around $16–$25 billion a year.

Methods of Attack

Pirates from local villages attack with the latest weaponry and best equipment. Most pirate attacks occur at night from 1:00–6:00 a.m. while the crew is asleep. The pirates are usually organized along gang lines named after the leader, like the Peter Hong gang, for example. Generally, pirates attack from behind a ship or may surround a ship with numerous smaller pirate boats in a sophisticated military attack. They take over the bridge, and then seek out the captain. Within minutes of boarding a ship, pirates go after the safe, crew, and cargo. At night, barefoot pirates hoist themselves over the sides of yachts, demanding TVs, stereos, and clothes. They will climb over the sides of oil tankers, holding guards at knifepoint and demand a safe be opened. Torture is also used to achieve results.[19]

Phantom Ships

Pirates with automatic weapons begin by overtaking a crew, usually killing them as they hijack a ship, then they quickly repaint and rename the vessel. They unload and sell the haul, which could be worth millions of dollars and then con unsuspecting shippers at the new ports into giving them new cargoes that never make it where they are intended to go. By the time the shipper has realized there is a problem, the "phantom" ship has been renamed, repainted, and has new registration papers. Hundreds of ships disappear this way every year. According to Andrew Linington of the UK Maritime Union, "The number of attacks on ships is staggering; by the end of the 1990s it was about 500 attacks a year. And that's just the tip of the iceberg. Conventional wisdom holds that the real number of attacks is at least four times more than what's reported."[20]

Technology allows merchant ships to be at risk via information sharing. Pirates armed with palm pilots and laptops can obtain the manifest of a ship, know the cargo and destination, and track a ship with GPS imagery and tracking capabilities. In terms of hideouts, pirates can hide on the island of their choice with a small craft. Indonesia alone has over 17,000 islands in which pirates can hide. With a small craft, a local villager in a key pirate area can rob a ship once and make more money and profit than they would ever make in their entire lifetime.[21]

It is not uncommon for pirates to pose as foreign military or law enforcement groups that get close and then attack. A merchant ship captain may think the ship radioing them with proper authorization codes is not a threat. It is also important to understand that maritime pirates change operations to fit the environment.

As in the case of the Barbary pirates, kidnapping has also now become a profitable business venture for pirates. Corporations are now paying on average $50,000 for the return of the captain and chief engineer of a merchant vessel. Pirates steal paperwork from the business so they have contact information to send kidnapping demands. Negotiations between businesses and pirates generally take three to four days. Once companies pay, the hostages are released two to three days later. Most of the kidnappings are not reported to local authorities. Businesses, particularly shipping companies, do not like to admit any kidnapping ever took place.[22]

The Affluent at Risk

International travel by sea for the wealthy members of society has become commonplace.

Some of the most common purchases for the affluent are yachts and custom luxury seagoing vessels. New boat sales were up over 20% in 2004, and custom boat building is up over 14%. These ocean-going vessels provide an escape for the affluent from the pressures of society. They provide quiet, remote places where business can be discussed in a peaceful setting outside of the office. However, the calmness and remoteness of the vast sea creates an illusion of safety. New statistics indicate that the number of pirate attacks worldwide has tripled in the past decade. For the affluent, the potential for the entire crew and passengers aboard a ship to be killed or held for ransom by organized crime syndicates or local pirate gangs is high. Affluent sea goers who survive a pirate attack and report it to the authorities of the nearest jurisdiction may discover that law enforcement personnel, officials, and port workers are involved in the attack and distribution of wealth. Grossly underpaid maritime security personnel have also begun to enter the business; many are complicit, and some are actively involved in attacks. For the affluent, it is recommended that private security personnel familiar with sea-going attacks by pirates and terrorists be aboard to protect the crew and passengers of a yacht or custom luxury ship.

Private Security In the News In 1998, the merchant vessel *Chang-Sun* in the South China Sea heading to Malaysia with a crew of 23 people was stopped by uniformed customs officials off of Taiwan. The "customs officials" killed each member of the crew and threw their bodies into the sea. The Chinese government moved quickly to raid Chinese pirate havens, and arrested 38 people involved directly or in support roles to pirates. Thirteen pirates were promptly executed and, overnight, pirates began avoiding China.

Security Precautions

As a private security guard assigned to a ship, a pirate attack can either turn into a moment of quick action and safety for all aboard or into a quick panic. Even a private security guard without nautical experience can offer some information to assist and guide the captain and crew of a ship. The following is a list of suggestions for the crew of a ship:

- Captains should take evasive action with the vessel to dodge the pirate ship or make fast turns at higher speed to create wakes that may disrupt the smaller pirate vessel.
- Sound an alarm and wake the crew.
- Turn on the lights of the boat.
- Use fire hoses to repel ships and boarders.

Private security guards can also walk along a vessel where they are visable from other ships in preparation for a future attack. If one ship looks ready for pirates and another target does not, then the least prepared ship becomes the new target. It is important for private security personnel to seek out up-to-date intelligence on pirate activity and to train and drill crew members in responding to a pirate attack. Locking a ship down and locking the crew in their rooms can prove to be an invitation for disaster.

How Far Do You Take Defense?

One of the most controversial issues involves allowing crew members and private security personnel to possess weapons aboard a ship. Weapons aboard ships raise major legal issues. International law forbids the possession and use of weapons aboard ships when traveling from jurisdiction to jurisdiction without informing the local authorities about weapons on board.

However, when faced with gunfire, the reality is that a crew may want to fight fire with fire. It is also important to realize that the cargo of a ship (such as liquid nitrogen) may require that access and use of weapons is restricted to the trained private security group in the event of a pirate attack. Most seafarers do not have marksmanship training nor have they experienced the stress of a shoot-to-kill attack.

A security expert must question whether seafarers can handle pirates. A small personal vessel may face 4 to 10 pirates. A major merchant ship may be attacked by upwards of 70 or more pirates with automatic weapons and military training. Three or four crew members are not enough to handle such a large assault. Therefore, private security firms and professional security agencies are more suited to the special needs of ships.

Currently, it costs anywhere from $20,000 to $100,000 for a security firm to escort a ship through a location such as the Malacca Straits. Most companies balk at the idea of such costs. Privately hired security personnel fall under the Law of Asian Nations as private citizens. However, the reality in terms of the response of law enforcement is the old saying "crime ends at the water." No cruise ship will admit armed guards are present on current vessels as it is considered bad business practice and would scare passengers.

Controversies in Private Security   The possession of weapons by private security personnel poses a major legal issue that warrants a further discussion of maritime law. The nationality of ships is governed by the United Nations Convention on the Law of the Sea. Under international law, each state may determine for itself the conditions on which it will grant its nationality.

The basic principle under customary international law is that only the flag state is entitled to exercise jurisdiction over a ship or yacht on the high seas. Therefore, there is no legal prohibition on having firearms onboard on the high seas when a ship is in its own territorial waters provided all laws and restrictions are obeyed.

However, when a ship from one country enters the waters of another country, a legal problem emerges. Although many ships as a matter of safety (especially yachts) carry weapons, most countries do prohibit the entry of ships carrying firearms into their jurisdiction unless they declare them on arrival and they are suitably secured onboard and sealed during a port stop. Generally, carrying weapons is trouble-free as a matter of practical application. However, keep in mind the following factors that private security employees should consider:

- Location where your ship is registered and where it is moored
- Countries you are planning to travel to and from
- Type of firearm you intend to carry

If private security personnel defend themselves from pirate attacks (especially with assault weapons) and then later engage with local law enforcement from a foreign government for assistance, they discover the hard way that they are in violation of the specific nation's code on the use and containment of weapons and can even suffer fines and punishment. Also, the nature of the type of vessel, especially a ship like a liquefied natural gas (LNG) carrier, makes weapons aboard an additional risk based on the nature of the cargo.

Maritime Terrorism

While commercial aviation has seen major security changes, the maritime industry is still the soft underbelly of US security preparedness. The attack on the *USS Cole* on October 12, 2000, is known by most experts, but many do not realize that al Qaeda attacked the *USS Sullivan* earlier that year. In January, 2000, al Qaeda attempted to ram a boat loaded with explosives into the *USS Sullivan* in Yemen waters. The attack failed only because the boat sank under the weight of its lethal payload. After this initial failure, al Qaeda suicide bombers in a speedboat packed with explosives blew a hole in the *USS Cole*, killing 17 sailors.[23]

In October, 2002, an explosives-laden boat hit the French oil tanker *Limburg* off the coast of Yemen. In February, 2004, the southern Philippines-based Abu Sayyaf terrorist group claimed responsibility for an explosion on a large ferry that killed at least 100 people.[24] In June, 2002, the Moroccan government arrested a group of al Qaeda operatives suspected of plotting raids on British and US tankers passing through the Strait of Gibraltar. In fact, since September 11, 2001, strikes on oil targets have become almost routine. In October, 2001, Tamil Tiger separatists carried out a coordinated suicide attack by five boats on an oil tanker off of northern Sri Lanka. Oil facilities in Nigeria, the United States' fifth-largest oil supplier, have undergone numerous attacks. In April, 2004, suicide bombers in three boats blew themselves up in and around the Basra terminal zone, one of the most heavily guarded facilities of its kind in the world.[25]

Maritime Ships Used as Floating Explosives

Terrorists seek the biggest bang for their buck when it comes to causing a major incident. Al Qaeda or another terrorist organization could easily seize a ship and crash it into a supertanker. The more frightening scenario would be a ship hijacked and used as a floating improvised explosive device.

When considering the likelihood of a ship being hijacked for later use as a floating bomb, a number of key factors must be considered both by government agencies and security professionals involved in the safety of the ship. The carrying capacity of the vessel along with the sensitive nature of its cargo must be examined when contemplating the possibility of an actual impact on a facility or port.

In a visit to Malaysia in 2005, Vice Admiral Terry Cross of the US Coast Guard told participating media groups that the vulnerability of merchant shipping in the Malacca Straits could "alert terrorists to the opportunities for seizing oil tankers" and that "these could be used as floating bombs."[26] Merchant shipping carrying hazardous materials could also pose a major threat. The 1289-ton *MT Tri Samudra* was boarded by pirates in the Malacca Straits. The *Tri Samudra* is a chemical tanker that was carrying a full cargo of flammable petrochemical products when it was hijacked. The regional manager of the International Maritime Bureau was quoted as saying: "This is exactly the type of tanker that terrorists would likely use to attack a shore-based port or other facility."[27]

If the vessel chosen was an oil tanker carrying crude oil or petroleum products, its explosive capability would depend on whether the vessel had a full load in its hold and the nature of the petroleum products. Crude oil itself is difficult to ignite; its vapor, however, which may remain in the tanks after the vessel has unloaded its cargo, is more easily ignited. Localized fires or oil spills resulting from an attack are the likely concerns for port security professionals.[28] Merchant ships containing chemical products have unique safeguards that are not found on most oil tankers. The chemical vessels maintain space between tank walls to prevent incompatible cargos from coming into contact with each other.[29] Such vessels, however, can be subjected to sabotage by crew members who are actually terrorist operatives.

Liquefied natural gas (LNG) carrier ships and their potential role in a scenario of this kind have probably received the most attention in recent years. In its liquid state, natural gas is not explosive, and it is in this form that it is shipped in large quantities via refrigerated tankers. Once in the open air, however, LNG quickly evaporates and forms a highly combustible visible cloud. It has been reported that, if ignited, the resulting fire could be hot enough to melt steel at a distance of 1200 feet, and could also result in second-degree burns on exposed skin a mile away.[30] A fire of this magnitude would be impossible to extinguish. It would burn until all its fuel was spent.

A liquid nitrogen gas shipping vessel could be hijacked, and once in a port and awaiting the harbor pilot, it could be put on autopilot and made to crash. A conventional explosion onboard the vessel could be created as the ship crashed into the target. If powerful enough, this could rupture the hull and cause the gas to escape. The force required to breach the hull and tank, however, would almost certainly cause a fire at the tank location which would ignite the gas as it escaped rather than causing a cloud of fire or plume.

Such a release of 33 million gallons of fluid gas would result in thousands of deaths, the equivalent of a small nuclear device going off. Singapore's Foreign Minister, George Yeo, stated in a speech given to the ASEAN Regional Forum on July 29, 2005: "Terrorists could hijack a liquefied natural gas tanker and blow it up in Singapore harbor. Singapore, of course, would be devastated. But the impact on global trade would also be severe and incalculable."[31]

Additional Maritime Terrorism Scenarios

Ship Sunk to Block the Straits of Malacca. The narrowest point of the Malacca Straits is at One Fathom Bank, which has a width of 0.6 nautical miles. Singapore's major broadsheet newspaper, the *Straits Times* printed on March 27, 2004, noted that "If terrorists want to mount a maritime strike here [Southeast Asia], sinking a ship in the Malacca Straits is the likely attack of choice." Any blocking of the major sea lanes in this region of the world would result in major economic havoc upon the American and Western European economies."[32] This attack is unlikely. Although the narrowest point of the marked channel is 0.6 nautical miles, a ship sunk in this area would not cripple shipping lanes. Merchant ships would continue to use the waterway by simply navigating around the sunken vessel.

Missile Launched at Aircraft from Vessel. It is possible for terrorists to launch a surface-to-air missile (SAM) purchased on the black market from a ship or shore location to bring down a commercial airliner or to attack another ship with incendiary cargo. SAMs can be purchased on the black market for a starting price of $10,000 and have a range that put aircraft that are landing or in a holding pattern waiting to land well within their targeting capability.[33] In Asia, the missile could be launched from one of the many hundreds of small vessels transiting the Singapore Straits. Short of inspecting the contents of every ship that passes though the Singapore Straits, law enforcement agencies of different jurisdictions can do very little to reduce this particular threat. Private security forces for a company are in a much better position to prevent such an attack in this possible scenario.

The threat of maritime piracy is one that will continue to grow and affect the safety, economy, and security of nations. A greater understanding of this least known area of terrorism by private security personnel will help prepare both seafarers and law enforcement personnel for threats on the high seas.

Private Security in the News

- Of the 450 boats that fled from Vietnam to Thailand in 1981, over 75% of them had been raided by pirates. Over 600 people were killed, and over 600 people were raped.
- There were 445 reported cases of piracy attacks in the Malacca Strait in 2003.
- At least 400 people were murdered or captured from ships in the Malacca Strait in 2004.
- November 2, 2006, the *Seaborne Spirit* cruise ship with 151 passengers going from Egypt to Kenya was attacked at 5:30 a.m. by Somali pirates with automatic rifles and RPGs. Luckily, the RPGs didn't detonate and the captain was able to deploy an LRAD (long-range acoustical device) that deafened the pirates with sound while he took evasive action to escape the pirates.[34]

■ Conclusion

Preparation and training for demonstrations and riots can save millions of dollars and prevent injuries from occurring to employees or guests of a business. Awareness of domestic terror groups that could strike American businesses is important for those wishing to work in the private security field. Likewise, the crucial nature of maritime shipping now requires private security personnel to be aware of the rigorous and often unreported nature of piracy and terrorism in the maritime shipping industry.

■ Chapter Review

- Demonstrations require private security personnel to be aware of possible disruptions to a business or organization.
- Domestic terrorist organizations operate and attack targets within the United States.
- Organizations such as the ELF and ALF target businesses for criminal activity and cause millions in damages.
- Private security employees must engage in specific countermeasures when terrorism signs are present to prevent domestic terrorism from occurring at specific locations.
- Maritime piracy and terrorism is a major threat to the security of American businesses.
- Private security personnel can assist a captain and crew when under attack by pirates or terrorists at sea.
- Being armed on a ship creates a number of possible legal and safety issues.

■ Answers to Case Studies

Case Study 1

1. What possible unusual situation may occur at this retail store? Based on the time of day, season, or demand for an item that not every retail customer will receive, the possibility of a small riot or mob could develop. Private security personnel should consider taking steps in conjunction with employees to ensure, in an organized fashion, that people can receive the items they desire without being pushed or trampled. In addition, direct communication with the crowd to diffuse anger may be an option. Making people aware of the reality of the shortage of the item but also providing them with information on when they can expect the next shipment may help ease some of the tension in the crowd.

2. What are some common occurrences that could occur at a store? Depending on the nature of the store or location, a riot or demonstration in front or near a store is always possible.

Case Study 2

1. What is the nature of domestic terrorism in the United States? While many Americans fear an attack by Islamic militant groups, numerous domestic terror groups operate within the United States. Right-wing, left-wing, environmental, racial, and animal rights organizations and individuals engage in criminal activity against American businesses and government locations.

2. What scenarios would warrant a private security guard to be on heightened alert for a possible domestic terror attack? Suspicious activity such as a suspicious letter or package that arrives in the mail, someone suspiciously entering or exiting a secured nonpublic area, any type of activity or circumstance that seems frightening or unusual within the normal routines of the workplace, or someone unfamiliar loitering in a parking lot of an area are just some of the possible signs that a heightened private security response is required. Also, unusual activity of employees at a location may require heightened security or an investigation.

Case Study 3

1. What steps should be taken to protect the ship and its crew? Private security employees should consider advising the captain to increase the speed of the ship and take evasive action. Often, the wake caused by a large, fast moving ship can sink or turn a smaller pirate vessel. An alarm should be sounded and the crew awoken. All lights of a vessel should be turned on along with any fire hoses or security technology devices used against attackers.

2. What criminal activity will maritime pirates or terrorists engage in if they can board the vessel? Pirates are likely to assault the crew, rob them of possessions, steal whatever is available in a safe or the cargo hold, then leave. They may take key members of the crew such as the engineer or captain hostage. They also may kill everyone aboard or torture individuals for information. Terrorists may steal information about a ship or may in fact target a ship with weapons in order to sink it.

■ Key Terms

Activism   Involvement in actions to bring about change, be it social, political, environmental, or other type.

Animal Liberation Front (ALF)   The name used internationally by an organization whose members engage in terrorist activity to oppose the use of animals as property or resources, or used for capitalist profit and experimentation.

Aryan Race Groups   White power organizations often based in Nazi ideology.

Demonstration   A gathering of people to express a concern over a particular topic or issue.

Domestic terrorism   Terrorist actions originating from persons and influences within the country they are targeting. It involves the unlawful use, or threatened use, of violence by a group or individual based and operating entirely within the target country or its territories without foreign direction.

Earth First   An organization that began in the 1980s as a disaffected radical environmental group that is now much more militant and dangerous.

Earth Liberation Front (ELF)   The name of a group that uses guerrilla warfare to stop the exploitation and destruction of the natural environment in the United States, Canada, and the United Kingdom.

Left-Wing terrorists   Terrorist groups that are usually driven by anti-Christian, anti-government, race, pro-abortion, right wing and other conspiracy beliefs, and are also cult practitioners.

Maritime piracy   Criminal acts of violence, detention, or depredation committed for private ends by the crew or the passengers of a private ship directed on the high seas against another ship, aircraft, or against persons or property aboard a ship.

Oklahoma City Bombing   The bombing on April 19, 1995 of the Alfred P. Murrah Federal Building that resulted in 168 lives lost and left over 800 people injured, was the deadliest act of terrorism on US soil until the 9/11 attacks.

Right Wing terrorists   Terrorists driven by mainstream and non-mainstream Christian beliefs, anti-government ideology, anti-abortion beliefs, race, end-of-time and world-order conspiracy beliefs.

Riot   A form of civil disorder with disorganized groups lashing out in a sudden and intense rash of violence, vandalism, or other crimes.

■ References

1. Herman, M. 1994. When strikes turn violent, somebody's going to pay. *Security Concepts*. *See also* Mallory, J. 1990. Demonstrations. *Law and Order*, September. Kouri, J. 1992. A system for safe strikes. *Security Management*, September. Oliver, C. 1993. Building the BEL system. *Security Management*, May.
2. Ibid.
3. Ibid.
4. Ibid.
5. Ibid.

6. Nacos, B. 2006. *Terrorism and counter-terrorism*. Pearson/Longman. *See also* Spy-Ops. Domestic terrorism. Vol 4. TB 19. http://www.Spy-Ops.com. Griest, P., and S. Mahan. 2003. *Terrorism in perspective*. Thousand Oaks, CA: Sage.

7. Ibid.

8. Ibid.

9. Griest, P., and S. Mahan. 2003. *Terrorism in perspective*. Thousand Oaks, CA: Sage. *See also* FBI report on ALF/ELF. http://www.fbi.gov/congress/congress02/jarboe021202.htm. CNN report on ALF/ELF. http://www.cnn.com/2005/US/05/19/domestic.terrorism/index.html.

10. Ibid.

11. *See* note 6.

12. United Nations. 1982. Convention on the Law of the Sea (UNCLOS) of 1982.

13. Burnett, J. S. 2003. *Dangerous waters: Modern piracy and terror on the high seas*. New York: Plume.

14. Koknar, A. 2004. Terror on the high seas. *Security Management* 48(6):75–81.

15. Chalk, P. 1998. Contemporary maritime piracy in Southeast Asia. *Studies in Conflict & Terrorism* 21(1).

16. *See* note 13.

17. ICC Commercial Crime Services. 2007. IMB's Piracy Reporting Centre to ships in Atlantic, Indian and Pacific Ocean regions on the SafetyNET service of Inmarsat-C from 7 January to 13 February 2007. http://www.icc-ccs.org/prc/piracyreport.php.

18. Elegant, S., and K. Sepetang. 2004. Dire straits. *Time*. Nov. 29. http://www.time.com/time/magazine/article/0,9171,501041206-832306,00.html.

19. Rossi, M. 2002. *What every American should know about who's really running the world*. New York: Plume.

20. Ibid.

21. *See* note 18.

22. *See* note 13.

23. *See* note 18.

24. Banlaoi, R. C. 2005. Maritime terrorism in Southeast Asia: The Abu Sayyaf threat. *Naval War College Review*, Autumn.

25. Luft, G., and A. Korin. 2004. Terrorism goes to sea. *Foreign Affairs*, November/December.

26. Ibid.

27. Raymond, C. 2006. Maritime terrorism in Southeast Asia: Potential scenarios. *Terrorism Monitor* 4(7).

28. Schoen, J. 2004. Ships and ports are terrorism's new frontier. *MSNBC.com*, June 21. http://www.msnbc.msn.com/id/5069435.

29. *See* note 27.

30. Ibid.

31. Ibid.

32. Ibid.

33. Ibid.

34. Ibid.

School Security Issues and Techniques

▶ ▶ OBJECTIVES

- Understand the nature of school violence.
- Become familiar with cyberbullying techniques.
- Understand the nature of child exploitation.
- Become familiar with school bomb threats.
- Understand street gangs.

■ Introduction

In previous decades, the need for heightened security at the elementary, secondary, and college level would have been unthinkable. Events such as the Columbine High School and Virginia Tech shootings have pushed for a larger demand for private security personnel to be employed at educational institutions. Educational environments pose a difficult environment for providing security. A school at any level is meant to be a place of learning and openness. At the same time, teachers, administrators, and security are working to ensure that the environment of learning doesn't allow an opportunity for violence or crisis situations. The nature of protecting students and teachers also raises a number of possible litigation issues if security is not provided in a proper manner or if techniques are employed incorrectly. In addition, technology in schools allows both students and outside criminals to pose a security threat to individuals who are involved with an educational institution. The rise of gangs in the United States that tend to reside and operate near schools also presents a difficult threat to private security employees. This chapter will serve to bring you up to date on current trends and issues regarding the nature of school security.

■ School Violence

▶ ▶ CASE STUDY 1

You have recently been hired by a major private security company to provide security at a local high school. You have just completed an orientation regarding specific problems found at the school that threaten the safety and operations for administrators, teachers, and students. By your second week of guarding and patrolling at the school, you have been asked by administrators to serve on a number of school safety committees. In addition you are expected to provide detailed information on ways to provide continual information on how to prevent school violence incidents.

1. What specific background work should you do when beginning work at a school?

2. How can a you help in the creation of security policies that protect employees and students from harm as well as mitigate the possibility of future lawsuits?

3. What advice would you provide to teachers who may suspect one of their students is a future school shooter?

Controlling and preventing violence among young people is a daunting task for any security person to face. The current trends in school violence are not favorable. Fifty-seven percent of public elementary and secondary school principals stated that one or more incidents of crime or violence were reported to the police. Ten percent of all public schools had one or more serious violent crimes (murder, rape, sexual battery, suicide, physical attack or fight with a weapon, or robbery). According to a major survey, 84% of public schools have a "low security" system in place.[1]

Beginning in a School Security Setting

One of the first steps in providing security at school is to know the level of criminal activity or potential problems on campus. This information can be obtained from local law enforcement agencies but you should also meet with the administrator in charge of discipline and teachers to understand the nature of any current problems. When working at a school for the first time, it is important to uncover possible sources of information regarding school activity. Every school is its own **microcosm** in which specific people, groups, leaders, and personalities all come together. It takes a little bit of time before you can understand the nature of the way people think at a school. This also allows a private security employee to note the specific viewpoints towards discipline held by the school as the priority concerns of the institution. Any attack that involves **assault,** the crime of violence against another person, is a major concern as fights among students can be commonplace. Ultimately, most school teachers and administrators are focused on maintaining a safe and productive environment with a good degree of discipline and social control. Besides safety however, private security employees are also part of the process of preventing possible lawsuits against school institutions. [2]

Early on you should conduct an assessment to determine the level of security technology in place such as cameras, fences, locks, alarms, and other security tools. Building infrastructure and safety should also be checked to understand the nature of the conditions that could assist or impede security. This would include the nature of lighting, hallways, basements, rooftops, and other locations that are of significance.

School Violence and Litigation

Educational institutions focus on security being improved not just for the sole purpose of protecting individuals. School violence incidents, whether it is a fight between two teenagers, a student found in possession of a weapon, or a horrible scenario in which lives are lost, all raise the potential for parents, administrators, and school institutions themselves to be subjected to lawsuits that can cost thousands of dollars and result in damaging the economic security and reputation of individuals. School security serves to prevent or to mitigate any incident that may lead to a future lawsuit from an aggrieved party. Understanding the nature of school security-related lawsuits can help an entry-level security person determine the correct course of action as well to recommend to other school employees the correct procedures when facing difficult situations. [3]

While suing another person or group in the United States is a complex process, understanding the nature of school security-related lawsuits is not difficult. Suppose a new private security employee was asked how to provide security on campus in a way that prevents a lawsuit against a school should a violent crime occur. A private security employee could explain confidently that any incident of school violence or crime first must be examined to see if it was a **foreseeable risk and threat**. A foreseeable risk and threat is a danger that a reasonable person should anticipate as the result of their actions or inactions. In the case of school violence incidents, an educational institution would have to look at past events, the status of the community, feedback from personnel, and information from private security employees and law enforcement agencies regarding whether a particular school incident would be foreseeable. [4]

Unfortunately, incidents of gang violence, sexual assault crimes, weapons possession, and school shootings are all foreseeable risks and threats for an educational institution, and even more so when acts have occurred previously on the campus or nearby. If a school violence incident is a foreseeable risk and threat, then the question becomes whether an educational institution was negligent in preventing and responding to the incident. **Negligence** is the failure to use such care as a reasonably prudent and careful person would use under similar circumstances.

Negligence is also the doing of some act or the failure to do some act that a person of ordinary prudence would or would not have done under similar circumstances. Conduct that falls below the standard established by law for the protection of others is unreasonable risk of harm; it is a departure from the conduct expected of a reasonably prudent person under like circumstances.[5]

Litigation affects the cost of insurance and the products and services of the industries sued. The American civil liability (tort) system cost $260 billion in 2005, a $14 billion rise from the previous year.

Most lawsuits are settled out of court. Of those that are tried and proceed to verdict, jury verdict research data show that in 2005 the median plaintiff award in personal injury cases was about $38,000 per plaintiff.

Ultimately, a private security employee offering information to a school would be able to note that specific school violence and criminal acts if foreseeable could result in negligence when ignored by teachers and administrators. For example, if the threat of gang activity on school property is a foreseeable risk based on current information or previous incidents, a school could be negligent if they did not take key security measures or allow private security employees to conduct patrols that prevent such activity from taking place. A private security employee can have a basis for making valid legal statements regarding the nature of current and future security activity at a school.

Negligence can further be analyzed by breaking it down into its operational legal components. Courts in the United States follow a simple formula for determining school liability through negligence. For a case to be successful, a party suing an educational institution at any level must be able to show all of the following elements:

1. Duty—Did a school system or employee fail to perform as a reasonably prudent and careful person in regards to a specific situation?
2. Breech—Was there in fact a breech of that duty?[6]
3. Causation—Was the breach a result of a failure to conform to an assigned duty?
4. Damages—Was a person in fact harmed in any form?

One of the key components of this formula is the word *reasonable*. The standard of reasonableness is a confusing term as it is vague and subject to interpretation. For example, how would a court determine that a private security employee breaking up a fight is reasonable compared to a teacher using some degree of force for breaking up an altercation? The concept of **reasonable**, what a person under a set of circumstance and position should properly do when faced with a situation, can be determined through a number of sources:[7]

- Teacher/professor handbooks
- School union rules
- District/building codes
- Contract stipulations
- Private security guidelines
- Legal restrictions
- School safety plans
- Common sense

Going back to our previous example, if the school policy is that only trained security personnel should break up fights, a teacher that breaks up an altercation and possibly injures a student may have acted in a manner that places the school at risk for a lawsuit. Putting everything together, a private security employee can consider the following: (1) Was a fight on school property foreseeable? (2) Would the school be considered negligent because a teacher had a duty to act as a reasonably prudent and careful person, failed to perform at a reasonable level, and in fact damaged the student?

Being able to think in this matter as an individual who works as a security employee at an educational institution can help determine the correct response to activity as well as to provide information and policy suggestions that can help prevent and mitigate school incidents while legally protecting the client.[8]

School Threats

Private security employees working in educational institutions are expected to be aware of threats to administrators, teachers, students as well as the educational institutions themselves. You will likely be tasked with investigating these threats. Threats of violence arise from feelings or ideas that range from the mean-spirited to the messianic. Sometimes a threat is backed by the will and capacity to do harm; at other times, a voiced threat may amount to nothing but emotional "venting."[9] It is important for educators, staff, and security professionals to be able to recognize the difference between "making" and "posing" a threat.

Recognizing Threats

In general, threats can be classified in four categories: direct, indirect, veiled, or conditional. A direct threat identifies a specific act against a specific target and is delivered in a straightforward, clear, and explicit manner: "I am going to place a bomb in the school's gym and kill everyone on Monday." An indirect threat tends to be vague, unclear, and ambiguous. The plan, the intended victim, the motivation, and other aspects of the threat are masked or equivocal: "If I wanted to, I could kill everyone at this school!" The key difference here is the "implied" word being used by a student. While violence is implied, the threat is phrased tentatively—"If I wanted to"—and suggests that a violent act could occur, not that it will occur. A veiled threat is one that strongly implies but does not explicitly threaten violence. "We would be better off without you around anymore," clearly hints at a possible violent act, but leaves it to the potential victim to interpret the message and give a definite meaning to the threat. The fear of the "unknown" activity of a student can cause as much fear and concern as a direct threat. A conditional threat is the type of threat often seen in extortion cases.[10] It warns that a violent act will happen unless certain demands or terms are met: "If you don't pay me $1 million, I will place a bomb in the school."

Every security employee should speak with school administrators and teachers for the purpose of developing a system that monitors and provides specific guidelines for identifying threats. This system should also identify risks of an event and the magnitude of impact if an event were to occur. Everyone working at an institution should be familiar and comfortable with the guidelines.

Responding to Threats

Understanding the difference between risks and threats is important because it can determine the appropriate response from private security employees or guide educational institutions on how private security personnel should be operating on a campus. Threats of a bomb going off in a bathroom from an anonymous caller would warrant heightened vigilance of bathroom areas by all school personnel as well as private security employees.

Private security employees beginning work at a school location should learn the official action responses to specifics threat and violent situations. This would include the specific response required of school administrators, teachers, and private security personnel when facing:

- A student fight
- A student threatening a teacher or administrator
- A bomb threat
- Gang presence near school
- A school shooting incident
- Possession of weapons or drugs by a student
- A student threatening suicide while on school grounds

In addition to having laid out and understood plans in a school, serious threats should be reported to law enforcement agencies that can also respond and investigate possible criminal activity.

Security Planning Committees

As a private security employee, there is a good possibility you will be placed on a **school planning committee** that offers advice and helps create the policy guidelines for handling any type of school crisis or criminal activity on a campus. Since 9/11 many states now require planning to be in place at two major levels, on a school district or county level, and on a building-by-building level.

Regardless of if the committee is tasked with just creating plans for one building or an entire campus or district, security planning committees are focused on creation of the documents that determine how a school responds to any difficult situation. As a private security employee, there is an expectation you are able to do more than assist others with the formation of documents that can save the lives of school employees and students as well as prevent lawsuits. Private security employees are also expected to provide candid and honest answers regarding the negatives or shortcomings of security planning or security programs at an educational institution. The following is a simple set of questions to allow a private security employee to be successful at completing security planning at the school level regardless of the size of the institution or the specific problems it faces.[11]

1. Statement of the problem—It should answer the following question: What are the threats and risks for the school? A school may have difficulties with gangs, drugs, copy-cat school shooting incidents, or a whole host of unique problems.

2. Solution options—This section should be an identification and investigation of the possible solution options to reduce each of the threats or risks that have been identified. This is where teachers, administrators, and security personnel will spend a great deal of time coming up with new ideas and possible solutions.

3. Selected approach—A clear statement of which options have been selected, and why, is important for providing the reasoning why a particular approach seems to be the correct course of action in dealing with particular problems.

4. Specific actions—This is a chronological listing of specific actions planned to carry out the selected approach. They should be stated briefly but in enough detail to make clear their function and what they entail and when they would be completed.

5. Risk reduction projection—This section should indicate the projected reduction of risk from the value noted above. This is a difficult section because you are attempting to provide information on how you will be able to show that the chosen solution(s) are in fact adequate.

6. Estimated cost—This is a statement, by fiscal year, of funds required to accomplish the plan developed by the committee.

School Violence Profiling

One of the biggest challenges for private security personnel at an educational institution is determining who might be a potential perpetrator of violence. Perpetrators of violence often have a traceable history of problems, disputes, and failures. They are students who have been repeatedly in conflict with the school system, disciplined by administrators, and evaluated negatively by teachers and school psychologists. Violent behavior in an educational institution may be triggered by these individuals' perception that it provides a means to rectify or avenge an injustice or wrongdoing. Feelings of being outside the mainstream of the school can drive a person to attack others believed to be part of the mainstream. By creating videos or leaving messages, potential shooters or bombers within a school setting can earn their 15 minutes of fame after carrying out violent activity against a target. The Columbine and Virginia Tech shooters provide clear examples of such individuals with those particular feelings and notions. Targeted violence can be premeditated in that the perpetrator has spent considerable time planning and executing a school violence incident. School violence can also be opportunistic when a situation arises that facilitates school violence activity or when a lack of security permits the violence.[12]

Schools are possible targets for terrorism. As more Islamic terrorist organizations call for attacks on American schools, the possibility of an incident in which terrorists take hostages is not out of the realm of possibility. Students and teachers in the Beslan School in Russia were taken hostage by terrorists on September 1, 2004. The end of the attack left 344 people dead, including 186 children.[13]

For educational institutions, discovering a possible future perpetrator of school violence can be difficult. Privacy law restrictions at the state and federal level create problems in freely sharing information about employees or students. In addition, the creative process of young people or behavior of students going through normal everyday scenarios can easily be mistaken for people on the verge of violence if misunderstood by those in authority. Therefore it is important for private security employees to proceed with caution when studying individuals to determine if they may be a potential threat. Figure 10-1 is a checklist of behaviors to monitor that could indicate a potential violent attacker at an educational institution.[14]

It is important to note that information from students and teachers is critical. While four out of five school shooters tell another about their plans, violent acts can be committed when no prior threat has been uttered.

_____ Has a history of tantrums and uncontrollable angry outbursts.

_____ Dramatic change in their behavior.

_____ Has become detached or withdrawn.

_____ Characteristically resorts to name calling, cursing or abusive language.

_____ Habitually makes violent threats when angry.

_____ Has previously brought a weapon to school.

_____ Has a background of serious disciplinary problems at school and in the community.

_____ Has a background of drug, alcohol, or other substance abuse or dependency.

_____ Is on the fringe of his/her peer group with few or no close friends.

_____ Is preoccupied with weapons, explosives, or other incendiary devices.

_____ Has previously been truant, suspended, or expelled from school.

_____ Displays cruelty to animals.

_____ Has little or no supervision and support from parents or a caring adult.

_____ Has witnessed or been a victim of abuse or neglect in the home.

_____ Has been bullied and/or bullies or intimidates peers or younger children.

_____ Tends to blame others for difficulties and problems s/he causes her/himself.

_____ Consistently prefers TV shows, movies or music expressing violent themes and acts.

_____ Prefers reading materials dealing with violent themes, rituals and abuse.

_____ Reflects anger, frustration and the dark side of life in school essays or writing projects.

_____ Is involved with a gang or an antisocial group on the fringe of peer acceptance.

_____ Is often depressed and/or has significant mood swings.

_____ Has threatened or attempted suicide.

_____ Is being monitored as part of the Juvenile Justice system in a given area.

_____ Is from a family that is being monitored by the criminal justice or Family Court system.

Figure 10-1   Checklist of Behaviors for a Violent Student

■ Cyberbullying

▸ ▸ CASE STUDY 2

You are working on a normal shift at a public high school in an American city. You are asked to attend a meeting with the school principal. Walking into the meeting, you notice that a group of parents are present in the office along with two teachers and the principal. The parents present in the room have asked the principal to take steps to prevent their children from continually being bullied online by students using computers on the school campus. The principal agrees with their request and now asks you for steps to prevent such activity from taking place in the future.

1. What can be done to prevent cyberbullying from taking place at an educational institution?

2. What are some of the ways in which young people victimize other people while on a school campus or at home?

Young people have been bullying their peers since the beginnings of humankind. Generally the reason for it comes down to one word: *power*. Bullying in any form involves a power play upon someone to make that person feel weak or helpless while inflating one's own self-worth. However, bullying has taken on a new and perhaps even more sinister form in schools today. Private security personnel are now being asked to investigate or to counter the growing problem of cyberbullying. Through the use of technology applications, young people are threatened, harassed, and embarrassed in ways that go beyond the realm of acceptable school behavior. Through technology, a young person has the illusion of anonymity. This is key to understanding why cyberbullying is on the rise. Through a technology application such as a cell phone, young people have the courage to say horrible things to another minor that they would never be able to do in public. The use of computers and cell phones to attack a student causes young people to become depressed and angry. Many experts believe it is a major contributing factor why students may perform poorly in school or harm themselves and others.

Private security personnel must be ready to meet the challenge of helping schools prevent and respond to such incidents as well as assist parents who hire private security personnel to assist their children when attacked. Therefore a complete understanding of cyberbullying is important to private security employees working in an educational setting. For a private security employee faced with sudden complaints of technology on a school campus being used to attack others, the response will have to be appropriate and thorough.

What Is Cyberbullying?

Cyberbullying is the use of technology to frighten, embarrass, harass, or otherwise target a minor. It is important to understand that it involves more than just the use of the Internet or a computer. Cyberbullying includes any cybercommunication or publication posted or sent by a minor online, by instant messaging, e-mail, Web site, diary site, online profile, interactive game, handheld device, cell phone, or other interactive device.[15] This is very different from a situation in which an adult sends a message to a child or young adult. If an adult is involved in sending out messages to a minor, it is considered cyberharassment, not cyberbullying. Also it must be understood that a one time rude or insulting communication made by a minor directly to another may not rise to the level of cyberbullying. For an act to be cyberbullying, it generally needs to be repeated or a one time serious threat of bodily harm or a public posting designed to hurt, embarrass, or otherwise target a child.[16]

The experts in the educational field have reported some alarming results when students are polled and questioned on cyberbullying. Ninety percent of the middle school students in one study admitted to having had their feelings hurt online or through the use of technology. Seventy-five percent of the preteen and young teen students polled reported being involved directly or indirectly in a cyberbullying incident. Sixty percent have heard of or seen a Web site bashing another student in their school, and 45% have visited a bashing Web site. Forty percent have either had their password stolen and changed by a bully (locking them out of their own account) or had communications sent to others posing as them.[17] The difficulty for many researchers and educators is knowing how to ask students if they are facing cyberbullying problems. Many studies that ask kids if they have been cyberbullied fall short of measuring the real problem in a community by failing to ask the right questions.[18] It may seem at first that cyberbullying should not be a concern for private security employees. The reality is that children and young adults who are bullied are more likely to engage in violent acts towards themselves or to reach a boiling point in which they attack others. Young people can easily give in to their feelings of frustration and anger. The majority of major school violence incidents over the past few years were conducted by individuals who were in fact victims of bullying.

Methods of Attack

It is very easy to disguise your identity and pretend to be someone else. Today even 12-year-olds know how to create an e-mail account with a specific ISP, make up a new screen name, and post comments about others with little consequence. Web sites such as Myspace and Facebook allow young people to easily create Web sites that reveal personal information and allow the entire world to post comments or send messages within seconds. Such Web sites are some of the most trafficked on the Internet.[19]

The following is a list of common methods of cyberbullying at work in the United States:[20]

- Hate/threat messages—Young people may send or forward hateful or threatening messages to others without realizing the strong nature of the content. While not said in real life to a person face to face, the messages are unkind or threatening messages that are to be taken seriously.
- False screen names—A child or teen may create a screen name that is very similar to another kid's name but implies a negative message. The name may have an additional *i* or one less *e* but has a message for all to see such as "Robwilldietomorrow24" or "JennyFrankoverweight."
- Cell phone text wars—A group of children can gang up on a victim by sending thousands of text messages to a chosen victim's cell phone or mobile device. This results in aggravation, loss of phone service from the constant messages, and a huge phone bill.
- Instant messaging/text threats with photos—Children can use **instant messaging (IM) programs**, a form of real-time communication between two or more people based on typed text, to send pictures or text messages to threaten or embarrass a chosen victim.
- Password theft—By stealing another child's password, the bully can change the password so a victim has no access to a phone or computer program or any online account. In addition they can chat with other people, pretending to be the victim and offend and anger as many people as possible. Also if a young person has a Web site, with the password the bully can change their profile to include sexual, racist, and inappropriate things to offend people.
- Blogs—A **blog** by definition is a Web site where entries are made in journal style and displayed in a reverse chronological order. However, a blog can be used to damage a child's reputation or to post sensitive information that is embarrassing. Also a bully can set up a blog pretending to be the victim and say humiliating things for all to read in graphic detail.
- Web sites—Children now using Web sites of their own design or through sites such as Myspace or Facebook can create pages that are specifically designed to threaten or humiliate a chosen victim or group of victims. Also by posting personal information about a chosen victim on a Web site, it increases the risk of that person being contacted or found by those who may do further harm to a victim.
- Internet polling—A fairly new bullying tactic, Internet polls created by young people are designed to be offensive or bully other children. Posting questions on a website "Who is the fattest kid or biggest slut" can severely hurt a child.
- Interactive games—Computer games such as "World of Warcraft" or gaming devices such as Playstation 2 or X-Box allow a child to play and communicate via the Internet. In video games, children get computer-generated characters

(avatars) they can manipulate and control. In this online world, characters can gang up, threaten, and use offensive language towards a victim. Also bullies can lock others out of a game, passing false rumors or find a way to hack into their account and change information.

- Malicious programs—Children can also send spyware and viruses to disrupt and harm a child's computer. Trojan horse programs allow the cyberbully to control their victim's computer remotely, and can be used to erase the hard drive of the victim.
- Junk e-mail/pornography—A cyberbully can sign a chosen victim up for e-mails from marketing lists and also from porn sites that can result in thousands of e-mails that prevent a person from using the Internet or simply distresses them based on the content of the e-mails.

Cyberbullying by Proxy or When Forwarding an E-mail

Often people who use the Internet to target others do it using chosen and easy-to-manipulate accomplices. These accomplices often do not recognize the cyberattack against the chosen victim. The attacker simply creates indignation or emotion on the part of others that causes them to act, and then the attacker can sit back and let others do their dirty work. The bully then can argue that he or she did not instigate any attack and blame the accomplices, such as other students. According to Parry's Guide to Cyberbullying, it is one of the most dangerous kinds of cyberharassment or cyberbullying. For private security personnel doing an investigation, tracing back these communications can be challenging. It generally can be done in the following three ways:[21]

1. A cyberbully sends a message to a chosen accomplice or group of accomplices that he or she has been harmed by a future victim. Children then rally to the aid of their friend and begin using the Internet or any technology application to attack a victim.

2. A cyberbully sends a statement or statement and picture regarding a future victim to a third party. The third party forwards the message to dozens of people. The bully can stand behind the argument that they sent a private message to someone else and not the victim. The accomplice unknowingly is in trouble for the forwarding of the message.

3. Children often use AOL, MSN or another ISP as their "proxy" or accomplice in warning wars. When they engage in a "notify" or "warning" war, they can get the ISP to view the victim as the provocateur. A notify or warning war is when one child provokes another, until the victim lashes back with obscene or threatening language. When they do, the real attacker clicks the warning or notify button on the text screen. This captures the communication and flags it for the ISP's review. If the ISP finds that the communication violated their terms of service agreement (which most do), they may take action.

While designed as a security tool or shield, it can be used as a way to disrupt service. Some accounts allow several warnings before formal action is taken. But the end result is the same. The ISP does the attacker's dirty work when they close or suspend the real victim's account for a terms-of-service violation. Most knowledgeable ISPs know this and are careful to see if the person being warned is really being set up.

Word to the Wise   Warning signs of a child victim:[22]
- Has few friends
- Seems afraid of going to school
- Has suddenly lost interest in school or begins to do poorly in school
- Appears sad, moody, teary, or depressed
- Complains of frequent headaches, stomachaches, or other physical ailments
- Has trouble sleeping
- Experiences a loss of appetite
- Appears anxious and/or suffers from low self-esteem

Using Parents in Cyberbullying

Sometimes children use the victim's own parents as unwitting accomplices. They provoke the victim and when the victim lashes back, they save the communication and forward it to the parents of the victim to let them know the nature of their child. The parents often believe what they read, and without having evidence of the prior provocations, think that their own child created the initial conflict. That's why those in authority should never take any cyberbullying at face value before doing a complete investigation into the whole situation and major examination of all parties involved in a case. For private security personnel contacting parents, it is important to tread carefully.[23]

Combating Cyberbullying

School administrators, teachers, and parents who are not familiar with cyberbullying until it occurs are likely to ask for security advice from private security personnel. The good news is that there are many steps that even entry-level private security personnel can take to help combat cyberbullying. The first and most essential thing a victim of cyberbullying must do is to never respond to the bullying. A victim should not answer e-mails, respond to blog or Web site posts, reply to phone texts, engage in a chat room or IM exchange, or post a fake profile of the bully. Any communication should be saved and if possible printed out so parents, school officials, Internet service providers (ISPs), and law enforcement personnel can properly investigate the matter.

Prevention of Cyberbullying

As a private security employee you can help mitigate any cyberbullying problem by providing clear policy guidelines. You should share the following checklist with administrators, teachers, and parents before any report of problems. These steps can be taken in the classroom and on campus:[24]

1. Instruct students as to what behavior is unacceptable. Ask them how they would feel if someone posted online that they were fat, stupid, and ugly.
2. Have a clear policy as to what is cyberbullying.
3. Learn what parental security and control options are available from the local Internet service providers.
4. Have consequences for children who violate rules regarding the use of technology.
5. Control or minimize the use of cell phones and the Internet on the school campus.
6. Watch for signs of a victim of cyberbullying, such as nightmares, school avoidance, or sudden disinterest in the computer.
7. Develop a clear and understandable policy regarding the use of technology on or off school property.
8. Establish a relationship with local police regarding cyberbullying.
9. Teach ethics as part of any computer instruction given at a school.

It is important to send a clear message that private security can only do so much to prevent or mitigate cyberbullying. You can serve in an advisory role in helping a school create guidelines on the use of technology on campus or in monitoring how children are using computers, cell phones, and other pieces of technology. However the real battle against cyberbullying must take place in the classroom and with parents at home.

■ Child Exploitation

▶ ▶ CASE STUDY 3

As a private security employee, you receive a notice from local police that there has been a rise in the number of pedophiles moving into the area around the educational institution where you provide security services. Parents have begun contacting the educational institution to request information concerning safeguards to prevent their children from being harmed. The superintendent of the school district has now asked that private security employees provide detailed information on how they can assist the school.

1. What are the ways that children are exploited in the 21st century?
2. In what ways can you help to prevent children from becoming victims?

Each day our children are at risk of becoming victims of **pedophiles**, those individuals with a sexual interest in children. The reality is that victimization of children or exploitation is not a new phenomenon. Unfortunately, the rise of the Internet has provided the way for pedophiles to communicate online and to become more organized in their attacks on children. However, the use of the Internet is only one way in which a child going to school can become a victim of a sexual attack. The magnitude of this problem is overwhelming to law enforcement, Internet companies, and security agencies around the world. Approximately 1 in 5 girls and 1 in 10 boys are sexually solicited before adulthood. Only 35% of child exploitation is ever reported. Predators come in all nationalities, and immigration and customs enforcement reported 6600 child predators who have been identified and deported. Currently, there are approximately 1500 cases of child exploitation pending in the United States. This is very minimal when compared to the estimated number of pedophiles. Only about one-third of child sexual exploitation incidents are reported.[25]

Many companies and institutions are seeking employees who understand the complex nature of those individuals who victimize children. Therefore a basic understanding of how children become victims, the signs of sexual exploitation, and a profile of the sexual predators, along with strategies to help children, is important for private investigators, computer security experts, and school security personnel.

> The use of the Internet as the primary distribution channel for child pornography has exploded. There are already over one million IP addresses identified as participating in online child exploitation. An estimated 12 million pornographic images of children exists today, and there are an estimated seven million users of child porn sites (National Center for Missing and Exploited Children).

The Nature of Pedophiles

As mentioned above, adults who have a sexual and possible violent interest towards children are known as pedophiles. While many pedophiles have been prosecuted and are serving or have served prison terms for their offenses, the large worldwide market for child pornography suggests that pedophilia is more common in the general population than prison statistics would indicate. In addition, pedophiles have a high rate of revictimization; the chances of them continually engaging in criminal activity is likely. There have been efforts by some individuals to legalize the victimization of children by fostering pedophile activism in communities. Often called childlove, its proponents think of it as a social movement that encompasses a wide variety of views, but generally advocates one or more of the following: social acceptance of adults' romantic or sexual attraction to children; social acceptance of adults' sexual activity with children; and changes in institutions of concern to pedophiles, such as changing age-of-consent laws and mental illness classifications. Another such organization is the North American Man-Boy Love Association. NAMBLA was once the lone voice lobbying for the normalization of pedophilia. For those interested in protecting children, it is now becoming paramount that a need for more security personnel is necessary.[26]

The exact number of pedophiles in any given location is unknown unless the pedophiles have been caught on a previous occasion. At any given moment, experts believe there may be over 50,000 predators online and possibly more lurking around schools and playgrounds. In some jurisdictions, about 50% of men arrested for pedophilia are married. About 30% of those who sexually abuse children are relatives of the child, such as fathers, uncles, or cousins. About 60% of perpetrators are nonrelative acquaintances, such as a friend of the family, babysitter, or neighbor. The remaining 10% of perpetrators that abuse children sexually are total strangers.

Pedophiles are constantly evolving in their ways of choosing victims. Pedophiles have been known to collect significant amounts of information about a specific child and target that child through online information or through invading the privacy of a home. Web cameras, instant messaging profiles, and in some cases school Web sites have provided data that is used to stalk and target the victims.[27] Sexual predators use digital cameras to stalk or exploit children and to share pornography.

Children Most at Risk

For a security employee working in a school or those who conduct investigations, it is important to note which individuals may be potential victims by pedophiles. As noted before, nonrelative acquaintances who have access to a child may engage in criminally sexual behavior. Every child is at risk, however. About 10% of boys and 25% of girls, infants to teenagers, will become targets. Some children are more susceptible than others. Children who are easily influenced and submissive to authority figures as well as those who have had the following experiences are most susceptible:[28]

- Have experienced maltreatment on previous occasions
- Are emotionally immature or shy for their age
- Have low self-esteem or peer problems
- Are troubled or depressed at home or in school
- Have a strong respect for adult status
- Are willing to cooperate for a desired reward from an adult
- Are materialistic

Victimization Methods

Child Prostitution

Pedophiles are able to victimize children through a number of techniques. Firstly, child **prostitution**, providing sexual favors for hire, is a way many pedophiles can receive sexual favors from young people. By operating online, at shopping malls, near educational institutions, and at other public areas, adults can offer to purchase sexual services from a person less than 18 years of age. The purchase need not be for cash, credit cards, or digital cash. The sexual services may be purchased with anything (e.g., drugs, food, or even the promise of a ride home). It also can entail procuring, encouraging, enticing, or forcing a person less than 18 years of age to become a prostitute by portraying the prostitution field as an alternative to their current home life situation.

Luring

Luring is defined as activities conducted by a predator that tempts or attracts a targeted child with the promise of a pleasure or reward. Once a child is lured to a location chosen by the pedophile, an adult can engage in sexual activity with a minor against their will. An adult can promise to take a child to an exciting place or to provide some desired item such as fast food. In some cases, gift cards, online wish lists, PayPal money transfers, and other mechanisms can and have been used to entice targeted children to perform various acts. Luring can take place online or through in person communication between an adult and a chosen victim.[29]

Child Sex Tourism

Sex tourism is defined as traveling to a foreign country to engage in sexual activity with a child. The destination is most often a third-world country, especially in Asia. Sex tourism has become a well-developed component of the commercial child exploitation trade. Significant marketing efforts have evolved and include brochures as well as Web sites and all-inclusive advertising packages for travelers, complete with airfare, hotel, and directions to local brothels.

Webcam Exploitation

Webcam exploitation, the use of Webcams to entice young people to engage in recordable sexual acts, has become another new form of victimization. Web cameras are one of the new and highly prized electronic toys used by predators. A predator generally offers a child some type of payment for posing in front of a Web camera. It is important to note that the widespread adoption of broadband and wireless broadband has increased Webcam use in general, thus causing an increase in Webcam exploitation.

Cell Phone Exploitation

Cell phones now allow pedophiles additional methods for victimizing targets. Cell phones are rapidly evolving into a significant distribution channel for all types of pornography including child porn. Most cell phones today come with a digital camera or the ability to record live video. This allows pedophiles to easily snap images or record video of young people without their knowledge. In addition, they can quickly post any recorded data online for other pedophiles to enjoy or for profit on an Internet pornography site. In a *Wall Street Journal* report, worldwide revenue in 2005 from mobile phone pornography was expected to rise to $1 billion and could grow to three times that number or more within a couple of years.[30]

Summary of Victimization Methods
- Child pornography
- Luring
- Child sex tourism (traveling)
- Child prostitution
- Webcam exploitation
- Cell phone exploitation

Understanding the Signs of Child Victimization

Finding children who have been victimized can be challenging. Often children, even when speaking with adults that they trust such as family members, may not reveal that they have been a victim of child exploitation. However, there are general signs that victims of sexual abuse do manifest for observers or investigators to note. The most common signs exhibited by children who have been sexually abused include the following:[31]

- Unusual interest in or avoidance of all things of a sexual nature
- Sleep problems or nightmares
- Depression or withdrawal from friends or family
- Seductiveness
- Statements that their bodies are dirty or damaged
- Fear that there is something wrong with them in the genital area
- Refusal to go to school
- Delinquency and/or conduct problems
- Secretiveness
- Aspects of sexual molestation in drawings, games, fantasies
- Unusual aggressiveness
- Suicidal behavior

Prevention Steps

For private security personnel, there are a number of techniques that can be used in the investigation and prevention of child exploitation.[32]

- Ensure that parents and teachers talk to children.
- Suggest to parents that a computer in a household be located in an easily supervised central area.
- Monitor all Web sites visited by children.
- Invisibly record all online conversations a child has on the computer.
- Log instant messages and chats to prevent your children from having dangerous online contacts.
- Capture all typing done by children by using a **keycatcher** device, a device that records every keystroke made on the computer on which it is installed.
- Save and copy all e-mail activity sent and received by a child.
- Use parental controls built into the many of the systems.
- Use spam filters to block sexually explicit materials and unwanted contacts.
- Use a firewall to protect a computer and data.
- Use spyware prevention software.
- Keep software up to date with security patches and new releases.
- Instruct children not to stay up late at night talking to friends online.
- Instruct parents to watch for excess money or new items.
- Instruct parents and teachers to look for significant changes in a child's possessions that appear to be at odds with the financial means of the family.

For private security personnel involved with child exploitation issues, the reality is that pedophiles are constantly discovering new ways to communicate and victimize children. Therefore continued education and cooperation with public-serving law enforcement agencies is required to stay one step ahead of pedophiles.

■ Bomb Threats

▶ ▶ CASE STUDY 4

You are working as a school security guard when you are called into the principal's office along two other members of your security guard team. The front office at the school received an anonymous call that a bomb has been placed on campus. Local police have been notified that a bomb threat has been made. This bomb threat is the second of two bomb threats communicated to the school in the past few weeks.

1. What considerations should be made in light of this recent bomb threat?

2. What activities can you take to help the local police that are on their way?

The unfortunate reality is that bomb threats in schools are on the increase. Whether the threats are intended to be a prank to break up a school day or are in fact a serious threat by future offenders, the response by security personnel must take into account the possibility that people will be injured or killed. Before an incident occurs, private security personnel should meet with administrators and public-serving law enforcement agencies to determine the best course of action when a bomb threat is received. While at first an evacuation of a campus may seem to be the easiest and simplest solution, evacuating a school can cause a panic and result in others being injured. It raises concerns among the general public, media, and parents that an educational institution is a dangerous place. Such a notion can be hard to shake and can result in a negative end result such as withdrawal of students and increased scrutiny from numerous state and federal agencies. If people know that an evacuation will take place every time a bomb threat is called into a school, then the likelihood of bomb threats can increase because students may call in bomb threats just to get a day off. Many young people today realize that you can purchase a prepaid cell phone at a retail outlet that is untraceable and make a bomb threat very easily to a school administration office without law enforcement ever finding out who was responsible. There is also the concern that a bomb threat may be the first step towards carrying out a mass shooting. A shooter may be calling in the threat so that school personnel and students evacuate and gather in locations outside, where they can be more easily attacked.

The Nature of Bomb Threats

Bomb threats to educational institutions are delivered in a variety of ways. The majority of threats are called in to the target, namely the educational institution itself. Occasionally these calls are through a third party. Sometimes a threat is communicated in writing or by a recording. There are two logical explanations for reporting a bomb to an educational institution:

1. The caller has definite knowledge or believes that an explosive or incendiary bomb has been or will be placed and he or she wants to minimize personal injury or property damage. The caller may be the person who placed the device or someone who has become aware of such information.
2. The caller wants to create an atmosphere of anxiety and panic that will, in turn, result in a disruption of the normal activities at the facility where the device is purportedly placed.

Whatever the reason for the report, there will certainly be a reaction to it. Through proper planning, the wide variety of potentially uncontrollable reactions can be greatly reduced. Training is essential to deal properly with a bomb threat incident. Private security personnel should instruct all personnel, especially those at the telephone switchboard, what to do if a bomb threat is received at the educational institution.

School Bomb Planning

In preparing to cope with a bomb threat at a school, it is necessary as a private security employee to develop two separate but interdependent plans, namely a physical security plan and a bomb incident plan. A **physical security plan** provides for the protection of property, personnel, facilities, and material against damage, sabotage, or other illegal or criminal acts by students or outsiders to the educational facility. The physical security plan also deals with prevention of unauthorized entry and control of access to the building. In most instances, some form of physical security may already be in existence, although not necessarily intended to prevent a bomb attack. The **bomb incident plan** provides detailed procedures to be implemented when a bombing attack is actually executed or threatened against a school.[33]

Only by using an established organization and procedures can the bomb incident be handled with the least risk to all concerned. Private security supervisors, deans, and principals all have authority in a school setting. In planning for the bomb incident at an educational facility, a definite chain of command or line of authority must be established.[34] The possible confusion that can ensue among such personnel without clear guidelines could be extremely high. Therefore a clearly defined line of authority will instill confidence and avoid panic if a bomb threat situation does in fact occur.

Sample Bomb Incident Plan[35]
1. Designate a chain of command.
2. Establish a command center.
3. Decide what primary and alternate communications will be used.
4. Establish clearly how and by whom a bomb threat will be evaluated.
5. Decide what procedures will be followed when a bomb threat is received or device discovered.
6. Determine to what extent the available bomb squad will assist and at what point the squad will respond.
7. Provide an evacuation plan with enough flexibility to avoid a suspected danger area.
8. Designate search teams.
9. Designate areas to be searched.
10. Establish techniques to be utilized during search.
11. Establish a procedure to report and track progress of the search and a method to lead qualified bomb technicians to a suspicious package.
12. Have a contingency plan available if a bomb should go off.
13. Establish a simple-to-follow procedure for the person receiving the bomb threat.
14. Review your physical security plan in conjunction with the development of your bomb incident plan.

Planning for a Command Center

An agreement should be worked out ahead of time between school administrators, private security, and local law enforcement for how a **command center**, or center for operations in case of a school crisis, should be specifically set up in terms of location and personnel. Private security personnel should be certain that all personnel assigned to the command center are aware of their duties. The positive aspects of planning will be lost if the leadership is not apparent. It is also very important to organize and train an evacuation unit that will be responsive to the command center and has a clear understanding of the importance of its role.[36]

Command Center Guidelines
1. Designate a primary location and an alternate location.
2. Assign personnel and designate decision-making authority.
3. Establish a method for tracking search teams.
4. Maintain a list of likely target areas.
5. Maintain a blueprint of floor diagrams in the center.
6. Establish primary and secondary methods of communication.
7. Formulate a plan for establishing a command center if a threat is received after normal work hours.
8. Maintain a roster of all necessary telephone numbers.

Word to the Wise Private security personnel should be aware that two-way radios may trigger a bomb if a bomb is on the grounds of a school facility.

General Bomb Threat Response Guidelines for Private Security Personnel

A private security employee should also follow a number of practical guidelines when faced with a bomb threat.[37]

1. Never disregard a threat as a hoax. All threats must be reported. When a threat is received (phone, e-mail, or letter), it must be recorded on a specific form.
2. The security site supervisor should be notified and an emergency procedure plan put into effect.
3. The police must be notified. Evacuation may be a possibility.
4. Avoid undue panic or hysteria.

5. Turn control over to police once they arrive,

6. All public, employee, and fire stairways should be thoroughly searched along with all restrooms, stalls, unlocked and locked closets, mechanical rooms, lockers, under and on top of desks, and any knapsacks and handbags, etc.

In addition to these practical guidelines, private security employees should continually seek the latest information on new bomb devices and the technology built into them, including new ways for detonation.

■ Gangs

▶ ▶ CASE STUDY 5

You have recently been reassigned to provide security at a school in a low socioeconomic neighborhood. Administrators begin to inform you that gang activity is a major concern for the school because young people are targeted as new recruits for the gang. You are not familiar with gang culture or the nature of such organizations.

1. What information concerning the nature of gangs is important for you to understand and be familiar with before working in school security?
2. What are some of the rising gangs in the United States that pose a threat to school institutions?

Private security is now on the frontline of protecting school institutions from possible intrusion by gangs and with prevention of gang violence on or near a school facility. Before a private security person considers working in an area with a high gang population, he or she should have a complete understanding of gangs. Street gang membership in the United States has reached estimated numbers around 700,000. Private security officers must be prepared for difficult work environments in which local gangs, if unchecked, may grow into organized armed groups capable of widespread violence and criminal activity.

Origins

At some point during the development of nearly all organized communities, there have been groups with different interests and activities outside the established mainstream society.[38] Often led by negatively controlling and charismatic leaders with different interests, they began a process of claiming territory, while encouraging members of a social group to engage in deviant acts.[39] It has been difficult if not impossible in this century, as it has been in the past, to develop an all-encompassing definition of such social organizations that ultimately emerge as gangs within a society. When individuals with a negative purpose begin to assemble on a regular basis, they are first seen as a distinct cluster by the members of a given community.[40]

Once assembled, the newly formed members begin to engage in activities that result in a negative response from the authorities and community at large. A labeling process and a new negative identity then becomes adopted by the assembled group as it moves toward learning new forms of criminal behavior.[41]

All gangs in the United States go through this process whether they are Caucasian or part of a minority population such as African-Americans or Hispanics. Regardless of race, gangs thrive when certain conditions in a community are present. Young people living in a working and lower-class population, whether rural or urban, are potential future gang members.[42] An area of the nation with continuous poverty, low education rates, decreased employment opportunities, and no positive social opportunities also can raise the potential for street gangs to emerge.[43] The neighborhoods from which individual members of gangs originate have a strong psychological impact on the lives of young people. Living in impoverished neighborhoods can create an atmosphere in which young people feel opportunities for advancement and respect are nonexistent, especially if the young people are first-generation Americans.[44] A "left behind" culture develops among potential and current gang members as others find ways to move up the economic and social ladder. Having little option or support from family, schools, or other social influences, the remaining young people are pulled together in a social vacuum struggling to find some identity among themselves.[45] A possible bad family or home life environment and a desire to belong to a larger societal group become motivations for young people to join gangs.

Juvenile gang delinquency and criminal behavior is a result of poor socialization and inability to accept the rules of society. The child is exposed to cultural and societal expectations by agents of socialization—parents, family, the schools, peers, the media, and religion—that should influence a young person to act in accordance with the law and ethical societal norms. The socialization that takes place at an early stage in a child's life is known as primary socialization. The primary influences on young people are parents and the immediate family.[46] The key here is that primary socialization is not always successful, as many families fail to properly socialize their children.[47] When parenting of a child is inadequate, a child's maturation process may potentially be damaged, and the end result is antisocial or criminal behavior by the young person.[48] Over time many young people develop voids in their social development that are ultimately filled by negative or socially undesirable beliefs and behaviors. If a young adult is devoid of opportunities for advancement, or for the possibility to earn respect and develop an identity or purpose in their lives, in addition to missing positive social influences, the young adult is left vulnerable to filling these voids through socially undesirable outlets. Gang culture is one realm in which these voids may be filled in a relatively immediate manner for these young adults. It gives them a sense of belonging, identity, and offers a purpose.[49] It allows a young person to be part of a society of "us vs. them" struggling to exist in an unfriendly and unforgiving environment.

It is also possible to describe the situation in terms of social disabilities. Social disabilities are manifested behaviors that are socially disabling and unacceptable. This is a key notion to understanding what fosters gang behavior, because in normal society, social disabilities effectively lower a person's self-esteem and make one view their society with a negative set of eyes.[50] It can lead to decreased participation in healthy social environments such as school and community functions thus resulting in outward rebellion against parents, teachers, police officers, and all those with authority. This also leads to an increased dependence on the acceptance of the gang and fuels any activity that might help an individual's status within the gang.[51]

A gang is any group of individuals who gather for an illicit purpose.[52] However, when rules, leadership, customs, and punishments become established and practiced within a gang, such a gang should be classified as a street power organization capable of terrorizing a local community, or "thug life street gang," such as the Bloods, Crips, Latin Kings, or MS-13. The word *thug* comes from the Hindustani word for deception. The original Thugee was an Indian thief terror gang. It is interesting to note that the Thugee gang provides us with an early example of an organized domestic terror gang whose psychological makeup was no different than current thug life street gangs.[53] A gang that doesn't reach the heights of becoming a major street power organization may develop and organize into a powerful street-based racial hate gang such as the current neo-Nazi/skinhead organizations

Delinquents who evolve their organization from a small group into a budding thug life street gang or a racial hate gang must change the makeup of the gang to grow. Like an onion, most thug life street gangs or racial hate gangs develop in layers. At the center is the leader(s) of a gang who determines at what level of criminal activity the gang will function and what strategic criminal objectives need to be accomplished in a given area. Characteristics of the leader(s) are reflected in the day-to-day criminal activities of the gang. The leader is all powerful. The next layer is the hard core gang members. They are usually the older gang members, the individuals who are culturally and criminally enmeshed in the gang and are at risk of being so for life. Most violent gang activity and crime as well as the majority of recruiting of young people emanates from this portion of the gang organization. Hard core gang members usually make up about 10–15% of the total gang membership.[54] This is followed by the associate gang members who have usually made a personal commitment to the gang culture and are dedicated to achieving the level of recognition needed to attain hard core status. The next level is the fringe level of gang participation. The fringe gang member is still able to function outside of the gang structure and has not made a total commitment to a life in the criminal gang culture. This type of member drifts in and out of the gang and seems to lack direction. The final level of gang membership is the entry-level or "wanna-be" caste. It is important to understand that "wanna-be" personnel are not actually gang members. They are youth who view the gang as an exciting place to be, a place where they could become "somebody" on the street. They are considered the future members of the gangs.[55] Wanna-bes may emulate gang dress, graffiti, hand signs, and other gang cultural symbols, and they may associate with known gang members, but they have not yet been accepted fully into the gang. Therefore they may in engage in violent acts like the hardcore members to prove themselves. For private security employees, wanna-be gang members may pose a serious threat even at the middle school level.

Each layer of a developed street gang has been found, in general, to have differences in measured intelligence, impulse control, school performance, and group dependence. It is interesting to note the organizational parallel between a street gang and the military. Rank, structure, and clothing indicators are important in understanding the power structure and allegiance to a group within both military units and street gangs.[56]

With such a structure in place, rules and customs set by the leader(s) allows the gang to develop its culture and propaganda, which serves as an alluring and attractive force for young people looking to fill the voids in their lives. As the culture and image of the gang develops, the gang is able to recruit in an organized fashion through the efforts of the hard core members. For a long time gangs have used a form of seduction to recruit new members. They create glorified fraternal myths about the gang that are very attractive to young recruits, and very often these myths become the foundation for young recruits.[57] For a group such as MS-13 or the neo-Nazi street gang, an easily communicated "us vs. them" emotional appeal is a powerful selling point on the merits of such organizations. Many armed gangs take the "obligation approach" by teaching young people that joining the gang helps the community.[58] The symbols of the gang (the graffiti, hand signs, colors, tattoos, clothing, etc.) can create a visual attraction for young people. Young people realize that with these symbols they are part of something organized and powerful. Parties are also very useful ways for recruiters to seduce young people into the gang. At the party they have fun, come under the influence of alcohol and drugs, and believe the rhetoric they are bombarded with by other gang members. In other cases, street gangs may use a coercive approach to recruitment through intimidation.[59] Coercion and intimidation may also include both physical and psychological tactics.[60] The most powerful lure of gang life trappings, however, are the promise of money, sex, and glamour.

For hate-based street gangs, we must make a major differentiation from other street gangs. All major established gangs have similar structure, psychological differences depending on the membership status of the individual in the group, and recruiting tactics. However, the development of hate-based groups goes beyond a need to fill voids. Hate-based groups have a greater social belief system structured around the "us vs. them" attitude. The development of this belief structure focuses on extreme hatred of a particular group in society and pushes them toward adopting and adhering to reactionary, racist, or religious prejudice ideology (such as anti-Semitism).[61]

From Street Gang to Organized Armed Group

Private security personnel should be aware of the seven stages of hate that represent the evolution from a small gang to a fully developed armed and organized criminal group. These seven stages, while developed to understand extremist groups, are easily applicable in understanding the development from a formation point early in the gang to the execution of its goals as a major armed street organization. A private security employee who witnesses or prevents criminal activity should know that such activity may be a sign that a gang is progressing from a small group of juvenile delinquents to a much more dangerous organization. As more and more members of a gang go through these stages, the more the organization gets dedicated members who will help the organization grow, engage in more daring criminal acts, and recruit new members for the future.

Stage 1

Hate is an emotional fire that more often goes cold over time. To maintain a state of hatred requires a constant rekindling of hate that is accomplished much more easily in a group setting. Irrational haters seldom hate alone. They feel compelled, almost driven, to entreat others to hate as they do. The establishment of a group, besides rekindling hate, also provides peer validation that bolsters a sense of self-worth while at the same time preventing introspection that reveals personal insecurities. Frustrated and angry, individuals that are otherwise ineffective as threats to others now become empowered when they join groups that also provide anonymity and diminished accountability for criminal hatred-driven actions.[62] The hatred against police, the community, and rival gangs can be constantly maintained by key members in a gang to keep personnel motivated and loyal to the gang.

Stage 2

A gang can form identities through symbols, rituals, and mythologies that enhance the members' status as having power while degrading the people who are a source of their hate. For example, skinhead groups may adopt the swastika, the iron cross, the Confederate flag, and other supremacist symbols. Thug life street gangs such as the Bloods or Crips use hand signals and specific graffiti symbols. Group-specific symbols or clothing often differentiate hate groups from original street gangs looking for money and respect.[63] Group rituals, such as secret hand signals and secret greetings, further fortify people as members of an almost mystical and religious organization.[64] Gangs then incorporate some form of self-sacrifice to their code, which allows members to willingly jeopardize their well-being for the greater good of the cause. Giving one's life to a cause provides the ultimate sense of value and worth to an individual that has fallen for ideology. Skinheads and neo-Nazi organizations often see themselves as soldiers in a race war and potential martyrs for the cause of a pure white race. Likewise Hispanic street gangs such as MS-13 or the Latin Kings foster the belief that they must strive against a white America that is denying them true liberty and opportunities.

Stage 3

Hate is the sustenance that emotionally and psychologically binds haters to one another and to a common cause. By constantly verbally debasing the object of their hate, haters enhance their self-image as powerful, as well as their group's status as legitimate. Graffiti done on buildings by thug life street gangs is demonstrative of this point. In fact, researchers have found that the more often a person thinks about aggression, the greater the chance for aggressive behavior to occur in a given society.[65] Thus, after constant verbal denigration of members of community or rival gangs, the gang members in an organization progress to the next stage of development.

Stage 4

Hate, by its nature, changes incrementally. Time cools the emotionally charged fire of hate, thus forcing the hater to look inward toward himself. To avoid introspection, leaders of a gang or the hard core gang members may use ever-increasing degrees of rhetoric and violence to maintain high levels of agitation and anger. Taunts and offensive gestures serve this purpose. In this stage, again using skinheads as an example, they typically shout racial slurs from moving cars or from afar. The hand signals and graffiti by thug life street gangs or hate-based groups that use Nazi salutes often accompany comments towards the targets of hate. Most gangs claim control of turf proximate to the neighborhoods in which they dwell. One study indicated that a majority of gang-related crimes occur when a gang member of a target group travels through the rival group's perceived turf.[66]

Stage 5

This stage is critical because it differentiates vocally abusive gang members from physically abusive ones. In this stage, the group becomes more aggressive, prowling their area seeking vulnerable targets. Violence unites a gang and further isolates them from mainstream society. Gangs, almost without exception, attack in groups and target single victims where opportunity for success is likely. Research has shown that physical violence, as an element of thrill seeking, is rampant in young delinquents. Researchers have found that 60% of hate offenders were thrill seekers.[67] The adrenaline "high" intoxicates the attackers. The initial adrenaline surge lasts for several minutes; however, the effects of adrenaline keep the body in a state of heightened alert for up to several days. Each successive anger-provoking thought or action builds on residual adrenaline and triggers a more violent response than the one that originally initiated the sequence of attacks. Anger builds on more anger. The adrenaline high combined with hate becomes a deadly combination when directed at a target. Hardcore members of gangs often keep themselves at a level where the slightest provocation triggers aggression towards others.[68]

Stage 6

Several studies confirm that a large number of attacks involve weapons. Some attackers use firearms to commit crimes, but some attackers prefer weapons such as broken bottles, baseball bats, blunt objects, screwdrivers, and belt buckles that increase the level of injuries on victims. These types of weapons require the attacker to be in close proximity to the victim, which further demonstrates the depth of personal anger, as opposed to discharging firearms at a distance, thus avoiding personal contact. Close-in onslaughts require the assailants to see their victims eye to eye and to become bloodied during the assault. Hands-on violence allows groups to express their hate towards the intended target in a way a gun cannot. Personal contact empowers and fulfills a deep-seated need to have dominance over a target.

Stage 7

The ultimate goal of people with hatred in a gang is to destroy the object of their hate. Mastery over life and death imbues the hater with feelings of omnipotence and power. With this power comes a great sense of self-worth and value. These are the very qualities that individuals lack and have desired from the beginning when they first associated with a local gang. However, in reality, hate physically and psychologically destroys both the hater and the target.[69]

Ultimately, upon reaching a high point in its development, a growing street gang can get to a stage where it wields influence over the political and cultural environment in a neighborhood for its own benefit. A gang can challenge legitimate democratic institutions to protect the values of its organization and its ability to engage in illegal activities. Street gangs, which began as youths who were the outsiders in the community, soon realize that the armed muscle of their organization can demonstrate power on many scales. For example, the thug life street gang previously known the Cribs as changed their name to Crips. While the origins of the name "Crips" is not clearly well known, it has been suggested by many that the gang's name change was made to reflect the new abbreviated motto and status of the gang when it reached a point of power as a "Community Revolution in Progress."[70]

Key Steps in Dealing with Gangs

For private security employees in a school setting, the key becomes understanding the size and scope of a gang. This requires speaking with administrators as well as having a tight knit relationship with local law enforcement agencies that have up-to-date information on activity. Law enforcement agencies in particular can provide private security personnel information that is crucial, such as whether a gang possesses automatic weapons and is possibly stepping up its recruitment at a school for a future gang war. You must be careful in patrolling or guarding a school. Depending on the nature of the threats, you may need to take extra precautions for safety. The school's exits and entrances should be guarded and watched closely for gang members who may try to infiltrate a school. A school should have a uniform policy that doesn't allow students to wear or display anything that indicates support or membership in a gang. Such a policy gives private security personnel a justification for intervening with students. In addition, areas close to the school during the evening may be the sites of criminal activity, recruitment, and gang initiations. Therefore the school may need additional private security personnel to patrol and guard key locations. You should also be aware of occurrences on the street, such as the death of a gang member or possible gang war that will require a heightened state of alert at a school. Students and faculty should be aware that any gang activity or information should immediately be communicated to private security personnel in a manner that is confidential.

A systematic approach to educational institution-wide security that is well designed, executed, and maintained will reduce many of the risks. Private security employees should also be seeking continuous training to update their awareness and knowledge about the ever-changing face of threats that will be faced today and in the future. Private security personnel in a school that has a potential gang problem should consider themselves part of a large team of administrators, teachers, parents, and law enforcement agencies that are working to prevent a gang problem from spreading. A focus should always be on communication and cooperation for the benefit of security at a school as well as the safety of the lives of everyone.

■ Conclusion

School violence incidents are a major concern for private security personnel at all educational institutions in light of recent tragic events. The nature of the violence raises the potential for administrators and schools to be subjected to lawsuits; therefore, it is a responsibility of the security person to help prevent or to mitigate any incident that may lead to a lawsuit. Technology has now allowed children to be victims of bullies or sexually assaulted by pedophiles. Bomb threats are a major concern that require in-depth planning and training for the protection of a facility and its people. Rising gang activity requires private security personnel to become familiar with the nature of gangs and be prepared for their threats to our educational institutions.

■ Chapter Review

- Private security personnel at educational institutions should be aware of the nature of school violence.
- A major focus for private security employees at an educational institution is to prevent lawsuits.
- School security requires understanding the layout of buildings as well the nature of people who work and attend an educational institution.

- School threats come in a variety of forms that require different responses from private security employees.
- Security planning committees are organizations to which private security personnel should be prepared to contribute.
- School violence profiling involves examining key characteristics that may indicate someone is likely to engage in violence at an educational institution.
- Students engage in cyberbullying through a variety of methods of attack that involve different areas of technology.
- Child exploitation is an unfortunate reality in this century.
- Pedophiles use a variety of methods to exploit and sexually assault children.
- Bomb threats are becoming a more common scenario faced by educational institutions.
- Physical security and bomb incident plans allow private security personnel to prepare a school for possible bomb threats.
- Private security personnel should be aware of the growing gang problem in America and take precautions when providing security services in high-risk gang areas.

■ Answers to Case Studies

Case Study 1

1. **What specific background work should you do when beginning work at a school?** Prior to reporting for work, you should become familiar with the location and mission of the school. Visiting Web sites or speaking with superiors will help give you an idea of the nature of the educational institution. Once at a location, you should become familiar with the physical layout of the campus and become aware of possible security difficulties. You should speak with as many employees or personnel as possible to get an understanding of the particular security issues that are priorities at the institution.

2. **How can you help in the creation of security policies that protect employees and students from harm as well as mitigate the possibility of future lawsuits?** You should work with school staff to determine the best policies and procedures that will avoid future lawsuits based on negligence. For example, you may be designated to break up fights because you have been trained in using nonlethal force. Allowing teachers to engage in such activity could prove to be negligent if a young person is harmed.

3. **What advice would you provide to teachers who may suspect one of their students is a future school shooter?** The teacher should communicate their

suspicions immediately. You are likely to work with a principal and faculty in determining whether there are possible signs or evidence that a student may engage in future violent activity.

Case Study 2

1. What can be done to prevent cyberbullying from taking place at an educational institution? You should work with administrators and teachers to discuss the legal and policy implications involved with cyberbullying. Computer specialists and computer companies that work with the school should be contacted for ways to minimize or prevent future attacks through computers. In addition, you can help implement and enforce a new policy regarding the use of cell phones and other pieces of technology.

2. What are some of the ways in which young people victimize other people while on a school campus or at home? The Internet provides a number of ways to cyberbully another young person, including the use of Web sites, e-mails, blogs, and instant messaging programs to harass, threaten, or embarrass another. Young people also use cell phones and other pieces of technology such as video game systems to conduct such activity.

Case Study 3

1. What are the ways that children are currently exploited? Children in the United States are often lured in person or via the Internet. They are turned into prostitutes at various locations at home and abroad. Technology is also used to communicate, exploit, and profit by victimizing children.

2. In what ways can private security employees help to prevent children from becoming victims? You can provide information, monitor the use of technology by young people, monitor suspicious adults in and around the school, and be aware of known pedophiles in the area.

Case Study 4

1. What considerations should be made in light of this recent bomb threat? You should consider the manner in which the threat was made as well as whether any additional threats or activity have taken place. Bomb threat incident plans should be implemented along with communicating with local police agencies. Security outside the building should also be taken into consideration if an evacuation must take place.

2. What actions can you take to help the local police that are on their way? You can provide leadership and guidance as a building is evacuated, as well as instructions to people, which will make the situation easier and safer for local law enforcement agencies as well as school personnel and students.

Case Study 5

1. What information concerning the nature of gangs is important for you to understand and be familiar with before working in school security? You should learn specifics concerning the local gangs that operate near an educational institution. You should speak with school administrators as well as law enforcement agencies for information that can assist you while on duty.

2. What are some of the rising gangs in the United States that pose a threat to school institutions? Bloods, Crips, MS-13, skinheads, and Latin Kings are just a few of the gangs that have continued to rise and operate in the United States near school campuses.

■ **Key Terms**

Assault   The crime of violence against another person. In some jurisdictions, assault is used to refer to the actual violence, while in other jurisdictions (e.g., some in the United States, England, and Wales), assault refers only to the threat of violence, while the actual violence is battery.

Blog   A Web site where entries are made in a journal or diary style of writing. Blogs can be used for personal use, to discuss a particular subject with individuals, or for other personal functions.

Bomb incident plan   Provides detailed procedures to be implemented when a bombing attack is executed or threatened.

Command center   A center for operations in case of crisis.

Cyberbullying   The use of technology to frighten, embarrass, harass, or otherwise target a minor. It is important to understand that it involves more than just the use of the Internet or a computer. Cyberbullying includes any cybercommunication or publication posted or sent by a minor online, by instant message, e-mail, Web site, diary site, online profile, interactive game, handheld device, cell phone, or other interactive device.

Foreseeable risk and threat   A danger that a reasonable person should anticipate as the result of his or her actions. Foreseeable risk is a common affirmative defense put up as a response by defendants in lawsuits for negligence (a tort).

Instant messaging or IM   A form of real-time communication between two or more people based on typed text. The text is conveyed via computers connected over a network such as the Internet.

Keycatcher   A device that records every keystroke made on the computer on which it is installed.

Luring   Activities conducted by a predator that tempts or attracts a targeted child with the promise of a pleasure or reward.

Microcosm   A small, representative system having analogies to a larger system in constitution, configuration, or development.

Negligence   The failure to use such care as a reasonably prudent and careful person would use under similar circumstances; it is the doing of some act that a person of ordinary prudence would not have done under the circumstances or failure to do what a person of ordinary prudence would have done under similar circumstances. Conduct that falls below the standard established by law for the protection of others is unreasonable risk of harm; it is a departure from the conduct expected of a reasonably prudent person under like circumstances.

Pedophiles   Those individuals with a sexual interest in young children.

Physical security plan   A plan that provides for the protection of property, personnel, facilities, and material against unauthorized entry, trespass, damage, sabotage, or other illegal or criminal acts.

Prostitution   Providing sexual favors for hire.

Reasonable   What a person under a set of circumstance and position should properly do when faced with a situation.

School planning committee   Offers advice and creates the policy guidelines for handling any type of school crisis or criminal activity on a campus.

Sex tourism   Traveling to a foreign country to engage in sexual activity with a child.

Webcam exploitation   The use of Web cams to entice young people to engage in recordable sexual acts has become another new form of victimization.

■ References

1. Spy-Ops. 2006. *School violence training brief.* Vol 12. TB 58. *See also* Newman, K., Fox, C., Harding, D., Roth, W. 2004. *Rampage: The Social Roots of School Shootings.* New York: Basic Books. CNN Study on School Violence. http://www.cnn.com/us9908/04/school.violence. National Center for Injury Prevention and Prevention Control. http://www.cdc.gov/ncipc/factsheets/schoolvi.htm. Department of Health and Human Services Report. http://www.hhs.gov.asl/testifv/t990311a.html.

2. Ibid.

3. Ibid.

4. Ibid.

5. Ibid.

6. Ibid.

7. Ibid.

8. Ibid.

9. Ibid.

10. Ibid.

11. Ibid.

12. Ibid.

13. Ibid.

14. Spy-Ops. 2006. *School violence training brief.* Vol 12. TB 58.

15. Center for Safe & Responsible Internet Use. http://www.csriu.org. *See also* Wired Safety Organization. http://www.wiredsafety.org. I-Safe America. http://www.isafe.org. Media Awareness Network. http://www.media-awareness.ca. *Parry's Guide to Cyber-Bullying.* http://www.bebo.com/Cyber-bullying. *Stop Cyber-Bullying.* http://www.stopcyber-bullying.org.

16. Ibid.

17. Ibid.

18. Ibid.

19. Ibid.

20. Ibid.

21. Ibid.

22. Ibid.

23. Ibid.

24. Ibid.

25. Spy-Ops. 2006, *Online child exploitation training brief.* Vol 10. TB 50. *See also* National Center for Missing and Exploited Children. http:/www.missingkids.com.

26. Ibid.

27. Ibid.

28. Ibid.

29. Ibid.

30. Ibid.

31. Ibid.

32. Ibid.

33. Ibid.

34. Fay, J. 1994. Getting ready for the bomb in your building. *Security Management*, April. *See also* Jenkins, A. 1991. Bomb threat preparation: Defusing an explosive situation. *Security Management*, November. McCarthy, W., and Quigley, R. 1992. Don't blow it. *Security Management*, March. Seuter, E. 1991. Are you ready? *Security Management*, July. Learning for Life: Law Enforcement Study on Bomb Threats. http://www.learning-for-life.org/exploring/

lawenforcement/study/bomb.pdf. Ortmeier, P.J. 2005. *Security Management*. Upper Saddle River, NJ: Pearson Prentice Hall.

35. Ibid.

36. Ibid.

37. Ibid.

38. Ibid.

39. Ashbury, H. 2002. The gangs of New York. *In: S. Donahue, ed. Gangs*. New York: Thunder's Mouth Press. (Originally published in 1927 by Knopf).

40. Cohen, A. 1955. *Delinquent Boys: The Culture of the Gang*. New York: Free Press.

41. Williams, F., and M. McShane. 1994. *Criminological Theory*. Englewood Cliffs, NJ: Prentice Hall.

42. Sheldon, R., S. Tracy, and W. Brown. 2001. *Youth Gangs in American Society*. Belmont, CA: Wadsworth.

43. Kratcoski, P., and L. D. Kratcoski. 1996. *Juvenile Delinquency*. 4th ed. Upper Saddle River, NJ: Prentice Hall.

44. Duffy, L. 1996. Experts say gangs offer acceptance. *Syracuse Post-Standard*. November 7: A16.

45. *See* note 1.

46. Delaney, T. 2001. *Community, Sport, and Leisure*. Auburn, NY: Legend Books.

47. Padilla, F. 1992. *The Gang as an American Enterprise*. New Brunswick, NJ: Rutgers University Press.

48. Ibid.

49. Vigil, J. 1997. *Origins of Mexican American Gangs: Learning from Gangs*. The Mexican American Experience, Eric Digest. http://www.ed.gov/databases/ ERIC_Digests.

50. Siegel, L., B.C. Welsh, and J.J. Senna. 2003. *Juvenile Delinquency*. 8th ed. Belmont, CA: Wadsworth.

51. Thorton, W., and L. Voight. 1992. *Delinquency and Justice*. 3rd ed. New York: McGraw-Hill.

52. *See* note 1.

53. Savelli, L. 2000. *Introduction to East Coast gangs*. National Alliance of Gang Investigators Associations. http://www.nagia.org.

54. Reiner, I. 1992. *Gangs, Crime, and Violence in Los Angeles: Findings and Proposals from the District Attorney's Office*. Arlington, VA: National Youth Gang Information Center.

55. Ibid.

56. Schneider, E. 1999. *Vampires, Dragons, and Egyptian Kings: Youth Gangs in Postwar New York.* Princeton, NJ: Princeton University Press.

57. Delaney, T. 2006. *American Street Gangs.* Upper Saddle River, NJ: Prentice Hall.

58. Jankowski, M. 1991. *Islands in the Streets: Gangs and American Urban Society.* Berkeley: University of California Press.

59. Ibid.

60. Schafer, J. R., J. Navarro. 2003. *The seven-stage hate model: The psychopathology of hate groups.* FBI Law Enforcement Bulletin, March.

61. *See* note 1.

62. *See* note 60.

63. *See* note 60.

64. *See* note 60.

65. *See* note 60.

66. *See* note 60.

67. *See* note 60.

68. *See* note 60.

69. *See* note 60.

70. A&E Home Video. 2001. *History Channel Presents: Street Gangs – A Secret History.*

Technology Warfare, Biometric, and Bugging Issues

CHAPTER
11

▶ ▶ OBJECTIVES

- Become familiar with technology warfare.
- Become familiar with biometric security devices.
- Understand the threat posed by bugging.

■ Introduction

Technological warfare against American businesses and government agencies is a real possibility, as technology makes criminal and terrorist activity easier and more profitable. Advances in technology in the area of biometrics have made security more efficient; however, the use of bugging devices by criminals will continue to pose threats to these new effective security measures.

■ Technology Warfare

▶ ▶ CASE STUDY 1

You attend a joint training session between the private security firm that employs you and the FBI. In the training session, a special focus is placed on upcoming threats to technology within American companies. A recent land dispute between the United States and China has led to unofficial cyber and computer attacks on US government sites and against the American business community. A federal agent notes in his presentation that the United States is currently in an unofficial war with China.

1. What is the nature of technology warfare?
2. What events are likely to spark a technology conflict between two countries?

Few security policy makers truly understand the importance of technology in protecting and defending our national assets and human lives. This section discusses the role of technology as a method of current warfare threatening US businesses and critical areas. In particular, the role and increasing threats of espionage and cyberterrorism are discussed in greater detail than in the previous sections.

The objective of technology warfare is to gain a technological or economic advantage over your adversary through the unlawful acquisition of technology, information about technology, or information about the technical capabilities of the adversary. Technology warfare allows domestic and foreign businesses, as well as foreign nations and their state-controlled corporations, to avoid the high costs of research and development while exploiting the economic and strategic gains of others. An economic, financial, and possibly a military advantage can be gained by those using illegal technology warfare, whether they are a private business organization or a foreign government entity. Therefore, any domestic or foreign entity that illegally acquires a technological or economic advantage over an organization has engaged in technological warfare.

The current threat to US business organizations cannot be overlooked or avoided. Technology warfare is threatening US business at an increasingly alarming rate because it is easier than ever to commit. This is because it is extremely productive and is not easily understood by potential business targets. As previously noted, intellectual property (IP) is as valuable to any company or military institution as money, natural resources, and commodities. Intellectual property is at the center of any business's true value to investors and to the global economy. Companies compete with one another in markets to see who can create new services or products with a greater degree of value. This results in new IP being researched and developed by a business firm to maintain a lead in their respective market. Therefore, as much as 80% of a company's value can be in its intellectual property that is already developed or is in the early stages of development. The previously mentioned IP information, if obtained from a company, can ultimately lead to a company's failure and ultimate demise in the domestic and global market. Furthermore, stolen IP information can also lead to destabilization of the US economy and national security.[1]

Targets

It must be understood that is not just large corporate conglomerates, multinational banks, and defense firms that are targets. The illegal acquisition of information can occur within a business of any size and begin either with an entry-level person or at the very top of the executive chain of command. As long as a business has critical information that can change the balance of power in some manner, then it is a potential target. For example, businesses in the entertainment, communication, and information fields fear becoming targets due to their databases, proprietary information, and customer lists that share personal, financial, and social information. Almost half of the Fortune 500 companies have been victims of industrial espionage.[2]

While numerous corporations and foreign nations, including France, Israel, and Russia, have been implicated in seeking out sensitive IP here in America for an economic advantage, a recent US government investigation has unveiled an alarming trend in the area of technology warfare. There are a number of cases in which China has obtained sensitive and classified US weapons technology from US corporate firms in the past ten years. Chinese agents have illegally purchased or have been caught by authorities trying to obtain advanced electronic components, materials for precision guided missiles, radar equipment, advanced night vision technology, and computer technology, according to the Immigration and Customs Enforcement (ICE) officials who have been carrying out recent investigations. Immigration and Customs agents have approached about 6000 US companies that are known targets of illicit Chinese technology and equipment theft. In terms of threats to the US economy and national security, the stakes can be very high. For example, in the late 1990s, China engaged in one of the most damaging illegal technology exports ever to hurt US national security. China secretly obtained the advanced technology of the battle management system for the Aegis cruiser. By 2004, China had deployed its first two Luyang II guided missiles equipped with the Chinese version of the Aegis system.[3] Recently, two Lucent Technologies scientists were arrested by federal authorities and charged with stealing key telecommunication information for the purpose of transferring it to a state-owned Chinese company. Sensitive and critical technology information must be protected from criminal conspirators within a US business, foreign corporations, and foreign governments. The damage in this area not only can hurt American business interests but threaten national security as well.[4]

The world currently thrives on cutting edge technology that advances aspects of human development. Space technology, robotics, energy conduits, and communication equipment are major areas of research and development. In a globalized world, a business that can achieve even a small advance in such areas will land a financial and political windfall. In addition, a business is likely to secure the involvement of the federal government in the development of such IP.

New Hidden Risks for Businesses

The merger and acquisition of companies is commonplace and considered a blessing in some cases for shareholders. **Mergers and acquisitions** involve companies organizationally and financially coming together or being taken over by acquiring assets. There is, however, a downside to such business rearrangements that is often ignored by executives at the top. The rising trend has led to a significant rise in IP theft and technology warfare practices. Larger companies, especially foreign-based companies, have the potential to take advantage of small and medium-sized technology-based companies. A larger company during the merger and acquisition process may take steps that seem like gestures of good business negotiations and strategy, but are actually designed to observe and target technology, business processes, and trade secrets. Such areas make up 70–80% of the value of most small and medium-sized firms. Small and medium-sized firms eager to please a larger company may "show their cards," thereby exposing themselves to risk by revealing sensitive IP.[5] Also, employees within small and medium-sized firms are valuable assets that can be targeted and influenced to move away from a firm or divulge sensitive information during the merger and acquisition process. Failure to realize such threats can result in the value of the acquisition process being much less for small or medium-sized firms or IP value being completely taken away from a firm, leading to its ultimate demise or an inequitable acquisition process by a rival business.[6]

The following are the top areas of IP risk in the area of mergers and acquisitions:[7]

- Show and tell—A business that seeks to merge or be taken over by a larger corporation tries to assure the larger company of its value by revealing sensitive information (IP). This allows a dominating company or foreign company to possibly back out of the deal and now, with the advantage of new information, outmaneuver the small business in the market or beat them to the punch in production of a product or service.

- Derogatory information—Risks related to any potential unknown derogatory or controversial information within the background of the company being acquired and used to exploit a business during the merger and acquisition process. This is a form of blackmail where the concern is the image of a company and possibly the value of its shares if information was revealed to the public.

- Poor IP protection practices—If electronically stored and transmitted trade secrets, like proprietary source code and technical data, are not properly stored, such information may be observed during a tour of a facility or during the negotiation process of the merger and acquisition and used to the detriment of a company.

- Risky strategic partners—The target company's relationships with third parties such as contract manufacturers, consultants, technology developers, vendors, and licensees can potentially place the company at risk. Such third parties could be revealed during the merger and acquisition process and therefore new backdoor relationships may develop to the detriment of a firm. If a small company thrives because of a great relationship with a third-party contractor, then the company acquiring the smaller company could work out a side relationship making the company being acquired unnecessary. Also, a third-party contractor could be tricked into revealing information or turning over critical IP.

- Key employee retention—It is important for a company to retain key employees and technology contributors that, if lost, could significantly depreciate the intellectual capital under acquisition. A larger company could ask for a firm's employee to work on a project or to be on "loan" to a firm, only to later be lured away permanently.

There are three key data security tasks that should be completed during the acquisition process to protect a firm from future problems:

1. Search for file-sharing applications on the computer network, particularly any sharing applications to a company that is on the other side of the table in a merger/acquisition deal.
2. Develop an application inventory and compare it to the software licenses.
3. Conduct a penetration test of the acquired company's systems. The best way to determine the problems in a security system is to try and break it. A company may want to have employees try and get around security protocols or bring in outside consultants to test the security strength prior to any merger and acquisition negotiations taking place. This is not to say that in-house security personnel are not capable of protecting a business, but, like many other areas of business, a fresh set of eyes and a fresh voice that is honest and unrestrained from offering a true picture of the state of security may be more valuable.

Entry-level security personnel in this area of technology warfare often have a notion that IP is being taken from a business by a trained foreign operative or genius computer hacker. The reality is that penetration into a business entity can be completed with simple methods, even as simple as a phone call. Information written on a cocktail napkin given by one executive to another at a bar, or information said very loudly at a conference, needs to be protected as much as the hard drive of a research and development team. Focusing exclusively on computer and network security still leaves a large opportunity for victimization.

High-tech spying has become commonplace, and hackers and spies are being actively recruited to target companies. While the above list covers about 80% of the techniques used, industrial spies are very resourceful and use new, innovative techniques constantly. In particular, information on laptops with wireless Internet access needs protection from IP theft.[8]

The accessibility of information found on corporate databases, as well as open access to information networks in a company, makes it easy for workers to steal from their employers. Technology gives job-hopping employees an easy way to take reams of data with them when relocating to higher-paying firms. With a flash drive or a burned CD, a company's critical IP can be taken right out the door without security even realizing the possible breach. Even an iPod or a flash drive disguised as a piece of jewelry can be employed to steal information. Once information has been obtained from a business, you have a "broken arrow" situation. The likelihood of recovering information once it is in someone's pocket and on the move is almost impossible. Information can also be stolen from a company and sent out via a company's own computer to an undisclosed location creating a "broken arrow from within" situation.

Signs of Intellectual Property Theft in a Business Setting

While not all of the following is clear proof that technology warfare is about to occur at a business firm, there are certain signs that should raise a flag of possible theft by employees in the future:[9]

- An employee has been given a bad performance review by a superior.
- An employee is not given a raise when requested.
- A salesperson's key customer just canceled a business transaction or partnership.
- An employee changes work habits and starts coming in early or staying late when he or she has never done this in the past.
- Key employees who play major roles in the company begin leaving for no apparent reason.

It is important to realize that an honest employee may actually be acting as a corporate spy without even realizing they are transferring critical IP. Employees, consultants, temporary workers, and others who have direct access to sensitive information, or who may overhear conversations containing sensitive information, must be informed of their responsibility to maintain confidentiality. An employee talking to a colleague in another company and discussing their day at work may reveal critical information to a rival. It is often the case that current employees and even former employees are either willing or unwilling participants in IP theft during a job interview. They can reveal information during the interview or provide sensitive information on a resume. For example, in a recent incident, the proprietary data about the global expansion plan of one company was obtained from the resume of an employee seeking a new position. In similar incidents, industrial spies posing as recruiters interviewed candidates for a position and pressed them to obtain sensitive information about their current or past employer. In another case, an individual was pushed to answer questions about a classified project they participated in and the sensitive details.[10]

For corporate spies actively engaged in technology warfare, there are certain common profile characteristics. While everyone is a potential suspect, the following is a list of the more common characteristics of an active corporate operative who poses a threat to IP at a business:[11]

- 22–40 years old
- Female or male (especially females since males are generally regarded with more suspicion)

- College graduate (possibly from a university that is not well known) with a low-level degree
- Broad, short-term employment history. Their work background may be sporadic, and they may have numerous employment entries on their resume.
- Financial problems and bad credit history
- Military intelligence experience
- Considered a loner or outsider in the office
- Has acquaintances in law enforcement
- Romantic (and/or expensive) hobbies or interests (e.g., scuba, snow skiing, skydiving) along with expensive tastes in food and drink

A key point in this area is that for effective investigations and prevention, no one can be ruled out as a corporate spy. Experienced veteran employees may be conducting espionage activities within the organization despite their years of loyalty to an organization. Inside security and IT/communication personnel may also be involved in theft of information. It is therefore important to bring in outside investigators who will examine any suspected malfeasance by any employee. An in-house security person may be reluctant to accuse an executive at the top for fear of retribution.

A company has the power to decide how much investment they should make in their own protection and how many steps they wish to take to protect their IP. However, the general trend is to be reactive to a threat. Precautions require money, and money spent on security is money that cannot be used for other profit-driven purposes. In other words, a business generally takes precautions to protect IP once they discover a critical attack, instead of being proactive and preventing an illegal transfer from the beginning. A comprehensive security program must be in place that addresses physical security of a facility and information protection. A complete assessment of both must be completed as part of the due diligence to the company, employees, and shareholders.

Now, those skeptical about taking preventive measures prefer to allow lawyers to provide a remedy. If, for example, a rival Chinese company releases a product that was clearly produced through stolen IP from a victim company, many executives would argue that clear proof of theft or violation of a nondisclosure contract would allow a court victory. Keep in mind the reality. Court cases involving international or domestic theft can take years and cost a company gross sums of money, even without a victory. In civil action cases, less than 2% of the 7445 civil IP disputes disposed in 2002 were resolved by a trial verdict. Meanwhile, a business firm is being beaten in the market by the rival organization that successfully conducted technology warfare practices. Also, relying on a contract to protect your business interests works if the party follows the rule of law. In dealing with rival companies from foreign lands, it is going to be very difficult to acquire judgment and satisfaction in your favor. Instead, due diligence and proactive measures are the ways to protect your business firm.

For example, in the area of due diligence, consider sales and marketing personnel. Whether on the phone or at a trade show, anyone can obtain sensitive information from a sales and marketing person just by asking. Sales personnel are supposed to give out information, not protect it. As a matter of practice, when it appears that a major sale is in jeopardy of collapsing over the phone or at a meeting, a salesperson will reveal sensitive or critical information. A trained corporate operative knows how to pose as an interested customer and drag out a purchase negotiation long enough for a concerned salesperson to reveal the critical information.

Formal documents are protected, but drafts and rough copies are considered worthless and therefore receive little security scrutiny. Keep in mind with a rough draft, the information is the same as the formal copy; the organization and presentation are just different. Such information simply discarded in a wastebasket becomes invaluable. Likewise, travel tickets, invoices, hotel slips, shipment manifests, credit card receipts, and purloined appointment calendars can all reveal a possible merger or joint venture, as well as who a business has been dealing with or plans to work with in the future. That information, if obtained by a rival, makes a business vulnerable. Internal company correspondence in the form of newsletters, policy meeting minutes, project data, and company status updates that are simply handed out to the public at will, without any inquiry as to the request, can put a company in a disadvantaged position. Add the previous mentioned methods of intrusion and acquisition, such as hacking, dumpster-diving, eavesdropping, and active infiltration, and a business can be a sitting duck.[12]

While any security plan must be tailored to the individual business, and outside consultants and local and federal law enforcement agencies should be contacted to coordinate preventive methods, the following is a basic list of steps every security employee should consider regardless of the size or field of the business:[13]

1. Inventory all IP assets, including personnel with special skills.

2. Identify and label all IP assets and associated information appropriately.

3. Limit direct access and monitor all access to sensitive IP until a workable and reliable security measure is fully in place.

4. Perform a risk assessment on each of the IP assets and include IP as part of a risk assessment plan, whether it is conducted by an in-house or outside risk assessment firm. When discussing a business continuity plan, IP should at a minimum be discussed in the planning.

5. Develop a security program for each IP asset based on the determined risk.

6. Lock it up, encrypt it, keep it behind closed doors, limit access, track access, and monitor the area where it is stored and used. Keep a log of all those who access critical IP, which includes security personnel and top-level executives.

7. Make sure you take the protective steps necessary to obtain legal protection of the IP.

8. Educate employees of their responsibilities and the preventive steps to protect IP. This is one of the most important steps in protecting your IP assets and may require additional training or testing exercises.

9. Make sure there are nondisclosure agreements for all employees and visitors.

10. Ensure outside businesses in any business deal are contractually liable for taking or revealing IP.

11. Make sure all company information and assets are retrieved when employees and others leave the organization.

12. Look at leased electronic equipment such as computers, cell phones, PDAs, copiers, and fax machines that may store documents, and ensure that they are properly cleared of data before returning them.

13. Maintain all computers with up-to-date software and include firewalls, antivirus programs, and spyware protection.

14. Do not allow mail and packages to arrive on a Saturday when the business is closed without an available person to collect all mail. A business that is closed on Saturday, but has mail lying around, is at risk if someone else comes by and takes the mail.

15. Train multiple personnel in the threat of IP being stolen or misplaced.

Ultimately, technology warfare is all too common in the business world and a growing problem. Whether for financial or competitive advantage, or for military operations in a global theater, the intellectual property and technology base in American businesses is at risk. The executives in businesses that fall victim often do not report the damage that has been done for fear that it will affect their relationships with customers and ultimately the value of their business in the market. Ultimately, technology alone cannot protect technology. Even with the best security plan in place, a new employee can be tricked into sending out critical information to a predator. Employee screening, training, and testing must be implemented as well as other security policies. Furthermore, while no plan will work 100%, the key issue is awareness of possible threats. A potential victim company should harden itself for a technology warfare attack. In selecting a business as a target, offenders will choose the business that is the least prepared. This is why cooperation among domestic businesses and sharing of security methods helps protect the businesses, the US economy, and national security.

■ Biometrics

▶ ▶ CASE STUDY 2

As a private security team member at a corporate office building, you recently learn that the corporation has decided to invest in the installment of biometric security measures throughout the building. Corporate management has decided that biometric devices will allow extra security protection at various points in the building while also monitoring those employees entering or leaving.

1. What are some of the major benefits of using biometric devices?

Since the global war on terrorism began, increased emphasis has been placed on security, access control, and identification. **Biometric** technologies are defined as "automated methods of identifying or authenticating the identity of a living person based on a physical or behavioral characteristic." Historically, individuals were identified by some known piece of data or information, such as a social security number, mother's maiden name, or a personal identification number. Individual identification was also varied by things such as a driver's license, an ATM card, a work ID card, or a key to the building. Today, biometrics provides positive identification using fingerprint, iris, facial, hand, voice, and signature recognition.

All biometric systems work in the same manner. First, a person is enrolled into a database using a specific type of biometric identification device. Initially, information about a certain characteristic of the person is captured, for example, a fingerprint or hand geometry. This information is subsequently processed by an algorithm, coded, and stored in a database for future reference. When the person needs to be identified, the system will ask for specific personal information, translate it using an algorithm, and then compare the new code with existing database information. If a match is made, the identification process is complete.[14]

Much attention is being given to this technology that has been under development for decades. In fact, the first commercial biometric device was produced nearly 25 years ago, and there is a good chance many individuals have already come across one of these biometric identification and access control systems. As advances in this specific area of technology continue, adoption will grow and private security personnel may soon see a biometric identification system built into cars and computer keyboards. The best measurement of biometric advancement is the lowering price of verification.[15]

Biometric identification and access control systems are based on a number of different techniques and devices. These systems can be placed in one of two categories. The first category is physical biometrics, which uses physical characteristics, like the eye, for recognition. The second category is behavioral biometrics, which uses characteristics like someone's voice or handwriting for recognition. The following is a brief description of several of these biometric systems.

Fingerprint Recognition

Fingerprint-based **identification** is the oldest biometric technique, and has been successfully used in numerous applications. All human beings have unique, immutable fingerprints. A fingerprint is comprised of a series of ridges and furrows on the surface of the skin that covers the finger. The uniqueness of a fingerprint can be determined by the pattern of ridges and furrows as well as the small points in the fingerprint. These characteristics are compared against patterns stored in the access system and access is granted to those that match, while access is denied to those that are unknown. Contrary to what has been seen in popular movies and television shows, simply cutting off an individual's finger and placing it on the access device does not fool a biometric device. In many of the advanced fingerprint recognition systems, sensors have been included that can determine if the finger in the reader is attached to a living person or not. This is accomplished through temperature, moisture, and oxygenation sensors.[16]

Facial Recognition

Facial recognition analyzes specific characteristics of a person's face and captures the images with a digital video camera. It takes specific measurements of the overall facial structure, including distances between eyes, nose, mouth, and jaw edges. These measurements are retained in a database and used as a comparison when a user stands before the camera. This type of biometric system has been used widely in the fight against terrorism. Known measurements, stored in a database, are compared to measurements captured in real time, matches are identified, and appropriate access or service is provided when a person uses the device.

Iris Recognition

The iris is the colored ring of tissue in the eye suspended behind the cornea and immediately in front of the lens. Like a fingerprint, every iris is unique. While many mistake it for retinal scanning, iris recognition simply involves taking a picture of the iris; this picture is used solely for authentication. A matching algorithm of the iris recognition system analyzes the patterns in the iris that are visible between the pupil and sclera (white of the eye) and converts them into a digital template. These values are stored in a database and communicated to access control portals.

Retinal Recognition

Retinal recognition technology is used to measure the unique configuration of blood vessels in the eye contained in the retina. Retina images are captured using a digital camera. The pattern of blood vessels of the retina is mapped. These maps are compared against those stored in a database, and matching is done by an algorithm. Unlike other biometric technologies, retinal recognition is not yet widely deployed for commercial applications.[17]

Hand Recognition

Hand recognition was one of the first biometric systems proven practical in use across a variety of real-world applications. Hand recognition works by taking a 3-dimensional view of the hand in order to determine the geometry and measurements including finger length, height, and other details. Hand recognition systems with up to 90 different measurements are currently available. These measurements and metrics of the handprint are processed by applying algorithms and stored as a representative template for a specific individual.

Voiceprint Recognition

Every voice has enough individual characteristics to distinguish it from others through voiceprint analysis. Voiceprint recognition can be defined as a combination of both aural (listening) and spectrographic (instrumental) comparison of one or more known voices with an unknown voice for the purpose of identification or elimination. The uniqueness lies in the manner in which the muscles for talking are manipulated during speech.

Handwriting Recognition

Distinguishing one individual's handwriting from another individual's can also be accomplished through biometrics. This is quite different from optical character recognition (OCR), where a computer converts handwritten materials into electronic format. Complex computer programs look at spacing, slant, arcs, and other characteristics of handwriting samples and create a template that is stored in a database. These templates are accessed and matches can be identified. New devices that actually create a 3-D image of a signature, based on pressure exerted by the writer, have recently come on the market. They have great potential, but have yet to reach critical mass market usage.[18]

Biometric Smart Cards

Smart cards provide a complementary technology to biometrics. Smart cards augment the information contained on the magnetic strip on the back of the card with a substantial amount of data that can be read and written to a chip mounted on the surface of the card. The acceptance of these combined technologies in the US market is being driven by the significant increase in identity theft over the last few years. Application of these technologies is being considered in the national ID card initiatives currently being discussed in Congress.

Fingerprint-scan technology adds an additional security layer to a smart card system to help guard against identity theft. Earlier this year, the Department of Defense in the United States tried biometric smart card solutions in South Korea, Japan, and Europe. The Department of Defense's Biometric Identification System (DBIDS) places a digital fingerprint and photo on a smart card in a configuration that local authorities can adapt to their specific system requirements. Like retina recognition, this technology holds great potential, but interoperability remains a stumbling block for the foreseeable future.

Accuracy is the key to success in biometrics. Positive identification with an extremely limited number of errors is required and must be proven. This requires biometric systems to obtain high-quality, legitimate templates. These templates are the records used by the biometric-based authentication system. Without high quality, interoperability among systems, and industry standards, correct authentication cannot be guaranteed. Other areas that cause errors in biometric authentication include sensor noise, particularly in voice authentication systems, as well as the variability in biometric characteristics. In the fingerprint identification area, placement of the finger or hand on the sensing device is the single most critical factor in the accuracy of the identification system.[19]

No one biometric technique will serve all applications. The differences between physiological and behavioral methods are important for several reasons. The degree of intrapersonal variation in a physical characteristic is smaller than in a behavioral characteristic. For example, an individual's fingerprint is the same day in and day out, barring injury. A signature, however, is influenced by both controllable actions and less controllable psychological factors. Behavior-based systems, therefore, have a tougher job adjusting for intrapersonal variation and tend to have higher error rates. None of the techniques described above are perfect. Private security personnel must understand that such devices all have the potential to make mistakes. However, private security personnel must incorporate the strengths and weaknesses of biometrics as part of the overall security program at a location.

While still early in the technology maturity model, biometric systems are being deployed almost daily by governments and the private sector alike. Private security professionals agree that these techniques provide another barrier that can be used to secure information, materials, and physical sites. The use of these systems will become commonplace as technology continues to evolve, the systems become more reliable, and regulatory policies are developed in order to safeguard individual privacy.

■ Bugging

▶ ▶ CASE STUDY 3

A recent private investigation involving the corporation where you are employed as a security professional has revealed that confidential information is being leaked to a competitor. One of the corporate managers suspects that numerous offices in the corporate building have been bugged.

1. What are some of the indicators that a bug has possibly been placed at a location?
2. What are some of the appropriate responses if a bug is suspected or found?

Eavesdropping on people or groups no longer requires large and complicated devices. These devices are also no longer used by government personnel only. The manufacture, sale, installation, and monitoring of illegal surveillance devices is a multibillion dollar underground industry within the United States. The significant decrease in cost and the increased availability of this equipment has made electronic bugging all too common. In a study completed by the US State Department in 2000, it was estimated that at least $800 million of illegal bugging and eavesdropping equipment is imported and installed in the United States each year. A major Silicon Valley firm has noted that the cost to the US economy has been estimated at $59.5 billion a year.[20] The majority of this equipment is illegally imported from France, Germany, Lebanon, Italy, Canada, Israel, England, Japan, Taiwan, South Africa, and a host of other countries.

In the United States, over $6 million worth of surveillance devices are sold to the public each day.[21] Most of these products are sold by storefront operations, spy shops, attorneys, and private investigators located in major metro areas such as New York, Miami, Los Angles, San Francisco, Dallas, Chicago, and Minneapolis. This does not include the tens of billions of dollars spent each year on legitimate eavesdropping products purchased by law enforcement, military, and intelligence agencies. The equipment is commonly sold over the counter, via mail order, and through the Internet. Most of these bugging devices cost only a few dollars, but highly sophisticated, quality products may be purchased for less than $1000 each. In New York City alone, there are a significant number of companies that will not only sell you the eavesdropping device, but will also break into the target's office to install the device, and, for an additional fee, will provide a monitoring and transcription service. Additionally, anyone with a soldering iron and a basic understanding of electronics can build and install an eavesdropping device. Numerous books on the subject are available through book retailers. In addition, plans and schematics for these types of devices are available on the Internet. These plans range from a very simple wireless microphone to elaborate infrared audio transmitters. [22]

The raw materials needed to build these devices are easily obtained at Radio Shack, or salvaged from consumer electronic devices such as cordless telephones, intercom systems, and televisions. Bugs, wiretaps, and covert video surveillance are all techniques used to gather intelligence, trade secrets, and other valuable information and intellectual property. These techniques are typically referred to as espionage, the act of gathering information illegally.

Electronic Bugs

An electronic bug is a device that is placed in an area for the purpose of intercepting communications and transfers that communicate to a remote listening point. The eavesdropper can be just a few feet away or miles away from the target, depending on what device is used.[23] Without electronics, eavesdroppers have to rely on acoustic bugs that use simple tools to help the naked ear directly intercept a communication. This might involve using a water glass, stethoscope, or rubber tube to intercept the sound, and relies on areas where sound is leaking through soft spots around windows, structural defects, ventilation structures, poorly installed power outlets, and so on. An electronic bug can use several different kinds of technology: ultrasonic, radio frequency, optical, and hybrid.

An ultrasonic bug is a device used to convert sound into an electrical signal above the range of human hearing. The ultrasonic signal is then intercepted at a nearby position, and converted back to audio sound.

A **radio frequency**, or RF bug, is the most well-known type of bugging device. A radio transmitter is placed in an area or hidden in a device that would typically be found in the targeted area. The RF bug is extremely easy to detect, is inexpensive, disposable, and difficult to trace back to the person who planted it.

An optical bug is a bugging device that converts sound (or data) into an optical pulse or beam of light. It is rarely used, expensive, and easy to detect. The beam from some of these devices resembles that of a common laser, and is easily seen by the naked eye. Examples are active and passive laser listening devices.

Hybrid devices are the newest category of electronic bugs. A good example of this is a key capture device, connected between a keyboard and a computer. As the computer user types away, the key capture device stores each keystroke and sends it via the Internet to a listening point. It is important to note that wireless keyboards are extremely susceptible to covert eavesdropping.

> **Word to the Wise**   Many police-grade bugs and taps are presently being offered to the general public by a number of firms for very low prices, and many are smaller than an inch in diameter.

Warning Signs of Eavesdropping or Bugging

Bugging at a location is generally done in stages. Determining if such activity is occurring requires a number of careful steps. The first step is to determine if a person or group is a potential target. This is done by evaluating whether something in the location revealed in conversation or in writing would increase someone else's wealth or influence. If the answer is yes, then the location is a potential target. The higher the value of information, the more likely it is that a person or group can be a target. It requires asking a person or group of people protected by private security personnel to answer a number of important questions. The following list of questions can be used as a guide to determine the likelihood of bugging.

Do others seem to know your confidential business or professional trade secrets? Often, the loss of secrets will show up in very subtle ways, so people should always trust their instincts in this matter. When business competitors know things that

Courtesy of Tradewinds-Environmental Restoration

are obviously private, or the media finds out things they should not know, then it is reasonable to suspect technical eavesdropping or bugging.

Does information about closed meetings and bids seem to be widely known? Confidential meetings and bids are very popular targets for corporate spies. A client protected by private security personnel should consider what would happen if their plans became public knowledge. Copies of product designs can be of significant use to competitors, as well as knowing the quote another company has received for completing a possible project.

Have you noticed strange sounds or volume changes on your phone line? This is commonly caused by an amateur eavesdropper when they attach a wiretap, or activate a similar listening device. Surveillance devices often cause slight anomalies on the telephone line, like a volume shift or drop-out. Professional eavesdroppers and their equipment usually do not make such noises. If sound changes are occurring, an amateur eavesdropper is probably listening in.

Have you noticed static, popping, or scratching on your phone lines? This is caused by the capacitive discharge that occurs when two conductors are connected together (such as a bug or wiretap on a phone line). This is also a sign that an amateur eavesdropper or poorly trained spy is playing with your phone lines. It is hard for untrained individuals to determine if they are being bugged by professional eavesdroppers.

Are sounds coming from your phone's handset when it is hung up? This is often caused by a hook switch bypass, which turns the telephone receiver into an eavesdropping microphone (and also a speaker). If someone hears sounds in their handset, there is probably somebody within 20 feet of the phone listening to everything they say.

Does your phone often ring and nobody is there, or a very faint tone or high pitched squeal or beep is heard for a fraction of a second? This is an indicator of a slave device, or line extender being used on your phone line. This is also a key indicator of a harmonica bug, or infinity transmitter being used. These devices cause your phone to ring randomly. When a person answers, the device emits a faint tone and/or squeal/beep as it reverifies their user information.

Does your other electronic equipment suddenly develop strange interference? Many amateur and spy shop eavesdropping devices use frequencies within or just outside the FM radio band. These signals tend to drift and will "quiet" an FM radio in the vicinity of the bug. Private security personnel should look for the transmissions at far ends of the FM radio band, and at any quiet area within the FM band. Private security personnel should find a quiet band and then when the radio begins to squeal, slowly move it around the room until the sound becomes very high pitched. This is referred to as feedback detection, or loop detection, and will often locate the bug. The "stereo" function should be turned off so the radio is operating in "mono" mode, as this will provide a major increase in sensitivity. If a person finds a "squealer" in this manner, they should immediately contact a security professional and get them to your location *fast*.

Does your television suddenly develop strange interference? Television broadcast frequencies are often used to cloak an eavesdropping signal, but such devices also tend to interfere with television reception (usually a UHF channel). Televisions also "draw in" a lot of RF energy and, because of this, are very sensitive to any nearby transmitters (this is technically called "bandwidth," and TV signals use a lot of it). A small handheld television with a collapsible antenna may also be used to sweep a room. Carefully, security personnel should watch for interference around channel numbers 2, 7, 13, 14, 50–60, and 66–68 as these frequencies are very popular with eavesdroppers.

Have you recently been the victim of a burglary in which nothing was taken? Professional eavesdroppers often break into a target's home or office, and very rarely leave direct evidence of the break-in; however, occupants of the premises will often "pick up on something not being right" like the furniture being moved slightly.

Do electrical wall plates appear to have been moved slightly or jarred? One of the most popular places to hide eavesdropping devices is inside, or behind, electrical outlets, switches, smoke alarms, and lighting fixtures. This requires that the wall plates be removed. Private security personnel should look for small amounts of debris located on the floor directly below the electrical outlet. They should watch for slight variations in the color or appearance of the power outlets and/or light switches as these are often swapped out by an eavesdropper. Also, they should note if any of the screws which hold the wall plate against the wall have been moved from their previous position.

Has a dime-sized discoloration suddenly appeared on the wall or ceiling? This is a tell-tale sign that a pinhole microphone, or small covert video camera, has been recently installed.

Has anyone recently given you any type of electronic device, such as a desk radio, alarm clock, lamp, small TV, boom box, or CD player? Many of these "gifts" are actually Trojan horses that contain eavesdropping devices. Be very suspicious of any kind of pen, marker, briefcase, calculator, "post-it" dispenser, power adapter, pager, cell phone, cordless phone, clock, radio, lamp, and so on that is given as a gift. That little gift the salesman left behind may be a serious hazard.

Has a small bump or deformity appeared on the vinyl baseboard near the floor? This is a strong indicator that someone may have concealed covert wiring or a microphone imbedded into the adhesive which holds the molding to the wall. Such a deformity will often appear as a color shift, or lightening of the color.

Does the smoke detector, clock, lamp, or exit sign in your office or home look slightly crooked, have a small hole in the surface, or have a slightly reflective surface? These items are very popular concealments for covert eavesdropping devices. When the devices are installed in these items, the items are rarely replaced in their original position. Private security personnel should check these items for slight changes in their appearance, and watch out for items like this that "just appear."

Have you noticed white dry-wall dust or debris on the floor next to the wall? This is a sign that a pinhole microphone or video camera may have been installed nearby. It will appear as if someone has dropped a small amount of powdered sugar either on the floor, or on the wall.

Have you noticed small pieces of ceiling tiles, or "grit" on the floor or surface area of your desk This is a prime indicator that a ceiling tile has been moved around, and that someone may have installed a hidden video camera or other eavesdropping device in an office or near a desk. Also, private security personnel should look for cracks or chips in the ceiling tiles. Amateur and poorly-trained spies tend to crack or damage acoustical tiles. The ceiling tiles in any executive area should never contain any cracks, nicks, gouges, or stains. Any damaged ceiling tile should immediately be replaced. The cause of the damage should also be documented.

Have telephone, cable, plumbing, or air-conditioning repair people shown up to do work when no one called them? This is a very common ruse that eavesdroppers use to get into a facility. They fake a utility outage, and then show up to fix the problem. While they are fixing "the problem," they are also installing eavesdropping devices. Some of the more popular tactics involve power, air-conditioning, telephones, and even the occasional false fire alarm.

Have you noticed that your door locks suddenly do not "feel right," suddenly are "sticky," or have completely failed? This is prime evidence that the lock has been picked, manipulated, or bypassed. Security personnel should try to always encourage people to use biaxial locks with sidebars (such as ASSA or Medeco). Also, personnel at a location should only use double-sided deadbolts in all doors, good quality window bars on all windows, and a good quality door bar on all doors that are not used as primary entry doors.

Has your furniture recently been moved slightly, and no one knows why? A very popular location for the installation of an eavesdropping device is either behind, or inside furniture (couch, chair, lamp, etc.) People who live or work in a targeted area (such as cities and/or corporate and government buildings) tend to notice when furnishings have been moved even a fraction of an inch. Therefore, security personnel should pay close attention to the imprint that furniture makes on rugs and the position of lampshades. They should also notice the distances between furniture and the walls, as eavesdroppers are usually in a hurry and rarely put the furniture back in the right place.

Have things recently seemed to have been "rummaged" through? A "less than professional spy" will often rummage through a target's home for hours, and very rarely will they do it in a neat and orderly fashion. The most common rummaging targets are the backs of desk drawers and the bottoms of file cabinets, closets, and dresser drawers.

Have you received a copy of your private conversations? As simple as it seems, this is the strongest evidence of eavesdropping. An eavesdropper will sometimes send a victim a copy of a private conversation that they intercepted in an attempt at blackmail, or in an attempt to terrorize or stalk the victim. This is commonly seen in civil lawsuits, criminal court cases, marital problems, shareholder disputes, custody battles, and other situations where one side has a position of weakness and is trying to psychologically undermine their opponent.[24]

While there are many different things to look for, the key to success is to look for things that are out of the ordinary. If any of the multiple warning indicators above apply, or there is a general concern about eavesdropping, then it is up to private security personnel to take immediate action. Special precautions and behaviors must be practiced if you suspect bugging or wiretapping. The following should be used by private security employees as a general guide when suspecting a site is bugged:[25]

1. Immediately contact an electronic bug detection specialist. Handle the logistics of the inspection away from your office.

2. Use a phone away from your office or home. Never call from any type of cordless phone, cellular telephone, personal communications service (PCS) phone, or any other type of wireless device.

3. Consider having a complete sweep of the suspicious location. Have someone who specializes in technical counterintelligence do a bug sweep and make sure that this person is an expert with computers, telecommunications, and electronics.

4. Be very discreet. Watch what you say at home or at the office, and never discuss your concerns inside, outside, or near any suspect facility. Advise clients of possible bugging activity.

If an individual or group suspects they are being bugged, private security personnel should advise them to remember the following:

- Avoid using their office telephone to talk about suspicions.
- Avoid using their cellular or cordless phone to talk about suspicions.
- Avoid discussing their suspicions at the office, in the car, or at home.
- Avoid sending e-mails about suspicions.
- Do not try to find the bug or wiretap without security assistance.
- Avoid contacting the telephone company.
- Avoid contacting the FBI or Secret Service.

When a Bug Is Found

Finding a bug in a location either through an intensive search, or by pure accident, requires knowledge of the important steps to take following a bug's discovery. It is important for private security personnel to be aware that if they find a bug, they should leave the building, use a phone not associated with or used by the business or client, and contact a security professional with expertise in bugging for assistance. The key response when a bug is found is to not touch it, talk about it, or tell anyone about it with the exception of upper-level management and superiors on a security team.[26]

It may seem strange that the first call made by security personnel is not to local or federal authorities. The reality is that a bug carries major legal and confidential considerations that warrant heightened discretion and possible secrecy. For example, finding a bug should immediately raise possible questions that must be answered by private security personnel: (1) Is there a legal reporting requirement based on the nature of the business or client? (2) What type of professional should be used to do a thorough security audit? and (3) How will people react to the news? This is extremely important to corporations, as the hint of covert activities or risks might affect the valuation of the company, or brand value, if the information reaches the public.[27] Stockholders of publicly traded companies will be concerned about the impact on the stock price or even sell their stock, customers and employees will be concerned about loss of personal information and identity theft, and suppliers will be concerned that their confidential information or pricing may have been exposed.

A fourth question concerns the impact of the information that may have been compromised. Each bugging incident is different. The effect of the incident is dependent upon the value of the information that was garnered and how it can be used. The following questions must be asked: [28]

- What is the commercial value of the information?
- Could the information be used by criminals or those with criminal intent?
- Who stands to gain from having access to this information?
- Who has a motive to have done this?
- Who has access to the area where the device was found?
- Has anyone's personal security been put at risk by any of this information?

All of these questions must be answered in order to construct a plan to deal with an electronic bugging incident. Failure to follow these guidelines has the potential to compromise an investigation and further exposes the organization to other breaches in security.

The availability of electronic surveillance devices has dramatically increased the threat of bugging and actual instances of electronic eavesdropping. The signs of electronic eavesdropping are obscure occurrences that seem to be out of place. Often, only the vigilant eyes of private security personnel can recognize these signs and react before catastrophic consequences affect a business or client.

■ Conclusion

Advanced technology in this century is a double-edged sword for the security field. Advances in alarm security systems and biometric access control devices have made aspects of security programs easier and more efficient. At the same time, the use of bugging devices, which will continue to increase in the United States, has created additional security risks for security personnel seeking to protect information, people, and facilities. As communication and computer equipment continues to become more advanced in areas never before imagined, it is likely the private security field will adapt more technology to increase the effectiveness of security programs, as well as to foil any threatening uses of technology.

■ Chapter Review

- Technology warfare is likely to continue against the United States in years to come.
- Intellectual property faces continual theft.
- Current business practices open US businesses to security risks.
- Individuals who display signs of being possible participants in technology warfare practices should be watched carefully.

- Technology advances, such as biometrics, have given private security personnel additional ways to become more efficient and effective in providing security.

- Bugging has continued to increase and poses a threat to security in the United States.

■ Answers to Case Studies

Case Study 1

1. What is the nature of technology warfare? The nature of technology warfare has been a growing trend in terms of both information being stolen and the use of technology to disrupt government agencies and business systems.

2. What events are likely to spark a technology conflict between two countries? A conflict over resources, an international political issue, geographic tensions, and interactions with other respective allies may cause a conflict between two nations.

Case Study 2

1. What are some of the major benefits of using biometric devices? Biometrics and advanced identification technology create tougher security systems for criminals who will find it very difficult to penetrate security systems that require the fingerprints, iris, or other personal features of a person. They can be used on doors, computers, building access spots, safes, and other areas where heightened security is warranted.

Case Study 3

1. What are some of the indicators that a bug has possibly been placed at a location? A bug can be discovered by carefully listening to phone lines for possible changes in sounds, changes in the physical appearance of a location, or electronic devices, like radios or televisions, that are acting strange.

2. What are some of the appropriate responses if a bug is suspected or found at a location? Security personnel should work with a client or organization to ensure that a bug detection specialist is called in immediately. Maintaining confidence is key in ensuring that only essential people know that an area has been bugged. Investigating why a bug has been placed is also important to determine who may have bugged a location.

■ Key Terms

Biometrics Methods of identifying or authenticating an identity based on a physical or behavioral characteristic involving the use of different parts of the body, such as a fingerprint or the eye, as a password or form of identification.

Bugging   Intrusive surveillance whereby an eavesdropping device is installed in a target's home or car. There is a strict regime governing the use of this investigative technique.

Identification   Process of comparing a submitted biometric sample against all biometric reference templates on file to determine the identity of the person being scrutinized. The biometric system using the one-to-many approach is seeking to find an identity amongst a database, rather than to authenticate a claimed identity.

Mergers and acquisitions   When companies organizationally and financially come together or are taken over by one company acquiring ownership or control of assets of the other.

Photoelectric eye   A device that uses a beam of light that when broken triggers an alarm. There are two parts to a photoelectric eye, the transmitter, which sends out the light, and the receiver, which "sees" the light. The light used in today's devices is not visible to the human eye.

Radio frequency (RF)   A wireless transmission of signals.

■ References

1. *Spy-Ops. Corporate espionage training brief.* http://www.Spy-Ops.com. *See also* Dempsey, J. 2008. *Introduction to private security.* Boston: Wadsworth. Notable industrial espionage cases. http://www.dss.mil./search-dir/training/csg/security/Spystory/industry.htm. World Intellectual Property Organization. http://www.wipo.int/about-ip/en/. George Smiley joins the firm. 1988. *Newsweek,* May 2. Economic Espionage Act of 1996. http://rf-web.tamu.edu/security/secguide/T1threat/legal.htm#Economic%Espionage

2. Ibid.

3. Ibid. *See also* Gertz, B. 2000. *The China threat.* Washington, DC: Regnery.

4. CNN. 2001. *High tech spying fears.* May 4. http://edition.cnn.com/2001/BUSINESS/05/04/espionage/index.html.

5. *See* note 1.

6. *See* note 1.

7. *See* note 1.

8. *See* note 1.

9. *See* note 1.

10. Keith, M., C. Piligian, and D. Swierczunsky. 2003. *The spy's guide: Office espionage.* Philadelphia: Quick Books.

11. *See* note 1.

12. *See* note 1.

13. *See* note 1.

14. Coleman, K., *Biometrics*. Biometrics Spy-Ops training brief. Vol. 4. TB 20.

15. Ibid.

16. Ibid.

17. Ibid.

18. Ibid.

19. Ibid.

20. Spy-Ops. *Electronic bugging training brief*. Vol. 3. TB 14. http://www.spyops. com. *See also* Keith, M., C. Piligian, and D. Swierczunsky. 2003. *The spy's guide: Office espionage*. Philadelphia: Quick Books. Notable industrial espionage cases. http://www.dss.mil./search-dir/training/csg/security /Spystory/ industry.htm. World Intellectual Property Organization. http://www.wipo. int/about-ip/en/. George Smiley joins the firm. 1988. *Newsweek*. May 2. Economic Espionage Act of 1996. http://rf-web.tamu.edu/security/secguide/ T1threat/legal.htm#Economic%Espionage.

21. Ibid.

22. Ibid.

23. Ibid.

24. Ibid.

25. Ibid.

26. Ibid.

27. Ibid.

28. Ibid.

Future Security Trends: Issues and Information

CHAPTER 12

- Understand the nature of weapons of mass destruction.
- Understand the nature of unrestricted warfare.
- Become familiar with hostage situations.
- Become more familiar with private military companies.

■ Introduction

The national and international political, economic, and social state of affairs are constantly changing. With these changes come new threats to security that are far larger than shoplifters, animal activists, or casino cheats. Low intensity warfare is the new buzzword and faceless terrorists are the new enemy. The nature of warfare on a global scale is likely to change as Russia and China expand their militaries and the seizure of natural resources in the world. Terrorist organizations are likely to continue to grow in power in various parts of the world. The use of weapons of mass destruction is still a real and frightening nightmare that America is likely to face in the near future. Hostage situations are likely to increase as a result of terrorists, workplace violence and criminal activity. Private military companies have also reemerged in this century as a form of private security. Ultimately, private security personnel must keep up with current events at home and around the world to be prepared for these new wars.

▶ ▶ CASE STUDY 1

You are working at a corporate office building on a typical day as part of a contracted security team. You take a lunch break outside. You hear a large boom, and the air becomes congested and cloudy. You rush into the building where

(continued)

▸ ▸ CASE STUDY CONTINUED

fellow co-workers are gathering near a television. The news is broadcasting a story about a weapon of mass destruction that has been detonated near your building. Outside, people begin coughing and crying uncontrollably. Some people fall down and begin convulsing. Already, news agencies have received confirmation of the attack from the terrorist organization that planned and executed the incident.

1. What are some of the immediate concerns for your security team facing this type of scenario?

2. What steps should you and your team take near a weapon of mass destruction detonation site?

■ The Future of Terrorism

Predicting future terrorist activity worldwide is a dangerous and sometimes futile process. There is little agreement among experts as to whether terrorism will continue or decline over time. New generations of terrorists have taken the field, compelled to escalate their terrorism to maintain public attention or to react to restrictive governmental power. Possibly, some terrorist groups will gradually decline as they recognize the futility of indiscriminate campaigns of violence that only alienate them from society. For example, the Irish Republican Army (IRA) had little success freeing Northern Ireland from British rule after three decades of deadly bombings and assassinations. The IRA eventually signed a ceasefire and agreed to scrap its weapons. On the other hand, Islamic terrorist groups may escalate the violence beyond levels that Americans cannot even imagine. Currently, al Qaeda is the major leading patron of terrorism against targets within the United States. While other Islamic groups have redirected their goals toward the recovery of Palestine or the destruction of Israel, al Qaeda still focuses on two distinct groups, the enemies of Muslims and the enemies of Islam.[1]

Many al Qaeda members are convinced they have been unfairly treated by Arab countries of the Middle East and have been manipulated by the West. Currently, al Qaeda is expanding its branches and networks outside of the Middle East. Al Qaeda had planned to use cyanide gas in an attack on the US embassy in Rome in March 2002; it had also planned to crash an explosives-laden aircraft into the American consulate in Karachi, Pakistan. While both plots were foiled, these plans illustrate the continued desire by al Qaeda to escalate the violence. Al Qaeda and other terrorist groups will continue to use technology to their advantage. Al Qaeda, in particular, has used videotapes and audiotapes to warn potential targets of impending attacks and to relay messages to its followers. The use of such tapes allows them to convey the message that the organizational structure of al Qaeda is still functioning, and that the organization is still capable of carrying out successful missions.

For private security in the United States, the focus on terrorism is much different. While experts disagree on the state of worldwide terrorism, the possibility of a

terrorist attack in the United States again is quite possible. The concern for private security personnel is the likelihood of an attack against a less secure target, such as a school or shopping mall. Terrorist groups continue to call for attacks against US targets outside the normal realm of homeland security planning.[2]

Lone terrorists are also likely to increase. Jose Padilla, who attempted to set off a dirty bomb in Chicago, is a prime example of how lone operators can pose a continual threat to security. New US domestic groups may emerge like the Rajneeshees cult that tried to spread salmonellosis, or the 2001 spread of anthrax to political leaders. In addition, the growing debate over illegal aliens in the United States is likely to lead to more attacks by organized domestic terror and extremist groups within the continental United States.

Low-Intensity Warfare and Conflicts

Low-intensity warfare is the new term coined by the United States for conflicts ranging from terrorism, revolution and counterrevolution, to limited small war operations conducted by political groups to achieve a major political goal. Such political goals can include an overthrow of the existing system and establishment of a new political or social order. The most common and damaging to the survival of democracies is terrorism/counterterrorism and revolution/counterrevolution. As American businesses seek to open and operate business centers overseas, private security personnel will face the increased possibility of providing security services in locations that may erupt into a low-intensity conflict.[3]

■ Weapons of Mass Destruction

You can easily remember all five categories of weapons of mass destruction incidents using the acronym B-NICE. This term stands for Biological, Nuclear, Incendiary, Chemical, and Explosive. Conventional explosives are very common threats but biological, chemical, and nuclear attacks are more complicated and often more dangerous to human life. Biological and chemical attacks are easier to create than nuclear attacks.[4] These three categories require more specialized knowledge of their nature and potential use.

Biological Agents

Biological agents include any bacterium, virus, or toxin that could be used in biological warfare. They are simple to produce and can be readily adapted for use as terrorist weapons. Their use dates back to at least the 7th century when the Assyrians used ergot, a fungal disease originating in rye that produces a hallucinogenic effect similar to LSD, to poison the wells of their enemies. Bioweapons pose a very serious threat because if they are not rapidly contained after release, large numbers of people can become infected and quickly spread disease, causing large numbers of casualties and overwhelming medical facilities. Biological agents have four possible routes of entry into the human body:[5]

- Inhalation of an aerosol
- Absorption by direct skin contact
- Ingestion of contaminated food or water
- Injection or a puncture wound

Bioweapons would most likely use inhalation and ingestion as the primary routes of delivery. Injection is less likely. Good personal hygiene would reduce the risk of exposure from direct skin contact. There are three types of common biological agents. These are bacteria, viruses, and toxins.

Bacteria

Bacteria are single-celled organisms that multiply by cell division. Not all bacteria cause disease, but the ones that do are referred to as pathogenic bacteria. The potential for harm is limited only by the bacteria used, a terrorist group's ability to produce large quantities undetected, and the delivery method. Aerosolized bacteria pose the greatest threat. Aerosols can be delivered from the air undetected and the drifting cloud can infect a great number of people. The microorganisms that cause cholera and typhoid can be deliberately added to an unsecured water supply. It's also possible to infect a population using the animals (vectors) that carry the disease. Japan released fleas infected with plague and flea-carrying rats into China during their conflicts. Examples of other bacteria-caused diseases that could be used by terrorists are botulism, tularemia melioidosis, Q fever, and anthrax.[6]

Anthrax has become the latest "bomb scare." More than 400 hoaxes have been reported since the late 1990s. Anthrax is an infectious, usually fatal disease of warm-blooded animals transmitted to humans through contact with contaminated animal substances, such as hair, feces, or hides, and is characterized by ulcerative skin lesions. The spores of anthrax are tiny and can remain in a dormant state for many years. In normal veterinary circumstances, inhalational anthrax is very rare. Purposeful dissemination of aerosolized anthrax spores was used by Iraq in its war against Iran. Transmission by spore inhalation causes the most dangerous forms of anthrax, pulmonary and meningeal anthrax, which are 90% fatal, despite therapy. Dermal anthrax is caused by handling contaminated hair, wool, hides, or flesh of infected cattle, sheep, or horses. Infection by ingestion of infected meat is rare in Western countries where livestock are routinely immunized.[7]

Procedures for Anthrax-Contaminated Mail
- If a suspected package is sealed, private security personnel should take no action and should immediately contact authorities.
- If opened, personnel should wash their hands with soap and water, and medical personnel should be contacted to assess personnel exposure.
- In the unlikely event that a package containing actual spores causes contamination, it is likely to be localized to the immediate area.
- Authorities will isolate the area and treat it as a crime scene.

Viruses

Viruses are the simplest microorganisms and lack any system to support their own metabolism. They depend upon living cells to multiply and cannot live for an extended time outside a host. The smallpox virus causes 30% mortality in infected individuals who fail to receive the vaccine within four days of exposure. Large-scale smallpox vaccination in the United States ended in 1972. An unintended consequence of the successful worldwide smallpox eradication is that the general population has little more immunity than the Native Americans receiving infected blankets distributed by the British army during the French and Indian War of 1754–1763. Other viruses that could be readily used for biological agents include Venezuelan equine encephalitis and viral hemorrhagic fevers, such as the Ebola and Marburg viruses and Lassa fever.[8]

Toxins

Toxins are toxic substances of natural origin produced by animals, plants, or microbes. They differ from chemical agents in that they are not man-made and are typically much more complex. Common toxins that have been used as biological weapons include botulism, found in improperly canned food; biological agents such as staphylococcal enterotoxin B and mycotoxins; and ricin, derived from the castor bean plant.[9] Toxins can be easily extracted for use as a terrorist weapon, and are usually far more toxic by weight than many chemical agents. The lethal dose of type-A botulinum toxin for an adult male is one millionth of a gram.[10]

Nuclear Devices

It has been noted previously that the detonation of a nuclear weapon in the United States could happen at any time. A **nuclear weapon** is a device such as a bomb or warhead whose great explosive power derives from the release of nuclear energy. Many terrorist organizations, such as al Qaeda or Hezbollah, call for such an attack in the United States on a regular basis. With more nations currently pursuing nuclear technology, the possibility of uranium and other materials getting into the wrong hands increases greatly. Nuclear terrorists could require as little as 4 kilograms of plutonium or 11 kilograms of highly enriched uranium to construct a crude fission bomb that would produce an explosion equal to 100 tons of TNT. The device would be small enough to transport in a compact automobile.

The number of nations with nuclear weapons capability is small, and each places a high priority on control of its nuclear weapons. Even if a nation supporting terrorism developed nuclear capabilities, it is implausible that such a nation would turn a completed weapon over to a group that could possibly use it against them. The theft of a completed nuclear weapon is also unlikely. Therefore, the greatest potential terrorist threat from a nuclear weapon would be to use a device in the form of extortion. Another likely scenario is the use of a conventional explosive

Radioactive Materials Used in a Nuclear Weapon or Dirty Bomb[11]
- Enriched uranium—contains a U-235 concentration, which is the only naturally occurring fissile isotope.
- Plutonium 239—a fissile isotope created through the use of U-238 in nuclear power plants. It is an excellent material for the construction of nuclear weapons.
- Special nuclear material (SNM)—fissionable material in the form of uranium-enriched isotopes consisting of uranium-233 and uranium-235 or plutonium-239.
- Weapons-grade plutonium—contains less than 7% of plutonium-240. Pu-240 is considered a contaminant.

device to disperse nuclear material, which is known as a "**dirty bomb**," or radioactive dispersal device.

Nuclear Weapons vs. Dirty Bombs

Private security personnel must understand the fundamental difference between the threat posed by nuclear weapons and the threat posed by a dirty bomb. The threat of detonation of nuclear weapons is often used by nations as a way to cause fear. The atomic explosions that occurred in Hiroshima and Nagasaki were conventional nuclear weapons involving a fission reaction. The threat of nuclear weapons can also be used as a form of extortion. Currently, there is no known instance of any known terrorist or criminal organization obtaining or producing a nuclear weapon.

A dirty bomb, however, is a different type of nuclear device. Dirty bombs involve the detonation of a conventional explosive to disperse radioactive material and contaminate a small or large area. A bomb positioned near a source of radiation such as a nuclear power plant or nuclear cargo in transport is considered a dirty bomb. A conventional bomb can also be packaged with radioactive material, which would be dispersed in the explosion. Radioactive material is relatively easy to obtain. While most nuclear facilities are under extreme security, there are over 21,000 organizations in the United States licensed to use small amounts of radioactive material. These more accessible sources of radioactive material are:

- Hospitals
- Construction sites
- Food irradiation plants
- College and high school laboratories
- Research facilities
- Smoke detector manufacturers

This form of nuclear incident is a real and frightening possibility in terms of terrorists or criminals dedicated to achieving their objectives.[12]

© AbleStock

Impact of a Dirty Bomb

A large enough dirty bomb attack in this country could force people to move from key US cities, damage the economy, increase the deprivation of civil liberties, possibly increase depression and mental illness among people, and lead to increased political and social strife at home. The use of a dirty bomb in an area can have different effects based on a number of key factors. Knowing these key factors can help private security personnel understand the potential impact of such a device should the government declare that a dirty bomb has been placed by a terrorist or criminal organization.

The extent of impact would depend on the following factors:[13]

- Location
- Size of the explosive
- Weather conditions
- Density of population
- Type of radioactive material

Terrorists or criminals seeking to use a dirty bomb are going to choose specific targets that make detection difficult, as well as areas that could result in the greatest victimization. Potential dirty bomb targets are usually highly populated public areas such as malls, subways and trains, amusement parks, restaurants, and airports. Ultimately, you should keep in mind that any place where large numbers of people pass or gather is a potential target for a dirty bomb attack.

Three Types of Nuclear Radiation

There are generally three types of nuclear radiation: alpha, beta, and gamma radiation. **Alpha radiation** particles are the heaviest, most highly charged form of radiation. They can be stopped by an ordinary sheet of paper. The outermost layer of dead skin can stop even the most energetic alpha particle. However, if ingested, alpha particles become an internal hazard.

Beta radiation particles are smaller than alpha particles and can penetrate several millimeters of living tissue, but generally do not penetrate far enough to reach vital organs. If the skin is exposed to large amounts of beta radiation for a long period, the skin will be burned. If removed from the skin shortly after exposure, beta emitters will not cause serious burns, but, like alpha particles, they are an internal hazard if ingested by breathing contaminated dust, eating or drinking contaminated food or water, or if contaminated dust contacts open wounds.[14] Anyone exposed should wash thoroughly with soap and water and use hazardous waste procedures to dispose of contaminated clothing.

Gamma radiation travels great distances, penetrates most materials, and causes the most harm in humans. Without substantial shielding, gamma radiation can attack all tissues and organs. Acute radiation sickness occurs when an individual is exposed to a large amount of gamma radiation within a short time. Symptoms include skin irritation, nausea, vomiting, high fever, hair loss, and dermal burns.

Private security personnel should understand that traditional training in hazardous material response builds on the notion of TDS, which stands for Time, Distance, and Shielding. However, the explicit link to terrorism and weapons of mass destruction is often not made.[15]

© WilleeCole/ShutterStock, Inc.

Hazardous Material Release Response—TDS[16]

Time—Always spend the least amount of time in the hazardous area to minimize exposure.

Distance—Always distance yourself from the hazard. Do not neglect the fact that chemical or biological agents can be airborne or be heavier than the surrounding air, being more persistent in low areas with poor air circulation. You must not only seek distance from the hazard to minimize exposure, but move uphill and upwind from the source.

Shielding—Seek substantial physical barriers between yourself and the hazard.

What to Do If a Dirty Bomb Attack Occurs

The safety of employees, clients, and other individuals such as members of the general public may fall upon your shoulders when an attack occurs. You should be aware of a number of key points that can help you stay alive, as well as to protect the lives of others who are likely to seek out a security person for guidance during such a crisis.

If private security personnel are ever faced with a dirty bomb attack, they should immediately follow a strict set of steps to ensure they are protected and can help protect other individuals.

- Move away from the immediate area at least several blocks and go inside a building—this will limit exposure to airborne radioactive dust.
- Remove clothes and place them in a sealed plastic bag. Save the contaminated clothes for testing.
- Take a shower to wash off the dust and dirt. This will reduce total radiation exposure absorbed through the skin.
- Turn on local radio or TV channels for advisories and instructions from emergency personnel.
- Note any injures you may have sustained during a hurried escape from your previous location.
- Tend to any first aid needs of others if you are leading a group of people.
- Observe for any signs of radioactive poisoning in yourself and others.

Scene Management in Case of a Dirty Bomb

It is important for private security personnel to understand the nature of a dirty bomb detonation in their area, and what steps can be taken to minimize injury and the loss of life. When such an attack occurs, public safety officers (fire and police) are ultimately in charge of responding and handling such a difficult situation. However, private security personnel are likely to find themselves assigned to assist in an impact area if they are in or near the location. If called upon to provide assistance to law enforcement officers, private security personnel should maintain a perimeter around the incident. By designating and maintaining strict hot, warm, and cold zones based on the nature of the radiological activity, interaction between those who have already been exposed and others who have not been exposed can be limited. Private security personnel may also be tasked by public safety officers to provide medical triage to help prioritize the level of medical care needed by the victims of a dirty bomb attack.[17]

The Risk of Cancer

The unfortunate long-term side effect of a dirty bomb attack is sickness and death due to radiation exposure, often through **cancer,** a biological condition involving malignant neoplasm around healthy tissue. However, it should be noted that just because a person is near a radioactive source for a short time or exposed to radioactive dust does not automatically mean they will get cancer. Ultimately, doctors will be able to determine appropriate counteractive measures once the source and exposure level can be determined.[18]

Summary of Dirty Bomb Security Issues

- Radiological attacks constitute a credible threat, especially following the September 11, 2001, tragedies.
- Many radiological bomb-making materials are easily accessible with little or no security measures present.
- Dirty bombs likely would result in some deaths, but not nearly as many fatalities as could be seen with the use of conventional high-power explosives.

Incendiary Devices

An **incendiary device** is any mechanical, electrical, or chemical device used intentionally to initiate combustion and start a fire. It consists of three basic components: an igniter (fuse), a container, and an incendiary (fuel) material or filler. The fuel material is designed to produce enough heat and flame to cause surrounding combustible materials to burn once it reaches ignition temperature. Incendiary devices may be simple or elaborate and come in all shapes and sizes. The type of device is limited only by the ingenuity of the terrorist. A device containing chemical materials usually will be in a metal or other nonbreakable container. An incendiary device that uses a flammable liquid accelerant will usually be in a breakable container. Devices of this nature can be very low-tech, such as a modified gas container with a homemade fuse or a Molotov cocktail in a glass jar designed to explode and set fires upon impact with a hard surface.

Incendiary devices may be used individually or in combination. Handling of suspected incendiaries by those who are not specially trained can result in ignition, injury, and death, and could also damage evidence needed for the crime scene investigation. An incendiary device usually warrants extra precautions for private security personnel.[19]

Chemical Agents

The thought of a chemical attack targeting and killing Americans keeps many security personnel up at night worrying about how to protect critical infrastructure and the lives of everyday people. Japan learned firsthand the effects of such weapons on a civilian population. Just after 8 a.m. on Monday, March 20, 1995, several passengers on different trains of the Tokyo subway system placed vinyl bags containing a sarin nerve agent onto the floor, pierced them, and exited the train. The resulting aerosols killed 12 people and injured 5498 others.[20] Multiple victims with similar symptoms are an important early warning sign of the use of nerve agents. This murderous act was a wake-up call for police and security agencies around the world.

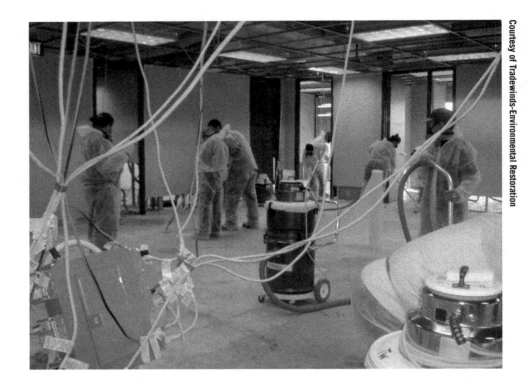

It is important to understand the primary routes of exposure for all chemical agents. Knowing these routes can help security personnel protect themselves from potential exposure. The primary routes of exposure for chemical agents are usually inhalation and skin absorption. Injection is possible through a puncture wound or through contact of the chemical agent with an open wound, but is less likely. Accidental ingestion by contamination of food or drink is possible, but also less likely.[21]

General Signs of Victims of a Chemical Attack
- Runny nose, nasal congestion
- Profuse tearing, dimmed or blurred vision
- Pinpoint pupils, eye pain aggravated by sunlight
- Excessive salivation, abdominal pain, nausea
- Involuntary urination and/or defecation
- Chest pressure, cough, difficulty breathing
- Excessive sweating
- Muscle tremors, involuntary twitching
- Giddiness, anxiety, difficulty in thinking or sleeping

Personal protective measures for any chemical hazardous material exposure include respiratory protection and splash protection. If private security personnel are lacking proper training and protective equipment, they should leave the affected area immediately and seek decontamination, medical assessment, and appropriate treatment.

Generally, chemical agents fall into five classes:

- Nerve agents disrupt the central nervous system.
- Blister agents are vesicants that cause severe burns to the eyes, unprotected skin, and respiratory tissues.
- Blood agents interfere with the ability of blood to transport oxygen.
- Choking agents severely stress respiratory tissues.
- Irritating agents incapacitate by causing tearing, respiratory distress, and pain, especially in moist areas of the body.

Nerve Agents

Nerve agents are odorless liquids, resembling water or light oil in pure form. They are toxic in small concentrations and typically dispersed as aerosols.[22] A nerve agents is given two designator letters. The first letter usually refers to the country of origin and the second the order of its development. GA, GB, and GD were developed by Germany during World War II. In the case of VX, the V stands for *venom* while X represents one of the chemicals in the specific compound. Common nerve agents include sarin, (GB), which was used in the Tokyo subway incident and by the Iraqis against Iran, Soman (GD), Tabun (GA), and V agent (VX). [23]

The primary indicators of a probable nerve agent attack include small explosions; multiple nauseous victims who twitch, convulse, are sensitive to light, and have lost bladder and bowel control; equipment to generate mists; and, if outside, many nearby dead animals.

Blister Agents

Blister agents, such as mustard agents (H, HD) and Lewisite (L) are heavy, oily liquids typically dispersed by aerosol or vaporization. These agents are similar to other corrosive materials that first responders encounter in hazardous material incidents. They readily penetrate layers of clothing and are quickly absorbed into the skin. All are very toxic, although much less so than nerve agents. A few drops on the skin can cause severe injury. Three grams absorbed through the skin can be fatal.[24]

Symptoms from blister agents resemble those resulting from other types of hazardous material releases. Because clinical symptoms may not appear for hours or days, or be immediately obvious, it may be difficult to attribute them to a target event, but eye and respiratory irritation, digestive complaints, and often skin irritation are the most common. The indicators of a probable nerve agent attack include small explosions, nearby spray equipment, or report of a garlic odor in the case of mustard gas. As in the case of nerve agents, similar symptoms will occur among many individuals exposed.

Symptoms of Blister Agents

- Eyes, within 1 hour
  - Reddening, tearing, burning, 'gritty' feeling, pain
- Skin, within 1 1/2 hours
  - Itching, redness, tenderness, burning pain, blisters; symptoms most intense in warm, moist areas of the groin and armpits
- Respiratory, within 2 1/2 hours
  - Burning sensation in nose or throat, hoarseness, profusely running nose, severe cough, shortness of breath
- Digestive, within 2–3 hours
  - Abdominal pain, nausea, bloody vomiting and diarrhea

These indicators and symptoms should be heeded as immediate outward warning signs. Call 911, report an unknown hazardous material exposure, and evacuate the area. Emergency decontamination procedures and prompt hospital treatment are required.

Courtesy of Tradewinds-Environmental Restoration

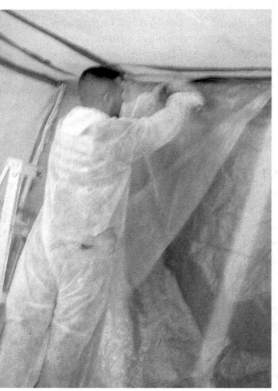

Blood Agents

All blood agents are toxic at high concentrations and lead to rapid death. **Blood agents** interfere with the ability of the blood to transport oxygen and result in asphyxiation. Common blood agents include hydrogen cyanide, also known as AC, and cyanogen chloride, known as CK. Cyanide and cyanide compounds are common industrial chemicals and are readily available. Precursor chemicals are typically cyanide salts and acids. All have characteristic odors of bitter almonds or peach blossoms, are common industrial chemicals. Blood agents are gases in pure form, but are usually transported as pressurized liquids. Effected persons should be moved to fresh air immediately and transported to a hospital for respiratory therapy. Clinical symptoms of people affected by blood agents are respiratory distress, vomiting, diarrhea, vertigo, and headaches.

Choking Agents

Choking agents stress the respiratory tract and cause formation of fluid in the lungs (edema) that can result in asphyxiation resembling drowning. Chlorine and phosgene are common industrial chemicals that can be used as choking agents. Clinical symptoms include severe eye irritation, coughing, and choking. Most people recognize the odor of chlorine. Phosgene has the odor of freshly cut hay. Both materials are gases commonly stored and transported in pressurized bottles or cylinders.[25]

Irritating Agents

The public in areas adjacent to civil unrest may be exposed to **irritating agents** known as riot control agents, such as tear gas. Many irritating agents are available over-the-counter for personal protection and are generally nonlethal. When used improperly in high concentrations asphyxiation can result; so caution is required, particularly in confined spaces. Common irritating agents include chloropicrin, MACE (CN), tear gas (CS), capsicum/pepper spray, and dibenzoxazepine (CR). Clinical symptoms include burning, irritation and tearing of the eyes, coughing, choking, difficulty breathing, nausea and vomiting if in high concentration.[26]

How the Local and Federal Government Will Respond to a Weapon of Mass Destruction Incident

Once a terrorist incident occurs, law enforcement and emergency management agencies activate their **emergency operations centers** (EOCs), mobilize their personnel, and begin to implement their emergency plans. At the federal level, the principal response agencies during terrorist events are the following:

- FBI
- FEMA
- Department of Homeland Security
- Department of Defense
- Coast Guard
- Department of Health and Human Services (particularly the Public Health Service)
- US Military forces
- Environmental Protection Agency
- Department of Energy

As in other kinds of disasters, the initial emergency response will include nonprofit organizations, such as the American Red Cross and the Salvation Army, and volunteers who will converge on the disaster site to help victims and to support the emergency response units. The response will likely include off-duty police officers, firefighters, emergency medical services personnel, and other medical personnel (e.g., doctors and nurses) who happen to be in the area. Volunteers will assist with search and rescue and may provide some assistance with the injured. Local agencies may have to secure the disaster scene, including dealing with terrorists who may be holding hostages or occupying a building, and provide emergency medical services until federal law enforcement and other agencies arrive on the scene. Fire services and police departments will likely establish their incident command centers and designate their incident commanders to coordinate emergency operations.[27] Emergency responders can anticipate some of the problems that they will encounter following a major bombing. Private security personnel and people near an attack site are likely to suffer from a number of common injuries, including the following:

- Blast injuries from the blast wave, which damage victims' inner ears and lungs
- Eye injuries caused by dust and larger particles
- Flash burns, which tend to be extensive but superficial because the heat dissipates quickly
- Lacerations and other shrapnel injuries from glass and debris
- Traumatic amputations from shrapnel
- People having "acute distress reaction" during which they are unable to speak or understand what to do
- Crush injuries if victims are buried in collapsed buildings

If the incident is a large one, such as the Murrah Federal Building bombing in Oklahoma City in 1995, volunteers may come from surrounding communities as the news media describes the disaster. Private firms also may be involved in the response as contractors providing public services, vendors selling specialized services, or as volunteers. State agencies will delegate personnel from law enforcement agencies, health facilities, environmental agencies, and other areas to assist with the response effort. Some units of the National Guard may be activated to assist with security and/or to help with other aspects of the disaster response. Local National Guard units are generally not activated because many law enforcement officers and other emergency services personnel may be members of local units already involved in the response. Instead, units are called up from other parts of the state, which may result in a delayed response by the National Guard. The response is a combination of well-defined and, it is hoped, well-rehearsed emergency operations and more spontaneous as-needed activities by government agencies, non-governmental organizations, private firms, and volunteers.[28]

Private Security's Role in Preparation and Response to a Weapon of Mass Destruction Attack

Large-scale attacks involving nuclear weapons, biological agents, chemical agents, or radiological materials may be far more difficult to manage than private security personnel can handle and certainly cannot be managed by one or even a few local or federal agencies. The reality is that resources of the federal, state, and local governments, as well as nonprofit and private businesses organizations, may be needed in the event of a large-scale attack. With the mobilization of so many different organizations, coordination of efforts will be one of the biggest challenges.

Since 9/11, the focus has been on developing joint training and education between businesses, universities, and public-serving agencies through a comprehensive preparedness approach to security. Preparedness programs between private security personnel and governmental agencies prior to an attack typically include the following:

- Assessment of the risk from particular hazards
- Mutual aid agreements to facilitate intergovernmental cooperation

Courtesy of Tradewinds-Environmental Restoration

- Contingency plans to deal with specific disaster requirements, such as mass evacuation
- Designation of lead agencies to coordinate aspects of the disaster response and recovery effort (e.g., evacuation or emergency sheltering)
- Development of resource inventories (e.g., heavy equipment, trauma facilities, beds)
- Development and maintenance of communications networks
- Training programs for responders, public officials, and others
- Exercises and drills to test and modify plans

For private security personnel, the reality is that such a weapon of mass destruction attack in the United States may occur. It will first be evident by a sudden emergence of multiple victims who exhibit the rapid onset of similar symptoms. This should always be heeded as a primary indicator of a probable "target event." If a private security person observes multiple people with any of the previously mentioned symptoms, it is time to retreat to a safe refuge at least 1000 feet away and call the local authorities immediately. It is absolutely necessary that the emergency medical system be alerted to a suspected release or detonation of any suspected weapon of mass destruction. Information from government authorities will also be made available quickly.

■ Unrestricted Warfare

▶ ▶ CASE STUDY 2

As a private security person, you are sent to attend a training workshop regarding future events that can destabilize the security of the United States. At this lecture, you learn of discussions on how recent events in the world arena may have an impact on security for American businesses.

1. Why is unrestricted warfare an often misunderstood security concept?
2. How do unrestricted warfare concepts have an impact upon private security personnel?

Unrestricted warfare (URW) is a relatively new concept and was first defined by two Chinese colonels in a book written in the late 1990s for the Chinese People's Liberation Army.[29] In this book, they described unconventional tactics that could be used by an enemy on a larger, more powerful target such as the United States. The book points out that the United States has not considered the wider picture of military strategy, which includes legal, economic, and cultural factors as methods of warfare. This concept has continued to evolve and now consists of 15 different modalities of warfare employed against an enemy. The concept poses a unique threat to the United States and other leading world powers that have increasingly been targeted with small-scale, stealth, and focused attacks on nonmilitary targets. Since no consideration has been given to modalities , the United States currently is highly vulnerable to attack along these lines. As the private security industry continues to grow, the need to prepare for future conflicts in this arena is imminent. An understanding of unrestricted warfare, therefore, must be explored and illustrated in detail. Private security personnel working at key locations in critical infrastructure, energy services, schools, landmarks, banking centers, or retail stores are all affected by shrewd unrestricted warfare practices and are on the front line in guarding and protecting such vital areas to the United States.[30]

Warfare is defined as organized conflict between groups for political, economic, or religious purposes.[31] Each group in a conflict is motivated by a common purpose. When we describe warfare, we can categorize it using modalities. Modalities are the types or modes of warfare. Traditionally we have only considered two types of warfare—conventional and weapons of mass destruction. Conventional warfare is fighting between two states by the armed forces from each state following a legal declaration of war, as defined by international law. Land fighting occurs with foot soldiers and land resources such as tanks, artillery, and other ground vehicles. Guerilla warfare is the use of unconventional fighting tactics for advantage in a conflict. Sea fighting is based on ocean-going vessels such as aircraft carriers, destroyers, and other naval assets. Undersea warfare is the use of submarines to attack ocean-going vessels of an adversary in a conflict. Air fighting uses planes, missiles, and other air vehicles. Weapons of mass destruction (WMD) were defined in an earlier chapter.[32]

The 15 modalities that represent the additional types of warfare that make up the category of unrestricted warfare are as follows:[33]

1. Cultural warfare refers to actions and tactics designed to bring about changes that target human activities, knowledge, customs, and arts of a group of people.
2. Economic warfare refers to actions and tactics designed to bring about changes that target the organization of production and distribution of goods and services within a state-governed system. Increases and decreases in economic aid are tactics of economic warfare.
3. Environmental warfare refers to actions and tactics designed to intentionally spoil the natural environment or modify the ecological systems of an adversary.
4. Financial warfare refers to actions and tactics designed to undermine, or create a loss in confidence in, the monetary or financial systems of a nation including its currency, banks, and the stock market.
5. Illegal drugs warfare refers to actions and tactics designed to flood an adversarial state with addictive controlled substances.

6. International law warfare refers to actions and tactics designed to undermine the regulations and/or policies of international or multinational organizations or to provide an adversarial nation with a major strategic advantage over another.

7. Information and media warfare refers to actions and tactics designed to influence the opinion of people and foreign news media by manipulating information distributed openly.

8. Telecommunication and network warfare refers to actions and tactics designed to disrupt electronic transactions or communication of a targeted adversary.

9. Political warfare refers to actions and tactics designed to bring about regime or policy change within an adversarial nation state.

10. Psychological warfare refers to actions and tactics designed to target the morale, mental aspects, or emotional components of an adversary.

11. Resource warfare refers to actions and tactics designed to inhibit access to critical supplies or natural resources needed by an organization, group, or nation.

12. Smuggling warfare refers to actions and tactics designed to flood an adversary's markets with illegal, counterfeit goods or products in an effort to create economic loss.

13. Technological warfare refers to actions and tactics designed to capture intellectual property associated with civilian or military technology that creates economic or technical advantage.

14. Terrorist warfare refers to the unlawful actions and tactics designed to intimidate governments or societies, often to achieve political, religious, or ideological objectives. For example:

    • Small arms are weapons carried into battle by individual infantry soldiers, including pistols, rifles, and machine guns.

    • Car bombs are bombs placed in cars or trucks and intended to be exploded while inside the vehicle.

    • Improvised explosive devices is the formal name for explosive devices used in unconventional warfare by terrorists, guerrillas, or commando forces.

    • Suicide bombers attack people or property, knowing the explosion will cause their own death.

15. Gang warfare refers to actions and tactics of a group of individuals who share a common identity (gang) to conduct acts of violence or intimidation.

The threats America currently faces represent a new way of thinking about conflict and warfare. What it takes to successfully defend against and offensively leverage this new era of unrestricted warfare is radically different from that which determined success in asymmetric warfare in the past. The battlefield now includes cyberspace. It is a battle for the minds of individuals, as well as for influence over culture, values, and beliefs. Multiple aspects of life are attacked in an effort to influence and bring about change. There are many other objectives besides killing people. These tactics include disruption of everyday life and destruction of cultural symbols that are core to the opponent's way of life. It is important to note that traditional forms of warfare will not disappear anytime soon. Most likely, any conflict will include both traditional and URW techniques. In this context, nuclear, chemical, and biological weapons fall under the definition of traditional warfare.

The reality is that a small, isolated group with only moderate training and financing can create a significant impact by launching an attack using one or more URW modalities from anywhere in the world against a stronger and more powerful nation. Creating the capacity to address these threats is arguably our nation's biggest challenge. Equally as challenging, is creating the weaponry for the "digital warrior" needed to combat these threats, as well as an early warning system to detect when one or more of the stealthy URW attacks are launched against our nation's critical infrastructure or other areas of vital importance.

In unrestricted warfare, there are no declarations of war and no uniforms. The blind attacks are not designed to control areas but rather to inflicted damage, influence public opinion, and political policies. When contemplating URW, it is important for private security personnel not to fall victim to singularity. It is uncommon for only one modality to be used in an assault or an attack. Multimodal attacks will become the modus operandi of URW warriors who are likely to cause situations in which private security personnel in various parts of the industry are going to have to react and respond.

■ Hostage Taking

▶ ▶ CASE STUDY 3

While working at a bank as a security guard, two men drop their coats and reveal themselves to be bank robbers. They begin to shout at people to get on the ground and obey their orders. As an armed private security guard, you draw your weapon and identify yourself. As one of the robbers turns in your direction with the intent to fire, you fire off a round. You quickly hear local police outside of the bank that have been alerted to this incident. The second bank robber has now grabbed a female patron of the bank and is holding a gun to her head. You are maintaining a position in which your gun is pointed in the direction of the bank robber and the hostage.

1. What are some key facts regarding hostage situations?
2. What are some of the critical aspects of dealing with a hostage situation as a private security guard?

Hostage situations can occur at any time and at any location. A criminal put in a desperate situation, someone with a mental illness, or a terrorist in a carefully planned attack can all take hostages. Private security employees must acquire the appropriate knowledge and learn the safest and most professional ways in which to respond in case an incident occurs while they are on duty.

Police statistics have revealed that nearly 2000 people throughout the world have been taken hostage in the last decade. However, the actual number may be several times this.[34] Some common sites at risk for hostage situations are government buildings, jails, prisons, airplanes, and locations of significant events. There are five types of hostage taking situations that are common to criminals and terrorists.

1. Prison takeovers
2. Seizures of business executives, diplomats, athletes, and cultural personalities
3. Aircraft hijacks
4. Armed robberies in which hostages are taken to effect an escape
5. Seizures of hostages by mentally disturbed individuals seeking personal recognition

Hostage takers generally fall into three major categories: The mentally ill hostage taker, the criminal hostage taker, and the social, political, religious, or ethnic crusader hostage taker (terrorist).[35] To put it another way, a hostage taker is either someone seeking to escape from something or somewhere, someone seeking personal gain, or politically motivated.

The mentally ill hostage taker most often seeks recognition from the intense media exposure that follows a hostage episode. They can exercise considerable power over the police, especially by threatening suicide. Criminal hostage takers, on the other hand, are the most rational and predictable. They are easy to negotiate with because they do not want to be arrested. Criminal hostage takers account for approximately 60% of all hostage-taking incidents and can be defused by delineating the seriousness of the crime of kidnapping and other criminal charges. The terrorist hostage taker has a strong commitment to a cause or a political ideology and seeks social or political change along with other demands. They are difficult to negotiate with due to their commitment to their cause. The ethnic crusader is usually rational and can enter a hostage situation with preconceived demands. They will identify limits as to how far the negotiator can be pushed in meeting the stated demands.[36]

The last decade has shown that hostage taking is a preferred tactic of political terrorists. For political terrorists, the strategy of taking high-ranking corporate business officials accomplishes four major objectives for a terrorist organization.[37]

1. The organization acquires large sums of ransom money needed to finance further terrorist activities.
2. The publicity generated by media attention brings the group national and international recognition.

3. The victim is often viewed as exploiting the poor people, which translates into much needed grassroots community support.

4. The free enterprise system is weakened by the intimidation of foreign investments.

For private security personnel, understanding the nature of the hostage taker can help security team members understand the nature of the threat to employees and other individuals when an incident occurs. In any hostage situation, the first few minutes when emotions are high and behavior is unpredictable are the most dangerous. Generally, the longer the hostage-taking incident continues, the greater the probability that the hostages will be released unharmed.

Guidelines for Hostage Events

It is important to realize that private security personnel are not likely to be placed into the role of formal hostage negotiators. However, there are steps you can take if you must engage the hostage taker while the authorities are in route to the scene. Stalling for time is a must. As a private security negotiator, it is important to do the following:

1. Ask about the health and safety of the hostage(s).

2. Discuss the family responsibilities of the hostage(s) with the hostage taker.

3. Request information on the treatment of the hostage(s).

To develop trust and a rapport with a hostage taker, any talks you have with the hostage taker should focus on the following:

- Self-disclosure
- Empathy
- Being a good listener
- Being understanding and showing personal interest in the hostage taker's situation
- Reflecting on the hostage taker's feelings
- Avoiding or rejecting outright demands

Over the years, the police have focused on ways in which formal police negotiators should operate. Private security employees should be aware of how police negotiators operate so that they can either be of assistance or at least avoid doing something that would prove to be detrimental. Police agencies generally follow these guidelines when handling hostage situations:

1. Negotiators should be trained in hostage management strategy, terrorist ideologies, and the psychology of hostage takers.

2. Negotiators should always be middle-level employees who report to a higher authority so they can stall for time or say a decision came from higher up.

3. Cooperate with the media and convince them not to air the negotiating strategies and actions being taken.

4. A chain of command must be established to ensure free and clear communication.

5. Hostages and hostage takers must be identifiable and differentiated from each other.

6. The exact number and identity of hostage takers must be ascertained immediately.

7. The negotiator should avoid any shift in the location of hostages by the hostage takers.

8. Avoid satisfying requests by the hostage takers for others to come to the scene (friends, clergy, family, etc.).[38]

9. A negotiator should avoid promising to meet demands that cannot be met.

10. A style of negotiation or overall hostage strategy based on mutual concession, compromise, and problem solving is recommended.

Most importantly, certain issues are nonnegotiable.

1. There will be no exchange of hostages.

2. No concessions are to be made without getting something in return.

3. Giving drugs or alcohol to hostage takers is unacceptable.

A private security employee put in a hostage negotiating role by the circumstances of an event must remember that these police guidelines have been shown to be effective in hostage situations. A more confrontational style, in which the hostage taker is forced to the point where they have no recourse but to release the hostages, is not usually recommended.

Hostages

During the passage of time in a hostage situation, something known as the Stockholm Syndrome can be manifested. This is the unconscious emotional response to the traumatic experience of victimization. A positive bond actually develops between the hostages and hostage takers, which serves to unite them against the outside influence of authorities. It generally manifests itself in three ways:[39]

1. Positive feelings of the hostages toward the hostage takers

2. The reciprocal positive feelings of the hostage takers toward the hostages

3. The negative feelings of both the hostages and hostage takers toward the police and government

The positive feelings act as a defense mechanism to ensure the survival of the hostage. The positive contact between hostage taker and hostages is largely determined by the absence of negative experiences during the hostage-taking incident (no beatings, rape, etc.). Unless a victim or hostage has been completely dehumanized in the eyes of the hostage taker, this syndrome can work for the benefit of the authorities.

Another hostage-related syndrome is known as the London Syndrome. This involves a situation in which a hostage continuously argues with or threatens the hostage takers, and unfortunately winds up getting killed (the best example is Leon Klinghoffer and the *Achille Lauro* affair of 1985).[40]

What to Do If You Are Taken Hostage

In the private security field, preparing for captivity is just as important as preparing tighter security measures to avoid being captured. The nature of being a hostage carries with it certain actions that can mean the difference between life and death. As a security guard, there is the possibility of becoming a hostage during a situation. At the initial phase of captivity, the hostage should decide whether or not to resist. This is a personal decision based upon the circumstances and the amount of danger involved in trying to escape. If surrendering to a hostage taker, the hostage should reassure the hostage taker that they will cooperate. The hostage should also be prepared to cope with blindfolds, gags, being bound, and being drugged. Blindfolds and hoods are used to disorient and confuse a hostage. Gags prevent talking or shouting, and being bound by hand and food prevents escape. Being blindfolded, gagged, and bound, the hostage then becomes a mere object, less than a human, making it easier for the hostage taker to assault the hostage.

If in captivity, a hostage must adjust. Recommendations include the following:[41]

1. Exercise when possible to keep fit (especially keep stretching).

2. Keep a sense of humor by remembering that others have survived worse situations.

3. Try to establish a routine (this gives a hostage a sense of control over his or her environment).

4. Keep recording in your mind information about your environment and your captors.

5. Don't appear weak or let hostage takers dehumanize you.

6. If beaten, don't be a hero, show pain.

7. Don't try to escape unless there is a high probability of success.

The most critical points of any type of hostage situation come at the moments of capture and release. The most important thing to remember is to remain calm and not to panic. Seventy-five percent of all hostage casualties occur during release or a tactical rescue attempt by authorities; so if a rescue attempt begins or shots break out, hit the floor and lie as flat as possible.[42]

Five General Hostage Responses[43]
1. Outcry: Fear, sadness, anger, rage
2. Denial: This can't be happening to me
3. Intrusion: Involuntary thoughts of the event
4. Working through: Facing the reality of the situation
5. Completion: Going on with life

Private security employees have a responsibility to understand the role that police will play and the steps that can be taken to save lives during a hostage situation. Other hostages will model their responses on your behavior.

■ Private Military Companies

▶ ▶ CASE STUDY 4

As a recent graduate of a local university and a former war veteran, you have received a phone call regarding possible employment as a private security employee for a well-known private military company. Based on your criminal justice and military experience, you are hired as a well-paid security consultant and security guard. You have been informed that training at a facility in the United States will be required as well as the possibility of work overseas.

1. What are some of the characteristics of private military companies?
2. What are some of the major concerns with private military companies?

Privatized military-style guards have returned in the form of **private military companies**. As mentioned in the historical section of this book, individuals providing military-style security have been in existence for thousands of years, and we are now repeating a historical cycle. Following the cold war, more Western nations have been decreasing the size of their military forces. Meanwhile, private military companies, the newest incarnation of mercenary units, have flourished, especially after the 2003 invasion of Iraq. The conflicts in Iraq and Afghanistan, along with the war on terror, have now led former military officers and soldiers to join corporate security groups like Blackwater and DynCorp to provide security services alongside conventional military forces. Currently, there are over 48,000 security personnel from over 177 security firms.[44] This is due, in part, by a need to provide security in light of shortages in manpower of an all-volunteer US military. In addition, the concept of compensation for private security work has also reemerged. Despite contentions by Machiavelli, it is now firmly established in the corporate world that a member of a security team that works within a company and desires the company to be successful is generally going to be paid less than an outside security consultant brought in to increase security at the same location. This has also been a major reason people seeking employment have pursued independent corporate security firms.

The change just in the last few decades has shown an additional return to more medieval practices besides the mercenary units previously mentioned. In the 1900s, private security personnel were often guarding or protecting the specific needs of wealthy citizens and companies around the world. However, the use of specialized and military-style protection is once again found in private security firms and companies that can tailor advanced, trained personnel to meet specific needs of a paying client, The use of a private military can be temporary or on a contracted permanent basis.[45]

It can be argued that paramilitary forces under private control of a corporation or business organization are functionally illegal mercenaries instead of security guards or advisors. Today, many private military companies desiring to showcase their services in private security use such terms as "conflict resolution specialists" or "operational support" experts. Private military companies, such as Blackwater, emphasize that their professionalism stems from their ranks full of formal security officers, police officers, and former members of military units.[46]

In the 1990s, private military companies began to also see an increase in business from foreign governments seeking out experts to provide security services.[47] The following is a list of some of the major private military companies that have security activities abroad:[48]

- Blackwater—Iraq, Afghanistan, and other locations around the world
- Executive Outcomes—Angola, Sierra Leone, and many other locations around the world
- Sandline International—Papua New Guinea, Sierra Leone
- Gurkha Security Guards Ltd—Sierra Leone.
- DynCorp International—Bosnia, Somalia, Angola, Haiti, Colombia, Kosovo, Kuwait, Afghanistan (active)

The question that arises when discussing these organizations is what private security-related functions they carry out at a location. In perspective, they provide the same services as soldiers do in an area. They are involved in battlefield support, embassy security, bodyguard and personal protection, and protection of critical infrastructure. Members of private military companies face the same risks, in many cases, as soldiers. For example, in March 2004, four employees of Blackwater USA were attacked and killed in Fallujah, Iraq, while guarding food shipments.[49] Private military companies also pose a legal quandary in terms of who supervises or commands members in their ranks and whether their actions can be disciplined under US military regulations or international law when they engage in activities that jeopardize the US military mission in an area. In September 2007, Blackwater came under the scrutiny of the world community after the infamous intersection shootout in Baghdad in which innocent civilians were killed.

The use of private military companies and their growth is likely to continue. In particular, foreign nations are likely to continue to rely on such organizations where police and military units are scarce or when governments are not willing to commit troops or police officers to dangerous peacekeeping missions. Also, as American businesses become more globalized and establish themselves with offices and buildings in locations around the world, private military companies may be called upon to provide security-related services.

■ Conclusion

In general, continual threats to the security and safety of America are increasing over time. Weapons of mass destruction used by criminals and terrorists and new forms of global warfare all threaten peace and security for the nation. For private security the focus will be living in a continual cycle of work, training, and executing, followed by retraining and new activities depending upon the threats rising in the nation. Growth in the specialty areas is likely to continue. For the entry-level security person, there are more techniques, knowledge, and experience that must be gained to become a successful practitioner in this changing period of world history.

■ Chapter Review

- Private security personnel face the possibility of being on the front line of a weapons of mass destruction attack in the United States.
- Biological, chemical, and nuclear attacks have caused a variety of different reactions and damage to individuals.
- Local and federal government agencies have plans in order to handle catastrophic events.
- Private security personnel must work with public-serving agencies to prepare for a WMD attack.
- Unrestricted warfare is a new form of waging war against an adversary through unconventional means.
- The United States has already experienced unrestricted warfare practices.
- Unrestricted warfare poses a threat to the security of US businesses and the American way of life.

- Hostage situations are new threats likely to be faced by private security personnel.
- Understanding the role of police can assist private security personnel in a hostage situation.
- Private security employees must understand the experiences that will be faced by hostages.
- Private military companies are one of the most controversial areas of the private security field.
- Private military companies are likely to continue to grow in number and use by government agencies.

■ Answers to Case Studies

Case Study 1

1. What are some of the immediate concerns for your security team facing this type of scenario? In a situation such as this crisis scenario, a major focus is on the type of attack that has just taken place. If training and drills have been completed and rehearsed, the security team can confidently know what to do in terms of securing the building and its people. The area where the attack took place is also of concern, since the building may be close to the heart of the attack. While members of the security team are likely to be in communication with upper management, they are also going to be communicating with public safety agencies such as the local police in terms of seeking a suggested course of action. Employees or visitors to the building are likely to ask questions regarding the attack and their safety. The building will also have to be more tightly secured and watched for fear of contaminated individuals still entering or leaving the building. For the security team and the people in the building, the main goal is following a plan that will keep them safe and that is in sync with the governmental response that is likely to follow such an attack.

2. What steps should you and your team take near a weapon of mass destruction detonation site? The private security team is likely to assess the security of the building along with the personnel inside. They are likely to consider certain courses of action based on the type of attack and its location. They may possibly evacuate the building or follow through on a plan previously executed with public safety officers. In addition, based on newly emerging information or situations, they may have to address concerns or needs not previously considered when creating their own emergency response plans. Primarily, the focus is on taking steps to mitigate injuries and to ensure safety for as many people as possible.

Case Study 2

1. Why is unrestricted warfare an often misunderstood security concept? Unrestricted warfare involves targeting vulnerable areas of a nation for attack without formally declaring a state of war. It is warfare without using a conventional military, but through more deceptive practices designed to attack critical areas of a nation such as its resources, telecommunications, international image, and economic system, to note a few of the unrestricted warfare modalities.

2. How do unrestricted warfare concepts have an impact upon private security personnel? By working at key locations in critical infrastructure, energy services, schools, landmarks, banking centers, and retail stores, private security personnel are affected by shrewd unrestricted warfare practices and are on the front line in guarding and protecting such vital areas to the United States.

Case Study 3

1. What are some key facts regarding hostage situations? A private security employee should consider that hostage situations can occur anywhere, although locations such as banks or government buildings have a higher probability of an incident occurring. Understanding the types of hostage takers and their motives is critical in determining the level of threat facing a private security employee. Awareness of the steps that are to be taken by law enforcement agencies can prevent private security employees from making the wrong decisions, especially when interacting with hostage takers or hostages.

2. What are some of the critical aspects of dealing with a hostage situation as a private security guard? If placed in a position in which a private security officer must interact with a hostage taker, it is important to develop a rapport with the hostage taker, as well as to follow the actions a police law enforcement officer would take in a hostage negotiation situation. A private security person should not make promises to the hostage taker, or grant them requests that could lead to a dangerous response by a hostage taker.

Case Study 4

1. What are some of the characteristics of private military companies? Private military companies offer a chance for primarily former security, law enforcement, and military personnel to work in an area of the private security field with heightened risk. They are militarized in nature, and employees are often required to go through training at a private military company's own facility before working at a particular position.

2. What are some of the major concerns with private military companies? Just as mercenaries posed a number of problems in the Middle Ages, private military companies pose threats in this century. They work for profit while

providing many of the same services as the military. The issue of who can control them and whether they are accountable for any misconduct under federal or international law is still questionable.

■ **Key Terms**

Alpha radiation   The radiation of alpha particles during radioactive decay.

Anthrax   An infectious, usually fatal disease of warm-blooded animals transmitted to humans through contact with contaminated animal substances, such as hair, feces, or hides, and is characterized by ulcerative skin lesions.

Bacteria   Single-celled spherical, spiral, or rod-shaped organisms lacking chlorophyll that reproduce by fission; important as pathogens and for biochemical properties; taxonomy is difficult, often considered to be plants.

Beta radiation   Radiation of beta particles during radioactive decay.

Biological agents   Any bacterium, virus, or toxin that could be used in biological warfare.

Blister agents   Chemical compositions that can blister human skin and cause severe sickness or death.

Blood agents   Chemical compositions that can disrupt the blood flow and composition in the human body and cause sickness or death.

Cancer   Malignant neoplasm characterized by the proliferation of anaplastic cells that tend to invade surrounding tissue and metastasize to new body sites.

Chemical agents   Chemical compositions used to hurt or kill individuals.

Choking agents   Chemical compositions that attack the human respiratory system causing sickness and death.

Dirty bomb   A conventional bomb that leaves considerable radioactive contamination.

Emergency operations centers   (EOCs)   Centralized operating areas for the command and control of all public-serving personnel in an emergency crisis, such as responding to a terrorist attack or natural disaster.

Gamma radiation   Electromagnetic radiation emitted during radioactive decay that has an extremely short wavelength.

Incendiary device   A device using fuel material or a mixture that is designed to produce enough heat and flame to cause surrounding combustible materials to burn once they reach ignition temperature.

Irritating agents   Chemical compositions designed to irritate the eyes, ears, nose, respiratory system, and throat of an individual.

Nerve agents   Odorless liquids, resembling water or light oil in pure form, that can harm and kill humans and animals.

Nuclear weapon   A device, such as a bomb or warhead, whose great explosive power derives from the release of nuclear energy.

Private military company (PMC)   Provides security, logistics, manpower, training, and other services.

Toxin   Toxic substances of natural origin produced by an animal, plant, or microbe.

Unrestricted warfare   A new concept of warfare written about in a book in the late 1990s for the Chinese People's Liberation Army. In this book, they described unconventional tactics that could be used against a larger, more powerful enemy such as the United States.

Virus   Any simple submicroscopic parasites of plants, animals, and bacteria that often cause disease and that consist essentially of a core of RNA or DNA surrounded by a protein coat. Unable to replicate without a host cell, viruses are typically not considered living organisms.

Warfare   Organized conflict between groups for political, economic, or religious purposes.

■ **References**

1. Nacos, B. 2006. *Terrorism and counter-terrorism.* Pearson/Longman. *See also* Griest, P., and S. Mahan. 2003. *Terrorism in perspective.* Thousand Oaks, CA: Sage.

2. Flynn, S. 2005. *America the vulnerable.* New York: Harper Perennial.

3. Kaplan, R. 2000. *The coming anarchy.* New York: Random House. *See also* note 1.

4. *See note 2.*

5. Couch, D. 2003. *The U.S. Armed Forces nuclear, biological, and chemical survival manual.* New York: Basic Books.

6. Ibid.

7. Ibid.

8. Ibid.

9. Ibid.

10. Ibid.

11. Ibid.

12. Allison, G. 2004. *Nuclear terrorism.* New York: Times Books. *See also* Couch, D. 2003. *The U.S. Armed Forces nuclear, biological, and chemical survival manual.* New York: Basic Books. Griest, P., and S. Mahan. 2003. *Terrorism in perspective.* Thousand Oaks, CA: Sage.

13. Spy-Ops. *Dirty bomb training brief.* Vol. 3. TB. 12. http://www.Spy-Ops.com. *See also* Allison, G. 2004. *Nuclear terrorism.* New York: Times Books. Couch, D. 2003. *The U.S. Armed Forces nuclear, biological, and chemical survival manual.* New York: Basic Books.

14. Ibid.

15. Ibid.

16. *See* note 5.

17. *See* note 5.

18. *See* note 5.

19. Spy-Ops. *Improved explosive devices.* Vol. 4. TB. 18. http:/www.spy-ops.com.

20. Griest, P., and S. Mahan. 2003. *Terrorism in perspective.* Thousand Oaks, CA: Sage.

21. Ibid. *See also* Stahlberg, R. 1998. *The complete book of survival.* New York: Barricade Books.

22. *See* note 5.

23. *See* note 5.

24. *See* note 5.

25. *See* note 21.

26. *See* note 21.

27. *See* note 2. *See also Disaster Recovery Journal Online.* http://www.drj.com.

28. *See* note 21.

29. Liang, Q., and W. Xiangsui. 2002. *Unrestricted warfare: China's master plan to destroy America.* Panama City: Pan American. *See also* Gertz, B. 2000. *The China threat.* Washington, DC: Regnery.

30. Ibid. *See also* Spy-Ops. 2006. *Unrestricted warfare training brief.* Vol. 10. TB. 46. http://www.spy-ops.com.

31. Ibid.

32. Ibid.

33. *See* note 29.

34. Adam, T. 2004. *Police field operations.* 6th ed. Upper Saddle River, NJ: Pearson Prentice Hall. *See also* McNab, C. 2005. *How to survive anything.* McGraw Hill. Stahlberg, R. 1998. *The complete book of survival.* New York: Barricade Books. Piven, J., and D. Borgenicht. 2001. *The worst case scenario survival handbook: Travel.* San Francisco: Chronicle Books.

35. Ibid. *See also* Cronin, T. 2002. *Confronting fear.* New York: Thundermouth Press.

36. Ibid.

37. Ibid.

38. Call, J. 2003. Negotiating crises: The evolution of hostage/barricade crisis negotiation. *Journal of Threat Assessment* 2(3).

39. *See* note 35.

40. *See* note 38.

41. *See* note 38.

42. *See* note 38.

43. *See* note 38.

44. Soldiers of fortune then and now. 2007. *The Week* 7(332).

45. Ibid.

46. Ibid.

47. Avant, D. 2005. *The market for force: The consequences of privatizing security.* Washington, DC: George Washington University Press. *See also* Shearer, D. 1998. *Private armies and military intervention.* RoutledgeFarmer. Singer, P. 2004. *Corporate warriors: The rise of the privatized military industry.* Ithaca, NY: Cornell University Press.

48. Ibid.

49. *See* note 44.

Index

CPSIA information can be obtained
at www.ICGtesting.com
Printed in the USA
BVHW091406300120
570930BV00005B/30